Secrecy and Silence in the R

Feminist research is informed by a history of breaking silences, of demanding that women's voices be heard, recorded and included in wider intellectual genealogies and histories. This has led to an emphasis on voice and speaking out in the research endeavour. Moments of secrecy and silence are less often addressed. This gives rise to a number of questions. What are the silences, secrets, omissions and the political consequences of such moments? What particular dilemmas and the constraints do they represent or entail? What are their implications for research praxis? Are such moments always indicative of voicelessness or powerlessness? Or may they also constitute a productive moment in the research encounter? Contributors to this volume were invited to reflect on these questions. The resulting chapters are a fascinating collection of insights into the research process, making an important contribution to theoretical and empirical debates about epistemology, subjectivity and identity in research. Researchers often face difficult dilemmas about who to represent and how, what to omit and what to include. This book explores such questions in a stimulating collection of essays from international scholars.

Róisín Ryan-Flood is a Lecturer in Sociology at the University of Essex. Her research interests include gender, sexuality, kinship and migration. She is the author of *Lesbian Motherhood: Gender, Families and Sexual Citizenship* (2009). Her current research explores sexuality, citizenship and diaspora.

Rosalind Gill is Professor of Social and Cultural Analysis at King's College, London. She is author of *Gender and the Media* (2007) and is currently writing a book about mediated intimacy.

Transformations: Thinking Through Feminism
Edited by Maureen McNeil,
Institute of Women's Studies, Lancaster University
Lynne Pearce
Department of English, Lancaster University

Other books in the series include:

Transformations: Thinking Through Feminism
Edited by Sara Ahmed, Jane Kilby, Celia Lury, Maureen McNeil and Beverley Skeggs

Thinking Through the Skin
Edited by Sara Ahmed and Jackie Stacey

Strange Encounters: Embodied Others in Post-Coloniality
Sara Ahmed

Feminism and Autobiography
Texts, theories, methods
Edited by Tess Cosslett, Celia Lury and Penny Summerfield

Advertising and Consumer Citizenship
Gender, images and rights
Anne M. Cronin

Mothering the Self: Mothers, Daughters, Subjects
Stephanie Lawler

When Women Kill: Questions of Agency and Subjectivity
Belinda Morrissey

Class, Self, Culture
Beverley Skeggs

Haunted Nations
The colonial dimensions of multiculturalisms
Sneja Gunew

The Rhetorics of Feminism
Readings in contemporary cultural theory and the popular press
Lynne Pearce

Women and the Irish Diaspora
Breda Gray

Jacques Lacan and Feminist Epistemology
Kirsten Campbell

Judging the Image
Art, value, law
Alison Young

Sexing the Soldier
Rachel Woodward and Trish Winter

Violent Femmes
Women as spies in popular culture
Rosie White

Pregnancy, Risk and Biopolitics
On the threshold of the living subject
Lorna Weir

Feminist Cultural Studies of Science and Technology
Maureen McNeil

Arab, Muslim, Woman
Voice and vision in postcolonial literature and film
Lindsey Moore

Secrecy and Silence in the Research Process
Feminist reflections
Róisín Ryan-Flood and Rosalind Gill

Feminism, Culture and Embodied Practice
The rhetorics of comparison
Carolyn Pedwell

Sociability, Sexuality, Self
Relationality and Individualization
Sasha Roseneil

Working with Affect in Feminist Readings
Disturbing differences
Marianne Liljeström and Susanna Paasonen

Secrecy and Silence in the Research Process

Feminist reflections

Edited by
Róisín Ryan-Flood and Rosalind Gill

Routledge
Taylor & Francis Group
LONDON AND NEW YORK

First issued in paperback 2010

First published 2010
by Routledge
2 Park Square, Milton Park, Abingdon, Oxon, OX14 4RN

Simultaneously published in the USA and Canada
by Routledge
270 Madison Avenue, New York, NY 10016

Routledge is an imprint of the Taylor & Francis Group, an informa business

Typeset in Times New Roman by
Taylor & Francis Books

British Library Cataloguing in Publication Data
A catalogue record for this book is available from the British Library

Library of Congress Cataloging in Publication Data
Secrecy and silence in the research process ; feminist reflections / [edited by]
Róisín Ryan-Flood [and] Rosalind Gill.
p. cm – (Transformations)
1. Feminism–Research. 2. Social sciences–Research. 3. Feminist theory. I.
Ryan-Flood, Róisín. II. Gill, Rosalind (Rosalind Clair)
HQ1180.S436 2009
305.4201–dc22

2009009374

ISBN 978–0–415–45214–4 (hbk)
ISBN 978–0–415–60517-5 (pbk)
ISBN 978–0–203–92704–5 (ebk)

Contents

Notes on contributors

Bipasha Ahmed is a Senior Lecturer in the School of Psychology, University of East London. Her research interests are in the area of critical psychology, particularly issues relating to 'race', class and gender. She is currently involved in projects on understanding experiences of domestic and sexual violence within South Asian Communities. Publications include recent articles in *Feminism and Psychology*, *Journal of Community and Applied Social Psychology* and in K. Throsby and F. Alexander (eds) (2008) *Gender and Interpersonal Violence: Language, Action and Representation*.

Suki Ali is a Lecturer in the Department of Sociology at the LSE. Her work centralises the interplay between gender, sexualities, 'race' and class. Current research interests focus upon processes of racialisation with specific regard to 'racial science' and technologies, kinship and postcoloniality. Recent publications include a Special Issue of *Ethnic and Racial Studies* on 'Feminism and Postcolonialism' (2007) and *'Mixed-Race', Post-Race: Gender, New Ethnicities and Cultural Practices* (2003).

Feona Attwood teaches Media and Communication Studies at Sheffield Hallam University, UK. Her research interests include new pornographies, online sex practices, and controversial images. She is the editor of *Mainstreaming Sex: The Sexualization of Western Culture* (2009) and *porn.com: Making Sense of Online Pornography* (forthcoming, 2010) and the co-editor of journal special issues on 'Controversial Images' (with Sharon Lockyer, Popular Communication, 2009) and 'Researching and Teaching Sexually Explicit Media' (with Ian Hunter, Sexualities, 2009).

Meg Barker is a Lecturer in Psychology at the Open University and a sex and relationship therapist. She and Darren Langdridge have published *Safe, Sane, Consensual: Contemporary Perspectives on Sadomasochism* (2007) and are now editing a new journal, *Psychology & Sexuality*, with Taylor & Francis. Her research publications focus on sexualities and relationships.

Kathy Davis is Senior Researcher at the Research Institute for History and Culture at Utrecht University in The Netherlands. Born in the United States, she has taught psychology, medical sociology and women's studies at various universities in The Netherlands as well as in Europe and the US. She has published extensively on contemporary feminist approaches to the body, interaction between physicians and women patients, cultural constructions of beauty and beauty practices, and the political and ethical dimensions of surgical technologies. Her books include *Dubious Equalities and Embodied Differences* (2003), *Reshaping the Female Body* (1995), *Power Under the Microscope* (1988) and *Embodied Practices: Feminist Perspectives on the Body* (1997). She is co-editor of the *Handbook of Gender and Women's Studies* (2006). Her most recent book is *The Making of Our Bodies, Ourselves: How Feminism Travels Across Borders* (2007).

Deborah Finding is currently completing her PhD at LSE's Gender Institute. Her work focuses on narratives of sexual violence in popular music, and draws upon both trauma theory and feminist cultural studies, as well as many years of NGO work with abused women. Her research interests include gender and psychoanalysis, mediated post-trauma discourses and fan/community identifications. She also writes more widely on popular culture, including two publications in IB Tauris's 'Reading Cult Television' book series and several pieces for the *Guardian*.

Rosalind Gill is Professor of Social and Cultural Analysis at King's College, London. She is author of *Gender and the Media* (2007) and is currently writing a book about mediated intimacy.

Debra Gimlin is a Lecturer in Sociology at the University of Aberdeen. She is author of *Body Work: Beauty and Self-Image in American Culture* (2002) and numerous articles and chapters dealing with body management, narrative and gendered identity. Her next book, *Cosmetic Surgery Narratives: A Comparative Study of British and American Women's Accounts*, will be published in 2009.

Miriam Glucksmann is a Professor of Sociology at the University of Essex. She has research interests in the areas of gender, work and employment; the shifting boundaries between production, distribution and consumption; the interconnections between different forms of social divisions; and temporalities and spatialities. Her books include *Women on the Line* (1982, 2009), *Women Assemble: Women Workers and the 'New Industries' in Inter-war Britain* (1990) and *Cottons and Casuals: the Gendered Organisation of Labour in Time and Space* (2000), and the jointly edited *A New Sociology of Work?* (2005). She recently completed a three year research programme on 'Transformations of Work: New Frontiers, Shifting Boundaries, Changing Temporalities' as an ESRC professorial Fellow. This explored diverse forms of integration and differentiation of labour, through research on offshored work and call centres, European elderly care work, and ready-made food work. In 2005 she was elected a Fellow of the British Academy, and in 2007 the Swedish Research Council awared her the Kerstin Hesselgren Visiting Professorship at Stockholm University.

Sabine Grenz is a Postdoctoral Fellow at Gothenburg University, Sweden. She completed postgraduate degrees in gender studies at the London School of Economics and Humboldt University. Her research and theoretical interests include gender, sexuality, consumption and epistemology. She is conducting research on the re-construction of feminine nationality at the end of World War II, based on diaries from 1945. She is also concerned with feminist criticism of science, the history of sexuality, prostitution and research on masculinity. Recent publications include her book about the clients of prostitutes *Secret Desire: On the Consumption of Sexual Services* (2005) and articles in the journals *Signs: Journal of Women in Culture and Society* and *Zeitschrift für Sexualforschung*. She is currently co-editing a book entitled *Twilight-Negotiations: Aspects of Prostitution in Historical and Contemporary Contexts.*

Lynda Johnston is a Senior Lecturer in Geography at the University of Waikato, New Zealand. Her research interests include feminism and poststructuralism, gender, sexuality and embodiment, tourism and subjectivities, methodologies, constructions of geographical knowledge and cultural geographies. She has published extensively on these topics. Recent publications include *Queering Tourism: Paradoxical Performances of Gay Pride Parades* (2005).

Darren Langdridge is a Senior Lecturer in Psychology at the Open University and a UKCP-accredited existential psychotherapist. His research expertise is in sexualities and hermeneutic phenomenology. He has co-edited several books including *Safe, Sane, Consensual*, and has also authored a number of other books including *Phenomenological Psychology: Theory, Research and Method.* He is currently co-editing the new journal *Psychology & Sexuality* with Meg Barker for Taylor & Francis.

Gail Lewis is Reader in Identities and Psychosocial Studies at the Open University. Her research preoccupations centre on the constitution, experience and dynamics of 'race' and gender; subjectivity and inter-subjectivity; and the psychodynamics of group and organisational process. She draws on feminist social, cultural, postcolonial and psychoanalytic theory to explore these objects of enquiry. Her publications include 'Birthing Racial Difference: conversations with my mother and others', in *Studies in the Maternal* (2009), 'Racialising Culture is Ordinary' in *Cultural Studies* (2007), *'Race', Gender, Social Welfare: encounters in a postcolonial society* (2000), and *Citizenship: personal lives and social policy* (2004), which she edited and co-authored. She has contributed to numerous journals including *Feminist Review, Ethnic and Racial Studies* and *Mobilities.* She is co-editor (with Kathy Davis) of the *European Journal of Women's Studies.*

Henrietta L. Moore is the William Wyse Chair of Social Anthropology at the University of Cambridge and Director of the Culture and Globalisation Programme at the Centre for the Study of Global Governance, London

School of Economics. Professor Moore has a continuing long-term research engagement with Africa. Her books include *The Subject of Anthropology: gender, symbolism and psychoanalysis* (2007) and *Feminism and Anthropology* (1989).

Kate O'Brien is Lecturer in Criminology in the School of Social Policy, Sociology and Social Research, University of Kent. Her research and teaching is underpinned by a concern to understand the gendering of crime, transgression and social control. Her forthcoming book (2009) *Dealing Tac*, is based on a neighbourhood ethnography of young women's connections to drug supply. Kate has also published various book chapters and journal articles based on the findings of her recent collaborative study of female bouncers operating in British licensed venues.

Julia O'Connell Davidson is Professor of Sociology at Nottingham University. She started to research prostitution as a form of non-standard work in the early 1990s. She has undertaken extensive research on prostitution, sex tourism, child prostitution, migration and trafficking. Her publications include *Prostitution, Power and Freedom* (1998) and *Children in the Global Sex Trade* (2005).

Jane L. Parpart, formerly at Dalhouse University's departments of history, gender studies and international development studies, is currently visiting professor and graduate coordinator at the Centre for Gender and Development Studies at the University of the West Indies. She is the author of numerous edited collections, most recently with Marysia Zaleswki, *Rethinking the Man Question: sex, gender and violence in international relations* (Zed Books, 2008). She is currently working on masculinities, gender and violence in Southern Africa, approaches to empowerment and gender equality in an increasingly violent, unequal and gendered world and the emerging African middle class in Bulawayo, Zimbabwe.

Ann Phoenix is Professor and Co-Director of the Thomas Coram Research Unit, Institute of Education, University of London. She currently holds an ESRC professorial fellowship for a programme of research on 'Transforming experiences: Re-conceptualising identities and "non-normative" childhoods'. Her published books include: *Young Mothers*? (1991); *Black, White or Mixed Race? Race and racism in the Lives of Young People of Mixed Parentage* (1993/2002, with Barbara Tizard); *Standpoints and Differences: Essays in the practice of feminist psychology* (1998, edited with Karen Henwood and Christine Griffin); *Young Masculinities: Understanding boys in contemporary society* (2002, with Stephen Frosh and Rob Pattman); *Social Psychology Matters* (2007, edited with Wendy Hollway and Helen Lucey); and *Parenting and Ethnicity* (online, 2007, with Fatima Husain). She has co-edited (with Pamela Pattynama) a special issue of the *European Journal of Women's Studies* on Intersectionality (2006).

Róisín Ryan-Flood is a Lecturer in Sociology at the University of Essex. Her research interests include gender, sexuality, family practices and citizenship, on which she has published articles. She is the author of *Lesbian Motherhood: Gender, Families and Sexual Citizenship* (2009). She has edited several journal special issues on topics including feminist methodology, researching intimate life, and sexuality and visual culture. Her current research explores sexuality, citizenship and diaspora.

Jacqueline Sanchez Taylor has undertaken extensive international research on sex tourism with a particular focus on female sex tourism. Her research and publications have focused on theoretical questions about the intersections of race, gender, sexuality, age, economic inequalities in the global sex trade. More recently, she has applied this theoretical interest to the demand for cosmetic surgery. She is currently a lecturer at Leicester University.

Christina Scharff is a doctoral researcher based at the Gender Institute at the London School of Economics, conducting a comparative study of British and German women's relationship to feminism. Her research cuts across interdisciplinary boundaries and explores the themes of feminist (dis-)identification, postfeminism, neoliberalism, heteronormativity and difference from a critical, international perspective. Ros Gill and Christina Scharff are the editors of *New Femininities: Postfeminism, Neoliberalism and Identity* (2010).

Bruna Seu is a Lecturer in Social Psychology at Birkbeck College, London. Her main research interests concern gender, inequality, epistemology and psychoanalysis. She has a longstanding commitment to developing and applying qualitative research methods, in particular Grounded Theory and Discourse Analysis, to the investigation of social phenomena. She is currently conducting empirical work on bystanders' reactions to Human Rights abuses through the support of a Leverhulme Foundation Fellowship. She is the author of numerous articles and book chapters and also editor (with C. Heenan) of *Feminism and Psychotherapy; Reflections on contemporary theories and practices* (1998).

Karen Throsby is an Associate Professor in the Department of Sociology at the University of Warwick. Her research focuses on the intersections of gender, technology and the body, and she is the author of *When IVF Fails: Feminism, Infertility and the Negotiation of Normality* (2004) and co-editor (with Flora Alexander) of *Gender and Interpersonal Violence: Language, Action and Representation* (2008). Her current research is on people's experiences of obesity surgery, and she has also recently begun researching embodiment and long distance swimmers.

Rebekah Wilson works as a senior researcher at the National Foundation for Educational Research and is completing a PhD in Gender Studies at the

London School of Economics. Her doctoral research comprises a critical examination of the practice of surname change married women – and alternatives to this norm – by exploring personal accounts, public attitudes and by building on feminist perspectives of marriage and 'the family'. The research stems from her interest in gender relations, women's history, life-course transitions, and changing family forms and relationships.

Foreword

Secrets and silence in feminist research

Sara Ahmed

Professor in Race and Cultural Studies at Goldsmiths, University of London

This volume of articles offers a thoughtful and diverse set of reflections on how secrets and silence matter in feminist research. We might turn to this volume with confidence, assuming we already know how silence and secrets matter in feminist research: silence is what we must overcome through speech; secrets are what we must keep in order to protect those who speak out about silence. Reading these essays does what one hopes reading will do: it helps us to lose confidence. You realise that silence and secrets do matter, but that they matter in ways that challenge the value of silence and secrets (or the idea that they have a given value), as well the precise nature of their role and effects.

Sometimes silence can be a tool of oppression; when you are silenced, whether by explicit force or by persuasion, it is not simply that you do not speak but that you are barred from participation in a conversation which nevertheless involves you. Sometimes silence is a strategic response to oppression; one that allows subjects to persist in their own way; one that acknowledges that, under certain circumstances, speech might not be empowering, let alone sensible. Sometimes you might speak out to announce a disagreement with what is being said, sometimes not, as to speak can mean to agree to participate in a conversation that you don't agree with. Sometimes we might stay silent about some of the findings of our research because we do not have trust in how those findings might be used by other actors. A lack of trust can be reason not to speak: or you can speak about your distrust. The point of this 'sometimes' is that we learn that silence and speech have different even contradictory effects given their timing, which is a question not simply of their time, but also of the place in which we reside at a given moment of time, the worlds we find ourselves in. To recognise this contingency as a feminist ethics is to live and work in a state of suspension: we will not always know in advance (though sometimes we might) when it makes sense to be silent and when it does not.

Perhaps we can say the same for secrets. Sometimes when we are entrusted with a secret we must hold that secret, keep it, by not even declaring that we have been entrusted with it (for a secret to be secret it would not even be named or declared as a secret, a true secret disappears from the sign of the secret). Our desire to keep a secret is to preserve a bond with the one who has entrusted us with it (or, perhaps more instrumentally, we might keep a secret in order to preserve the possibility of our own research, if it depends on certain bonds). At other times, we might need to reveal a secret in order to refuse a social bond; in order to challenge the power of some to control information, as a form *of* control that ensures the power *to* control.

And yet of course 'secrets' aren't simply information or details that are passed or not passed. A secret might be something we keep from ourselves, something that is too hard or too painful to come to light. When we keep secrets from ourselves, we do not know we have them (or if we know, then it is that fuzzy kind of knowing, that uneasiness that doesn't quite surface as attention). Secrets might establish the limits of knowledge, reminding us that as knowers that if we don't know what we don't know, then we might not even know what we know. Some essays in this volume thus reflect not only on the process of doing research, but they return to research that has already been done not in order to reveal to us what had hitherto been concealed about that research, but in order to produce new understandings of why some things are difficult to reveal. Difficulties are, as ever, pedagogic.

As readers of this volume, it is helpful to think with the authors, and to ask about secrecy and silence in our own work. I write this foreword as a feminist researcher (I have learnt from Audre Lorde not to be afraid of this 'writing as' nor to assume that it can abbreviate an experience). I have mostly engaged in text-based rather than empirical work: reading texts from public domains (what we might call documents) as well as cultural texts (films, fiction, memoirs), creating my own archives out of these materials. The document itself is an interesting example in any discussion of silence and secrecy. Documents must be thought of as written as well as public forms of information. A document can be the cessation of a secret: it is the paper in the trail. Of course documents can be held without us knowing about them. In our legal context, we might assume that the point of the document is that it cannot be kept secret, even those documents that document the person, what we would ordinarily describe as personal data. The Data Protection Act of 1998 in the UK can be described as a security regime for data, a way of protecting individuals from the misuse of data gathered about them by organisations, which is data that must not be disclosed to third parties without consent. Subjects are given rights to data; rights to know what organisations 'hold' them, rights to correct mistakes in the information that is held; to require that what is held is not used in a way that causes harm or distress; or that their data is not used for direct marketing.

However, as with most protections from secrets (understood here as the withholding of information) there are exceptions, one of which is national security. In the latter Anti-Terrorism, Crime and Security Bill of 2001, this exception acquires its legal standing: this Bill enables 'communication service providers to retain data – not content – for reasons of national security or where it may be vital for criminal investigation'. The project of securitisation becomes the right of the state to keep secrets, and to keep secrets of a certain kind: personal data becomes a state secret. We know too well what follows from such rights. The right to keep documents secret becomes a defence of the nation state, a right to terrorise, we could even say, anyone suspected of terrorism, where the grounds for suspicion are weak enough to be offered as a ground. That the right of the person to the document of their person can be so easily suspended teaches us something about the document: that the control of its circulation, how it does and does not pass around, is rarely given up.

My own interest in documents came about partly in response to the culture of documentation produced by the new equality regimes. For example, the Race Relations Amendment Act of 2001 required all public bodies to have a race equality and action plan. What this meant in practice was the requirement to write a document (the plan). I was involved in writing the document at my university, as one of two Black and Minority Ethnic (BME – the abbreviation could also be a secret[1]) academic staff on a team. We used what I thought of as a critical vocabulary in writing a document: we took care not to produce a 'happy diversity' document in which diversity is imagined as what brings the organisation together through the proximity of bodies of different colours. We took care to describe whiteness as institutional; to reflect on inequalities and to give an account of racism as an ongoing set of practices that benefits some and harms others. I am undone. The Equality Challenge Unit that monitored the process for Higher Education ranks the document as 'excellent': the Vice-Chancellor interprets this ranking as a sign of being good at race equality; and congratulates staff at a meeting. It was a feel-good moment that did not feel so good. The document that documents racism becomes usable as a measure of good performance.

Documents that aim to reveal can be used to conceal what they reveal. We have to work hard to resist the social desire for some things to be open secrets, to be left unnamed or untalked about, even when many of us know they are there. We are asked to agree to look over some things or to overlook them; if we do what is asked of us, we might experience disorientation; we might become uneasy as things get fuzzy (the fuzziness reminds us that secrets can be shared if we agree to push certain things into the background). The figure of the whistle blower shows us how the one who refuses to overlook signs of organisational misconduct is often read as the cause of trouble: disloyalty becomes the failure to keep a secret or to keep some things secret. Just to name racism can be an act of disloyalty, which is at once a form of disobedience; an act which refuses the veil of secrecy offered by diversity.

Such acts are not finished as actions, what they do depends on how they get taken up. Paradoxes follow when you aim to reveal what tends to work through concealment. At this point, I became involved in a social-science project, with a team of feminists, and I interviewed diversity workers about the very processes that I had witnessed first hand. Time and time I was told about the problem of diversity pride: and how racism becomes treated as something that bruises the ego of organisations. Diversity pride gets translated into the demand that Black and minority staff express gratitude, by giving up the very vocabularies of racism. Our report on this research showed how technologies of race equality (such as good practice guides or toolkits) can work to conceal the existence of racism. What happens: they suppressed the report.[2] Some things are not revealed because they refuse to conceal what must be concealed to preserve a social order. So yes, sometimes, when we are entrusted with secrets, we must break the trust.

At other times, it might become important to reveal something, but not to reveal too much. We have to learn how much to reveal or not (it is not just a question of *whether* to keep or not to keep a secret, or to choose or not choose silence but is also a question of *how much*). I learnt this from Sally Morgan's autoethnography, *My Place*, which gives us an account of becoming Aboriginal, of finding out that you are Aboriginal and coming to learn what this means. Aboriginality had been kept secret: Sally and her siblings were told they were Indian in order to protect them from the consequences of being Aboriginal in Australia. I am reminded of Audre Lorde's *Zami*, which gives us an account of her mother explaining racist violence as a random act of people spitting in the wind (1982: 17–18). Not naming something because of racism is complicated; you cannot always be protected from what you don't know, especially if not knowing can protect those who cause harm, in the sense that it can stop the causes of harm from being revealed. These sorts of secrets are painful. We don't always know what to do with them.

We could think of *My Place* as the catharsis promised by revealing a secret: Sally finds out about her history, her land, comes to share in the memories she was not allowed to have. But it is not that simple. She talks to her family, and their stories are incorporated into her story. We learn about her grandmother. And we learn also about what will and must remain secret through her grandmother: 'Well, Sal, that's all I am gunna tell ya. My brain's no good, it's gone rotten. I don't want to talk anymore. I've got my secrets. I'll take them to the grave. There's some things I cannot even talk about. Not even to you, my granddaughter' (1987: 428). What cannot be revealed to her granddaughter also is not revealed to us, the readers of the text. There are secrets that Nan will take with her; her secrets are sacred.

Sometimes we need to know that all cannot be revealed to avoid positioning the others as revelations. I think this is especially the case as we respond to indigenous testimony: the desire to know the truth about the other can participate in, and reproduce, violence, as if 'they' could provide us with what we are missing. It is for this reason – the need to be responsive to what cannot be revealed – that Gayatri Spivak suggests that ethics involves secrets. She does not mean by this that ethics involves meeting in secret, but that it involves, or even that it *must* involve, recognising the limits of what one can receive from others, the limits, in other words, of knowledge. As she describes 'there is always a sense that something has not got across' (1995: xxv). This sense of what does not get across is not a sense of something in particular: the something here is not an object, but what cannot be contained as an object, what cannot be passed from one to another.

These limits of knowledge are not just constraints: they can be productive as sites of enquiry. Read together, the essays in the volume show us how feminist reflection on or about feminism is never simply self-reflection but reflection on the kinds of the worlds in which we live. Feminist research in asking questions of itself, also asks us to reflect on what it means to do feminist research, which also means a commitment to consider the location of the research, questions of power within research, as well as the limits of research ethics, whether defined negatively as not causing harm or positively in terms of promoting good. We learn that to make ethics difficult is to allow a different kind of conversation of the value of feminist work as well of the value of values (what is harm, what is good, for whom, when and where). And importantly we think about feminist labour – about research as a form of work that in the Marxian sense is also praxis: a way of knowing that transforms what is known, or that at least aims for such transformation.

Perhaps feminist researchers are secretaries. By this I point not simply to how academic divisions of labour become gendered divisions of labour, though of course feminists might have much to say about this: about the act of separation of administration from academic work in the creation of classes of persons who are administrators and academics, as well as about how amongst those who are designated as academics, some might be required to do the work of administration more than others (dare we say it, administration might be the work of women and feminised men), where that work is given less value, and thus compromises the capacity of some to accumulate academic value. I suspect we have quite a lot of stories we could share about these processes: and it is important to share them; to talk about the labour of the work we do, not to agree to overlook its consequences (to be secretive about what wears us down just adds to the wearing). But I say feminist researchers might be secretaries to evoke what is now a relatively obscure meaning of secretary: a secretary is one who is entrusted with secrets. Sometimes we need to keep the secrets and be worth this trust. Sometimes we need not to keep the secrets with which are entrusted even if this means we become untrustworthy. What we do with what we are entrusted – whether we speak or keep silent – remains an important question, one this volume helps us to pose.

Notes

1 I mean by this that when the abbreviation can work to conceal trouble: you don't use certain categories as a way of not hearing their effects. I am tempted to offer a new angle on Paul Gilroy's (1987) book title: 'There ain't no black in BME' (when the B is put in the place of black, the black disappears).

2 The report has never been published, and no official reason was given. In response to emails, all we received was silence. This kind of silence one must resist! We have uploaded the report onto my website at Goldsmiths and we encourage its circulation.

References

Gilroy, Paul (1987) *There Ain't No Black in the Union Jack: The Cultural Politics of Race and Nation*. London: Hutchinson.
Lorde, Audre (1982) *Zami: A New Spelling of My Name*. London: Sheba Feminist Publishers.
Morgan, Sally (1987) *My Place*. Freemantle: Freemantle Arts Centre Press.
Spivak, Gayatri (1995) Translater's Preface. *Imaginary Maps*. London: Routledge.

Acknowledgements

We are indebted to our family and friends for encouraging us throughout the development of this book: Andy Pratt, Bruna Seu, Gail Lewis, Lisa Baraitser, Ann and Seán Flood, Ulrika Nyh, Christina Bodin, Kellie Burns, Roona Simpson, Julie Shanahan, Giovanni Porfido and Scheherezade Soodeen. We would like to thank the organisers of the conference on Feminism and Methodology at the Centre for Gender Studies at Stockholm University for inviting us to participate in a roundtable plenary on secrecy and silence in the research process. Thanks also to Lynne Pearce and Maureen McNeil for their enthusiastic support of this project, and to Miranda Thirkettle at Routledge for all her help. Finally, thanks go to Fabienne Jung and Anna Watts for their invaluable assistance in preparing the manuscript.

Introduction

Róisín Ryan-Flood and Rosalind Gill

Let us begin with a bold claim: all research involves secrets and silences of various kinds, and these secrets and silences matter. That is the premise of this volume, which brings together twenty-one articles to explore the dilemmas and challenges presented by secrecy and silence in the research process. United by a shared concern to reflect upon secrecy and silence, the contributors discuss an extraordinary range of different aspects of research, from the moment in which a research idea is conceived to its publication and reception by the media – and every moment in between. In the process the essays presented here trouble, unsettle and destabilise any singular understanding of secrecy or silence. Secrets may be kept from research participants or kept for them, they may be misunderstood or disclosed, may become a currency of exchange or a means of exclusion. Silence, meanwhile, has radically different meanings dependent upon context and power and the affective relations of the research encounter: one may silence or be silenced, keep silent out of respect, rage, fear or shame, or even as a mode of resistance. What emerges from this collection is a sense of the diversity of ways in which secrecy and silence are implicated in research, and the different ways in which feminist researchers reflect upon this in their own practice. By highlighting this we locate ourselves within an ongoing tradition of feminist 'troubling' of the taken for granted in research, and hope to inspire further discussion of the ways in which secrecy and silence matter – ethically, politically and epistemologically.

Feminist research has a tradition of demanding that the unseen and the unacknowledged be made visible and heard. Early feminist work was primarily concerned with writing women's voices into history and recording their lives and narratives. The very act of treating women's experiences as worthy of academic research was in itself a revolutionary concept in the face of much theory by the 'founding fathers' of social science and generations of empirical work that assumed male perspectives and experiences were universal. Beyond introducing gender as an analytical concept in research, feminist work has played a key role in transforming the terrain of epistemology and ontology in the social sciences. It has highlighted the importance of attention to power relations in research, both in terms of reproduction of social power in research relations and attention to potential harm to participants. The myth of the objective, neutral observer who leaves the field without influencing the data, untouched by the research process, has been soundly critiqued by feminist social scientists. They have illustrated the messiness of social interactions and the embodied nature of research. Far from being a straightforward, clinical, easily manageable process, research inevitably presents numerous challenges at ontological, epistemological, political, ethical and personal levels.

In exploring the consequences of differences in subjectivity and location, feminist literature has transformed understandings of epistemology, methodology, subjectivity and agency in social research. Writings on gender and epistemology have problematised the positivist notion of objectivity, have highlighted how the interaction between the researcher and interviewee – especially shared empathy and rapport – affects the data produced, and have reconceptualised subjectivity as an embodied and plural process. Identity categories, such as gender, 'race', ethnicity, sexuality and age, are viewed as significant in the practice of research for both researchers and participants. The situatedness of the researcher and researched therefore affects the production of knowledge, which has been theorised as constructed, partial and situated.

Critical reflections on epistemology and methodology have foregrounded notions of voice and representation. This has been particularly important in feminist research that aimed to contribute to an emancipatory project of bringing women's voices in from the margins. Questions of who speaks for whom and about what, as well as the situatedness of the researcher and researched, constitute important concerns in contemporary work on methodology and epistemology. This reflexive engagement with research praxis has raised many important questions about ethics, epistemology, power, subjectivity and agency. Feminist writing has been at the forefront of this enterprise.

However, notions of silence, secrecy and omission have been less often directly examined. Research inevitably presents dilemmas, challenges and choices, which are not always explicated in writing up. Often the liberatory potential of research has been unproblematically assumed to be a linear move from silence to voice. In this collection, we trouble that assumption and explore what becomes the unsayable and the unspeakable as it relates to the research process. The complexity of human interaction often leads to difficult dilemmas for the researcher, who is ultimately the person responsible for writing up the research and making choices about who to represent and how, what to omit and what to include. Our own experiences as researchers and our shared discussions about some of the dilemmas we encountered in the lived practices of research led us to the topic of secrecy and silence in the research process. The process of reflecting on these experiences, both individually and in discussion, inspired us to invite other authors to consider how secrecy and silence might inform research praxis.

The contributors to this volume were invited to reflect on the following questions: 'What are the silences, secrets, omissions and erasures that take place during fieldwork and writing up? What are the epistemological, methodological and political consequences of such moments? What particular dilemmas and constraints do they represent or entail? What are their implications for research praxis? Are such moments always indicative of voicelessness or powerlessness? Or may they also constitute a productive moment in the research encounter?' The response to our call for contributions was extraordinary. Nothing could have prepared us for the huge interest and desire there was for discussing such issues. It was as if our questions had touched a nerve; there was a real hunger to talk about the tensions and dilemmas they produced. What was striking, too, was the diversity of different ways in which individuals responded to our 'prompts'; secrecy and silence emerged as having multiple meanings for our contributors. The resulting chapters represent an innovative engagement with questions of secrecy and silence in the research process and their implications for theories of feminist epistemologies, research ethics and representation.

Feminist epistemologies and research ethics

Feminist social research has long been concerned with questions of breaking silence and speaking out (Alcoff and Potter, 1993; Harding, 1993; Stanley and Wise, 1993; Ramazonoglu with Holland, 2002). This began with taking women's experiences as a productive starting point for theory and research. The ways in which social theory and research were informed by androcentrism was highlighted by feminist writers who explored the significance of gender in social life. This required considering the embodied, affective and power-infused dimensions of theory and research. The social researcher was not an objective neutral observer, but a social actor embedded and participating in social relations of power. The notion of objectivity came under sustained attack – an early women's movement slogan being 'objectivity is male subjectivity' (Spender, 1980). Feminist writers raised the suspicion that transcendental claims to truth often reflected little more than the experiences of white Western males and, latterly, white, middle-class, Northern feminists (hooks, 1982; Segal, 1987; Spelman, 1988; Ramazonoglu, 1989; Hill Collins, 1990).

Feminists also challenged the notion that the producer of knowledge is irrelevant, that it does not matter whether the researcher is male or female, black or white, middle class or working class, and so on. Moreover, they pointed out the contradiction between this 'scientific' view, and the notion that feminist researchers would somehow 'contaminate' the research process – as if only white, middle-class males would get 'authentic' results (Bhavnani, 1993). Patricia Hill Collins recounts how her academic training sought to eliminate all those aspects of her everyday life, which could, looked at differently, be seen as a valuable resource: 'Much of my formal academic training has been designed to show me that I must alienate myself from my communities, my family, and even my own self in order to produce credible academic work' (1990: xiii). Meanwhile, in *Breaking Out Again*, Liz Stanley and Sue Wise asked: 'How many other professions, we wonder, make such a fetish of *ignorance*, and elevate it into the only possible claim to professional competence?' (1993: 169).

In addition, feminist writers challenged the positivist model in social research by writing frankly about the realities of empirical work. Oakley (1982), in a ground-breaking article, pointed out that in interviews with new mothers, her own identity as a woman and mother played a significant role in the research encounter. Her participants asked her advice as they engaged with the experience of motherhood. In some instances, the research encounter extended into a friendship. Her discussion of the lived experience of research rendered the notion of an objective distant researcher absurd. Furthermore, she argued that the shared empathy and rapport she experienced with participants was of benefit to the research endeavour, resulting in greater openness on the part of participants. Yet this too can present dilemmas, in research settings of unequal power where empathy might potentially become a means of exploitation – extracting more from research participants, and generating expectations of friendship that may be impossible to sustain. Other writers, moreover, have highlighted that a shared gender is not enough on which to build a rapport in research. Other dimensions of difference, such as ethnicity, race, age and class, affected how participants and researchers responded to one another.

Discussions of difference within wider feminist theory have highlighted the importance of acknowledging positionality, and have pointed to silences within feminism itself – notably the silent privileging of the Northern, white, middle-class, heterosexual and able-bodied subject of some feminist theorising. Hill Collins (1990) refers to intersections of identities and power within the 'matrix of domination' in which differences in identity also represent relative degrees of power and social capital that may intersect in complex ways. Postcolonial and Third World writers have challenged the epistemological and emancipatory goals of Northern feminist work (Spivak, 1988, 1999; Spivak and Harasym, 1990; Mohanty et al. 1991; Alexander and Mohanty, 1997; Bulbeck, 1998; Mohanty, 2003). Sisterhood cannot be assumed to be universal. Rather, solidarity has to be created across difference, where the acknowledgement of differences in power, social identities and social capital becomes an intrinsic part of the feminist project. Recognising differences among women – differences of location relating to geography, class, 'race', ethnicity, sexuality, health status and able-bodiedness – is a necessary part of the struggle for equality. A generation of feminist research has developed in which analyses strive to incorporate an awareness of the situatedness of both the researcher and researched. Increasingly, differences in power are more openly discussed and acknowledged, where they are seen to inform the research encounter and participant narratives – though it is striking how often such discussions are 'relegated' to methodology journals and continue to be excised from published analyses in books and mainstream journals (a fact that may be related to another 'secret' feature of research: namely, the political economy of publishing).

One concern with dimensions of power in research is often referred to in terms of 'representing the Other'. This references concerns about how – and indeed whether – we should represent 'Others'. Should able-bodied researchers do research on/with disabled people? Should heterosexual women research queer experiences, and, if so, how to respond to the political imperative: 'Nothing about us, without us'? How to write about people from a different – often implicitly less powerful – social location in ways that are not patronising or offensive? How to carry out research with 'Others' and not reinscribe hegemonic social relations? How to present Others' voices? Such concerns have long animated feminist writing on epistemology and ontology (Kitzinger and Wilkinson, 1996). Dilemmas of epistemology, ethics and representation are not of course limited to researchers from different social groups to participants. 'Insider' researchers may also experience particular quandaries, especially when researching minority groups where access may be facilitated on the tacit assumption that their findings will be sympathetic to the interests of the participant group. It may also be uncomfortable for 'insider' researchers to present their research to the disciplining gaze of academia (see Barker and Langdridge, this volume).

Feminist writing has highlighted the centrality of reflexivity to research. It has long been used as a means of examining the ways in which identity, intimacy, affect and power shape empirical data and the wider research process. As Haraway (1988) argued, there is no view from nowhere, no 'God's eye view'. This reflexive engagement can be understood as an expression of academic rigour, where the social encounter, insights and emotions inspired by the research process are useful in the interpretation of data and critical reflections on research praxis. Another aspect of 'writing the researcher in' goes beyond a reflexive account of the research, as some authors even take their own self as the subject of study.[1] However, doubts have also been expressed about the reflexive turn in social research. Too often 'papers start with what seems to be little more than a ritual incantation of the identities occupied by the author with little or no attempt to reflect on the *significance* of those positions for the research' (Gill, 1998: 32). It is as if simply 'acknowledging' one's location is enough to eradicate its effects (see also Lewis, this volume). Skeggs (2004) also points out that reflexivity is itself profoundly classed, a product of late modernity that rests on a number of assumptions, including a discourse of rationality that is historically defined in opposition to femininity.

The feminist concern with egalitarianism and power relations can perhaps be summarised by Clark and Sharf's reference to approaching the research process with the intention that 'Above all, we must do them no harm' (Clark and Sharf, 2007: 400). However, they point out that this intention is 'anything but straightforward' (401). Plummer (2001) notes that researchers are often forced to consider the impact what we write about them has on those we study and refers to the process of negotiating ethics in social research as one marked by ambivalence and a 'struggling with the self' (2001: 229). He argues for the value of sharing the stories of these struggles, as it contributes towards the development of ethical guidelines for other researchers grappling with their own dilemmas.

Researchers often find themselves grappling with unforeseen dilemmas. For example, a commitment to anonymity is often seen as fundamental to respecting the privacy of participants. However, it may prove difficult to achieve in practice, no matter how desirable it may be in theory. Thus, Mauthner (2000) found it difficult to disguise participants' identities from one another in her study of relationships between sisters. Although she attempted to retain participants' anonymity, given their closeness to one another as relatives, it was difficult to hide their identities in the writing up of the research. At a time when Institutional Review Boards (IRBs) are issuing ever more stringent guidelines about what constitutes ethical practice in research, it may seem that the feminist concern with 'doing no harm' is entirely appropriate for this particular climate of ethical guidelines for contemporary research. Given that IRBs are more often motivated by a concern with preventing litigation however, this is not always an easy alliance. Sharf (1999) discusses this dilemma in an article reflecting on her experience of carrying out qualitative research drawing on material from a breast cancer listserv. Contributors to internet forums may feel resentful of their words being used for research purposes, as they have not given permission or may find it exploitative. The IRB guidelines prohibited her from revealing her presence as a researcher to the rest of the online group. In a later discussion of this scenario, Sharf asks what recourse the researcher has 'when their sense of ethics is at odds with the decisions of an IRB'? (Clark and Sharf, 2007: 410) (see also Glucksmann, this volume). The practice of social research often gives rise to complex dilemmas. There are no easy answers. This volume presents accounts of epistemological, ethical and affective experiences by a range of researchers. Their contributions help to clarify various strategies and provide reflections on the nature of research and social life.

Before we introduce the chapters that make up this book, however, we want to highlight one of the silences of this collection itself: its apparent erasure or elision of voices from outside the UK and US/Canada. In inviting contributors to reflect on secrecy and silence we sought, from the outset, to produce an international collection that would explore the way that these dilemmas play out in different global spaces. With this in mind, we adopted a pro-active method and approached individuals writing in different contexts to contribute to the book. In particular we wanted to include scholars working in the global South. As the deadline for chapters approached, however, our inboxes began to fill with apologetic withdrawals, citing pressure of work and other deadlines, as, one by one, our contributors from outside the

UK withdrew. For us this was profoundly disappointing. We sorely missed contributions from Africa, Asia and Latin America for the insights their chapters would bring. Moreover, we worried that our publisher would no longer recognise the collection for which we had been contracted, and would suggest that the resulting collection was 'less marketable internationally' (read: in the US) – an anxiety familiar to everyone who attempts to publish in the UK. The resulting volume however, does include contributors based outside the UK, with scholars working in Canada, New Zealand, Sweden and The Netherlands. The chapters also draw on fieldwork in a range of geographical contexts: for example, Jacqueline Sanchez Taylor and Julia O'Connell Davidson's chapter reflects on their experiences of fieldwork in Latin America and the Caribbean; Henrietta Moore's chapter presents an account of empirical work in Kenya; Christina Scharff and Sabine Grenz write about research carried out in Germany; and Róisín Ryan-Flood's chapter draws on empirical research in Sweden and Ireland. In addition, many of the chapters consider questions of difference, identities and positionality. Gail Lewis and Ann Phoenix explore processes of racism and racialisation in the research encounter. Bipasha Ahmed outlines some of the dilemmas encountered in research on domestic violence in South Asian communities. Meg Barker and Darren Langdridge interrogate silences in relation to research on marginalised sexualities.

Nevertheless it is worth reflecting on the absence of other voices – especially in a volume precisely concerned with silences – for it tells us something perhaps about the difficulty of working across boundaries and doing transnational feminist work. Have we – unwittingly – silenced potential contributors from outside the UK? Do the concepts and categories that we use implicitly speak to a particular national imaginary and not 'travel' transnationally? Alternatively might we understand the withdrawal of – initially enthusiastic – overseas contributors as an outcome of the operation of a global academic star system – a system so unequal that only a few scholars from the South get to be part of it, and once they do, become forced to carry an intolerable burden of representation that includes constantly being asked to 'speak from' their position as global Southern expert-subject. There are other possibilities too: perhaps a British book chapter lacks enough prestige as a publication in an academic system in which other rationalities now dominate (see Gill, this volume), or perhaps the withdrawal simply speaks of the difficulty for feminist scholars in a variety of locations to write or speak publicly about secret, silenced and taboo issues. In this sense, the project itself of reflecting on secrecy and silence may be seen as always already informed by a neoliberal politics of location. There is perhaps no simple or singular answer to the question of why so many contributors withdrew – but even in asking the question we draw attention to the silence and its impact, in a way that is emblematic of the project of this book as a whole.

Organisation of the book

The book is divided into four parts: 'Interpreting and Theorising Silence'; 'The Unspoken in the Research Process'; 'Silence, Secrecy and Telling Research Stories'; and 'Affective Dilemmas'. In the first part, the contributors reflect on some of the hermeneutic challenges associated with processes of secrecy and silence. Jane Parpart's chapter outlines how collective silences can strengthen women's position in a highly gendered social world, while individual silence can also be a form of resistance. In this she challenges deeply held assumptions about the importance of 'voice' and 'speaking out'. The following chapter by Henrietta Moore considers how a longstanding fieldwork relationship with a community is defined in many ways by secrecy and silence. Jacqueline Sanchez Taylor and Julia O'Connell Davidson outline some of the difficulties in researching harrowing topics with regard to their work on sex tourism in the mid-1990s. When initially writing up the research, they chose not to write reflexively about their experience of the research process as gendered and racialised subjects. In retrospect, they argue that this was the appropriate choice at that time and that 'silence can be golden'. In the next chapter Grenz reflects on her research interviewing heterosexual male clients of prostitutes. She compares her work to a similar study carried out by a male interviewer, concluding that their differential embodiedness did not make any difference to the findings produced. However, it did affect the research process and how the participants situated the interviewers, in ways that were gendered. The final chapter in Part I, by Meg Barker and Darren Langridge, considers silences by researchers in relation to silenced sexualities, or those that fall outside of heteronormativity, raising difficult dilemmas about when, whether and how to speak about marginalised identities or practices.

Part II considers the unspoken in the research process from a different perspective. Contributors consider some of the conscious and unconscious ways in which research praxis is shaped by tacit complicities and marginalised subjectivities. Christina Scharff explores the significance of class location in her interview research with working class women about feminist identification. Bipasha Ahmed's chapter considers how a researcher may be forced to negotiate a sense of being compromised, in relation to her research on South Asian women and domestic violence. Karen Throsby and Debra Gimlin's chapter provides a thoughtful account of the embodied nature of research and how participants situate the researcher, in their discussion of carrying out a study of obesity surgery. Kate O'Brien's chapter on carrying out covert research on nightclub bouncers outlines some of the ethical dilemmas of 'undercover' research, including participating in gendered practices that may be at odds with the researcher's personal values. The final chapter in this part, by Rebekah Wilson, illustrates some of the dramaturgical dilemmas encountered in carrying out quantitative survey research.

Part III addresses difficulties in telling research stories in different contexts. These chapters highlight the wider challenges in writing up sensitive material, where the subjectivity and agency of research participants comes into play at every stage of the research process. In addition, the potential readership of academic work is also salient. Kathy Davis describes the difficulties in doing research on a feminist collective that uncovers a conflict around racism in the organisation. The next chapter by Ann Phoenix explores the ways in which the interview narrative is inevitably shaped by intertextual understandings. Feona Attwood's chapter on researching sexually explicit material outlines the wider context for research work within academia and how researchers who write about particular topics may themselves be situated uncomfortably by colleagues. Róisín Ryan-Flood's chapter explores some of the practical difficulties in negotiating secrecy and silence. Her decision to keep participants' secrets regarding their illegal activities reflects how researchers negotiate the wider context for the presentation of their research findings. Miriam Glucksmann's chapter provides a stark account of censorship imposed by a publisher, when she was required to write her first book under a pseudonym in order to avoid legal action by the institutions she was writing about.

Part IV explores affective dilemmas in the research process. Gail Lewis's chapter illustrates some of the challenges of researching people and topics that may elicit considerable rage within the researcher, who is left grappling with complex feelings while continuing to negotiate contact with participants and the research field. Rosalind Gill reflects on some of the affective and experiential qualities of life in neoliberal academia, arguing that these are neither entirely secret nor completely silenced but are structured through a toxic individualism. Suki Ali's chapter on the role of confidant and confidentiality considers some of the difficulties in carrying out research with children and negotiating ethics and responsibility, where to speak in confidence may mean different things for the researcher and researched. Bruna Seu's chapter explores the significance of shame in relation to women's narrative accounts and possible readings of them. Deborah Finding's chapter considers the implications for the researcher of engaging with the media. In an age when many funding bodies actively encourage the dissemination of research findings through the media, the researchers may find themselves coping with negative publicity and hostility towards their work. Finally, Lynda Johnston's chapter considers the significance of place in researching identities and affect in both queer and heteronormative spaces.

The chapters collected in this book reveal that secrecy and silence play an important role in research praxis. They illustrate how silence and secrecy are central issues across different moments of the research process – including in the development of theoretical frameworks, during data collection, when presenting the research to different audiences, as well as in writing up. In putting this volume together, we have been struck by the enthusiasm of contributors, as well as audiences at seminar and conference presentations for the topic. Our impression is that we have struck a chord in choosing to explore secrecy and silence in feminist research practice. We hope that this collection represents a first step in opening up the concepts of secrecy and silence to wider debate.

Note

1 See Coffey (2002) for a full discussion of the pros and cons of the use of autobiography in research.

References

Alcoff, L. and Potter, E. (eds) (1993) *Feminist Epistemologies.* London: Routledge.

Alexander, M. J. and Mohanty, C. M. (eds) (1997) *Feminist Genealogies, Colonial Legacies, Democratic Futures.* London: Routledge.

Bhavnani, K.-K. (1993) 'Tracing the contours: feminist research and feminist objectivity', *Women's Studies International Forum*, 16(2): 95–112.

Bulbeck, C. (1998) *Re-Orienting Western Feminisms: Women's Diversity in a Postcolonial World.* Cambridge: Cambridge University Press.

Clark, M. C. and Sharf, B. F. (2007) 'The dark side of truth(s): ethical dilemmas in researching the personal', *Qualitative Inquiry*, 13(3): 399–416.

Coffey, A. (2002) 'Ethnography and self: reflections and representations', in T. May (ed.) *Qualitative Research in Action.* London: Sage.

Gill, R. (1998) Dialogues and differences: writing, reflexivity and the crisis of representation', in K. Henwood, C. Griffin and A. Phoenix (eds) *Standpoints and Differences: Essays in the Practice of Feminist Psychology.* London: Sage.

Haraway, D. (1988) 'Situated knowledges; the science question in feminism and the privilege of partial perspective', *Feminist Studies*, 14, 3: 581–607.

Harding,S. (1993) 'Rethinking standpoint epistemology: what is "strong objectivity?"', in L. Alcoff and E. Potter (eds) *Feminist Epistemologies.* London: Routledge.

Hill Collins, P. (1990) *Black Feminist Thought: Knowledge, Consciousness and the Politics of Empowerment.* London: Taylor and Francis.

hooks, b. (1982) *Aint I a Woman? Black Women and Feminism.* London: Pluto Press.

Kitzinger, C. and Wilkinson, S. (eds) (1996) *Representing the Other: A Feminism and Psychology Reader.* London: Sage.

Mauthner, M. (2000). 'Snippets and silences: ethics and reflexivity in narratives of sistering', *International Journal of Social Research Methodology*, 3(4): 287–306.

Mohanty, C. M. (2003) *Feminism Without Borders: Decolonizing Theory, Practicing Solidarity.* Durham, NC: Duke University Press.

Mohanty, C. M., Russo, A. and Torres, L. (eds) (1991) *Third World Women and the Politics of Feminism.* Bloomington, IN: Indiana University Press.

Oakley, A. (1982) 'Interviewing women: a contradiction in terms', in H. Roberts (ed.) *Doing Feminist Research.* London: Routledge.

Plummer, K. (2001) *Documents of Life 2: An Invitation to a Critical Humanism.* London: Sage.

Ramazonoglu, C. (1989) *Feminism and the Contradictions of Oppression.* London: Routledge.

Ramazonoglu, C. (with Holland, J.) (2002) *Feminist Methodology: Challenges and Choices.* London: Sage.

Segal, L. (1987) *Is the Future Female? Troubled Thoughts on Contemporary Feminism.* London: Virago.

Sharf, B. F. (1999) 'Beyond netiquette: the ethics of doing naturalistic discourse research on the Internet', in S. Jones (ed.) *Doing Internet Research: Critical issues and methods for examining the Net*. Thousand Oaks, CA: Sage.

Skeggs, B. (2004) 'Exchange value and affect: Bourdieu and the self', in B. Skeggs and L. Adkins (eds) *Feminism after Bourdieu*. Oxford: Wiley-Blackwell.

Spelman, E. (1988) *Inessential Woman: Problems of Exclusion in Feminist Thought*. London: The Women's Press.

Spender, D (1980) *Man Made Language*, London: Routledge & Kegan Paul.

Spivak, G. C. (1988) 'Can the subaltern speak?' in C. Nelson and L. Grossberg (eds) *Marxism and the Interpretation of Culture*. Chicago: University of Illinois Press.

Spivak, G. C. and Harasym, S. (1990) *The Postcolonial Critic: Interviews, Strategies, Dialogues*. London: Routledge.

Spivak, G. C. (1999) *A Critique of Postcolonial Reason: Toward a History of the Vanishing Present*. Boston: Harvard University Press.

Stanley, L. and Wise, S. (1993) *Breaking Out Again: Feminist Ontology and Epistemology*. London: Routledge.

Part I

Interpreting and theorising silence

1 Choosing silence

Rethinking voice, agency and women's empowerment

Jane L. Parpart

Introduction

Voice, or the act of speaking out, is often identified in the gender and development literature, and much of the feminist literature, as one of the key conditions demonstrating women's empowerment. Indeed, while silence has its defenders (Gal 1991; Mahoney 1996),[1] for most feminists women's ability to make choices and speak their mind has been seen as proof of agency and empowerment (Gilligan 1982; Olsen 2003 [1978]), while silence has been deplored as 'a symbol of passivity and powerlessness' (Gal 1991: 175). The language of choice/voice also frames the thinking and writing about women's agency and empowerment produced by development scholars, policy-makers and practitioners. Women who cannot speak out are seen as disempowered, unable to act and to effect change. The search for empowerment has thus become a search for women's voices, particularly the moments when women demonstrate agency[2] by speaking out against patriarchal authority (Kabeer 1999).

While keenly aware that a willingness to speak out and name oppressions and oppressors is a critical factor for challenging injustices, especially gendered injustices, I believe the assumption that voice equals agency needs to be rethought. The literature on women's empowerment, with its emphasis on voice and agency, is embedded in neo-liberal assumptions that individuals who speak hard truths will be protected by international and national institutions devoted to democracy, freedom of speech and human rights (Bishai 2004). Yet these assumptions are hard to sustain in a world where challenges to women's advancement and gender equality abound and where the World Health Organization warns of an epidemic of violence against women in 'private' and 'public' life (WHO 2002; UNRISD 2005). In such a world, can we assume that masculinist privilege can always be openly challenged?[3] Do we need to consider other forms of voice/agency/empowerment? Can silences and secrecy be legitimate and even empowering strategies for dealing with difficult situations?

This chapter argues that the uncritical identification of silence with disempowerment, and voice with agency/empowerment, so common in the gender and development literature (Cornwall and Brock 2005), as well as much of the wider feminist literature, dismisses and obscures the potential of many subtle strategies attempting to improve women's lives and to foster gender equality. The chapter explores the possibility that silences and secrecy may be essential strategies for negotiating gender relations (Kandiyoti 1998; Mohammed 2002), and considers the ethical, analytical and methodological implications of researching and writing about silence/secrecy as empowered choices/agency for women in an often masculinist, dangerous and conflict-ridden world.

Agency/voice/empowerment and development

Empowerment, particularly women's empowerment, has not always been regarded as a development issue. Initially associated with the critical thinking of educationalists such as Paulo Freire (1970), empowerment was seen as a tool for the liberation of the poor and marginalized, particularly women. While initially dismissed by mainstream development agencies as a minor sideshow to the real issues – economic growth and modernization – the failures of neo-liberal solutions, particularly structural adjustment programmes, encouraged a search for new solutions. By the 1990s, empowerment had moved into mainstream development discourse, affirmed by the 1995 Beijing United Nations conference on women, and supported by the United Nations and other key development agencies (UNDP 2003; Batliwala 2007).

Despite the notoriously slippery character of the term, a core set of assumptions/definitions about empowerment emerged, with an emphasis on the ability to choose, act and speak out. The UK Department for International Development (DFID) defines empowerment as 'individuals acquiring the power to think and act freely, exercise choice, and to fulfil their potential as full and equal members of society' (2000:11; Smyth 2007: 584). In a similar tone, Naila Kabeer, a well-known development scholar, argues that '[t]o be disempowered means to be denied choice, while empowerment refers to the processes by which those who have been denied the ability to make choices acquire such an ability' (2005: 13). The ability to voice concerns and to exercise choice in ways that challenge patriarchal power thus became the litmus test for 'true' empowerment (Cornwall and Brock 2005: 1055; Kabeer 2005: 13–16).[4]

The tone of this literature has been optimistic, even triumphalist; gender equality and women's empowerment are framed as laudable *and* reachable goals – encouraged by technical 'fixes' such as gender mainstreaming (GM) and micro-credit schemes. Women who fail to speak out and challenge masculinist power structures are portrayed as disempowered failures. The persistent, deeply held resistances to gender equality and women's empowerment are rarely discussed, despite repeated failures to achieve either of these goals (Heyser 2005; Rao and Kelleher 2005); nor is the fact that openly voicing dissent and opposition is often dangerous and even suicidal for many women (and men). Clearly new ways of thinking about agency and voice are needed, ones that take into account the many subtle forms of agency required to cope with an increasingly dangerous world.

The limits of voice: silence as a survival strategy

As we have seen, the discourses of gender equality and empowerment have focused on women's ability to make choices, to speak out, to choose and to challenge established gender hierarchies. This is understandable given development agencies' commitment to solving the problems of poverty, conflict and inequality, especially through expanded individual freedoms and democratic processes. Yet in many situations, particularly conflict and post-conflict zones as well as societies characterized by deeply masculinist practices, widespread criminal activities and gender violence, the choice to publicly challenge the powerful is often extremely dangerous and even foolhardy. Indeed, as Everjoice Win concludes for Zimbabwe, '[a]s any woman in a violent situation will tell you, there are no prizes for speaking out. If anything, you are ostracized by your own family and community. You are branded a bad woman, or worse, you are violated all over again for daring to open your mouth' (2004: 76). Often personal survival is all one can seek, especially in a subverted state with no active civil society (Chan 2005: 372). At the same time, choices and actions are made, if not in easily recognizable forms. As the WHO study on health and violence points out:

> Most abused women are not passive victims. ... Some women resist, others flee, while others attempt to keep the peace by giving in to their husbands' demands. What may seem to an outside observer to be a lack of positive response by the women may in fact be a calculated assessment of what is needed to survive in the marriage and to protect herself and her children.
>
> (2002: 95)

How do we understand women's agency and empowerment in an increasingly dangerous and often sexist world, particularly given the widening gap between poor and rich, the rise in civilian casualties in conflict and post-conflict societies and the world-wide increase in crime, gender-based violence and health risks? Wars, of course, have long been sites of violence against women. The supposed 'civility' legislated by the rules of engagement and codes of war in interstate conflicts has never stopped gender-based violence during war, and while some men suffer as well, most sexual violence in war is perpetrated by men against women, particularly rape. Indeed, both domestic violence and sexual violence generally increase in militarized societies, especially during wars (Enloe 1993: 127; Kelly 2000). The diary of a German woman caught in the Russian occupation of Berlin towards the end of World War II reveals the limits of voice in war conditions. Rape became an everyday experience, undermining women's sense of security and personhood. The threat of starvation, housing and safety soon drove many women, including the author, into the arms of Russian soldiers. The women she knew 'reached an unspoken agreement – all of a sudden no one is bringing up "that subject"' (Anonymous 2005: 18). Thus silence became a survival strategy for dealing with the horrors of rape and war. While shared moments discussing private traumas provided some solace, survival depended largely on learning to seal off feelings, to negotiate better conditions for sex and just keeping going (*ibid.*; Bletzer 2006). Speaking out was not an option; judicious silence was a key survival strategy in a dangerous and brutal world – a strategy that may not have changed conditions but did promote/enable healing and allowed some women to carry on.

Since the end of the Cold War, conflicts have become even more deadly, particularly for civilians. Often led by warlords and other adventurers, these new wars are sustained through terrorizing and looting civilians while also benefiting from global economic connections, both legal and illegal. Fought largely by young disaffected, under- and unemployed young men who see war as a way to gain prestige and money, and led by men seeking enrichment and power, these new wars are characterized by a strong, often adolescent sexualization of violence, 'ranging from almost daily orgies or veritable strategies of rape through to the ever more common mutilation of victims and the displaying of body parts as trophies' (Munkler 2005: 14–15; Kaldor 2001). Rape as an act of war continues to be a way to humiliate their male opponents by symbolically (and physically) 'marking' enemy women's bodies with semen and physical domination. Group rape is frequent, providing an opportunity to assault enemy women while also *performing* loyal masculinity to one's comrades (Kelly 2000). Indeed, rape camps in Bosnia were vehicles for educating/training reluctant soldiers in the practices of violence (Kaldor 2001: 44–53). Sexual violence is thus one of the key characteristics of the new wars around the world, with Liberia, Sierra Leone and Rwanda being particularly gruesome examples (Dolan 2002; Pederson 2008). For most women direct confrontation risks swift and terrible revenge. As in Berlin, silence and secrecy have been one of the few choices for negotiating survival. Even deliberate attempts to thwart authorities, such as girls' education under the Taliban, have only survived under conditions of strict secrecy (Hans 2004: 235; Armstrong 2002; Povey 2004).

Post-conflict societies have often proven little better for women and girls. Even the transition to peace has often been marked by increased sexual violence. In Liberia, both government and rebel forces engaged in a 'frenzy of rape' during the 'transition to peace' (African Women and Peace Support Group 2004). Yet, little has been done to address the epidemic of sexual violence characterizing many post-conflict societies, particularly when it has been and is being perpetrated by the new 'heroes of the nation' (Kelly 2000; Silber 2005; Jones 2008). Despite a supportive constitution and a significant female presence in parliament, post-apartheid South Africa has one of the highest rape rates in the world (du Toit 2005). Moreover, the much praised Truth and Reconciliation Commission for the most part ignored evidence of sexual violence (Goldblatt and Meintjes 1998), and young men continue to believe women out alone after dark are 'asking to be raped' (field notes, Cape Town 2006). In Rwanda, many rape survivors are trying to rebuild their lives in communities with the very people who raped them. 'There is little judicial redress and little sympathy from others', who blame them for choosing rape over death (Kelly 2000: 55). Sexual violence continues, often carried out by current government forces (Twagiramariya and Turshen 1998). Despite their key role in the peace process, and a woman president, post-conflict Liberia is experiencing an epidemic of violent rapes, particularly of young girls (Jones 2008; Pedersen 2008).

Many women and children have fled war and post-conflict zones,[5] yet refugee camps have provided disappointingly little protection. Sexual violence, particularly rape, is a common occurrence. Many refugee camps have become caught up in the new wars, inadvertently providing food and supplies as well as sex for marauding 'warriors'. Even the camp administrators and peacekeepers demand sexual favours. For many women refugees, sex has become one of the few commodities they can 'sell' for survival. Yet such activities are widely censured; once again, silence and secrecy are weapons for survival (WHO 2002; Hyndman 2004; Munkler 2005). Even applicants for political asylum often experience sexual violence, but tend to deny it publicly, both to deal with the trauma and to minimize the consequences of disclosure (Crawley 2000: 93).

Sexual violence, particularly rape, threads through all these stories. The development literature on women and empowerment urges rape victims to become empowered by speaking out, taking their persecutors to court and obtaining retribution. Yet this 'solution' has largely been empty rhetoric given the trauma of rape, the unreliability of police and courts and the widespread, entrenched cultures supporting sexual violence. In post-conflict Yugoslavia and Rwanda, for example, women have been encouraged to take their assailants to court, but no provisions have been made to protect them. Not surprisingly, most women have chosen to exercise agency 'by choosing to remain silent' (Kelly 2000: 54; Twagiramariya and Turshen 1998). An UNRISD study concluded that 'Somali women do not confess to having been raped because social rejection and divorce will follow' (2005: 215). South African rape victims are often reluctant to speak out in public (du Toit 2005). Public disclosure is particularly dangerous in societies where honour killing is the norm (Mojab 2004). For example, in 2002 almost half the women raped in Alexandria, Egypt, were killed by a relative after a rape (WHO 2002: 93). Thus, given the high cost of disclosing rape or sex with the enemy, the decision to remain silent cannot be dismissed simply as disempowerment. Indeed, silence and secrecy offer one of the few possibilities for rebuilding lives and renegotiating gender relations, if often in precarious, highly militarized contexts. Silence can also provide a private space to deal with trauma, to regain self-esteem and to build a sense of empowerment in an often unpredictable and dangerous world (El-Bushra 2000; Kelly 2000; Mojab 2004; Silber 2005).

Conflict and post-conflict zones are not the only danger zones for women. The rise in violence against women around the world, including beatings and non-consensual sex, is well documented (WHO 2002; Jejeebhoy et al. 2005). In South Asia, 'one in every two women faces violence in her daily life, and social customs and attitudes that support violence against women are entrenched and institutionalized at all levels – home, family, community, society, and the state' (Mehta and Gopalakrishnan 2007: 41). In Latin America, a study reported a fourth to a half of the women interviewed had been abused by their partners (Sagot 2005). Although patterns of gender-based violence vary by class, race, age and other factors, societies with rigid patriarchal hierarchies and established cultures of violence are the worst offenders (Armstrong 2002; Sagot 2005). For most victims, open challenges and public disclosure are dangerous strategies. Choosing silence and secrecy, policing one's voice and body, are well-established survival strategies. It seems unfair to dismiss these choices as passivity and disempowerment as they are often the best (and sometimes the only) tactics available for building internal strength, negotiating survival and sometimes for ultimately participating in more open challenges in a hostile world (Sagot 2005; Silber 2005).

Silence and secrecy also have a long history as survival strategies for women (and men) in marginal positions. Sexuality has been a key case in point. For example, Sarda discovered that in Latin America the reaction to disclosure of lesbian sexuality – with a few remarkable exceptions – goes 'from disclosure to firing'. Understandably, many choose to hide their sexual preferences, masking it by dating men, dressing in very feminine ways and avoiding talk about personal lives (2008: 113–17) The intersection of race and sexuality has been particularly toxic for Black women in racist societies. Pornographic stereotypes about Black sexuality have been met with steely silence – a tradition that has provided solace and a sense of community but has also encouraged reluctance to speak out against Black male patriarchy (Collins 1991: 92, 117). This same tradition has informed Black lesbians' reaction to widespread homophobia in both Black (and White) communities. With a few notable exceptions, this 'politics of silence', this tradition of 'silence, secrecy, and a partially self-chosen invisibility', has remained a key strategy for Black women dealing with racist and homophobic environments (Hammonds 1997: 171; Lorde 2007 [1984]; Collins 1991: 192–96). The HIV/AIDS pandemic has silenced many people as well. Gendered discourses blaming women/prostitutes for the epidemic in Africa have fuelled expulsion from families and communities, despite class, ethnicity or race (Win 2007). Not surprisingly, many African women (and men) deny their HIV/AIDS status, especially health care professionals (field notes, Zimbabwe 2005). Clearly these silences emerged under severe constraints, but are they merely symptoms of disempowerment? The evidence suggests that silence and secrecy can be crucial survival strategies, offering protection and sometimes spaces for renegotiating harmful gender relations and practices. While ideally voices should be heard and challenges launched, voice is not the only weapon available.

Challenging power/maintaining power through silence

Indeed, silence and secrecy can be a means for both maintaining and challenging gendered inequities. At an institutional level, secret societies reinforce the power of those who 'know' and exclude those who do not. They can build trust within groups while casting suspicion on others. This is often a gendered process. In Papua New Guinea, for example, while women gain some authority through their secret societies, overall secret societies have reinforced and legitimated the power of men over women (Herdt 2003: xii–xiii). Development agencies often use silence to stonewall controversial policies, especially regarding gender. The persistent gap between implementation and official support for gender mainstreaming and women's empowerment raises questions about commitment to gender transformation. Yet little is said about the possibility that subterranean resistance to GM may silence critics trying to implement GM. Indeed, Trunette Joseph (2008), in her study of UNDP/South Africa's gender mainstreaming policies and practices, discovered powerful unspoken resistances to GM at the highest levels. Her findings resonate with Ines Smyth's observation that, 'If words are important, silences are important too and a reflection of what is excluded from daily exchanges – verbal or written – among development practitioners and policy makers' (2007: 583). Thus silences can undermine official policies without openly challenging them, reminding us that they can control meaning/knowledge and thus deserve study in themselves (Kronsell 2006).

Oppressive regimes have often silenced critics and denied wrongdoings against women, thus perpetuating masculinist practices and gender hierarchies. During the Dirty War in Argentina (1976–83) the military junta carried on a secret war against its critics, kidnapping, torturing, raping and killing many young men and women. The struggles between the Palestinians and the Israeli government have also been marked by considerable gender-based violence – frequently denied by all parties. Nationalist movements, and the governments they form, have often refused to acknowledge widespread sexual abuse during and after conflicts, especially once victory has given them the power to define the 'truth' of the struggle (Chan 2005; Silber 2005; Cockburn 2007).

At the same time, silence and secrecy have sometimes played a critical role in challenges to oppressive regimes and social injustice. In circumstances where direct, vocal challenges cannot succeed, silent vigils, symbols and placards have proven effective weapons against tyranny, especially for women. Using their authority as mothers, women have found ways to publicly hold regimes accountable without saying a word. In Argentina, for example, some of the mothers of the disappeared (*Madres de la Plaza de Mayo*) gathered silently in the Plaza de Mayo, across from the presidential palace, where they walked silently round and round wearing white headscarves, symbolizing the diapers of their lost children. The Madres de la Plaza de Mayo grew in number, building awareness and gradually helping to bring down the government (Mellibovsky 1997; Anavy 2006). In Istanbul, Kurdish Mothers of the Lost sat silently every Saturday, providing a space for people to publicly condemn both state injustice and Kurdish patriarchal practices (Ahmetbeyzade 2007). Women in Black, established by a small group of Israeli and Palestinian women soon after the first Palestinian *Intifada* broke out in the 1980s, organized vigils once a week, at the same hour and at the same location – a major traffic intersection in Israel. The protestors dressed in black and held up a black sign in the shape of a hand with 'Stop the Occupation' written in white. Vigils soon sprang up throughout Israel and around the world, providing solace, shaping public opinion and strengthening solidarity against injustices (www.womeninblack.org). As Cynthia Cockburn reminisced:

> [T]here is something calming about vigilling, holding yourself in silence and stillness as city workers and tourists mill around you and the taxis and buses stream past. … What restores me as I stand there once again is the presence of other women at my shoulder … the carefully thought-out message we are trying to put across; and more than anything, the feeling that women are doing this in hundreds of similar vigils around the world. (Cockburn 2007: 51)

These demonstrations and vigils, and others like them around the world, illustrate both the power of collective silence and the importance of symbolic performances for challenging social injustice and mobilizing public opinion. The white headscarves symbolizing the diapers of the children of the disappeared reinforced the silent message of the Mothers of the Plaza de Mayo. At the height of the second Liberian civil war, for example, the Women in Peacebuilding Network (WIPNET) mobilized thousands of women around the country to protest against the war and deeper systemic disregard for women through silent protest, symbolic dress as well as media campaigns. They wore white t-shirts with the WIPNET logo and peace slogans on the back, traditional dress, no jewellery or make-up and lay on their bellies with their backs to the sun, fasting and praying. Sometimes they wore sack clothes and ashes for months. Their dress and manner deliberately highlighted their identification with traditional values, their rejection of class divisions and their group solidarity, particularly as mothers. These protestors' silent performance of resistance to the war and gender violence once again reminds us that voice is not the only form that empowerment and struggles for gender transformation can take (Pedersen 2008). As one member reported, it was sitting in the sun and rain 'that really caught people's heart … and played a major part in the peace process' (*ibid.*: 6).

Resistance also often takes the form of silent acts/performances in daily life. Just as wearing a veil may be a form of symbolic opposition to colonial rule or to the right-wing politics emerging in many parts of the world, particularly in opposition to Muslim minorities (Sullivan 1998: 228), so too are acts of resistance to patriarchal oppression around the world. In Afghanistan, for example, some women wear white socks, western clothes and platform shoes under *burqas* as silent challenges to Taliban rulings (Armstrong 2002: 3, 112). Wearing make-up and jewellery, painting one's toe-nails and other prohibited practices can be small signs of resistance in an oppressive situation. Afghan women in exile in India move about without veils, dress in the latest fashions and wear make-up (Hans 2004: 244). In French immigrant housing projects, for example, many young Muslim women challenge patriarchal authority over young women 'by continuing to wear revealing clothing, by dressing in fashion, by using makeup, sometimes outrageously. They want to live in a modern society, to exist as individuals, and to command personal respect on equal footing with young men.' For many young women in the housing projects, 'makeup has become war paint, a sign of resistance. It is their way of fighting' (Amara 2006: 75). They pay a price, often being roughed up, even raped. Some give up, others police their bodies to avoid rape, wearing a big sweater or baggy coats, which they then take off when they get to school (ibid.: 111–12).

While these institutional practices, vigils and performances may seem like small gestures, they can be powerful vectors for change (both individually and collectively). Some scholars and activists have questioned the transformative potential of silent protests. Blacklock and Crosby (2004: 45) argue that 'political contestation engaged in and through silence has not proved a unifying, cohesive strategy of resistance'. Indeed, they see silence as a defensive rather than a progressive strategy, arguing that Guatemala has changed little since the civil war. Highlighting the limits of silence and secrecy as a vehicle for social transformation, they ignore the importance of incremental change, particularly given the well-documented limits of revolutionary struggles for improving women's status (El-Bushra 2000: 163; Silber 2005). Silence and secrecy are by their nature, employed in contentious circumstances little given to dramatic transformations. Yet incremental change can occur. Daily performances of resistance can suggest new patterns of living and stabilize new patterns of empowerment – individually and collectively (Kesby 2005: 2052; Butler 2004). Silent vigils and symbols can disrupt and challenge the discourses of the powerful while providing space for solace, sharing and collective empowerment. While acknowledging the importance of voice, it is important to remember that 'silence can also be a means of resistance, a way of holding one's ground against the encroachments of oppression' (Stone 2002: 19). Moreover, as Audre Lorde (2007 [1984]) reminds us, silence 'is a site not only of resistance but also of transformation, the home where new dreams and visions are born' (cited in Stone 2002: 20). Silence and secrecy can be evidence of desperation and disempowerment, but they can also be strategic choices offering tools for gradual, subtle renegotiations of gender hierarchies and practices. The question remains: how can we discover and analyse such elusive and secretive strategies?

Researching silence and secrecy

As we have seen, silence and secrecy can take many forms and serve many purposes. They can reflect disempowerment as well as innovative strategies for survival in dangerous circumstances, mechanisms for renegotiating gender relations, collective challenges to oppressive regimes, ways to resist oppressive circumstances and to find space to breathe and find strength. They can foster performative challenges to the status quo and subtly undermine patriarchal and class hierarchies. The challenge facing researchers interested in investigating this realm are many. First, it is important to recognize that the use and expressions of silence and secrecy intersect with class, race, ethnicity and other factors. They are also shaped by specific circumstances over time and place (Das 2000).

Obtaining research permission may require lengthy diplomatic discussions with powerful gatekeepers. It also requires attention to local sensitivities, gaining support from local partners and careful pruning of contentious language in the research proposal (Thomson 2009). Gatekeepers in patriarchal institutions often block interviews or provide vague, unhelpful information. The researcher has to learn how to read silence and dissembling by deconstructing discourse and texts emerging from such institutions, paying attention to the unwritten, as well as what is 'between the lines' or expressed as symbols and in procedures (Kronsell 2006).

Once in the field, asking informants to reveal their secrets and silences is both difficult and ethically challenging. The research goals have to be explained immediately and complete anonymity guaranteed. Safeguards must be put in place from the beginning (Thomson 2009). Gaining trust takes time and consistency, requiring repeat interviews as well as efforts to engage in informal discussions wherever they occur. Sexuality and sexual violence are particularly difficult subjects to discuss openly (Hans 2004). Ethnographic and participatory methods are crucial, but patience and tact are required as well. Providing a safe, empathetic space for discussions, a leisurely pace that allows for silences, detours and tears is essential (Harrison 2006; Ghorashi 2007). Moreover, reading fragmented comments and bodily signs is crucial as the pain and fear associated with silence and secrecy often inhibit sustained open discussions (Das 2000).

Finally, evidence of secrets and silences must be carefully analysed and written up. For example, many women keep secrets from their husband and these secrets/silences are key survival practices. In Calcutta, many women keep their economic activities, especially their income, secret from their husbands. This money provides much needed goods as well as feelings of freedom and independence (Tenhunen 1999). Women admitting domestic violence or rape risk further violence and even death (Hans 2004; Sagot 2005; Mheta and Gopalakrishnan 2007). Such revelations place a responsibility on the researcher to write up their findings in ways that will not harm informants' lives. This ethical responsibility must inform information gathering, analysis and writing, whether by academic researchers or development analysts and practitioners aiming to facilitate change and improve lives.

Conclusion: rethinking agency and empowerment

The preoccupation with voice as a sign/symbol of women's agency is understandable given the long struggles of feminists to gain entry into male-dominated public spaces, to speak out and to be taken seriously. Yet, as this chapter demonstrates, open challenges to masculinist power are not always possible. Indeed, incremental steps towards gender transformation are often the most one can hope for. While silence and secrecy can be symptomatic of passivity and disempowerment, as well a means for reinforcing gender hierarchies, as we have seen, they can also provide the space for discovering and consolidating inner resources, questioning the status quo and developing long-term strategies for renegotiating gender relations. At an individual level, silence and secrecy can protect women from disempowering contexts where their voices have no institutional or collective power. Silent vigils and the use of appropriate symbols can reinforce group identity, build collective strength and subtly challenge oppressive behaviour. Everyday practices/performances, both individually and in groups, can also challenge long established gender practices (see also Gal 1991; Mahoney 1996).

These incremental, subtle strategies may not satisfy the goals of feminists calling for global gender equality. Nor do they sit well with development agencies' assurances that gender mainstreaming will transform gender relations and ensure women's empowerment. Yet in our increasingly unequal, often violent and masculinist world, such ambitious promises have limited purchase. Change at best is a messy, incremental and unpredictable process, often requiring a judicious mix of voice and silences/secrecy. To privilege voice over silence and secrecy as evidence of empowered agency ignores the transformative potential of a complex mix of choices. Indeed, Gal argues that the relationship between silence, speech, gender and power must be taken into account (1991). With their need to measure outcomes and 'prove' results, development policies and practices tend to privilege measurable behaviour and to ignore subtle, less obvious strategies for change (Alsop *et al.* 2006). The choice to speak out against gender oppression may be easy to measure, but as this chapter demonstrates, agency with a transformative agenda may take surprising forms, including the judicious use of secrecy and silence.

Notes

1 Both authors argue that silence can be a form of power and agency, although Gal emphasizes the relationship between silence, speech and power.

2 Kabeer sees agency as exercising choice in ways that challenge power relation (2005: 14). Feminists such as Kandiyoti (1998: 147) see it as 'embedded in the messiness of social reality'.
3 Of course, some women support masculinist privilege and 'necessary' violence against women.
4 Kabeer acknowledges the cultural, material and institutional constraints to empowered agency, but looks to education, employment and political representation for solutions – all spaces where voice is crucial for transformative agendas (2005). Participation, with its emphasis on voice, is also closely linked to empowerment (Cornwall and Brock 2005).
5 Over three-quarters of the world's 11+ million refugees in 2007 were women and children (www.unhcr.org).

References

African Women and Peace Support Group (2004) *Liberian Women Peacemakers*, Trenton, NJ: Africa World Press.

Alsop, R., Bertelsen, M. and Holland, J. (2006) *Empowerment in Practice: From Analysis to Implementation*, Washington, DC: World Bank.

Ahmetbeyzade, C. (2007) 'Negotiating silences in the so-called low-intensity war: the making of the Kurdish diaspora in Istanbul', *Signs* 33 (1): 159–82.

Amara, F. (2006) *Breaking the Silence: French Women's Voices from the Ghetto*, Berkeley: University of California Press.

Anavy, R. (2006) 'Hope ends 29-year March of Mothers of the Plaza de Mayo', *San Francisco Chronicle* (2 February).

Anonymous (2005) *A Woman in Berlin: Eight Weeks in the Conquered City*, trans. P. Boehm, New York: Henry Holt.

Armstrong, S. (2002) *The Hidden Power of the Women of Afghanistan*, New York: Four Walls, Eight Windows.

Batliwala, S. (2007) 'Taking the power out of empowerment – an experiential account', *Development in Practice* 17 (4–5): 557–65.

Bishai, S. L. (2004) 'Liberal Empire', *Journal of International Relations and Development* 7 (1): 48–72.

Blacklock, C. and Crosby, A. (2004) 'The sounds of silence: feminist research across time in Guatemala', in W. Giles and J. Hyndman (eds) *Sites of Violence: Gender and Conflict Zones*, Berkeley: University of California Press.

Bletzer, K. (2006) 'A voice for every woman and the travesties of war', *Violence against Women* 12 (7): 700–5.

Butler, J. (2004) *Undoing Gender*, London: Routledge.

Chan, S. (2005) 'The memory of violence', *Third World Quarterly* 26 (2): 369–82.

Cockburn, C. (2007) *From Where we Stand: War, Women's Activism and Feminist Analysis*, London: Zed Books.

Collins, P. H. (1991) *Black Feminist Thought*, London: Routledge.

Cornwall, A. and Brock, K. (2005) 'What do buzzwords do for development policy? A critical look at "participation", "empowerment" and "poverty reduction"', *Third World Quarterly* 26 (7): 1043–60.

Crawley, H. (2000) 'Engendering the state in refugee women's claims for asylum', in S. Jacobs, R. Jacobson and J. Marchbank (eds) *States of Conflict: Gender, Violence and Resistance*, London and New York: Zed Books.

Das, V. (2000) 'The act of witnessing: violence, poisonous knowledge, and subjectivity, in V. Das, A. Kleinman, M. Ramphele and P. Reynolds. (eds) *Violence and Subjectivity*, Los Angeles: UCLA Press.

DFID (2000) *Poverty Elimination and the Empowerment of Women*, Target Strategy Paper, London: DFID.

Dolan, C. (2002) 'Collapsing masculinities and weak states', in F. Cleaver (ed.) *Making Men Matter,* London: Zed Books.

Du Toit, L. (2005) 'A phenomenology of rape: forging a new vocabulary for action', in A. Gouws (ed.) *(Un)thinking Citizenship*, London: Ashgate Publishing.

El-Bushra, J. (2000) 'Transforming conflict: some thoughts on a gendered understanding of conflict processes', in S. Jacobs, R. Jacobson and J. Marchbank (eds) *States of Conflict: Gender, Violence and Resistance*, London and New York: Zed Books.

Enloe, C. (1993) *The Morning After: Sexual Politics at the End of the Cold War*, Los Angeles, CA.: University of California Press.

Freire, P. (1970) *Pedagogy of the Oppressed*, trans. M.B. Ramos, New York: Continuum.

Gal, S. (1991) 'Between speech and silence', in M. di Leonardo (ed.) *Gender at the Crossroads of Knowledge*, Berkeley: University of California Press.

Ghorashi, H. (2007) 'Giving silence a chance: the importance of life stories for research on refugees', *Journal of Refugee Studies* 21 (1): 117–32.

Gilligan, C. (1982) *In a Different Voice*, Cambridge, MA: Harvard University Press.

Goldblatt, B. and Meintjes, S. (1998) 'South African women demand the truth', in M. Turshen and C. Twagiramariya (eds) *What Women do in Wartime,* London: Zed Books.

Hammonds, E. (1997) 'Towards a genealogy of black female sexuality: the problematic of silence', in M.J. Alexander and C.T. Mohanty (eds) *Feminist Genealogies, Colonial Legacies, Democratic Futures*, London: Routledge.

Hans, A. (2004) 'Escaping conflict: Afghan women in transit', in W. Giles and J. Hyndman (eds) *Sites of Violence: Gender and Conflict Zones*, Berkeley, CA, London: University of California Press.

Harrison, M. (2006) 'Collecting sensitive and contentious information', in V. Desai and R.B. Potter (eds) *Doing Development Research*, London: Sage.

Herdt, G. (2003) *Secrecy and Cultural Reality: Utopian Ideologies of the New Guinea Men's Houses*, Ann Arbor, MI.: University of Michigan Press.

Heyser, N. (2005) 'Making the links: women's rights and empowerment are key to achieving the Millennium Development Goals', *Gender and Development* 13 (1): 9–12.

Hyndman, J. (2004) 'Refugee camps as conflict zones', in W. Giles and J. Hyndman (eds) *Sites of Violence*, Berkeley, CA: University of California Press.

Jejeebhoy, S., Shah, I. and Thapa, S. (eds) (2005) *Sex without Consent: Young People in Developing Countries*, London: Zed Books.

Jones, A. (2008) 'The war against women in Africa', in *Pambazuka News* (20 February).

Joseph, T. (2008) 'Mainstreaming women in development?', unpublished thesis, Political Science, University of Stellenbosch, South Africa.

Kabeer, N. (1999) 'Resources, agency, and achievements: reflections on the measurements of women's empowerment', *Development and Change* 30 (3): 435–64.

——(2005) 'Gender equality and women's empowerment: a critical analysis of the third Millennium Development Goal', *Gender and Development* 13 (1): 13–24.

Kaldor, M. (2001) *New and Old Wars: Organized Violence in a Global Era*, Stanford, CA: Stanford University Press.

Kandiyoti, D. (1998) 'Gender, power and contestation: rethinking bargaining with patriarchy', in C. Jackson and R. Pearson (eds) *Feminist Visions of Development,* London: Routledge.

Kelly, L. (2000) 'Wars against the women: sexual violence, sexual politics and the militarised state', in S. Jacobs, R. Jacobson and J. Marchbank (eds) *States of Conflict: Gender, Violence and Resistance*, London and New York: Zed Books.

Kesby, M. (2005) 'Retheorizing empowerment-through-participation as a performance of space', *Signs* 30 (4): 2037–65.

Kronsell, A. (2006) 'Methods for studying silences: gender analysis in institutions of hegemonic masculinity', in B. Ackerly, M. Sterns and J. True (eds) *Feminist Methodologies for International Relations*, Cambridge: Cambridge University Press.

Lorde, A. (2007 [1984]) *Sister Outsider*, Berkeley, CA: Crossing Press.

Mahoney, M. A. (1996) 'The problem of silence in feminist psychology', *Feminist Studies* 22 (3): 603–25.

Mehta, M. and Gopalakrishnan, C. (2007) '"We can": transforming power in relationships in South Asia', *Gender and Development* 15 (1): 41–49.

Mellibovsky, M. (1997) *Circle of Love over Death*, trans. M. Proser., Willimantic, CT.: Curbstone Press.

Mohammed, P. (2002) *Gender Negotiations among Indians in Trinidad, 1917–1947*, Basingstoke: Palgrave.

Mojab, S. (2004) 'No "safe haven": violence against women in Iraqi Kurdistan', in W. Giles and J. Hyndman (eds) *Sites of Violence: Gender and Conflict Zones*, Berkeley, CA: University of California Press.

Munkler, H. (2005) *The New Wars*, trans. P. Camillier, London: Polity Press.

Olsen, T. (2003, [1978]) *Silences*, New York: Feminist Press at CUNY.

Pedersen, J. (2008) 'In the rain and in the sun: women in peacebuilding in Liberia', mimeo.

Povey, E. R. (2004) 'Women in Afghanistan: passive victims of the borga or active social participants?', in H. Afshar and D. Eade (eds) *Development, Women, and War*, Oxford: Oxfam.

Rao, A. and Kelleher, D. (2005) 'Is there life after gender mainstreaming?', *Gender and Development* 13 (2): 57–69.

Sagot, M. (2005) 'The critical path of women affected by family violence in Latin America', *Violence against Women* 11 (10): 1292–318.

Sarda, A. (2008) 'Discrimination against lesbians in the workplace', in A. Cornwall, S. Correa and S. Jolly (eds) *Development with a Body: Sexuality, Human Rights and Development,* London: Zed Books.

Silber, I. C. (2005) 'Mothers/fighters/citizens: violence and disillusionment in post-war El Salvador', in S. D'Cruze and A. Rao (eds) *Violence, Vulnerability and Embodiment*, Oxford: Blackwell.

Smyth, I. (2007) 'Talking of gender: words and meanings in development organisations', *Development in Practice* 17 (4–5): 582–88.

Stone, E. (2002) *Rising from Deep Places: Women's Lives and the Ecology of Voice and Silence,* New York: Peter Lang.

Sullivan, Z. T. (1998) 'Eluding the feminist, overthrowing the modern? Transformations in 20th century Iran', in L. Abu-Lughod (ed.) *Remaking Women*, Princeton, NJ: Princeton University Press.

Tenhunen, S. (1999) 'Women's hidden work and agency in Calcutta', in K. Armstrong (ed.) *Shifting Ground and Cultured Bodies*, Lanham, MD: University Press of America.

Thomson, S. (2009) '"That is not what we authorised you to do … ": access and government interference in highly politicised research environments', in J. King, C. Sriram, J. Mertus, O. Martin-Ortega and J. Herman. (eds) *Doing Research in Difficult Situations,* London: Routledge.

Twagiramariya, C. and Turshen, M. (1998) '"Favours" to give and "consenting" victims', in M. Turshen and C. Twagiramariya (eds) *What Women do in Wartime: Gender and Conflict in Africa*, London: Zed Books.

UNDP (2003) *Transforming the Mainstream: Gender in the UNDP,* New York City, UNDP.

UNRISD (2005) *Gender Equality: Striving for Justice in an Unequal World*, Geneva: UNRISD.

World Health Organization (2002) *World Report on Violence and Health*, Geneva: WHO.

Win, E. (2004) 'Open letter to Nkosazana Dlamini-Zuma and other women in the South African Cabinet', *Feminist Africa*, 3 (October/November): 74–6.

——(2007) 'Not very poor, powerless or pregnant: the African woman forgotten by development', in A. Cornwall, A. E. Harrison and A. Whitehead (eds) *Feminisms in Development: Contradictions, Contestations and Challenges*, London: Zed Books.

2 Forms of knowing and un-knowing

Secrets about society, sexuality and God in Northern Kenya

Henrietta L. Moore

> One may say … that in all relations of a personally differentiated sort, intensity and nuance develop in the degree in which each party, by words and by mere existence, reveals itself to the other.
>
> (Simmel 1950: 307)

> There is no ethics without the presence of the other but also, and consequently, without absence, dissimulation, detour, difference, writing.
>
> (Derrida 1974: 139–40)

> In the social sciences the lore of objectivity relies on the separation of the intellectual project from its process of production. The false paths, the endless labors, the turns now this way and now that, the theories abandoned, and the data collected but never presented – all lie concealed behind the finished product.
>
> (Burawoy 1991: 8)

This chapter discusses the ways in which secrecy and silence have through various means defined the research I have conducted in an African community over the last 25 years. The discipline of anthropology has a long history of fascination with secrecy and secret knowledge, as exemplified in the very many studies of secret societies, esoteric knowledge and initiation rituals (e.g. Leiris 1948; Barth 1975; Murphy 1980; Bellman 1984; Ottenberg 1989; Kratz 1994; Herdt 2003; Crook 2007). In many such analyses, secrecy and secret knowledge are very often linked to political power and the maintenance of control of men over women and elders over youth. Anthropologists thus recognize the mutually constitutive relations of power and knowledge in the contexts in which they work, and they have discussed and analysed the ways in which the interconnections between knowledge and power shape their relations with their informants and with fieldwork more generally (e.g. Clifford and Marcus 1986; Stacey 1988; Abu-Lughod 1990; Mitchell 1993). What has been given less attention is the manner in which the idea of secrets dominates the imaginative construction of the domain of anthropology itself and acts as the evident, but nonetheless concealed, centre around which the desire of the anthropologist circulates (e.g. Bell et al. 1993; Rubenstein 2004). Anthropology as a set of disciplinary practices is discursively constructed in relation to the notions of fieldwork and participant observation and is actively depicted as a form of comparative knowledge production that involves an explicit oscillation between self and other. The self of the anthropologist is formed through multiple identifications with various subject positions, one of which is that of 'anthropologist'. The engagement with this subject position is, like all others, constituted by and through the workings of power: institutional, disciplinary and experiential. At the same time, it is set up in fantasy and connected for each individual to their experience of fieldwork and of self/other relations. Thus, the subject position 'anthropologist' is one which never entirely belongs – as is the case with all subject positions – to the individual who identifies with it, because it is the result not only of disciplinary training and institutional location and the engagement these have with the personal fantasies of the anthropologist, but is also the product of fieldwork, and of entanglements with the institutional and discursive structures of others, and most especially with their fantasies of otherness.

Otherness is a resilient and intoxicating site of power and desire both for the researcher and for the people they work with. The desire to be other to oneself is what drives many individuals to become anthropologists, and a similar desire to know the other and the secrets of their power is what motivates many people to engage with and work with anthropologists (e.g. Gable 1997; Lattas 1998; Rubenstein 2004). Much of the discussion about power differentials and hierarchies in fieldwork, and the unequal roles of the researcher and the researched in analysis and interpretation (e.g. McDowell 1992; Wolf 1996; Moss 2002), fails to acknowledge the unconscious processes at work in constructing the other – and their secrets – as an object of desire (e.g. Rubenstein 2004; Lovell 2007; Corin 2007). The desire for the other, the desire to be the object of desire for the other, finds specific inflection in the fieldwork situation, but is definitely not confined to it. The huge symbolic and emotional importance given in anthropology to being an 'insider', 'knowing another culture', understanding people in a way that others cannot, shows how powerful and important the drives for identification that underpin anthropological fieldwork are, and also explains the intense desire to know the secrets of others, to make them give them up, to find them out. This desire, which has been criticized by feminist social scientists for its masculine preoccupation with penetration, domination and objectification does demand serious self-reflection and critique as these scholars have suggested. However, the desire for recognition, for intersubjectivity is a constitutive element of all human interactions, whether in the research process or not. The feminist discussion of positionality, self-reflexivity, ethics and self-disclosure should thus be read as one way of acknowledging issues that are a key part of all forms of relationality, and which, whilst highlighted by fieldwork, are by no means produced only in and through the research process.

The positionality and partiality of our knowledge of others was raised by Simmel (1950) in his discussion of the secret and the secret society. His simple point is that we can never completely know another person; however, that this is not a matter of the mere quantity of knowledge, but of the fact that the situated character of self–other relations must necessarily make our knowledge of others partial (ibid.: 308). In all our relationships there are movements of concealment and revelation; some are within our conscious control and others are not. Simmel's focus here is on the intertwined nature of recognition and identification, and on how the ebb and flow of concealment and revelation are a consequence of the dynamic relation between these two processes (ibid.: 10). Our worlds are necessarily intersubjective; we recognize others, but what we reveal to them – consciously or unconsciously – are only 'fragments of our inner life', and these fragments are not in any way 'a representative selection, but one made from the standpoint of reason, value, and relation to the listener and his understanding' (ibid.: 312). Whatever we reveal cannot be a faithful and accurate representation of the totality our psychic life, but only aspects of it relevant to others, the context and our engagement with both. As Simmel suggests, '[w]e simply cannot imagine any interaction or social relation or society which is not based on this teleologically determined non-knowledge of one another' (ibid.: 312).

The secrets of society

Secrets are of many different kinds and Simmel's contention that social life is impossible without certain forms of 'unknowing' draws attention as I have suggested both to the mutual construction of secrets and knowledge, and to the fact that our knowledge of others is always partial. The fact that secrets (*ung'oot*) are not just an important but a constitutive part of social life is a self-evident fact for the members of the Marakwet community in Northern Kenya with whom I have worked since 1980. There are, of course, the specific secrets that families keep from outsiders, wives conceal from their husbands and children hide from the prying questions of their elders and betters. These may be such things as the details of financial transactions, the origins of sudden fortune, or the reasons for the loss of a goat or a pregnancy promised but never brought to fruition – the things, in short, that people in different ways and in different circumstances keep to themselves, the things that make up the ordinary stuff of life. However, these quotidian secrets and the experience of keeping them and revealing them are shaped by a much more powerful and diffuse understanding of secrecy which lies at the core of gendered subjectivity and the making of the social.

In Marakwet, the relationships of elders to youth, women to men and parents to children all involve secrecy in that they entail specific relations to forms of knowing and un-knowing. As one ages in Marakwet society, social relationships develop and shift, and all such movements are characterized by changing relationships to forms of knowledge. At the core of these transformations are the initiation rites for women and men. When I first began work in the Kerio valley in 1980, all boys and girls went through these rites. Today, these rites have undergone considerable change and while male circumcision is still held to be essential for boys, there has been a well-orchestrated campaign by an international Christian NGO to eradicate the practice of female circumcision which has received considerable support from certain sections of Marakwet society.

In the past, circumcision was the fulcrum of a rite of social transformation that prepared girls to be mothers and wives, and provided them with the maturity and the knowledge to produce children who were themselves the embodied link between the ancestors and the future well-being of the community. Intense secrecy surrounded the activities and teachings of kapkore, the girls' initiation house. These secrets were, however, a prelude to other secrets, other songs, dances and teachings that would be progressively revealed to married couples at different stages of the ceremonies associated with marriage, the last of which would not be performed until a couple had two or three children. These forms of knowledge were based on a model of revelation through progress, and initiation both for girls and for boys marked the assumption of social adulthood because it began that process of revelation.

Traditionally, girls coming from kapkore were said to know, to know what had been done and said in that place, to know that they were now social adults, and to know how to manage a marriage and a household. Kapkore was explicitly spoken of not just as a place, but as a set of teachings. The knowledge conveyed in kapkore was for the most part mundane, in that most girls clearly went to initiation fully cognizant of the practical activities required to run a household, of how to farm and were more or less aware of matters relating to menstruation, pregnancy, sexual relations and childbirth. The idea that the girls were being taught things that they did not know was a well-established one, but something of a conceit given that many of the teachings involved in this 'secret' rite turned out to be perfectly ordinary. What perhaps was more important was the overall relationship between knowing, hearing, seeing and speaking, the way in which the rite sought to transform through these embodied modes of engagement the very nature and character of the girls' relation to the world.

The Marakwet make an explicit contrast between adults and children and their modes of relating to the world. The work of initiation was to bring about these new modes of speaking and acting. Traditional initiation accomplished this through staged revelations, a set of enacted performances that conveyed the power and force of new ways of seeing, new knowledge. Such knowledge was revealed through the manipulation of concrete symbols in context and through forms of practical engagement with and participation in the ritual. The meanings conveyed in these different forms of praxis were rarely explicit and never univocal; they were intentionally adumbrated rather than clearly explicated. The initiands were transformed by participation in the rite itself, by the new relationship to knowledge and meaning it proffered and not per se by the content of the knowledge it contained (Barth 1990: 643).

Consequently, the nature and character of the secrets of the initiation house are encapsulated for the Marakwet themselves not by reference to the content of the knowledge (secrets) they acquire at initiation, but by the forms of personal and social transformation they expect the rites to achieve: 'when you come from that place you will be a grown up'; 'you will know how to speak in public and your words will be heard'; 'you will know how to look after your family'. Such statements are about the social achievement of adulthood and those who have never seen or heard what is done in kapkore cannot bear children for they are still children themselves. The importance of seeing, hearing and speaking is reinforced through the absolute prohibition on the uninitiated (and men) entering kapkore and seeing or hearing what takes place. This is reinforced by the fact that in kapkore (as in kaptorus, the boys' initiation house), the initiands are taught a special language in which ordinary everyday items and actions are designated by new words which only the initiated can know. In the past, on occasions when there were doubts about an individual, he or she might be tested by being asked the 'correct words used in those places'. The importance of language was reinforced in other ways through the absolute prohibition on 'telling out', speaking about what one has seen, heard and done, and through the link between initiation and language more generally.

One of the key issues surrounding circumcision – both for boys and girls – in Marakwet is the link between knowledge, authority, speaking and leadership. It is said of both boys and girls after initiation that 'their words will be heard', meaning that they can now speak about and deliberate on matters of community import. One of the key connections, within this general set of values, links circumcision and passage through the rite to community participation and leadership. In the past, if you were uncircumcised, you would never be able to command sufficient respect to be a leader, and because you could not marry you would be specifically excluded from the secrets and knowledge associated with the marriage ceremonies and thereby prevented from becoming a fully knowledgeable member of the community who would know what action to take in times of difficulty or decision. The Marakwet frequently refer to outsiders who are uncircumcised as lacking the capacity to speak, to conduct themselves appropriately, to demonstrate leadership through judgement. In the 2007 election campaign in Kenya, Raila Odinga, a Presidential hopeful (subsequently Prime Minister), had to tackle this problem during public pre-election meetings in Marakwet District because he is a Luo and uncircumcised. At one such meeting he was heard to say that what is important is to be 'circumcised upstairs', asking people: 'which is more important to be circumcised in the mind or in the flesh'? This distinction has been readily taken up by young people in the valley and others who can now be heard saying 'I want to vote for Raila. He's circumcised upstairs', meaning that he is educated, he is knowledgeable about the modern world and that he is clever.

The fundamental connection between initiation, language and adult judgement – the ability to know what to do and when – is reinforced during the periods of seclusion associated with the rites, not through explicit moral instruction, but rather by means of an altered relation to meaning(s). Through songs, practical demonstrations, the interpretation of clay drawings and other material symbols, recitations and a series of staged encounters – some involving 'mythical' beings – words, behaviours and objects are revealed in a new light. These fresh meanings are not about unveiling the true, hidden or esoteric meanings associated with key symbols and mundane practices, but rather about demonstrating the ambivalent, polyvalent character of words, actions and motives. Becoming an adult involves recognising the morally variegated character of the world and of human (and non-human) meanings and actions within it.

Beidelman, noting similar features within Kaguru initiation, describes adulthood as the 'acquisition of fuller skills in speech and thought', the 'development of a moral imagination for constructing and deconstructing different social scenarios as well as the motives and demands that animate them' (Beidelman 1997: 9–10). In the context of Marakwet initiation, matters relating to authority may be both reinforced and transgressed. For example, during teachings in kapkore in 1980, a woman who was instructing the girls about how to comply with the demands of their future husbands was repeatedly interrupted by other women, laughing and joking, saying 'you never did that with your husband'. The girls learn that there is a gap, a space between the moral precepts guiding women's roles in society and the actuality of intimate relations within a marriage. Much of what is learnt in seclusion is indirect, left open to interpretation and reinterpretation. The moral world is revealed as one where competing values and positions jostle alongside each other. What is required of the adult is the ability to exercise judgement, to know what to say and do, and when and how to act, when to speak and when to stay silent, when to conceal and when to reveal motives and preferences. In other words, adulthood is about the complex deployment of forms of knowing and un-knowing as part of an evolving set of relations between self and other, kin and non-kin, members of the community and those outside.

For the Marakwet, one of the key features of initiation is the constitution of the moral subject, a subject who can manage themselves and their relations with others. These moral subjects are differentially gendered, and the Marakwet make this explicit with reference to men's enhanced control over language and judgement as compared to women. In practice, individuals of both genders may be revered for their skills or denigrated for their lack of them, but what is key is the way initiation ties experiences and understandings of the gendered body both to the moral values of the community and to the fantasies, desires and fears of individuals. The constitution of the moral subject in Marakwet is indissolubly linked both to the social values assigned to sexual difference and to individuals' experience of that difference. Gendered subjectivity is intimately based on forms of knowing and un-knowing, of revealing and of concealing. If moral subjectivity has a gendered form, it is one based on the management and acquisition of secrets, secrets that one acquires over time, first in initiation and later in other ceremonies relating to marriage and death. At initiation, you are enjoined never to speak out on pain of death; that vow is very rarely broken because to do so would be to strike at the core of the self, of what ties the psyche to the social.

This is because secrecy in the initiation rites is not just about the development of the moral imagination, as Beidelman contends, but about the empowering and enlargement of the imagination more generally, through a sustained engagement with the cultural imaginary. This engagement is energized and internalized in the soma and psyche of the individual through a set of experiences and enactments that link the constitution of gendered subjectivity to the future of society through physical and cultural reproduction and to the acquisition of knowledge. Thus we must understand the literalness of the Marakwet statement when they say that those who have not seen and heard what is done in kapkore cannot bear children for they are still children themselves. The secrecy of initiation is something that changes both one's knowledge of the world and one's understanding of one's gendered and sexual self – what goes before is not like what comes after – and those transformations are tied to cultural understandings which make them foundational for the Marakwet sense of society and community. As Herdt says of Sambia initiation, ritual secrecy produces not only gendered ontologies but culture itself (Herdt 2003: 167). The secrecy of this process of production and transformation is based not just in seeing and hearing as abstract practices of knowledge acquisition, but in pain and fear, in traumatic surgery, in feeling and touching and sensing, in the sensate forms of knowledge that tie the desire for and experience of new knowledge to an embodied sense of gendered subjectivity that is made powerful culturally through its enhanced capacities for social and sexual reproduction.

The secrets of research

The very fact that the moral subject is constituted for Marakwet through forms of subjectification that locate secrecy and silence at the core of gendered subjectivity places various dynamic constraints on the practice and ethics of research, for it institutes a demand that we all – anthropologist, research team, informants – work with and refer to many things that we cannot speak directly about. This is most evident with regard to research on sex and sexual practices. A strong sense of moral etiquette governs issues of sex and sexuality, and parents and children never speak of such matters. In fact, young people learn most about sex and the mysteries of fertility and reproduction from their peers and from their grandparents. In so far as these matters are spoken of publically, it is mostly with regard to how they impinge on such things as kinship relations, the management of families, social relations within the village and questions of social status. Listening to stories and to gossip, matters of this sort are the stuff of narrative, humour and opinion, and they indirectly speak of sex and sexuality, but actual mention of body parts or sexual acts or passions or the experience of sex and its excitements and terrors are very rare. One of the most intriguing aspects of the campaign against girls' circumcision is the way in which religious and NGO leaders have been involved in developing new ways of speaking about and instructing girls and boys in matters of sex and sexuality. These new forms of discourse are not necessarily any less regulatory than those that preceded them, and they are only partially revelatory. They cannot speak, for example, in the context of a strong public commitment to Christian values and practices of contraception, but they are able to be more explicit about menstruation, about what circumcision for girls entails, and about the fact that circumcision may limit female sexual pleasure and cause problems during childbirth.

In some direct sense, the success and the shock of the anti-FGM campaign is the way that it has revealed things that would otherwise not be known until after circumcision, and has brought them into public view and made them a topic of instruction, if not actually discussion, in cross-sex groups. What is interesting in this context is the manner in which the local leaders involved in the eradication campaign have been able to draw on the discourses of social development, reproductive health and women's empowerment to link certain sorts of knowledge about sex and sexual practices to an aspiration for modernity and new forms of knowledge. Key to this is the explicit message – in all seminars, youth camps, alternative rites of passage, church sermons and the like – that the teachings of kapkore (the girls' initiation house) are useless. This statement, which trips easily from the lips of all young women who have refused initiation and circumcision, is to a very significant extent a self-fulfilling prophecy because in the past these matters were not made explicit until initiation, which meant that the rite contained a fundamental secret in that it held out the promise of a revelation and a kind of clarification about that most important of human matters, sexuality. It is not that children did not know about sex before initiation, but that the knowledge they had was thought of as an inferior sort, both morally and practically, the things that children know. In the contemporary moment, initiation has been superseded by modern knowledge, kapkore has lost its power to reveal. The relationship between power and knowledge has shifted in a powerful and determining way, but this does not mean that the sexual act and its problems and attractions are talked about in explicit ways. There are plenty of silences, but they are different ones.

These silences, old and new, all constitute ethical dilemmas to be negotiated by the anthropologist, the research team (drawn from the local community) and the informants (who may be elders opposed to the anti-FGM campaign, youth in favour of it, NGO and church leaders well versed in anthropology, social development initiatives and Christian theology). In such a context, revelation and concealment are about how power and knowledge constitute the domain of the political through their differential distribution. This distribution is hierarchical, but often cross-cuts social and economic advantage, rather than being congruent with it. The problem for all the actors involved is who knows what and what exactly is it that everyone knows. It is the non-congruence of forms of knowing that make each encounter, each step in the process of research a matter of ethics and of judgement for all the parties concerned. As a young NGO worker, you cannot speak directly to me as an older woman of matters concerning sex and sexuality, but you can use the language of development, seminars, training manuals and the anti-FGM campaign to allude to, and to assert the possibility of new forms of sexual and personal intimacy that do not depend on the cutting of young girl's bodies. I can talk to older women in the community about the importance of kapkore for the socialization of young women in the community, but we cannot speak directly of what takes place in kapkore because these things are not to be spoken of 'outside that place' and I cannot speak of what I feel about female circumcision in that context, of my visceral, embodied response to it. When we work as a team, we are women and men together, and yet if some aspect of women's knowledge needs to be discussed or if explicit reference needs to be made to body parts or sexual acts then the genders need to divide for that utterance to be made and recombine minutes later knowing what has likely been said, but not knowing it exactly. Much of the work concerns what is not spoken, and much of it is about our bodies and the bodies of others.

It is perhaps not surprising that secrecy and silence, revelation and concealment should have over time defined the research project, as well as the research process, since they both define the nature of the social and are at the core of the constitution of gendered subjectivity. However, the process of keeping and revealing secrets, of making moral judgements and being evaluated as a moral subject according to the management of self and knowledge has also become central to my own gendered subjectivity and to how I relate to and engage with the people I work with. I have kept the secrets of kapkore for nearly 30 years. Like all women who know them, I have never spoken of them and I have never published anything other than what is generally known and in the public domain. Part of my sense of self is now bound up – in practice and through the workings of desire and fantasy – with how I have managed these secrets. These secrets have in some important ways shaped the whole of my adult life and my career. They have also fashioned my relationships with everyone I know in Marakwet because they know I know, and they know I have kept the secret. This makes me, despite all the obvious differences of race and class, and increasingly now of religion, someone who is a legible moral subject to a certain extent, someone who can be understood to have managed themselves over time in a particular way. My legibility in this regard should not be taken to imply commonalities, the differences of experience, opportunity and privilege are all too salient for me, for my research team who come from the village where I work and for the people in the community who know me. Most particularly, my legibility should not be taken to mean that the exchanges of knowledge that take place between different actors within the research process are equal or mutual. They are very far from that. It is also the case that legibility should not necessarily be equated with positive valuations. It implies nothing about whether other individuals think me a good or a bad person, someone worthy of respect. What my partial legibility does do is to make me part of a community, an individual like others who both reveals and conceals aspects of themselves and their motives. In short, someone who is a social adult and who exercises judgement through the management of knowledge, making evident through their actions, as Simmel suggested, that '[r]elationships being what they are, they … presuppose a certain ignorance and a measure of mutual concealment … ' (Simmel 1950: 315–16).

What is ironic for me is that this is something that has a positive moral value in Marakwet but is quite differently evaluated by friends and colleagues in my other working environments. I have never been able to talk openly and accurately about my work on Marakwet, especially with my feminist colleagues, because the moral trauma of female circumcision has opened up an almost unbridgeable gap between us. One question I have been asked repeatedly but still find that I cannot answer honestly is 'how can you justify observing and participating in these rites since this implies to others that you are condoning them'? I rather weakly reply that I cannot imagine understanding anything without seeing it, engaging with it. This response sometimes make me wince, since I recognize the rather enfeebled and disingenuous ethics that cultural relativism has so often justified in anthropology. In this context, keeping the secrets of kapkore has diminished rather than enhanced my moral standing.

This is, as Derrida signals in the quote that opens this chapter, the contradiction inherent in the constitution of the ethical. Ethics is about a relation to an other, but one which is premised on difference, on dissimulation, on absence. It is this fact that makes the utopian hope of a thoroughly 'positive' or 'morally unimpeachable' fieldwork practice an impossibility, whether viewed from the perspective of informants, co-research team members, or colleagues in the broader working and disciplinary environment. What remains is the practice of judgement, the exercise and demonstration of moral subjectivity, the management of self in relation to others. When we work as a research team, we are discussing and recording the lives of others, and we are often in possession of information that is not generally known within the community at large. We know certain details of lives that, were they to be known, would not matter because of the content of the 'secret' itself, but rather because they would reveal family and kinship relations as they actually are. A certain woman in the village is visited in the evening by two men from a neighbouring village carrying a crate of fanta. At this moment, it is evident that these individuals are seeking to repair a relationship gone awry and to establish discussions about a potential marriage, and simultaneously it becomes clear that the daughter of the household has not actually been absent at school all these months, but rather has been living with the young man of her choice in his village. The facts of these matters may be known within the community, but they are not fully in the public domain. What takes place within the research team is the construction of a particular narrative surrounding these events, a set of decisions about whom to interview and how to gain supplementary data and check various details; the construction of a whole story, of a set of understandings and of social relations that elsewhere in the community is only known in fragments. At that moment, as members of the research team working together – with multiplex kinship links and loyalties within the village – we remind ourselves that what we do or say here is secret, is not to be revealed, is subject to moral and ethical judgment, that research, like initiation, is 'keiir nda kengalala kiir ngo' ung'oot', a matter of doing or saying something that should not necessarily be made public.

References

Abu-Lughod, L. (1990) 'Can there be a feminist ethnography?', *Women and Performance*, 5 (9): 7–27.

Barth, F. (1975) *Ritual and Knowledge among the Baktaman of New Guinea*, Oslo and New Haven: Universitetsforlaget and Yale University Press.

—— (1990) 'The guru and the conjurer: transactions in knowledge and the shaping of culture in Southeast Asia and Melanesia', *Man, New Series*, 25 (4): 640–53.

Beidelman, T.O. (1997) *The Cool Knife: Imagery of Gender, Sexuality and Moral Education in Kaguru Initiation Ritual*, Washington: Smithsonian Institution Press.

Bell, D., Caplan, P. and Wazir, J.K. (1993) (eds) *Gendered Fields: Women, Men and Ethnography*, London: Routledge.

Bellman, B. (1984) *The Language of Secrecy*, New Brunswick, NJ: Rutgers University Press.

Burawoy, M. (1991) 'Reconstructing social theories', in M. Burawoy, A. Burton, A.A. Ferguson and K.J. Fox (eds) *Ethnography Unbound: Power and Resistance in the Modern Metropolis*, Berkeley: University of California Press.

Clifford, J. and Marcus, G. (eds) (1986) *Writing Culture: The Poetics and Politics of Ethnography*, Berkeley: University of California Press.

Corin, E. (2007) 'Personal travels through otherness', in A. McLean and A. Leibing (eds) *The Shadow Side of Fieldwork: Exploring the Blurred Borders between Ethnography and Life*, Oxford: Blackwell.

Crook, T. (2007) *Anthropological Knowledge, Secrecy and Bolivip, Papua New Guinea: Exchanging Skin* (British Academy Postdoctoral Fellowship Monographs), Oxford: Oxford University Press.

De Jong F., Peel, J.D.Y., Heald, S. and James, D. (eds) (forthcoming) *Masquerades of Modernity: Power and Secrecy in Casamance, Senegal* (International African Library), Edinburgh: Edinburgh University Press.

Derrida, J. (1974) *Of Grammatology*, Baltimore, MD: Johns Hopkins University Press.

Ferme, M. (2001) *The Underneath of Things: Violence, History and the Everyday in Sierra Leone*, Los Angeles: University of California Press.

Franklin, S. (2003) 'Rethinking nature-culture: anthropology and the new genetics', *Anthropological Theory,* 3 (1): 65–85.

Gable, E. (1997) 'A secret shared: field work and the sinister in a West African village', *Cultural Anthropology*, 12 (2): 213–33.

Herdt, G. (2003) *Secrecy and Cultural Reality: Utopian Ideologies of the New Guinea Men's House*, Ann Arbor: University of Michigan Press.

Kratz, C. (1994) *Affecting Performance: Meaning, Movement and Experience in Okiek Women's Initiation Rituals*, Washington: Smithsonian Institution Press.

Lattas, A. (1998) *Cultures of Secrecy: Reinventing Race in Bush Kaliai Cargo Cults*, Madison: University of Wisconsin Press.

Leiris, M. (1948) *La Langue Secrète des Dogons de Sanga*, Paris: Institut d'Ethnologie.

Lovell, A. (2007) 'When things get personal: secrecy, intimacy, and the production of experience in fieldwork', in A. McLean and A. Leibing (eds) *The Shadow Side of Fieldwork: Exploring the Blurred Borders between Ethnography and Life*, Oxford: Blackwell

McDowell, L. (1992) 'Feminism, feminists and research methods in human geography', *Transactions of the Institute of British Geographers*, 17 (4): 399–416.

Mitchell, R. (1993) *Secrecy and Fieldwork*, London: Sage.

Moore, H.L. (2004) 'Global anxieties: concept-metaphors and pre-theoretical commitments in anthropology, *Anthropological Theory*, 4 (1): 74–88.

Moss, P. (2002) *Feminist Geography in Practice: Research and Methods*, Oxford: Blackwell.

Murphy, W. (1980) 'Secret knowledge as property and power in Kpelle society: elders versus youth', *Africa* 50: 193–207.

Ottenberg, S. (1989) *Boyhood Rituals in an African Society*, Seattle: University of Washington Press.

Rubenstein, S. (2004) 'Fieldwork and the erotic economy on the colonial frontier', *Signs: Journal of Women in Culture and Society*, 29 (4): 1041–71.

Simmel, G. (1950) *The Sociology of Georg Simmel*, New York: Free Press.

Stacey, J. (1988) 'Can there be a feminist ethnography?' *Women's Studies International Forum*, 11 (1): 21–27.

Taussig, M. (1999) *Defacement: Public Secrecy and the Labour of the Negative*, Stanford: Stanford University Press.

Wolf, D. (1996) *Feminist Dilemmas in Fieldwork*, Boulder: Westview Press.

3 Unknowable secrets and golden silence

Reflexivity and research on sex tourism

Jacqueline Sanchez Taylor and Julia O'Connell Davidson

Between 1995 and 2000, we jointly conducted fairly extensive research on sex tourism. Our early work on this topic was funded by a non-governmental organisation, ECPAT (End Child Prostitution in Asian Tourism), and involved field research to explore the attitudes, practices and motivations of tourists who paid for sex with children in Costa Rica, Venezuela, Cuba, the Dominican Republic, South Africa and India (O'Connell Davidson and Sanchez Taylor 1996). We then carried out ethnographic research, funded by the ESRC, which examined questions about gender, race and age and the informal tourist-related prostitution in Jamaica and the Dominican Republic (O'Connell Davidson and Sanchez Taylor 2001). In the course of these projects, we interviewed more than three hundred male tourists who paid for sex whilst on holiday, scores of Western expatriates who were directly or indirectly involved with the tourist-related sex trade in the countries we visited, and around two hundred local and migrant men, women and children who worked in prostitution and/or entered into other types of sexual-economic exchanges with tourists.

Though we have provided brief descriptions of the research design and methods in various reports and articles, we have never published any detailed discussion of the methodological issues and dilemmas we faced in the course of this research. Twice in the late 1990s, we started to write methods papers, both of which were strongly influenced by the then current emphasis on the value of open and reflexive accounts of research, and focused heavily on questions about identity and emotion in the research process. However, we abandoned both of the papers half-way through, because, whilst agreeing in principle that good research should account for the conditions of its own production (Stanley 1991; Stanley and Wise 1993), in practice we found it impossible to write reflexively about our research without also writing in a way that appeared to us as pointlessly self-indulgent, as well as either highly partial and selective, or personally and professionally damaging (or both).

When invited to contribute to this volume, we hunted out these old papers and re-read them. Our first reaction was relief that we had never completed or managed to publish them. Their tone was far more raw and angry than we had realized at the time of writing, and even though we had closely censored ourselves and left out much that we thought was interesting and relevant but also potentially risky to admit, some of the personal disclosures they contain would be a source of embarrassment today. Returning to these papers almost a decade later also made us appreciate how significantly the passage of time can change one's perspective. Looking back, it seems we only partially knew and understood the 'selves' we were trying to situate in the research.

This chapter explores why it was, and remains, so difficult for us to write openly about the experience of researching sex tourism. It opens with two 'tales from the field' to give a flavour of the range of interactions and relationships that the research involved.

'Desperate Dan'

Whilst conducting field research in a tourist resort in the Dominican Republic in 1996, we were approached by 'Dan', who was selling timeshare and took us for potential customers. We got talking, and took a genuine liking to Dan. He was an extremely intelligent, funny, well-travelled black American aged 35, who had been living and working in the Dominican Republic for two years. We explained that we were doing research on sex tourism and ended up talking to him for several hours. He then offered to take us to meet his Dominican wife in San Pedro, the nearby town where they lived, and to show us around the brothels there the next day.

We met up the following evening, and caught a bus with him, thinking we were going straight to San Pedro. Half-way there, he told us we were making a stop. We got off the bus and he took us into a casino where we stood by and watched him lose all the money he had with him. The casino provided him with a taxi home, and we sat in the taxi and listened to him agonize about his compulsive gambling. He was close to tears as he explained that he had just lost the rent money that was already some weeks overdue; that he had hoped to win enough to recover his wife's wedding ring from the pawn broker and pay the rent; that he was afraid his wife would leave him; that he didn't understand why he stopped at the casino every night on the way home from work, and so on.

We finally arrived at the run-down tenement block where he lived, and he took us upstairs to meet his wife, 'Dolores'. She was 21 years old, and had spent that day, like every day, sitting alone in the single room which was their home, waiting for him to return from work, hoping that he would not stop at the casino on his way. The couple had moved from her home town in the north of the country to San Pedro a couple of months previously when Dan had found his timeshare job, and because he could not afford a larger place to live, they had left her two children (from a previous relationship), aged 2 and 5, with her parents. Her children, parents and friends were all now a nine-hour bus journey away, and as neither she nor her parents had a telephone, she had not spoken to her children for two months. Dan told us that he did not want her to work, and also confided that he did not like the idea of her striking up new relationships with local people because he suffered terribly from jealousy.

When we walked into the room, Dolores was putting on make-up. Dan had told her the night before that he was bringing us to San Pedro and that we would all go out for a meal together. Meanwhile, Dan encouraged her to give us information that would help with our research, and she began talking about the situation faced by young girls in her home town, and how and why prostitution often became the only choice for them. As she talked, there was a power cut. Dan lit a candle and we continued chatting in virtual darkness for a while. Then Dan suddenly announced that we were leaving. We got up to go. Dolores asked, 'Am I coming?' Dan said 'No'. We left her there, sitting alone in the unlit room in her make-up and her best clothes.

Dan and a male friend of his then took us through the unlit, potholed, backstreets of San Pedro to two brothels, where Dan introduced us as researchers writing a book on prostitution. Following his introduction, we explained the nature and purpose of our research, and the owner of one establishment and eight sex workers agreed to be interviewed. Though we had always managed to secure interviews with third parties and sex workers working in tourist-related prostitution, we would not have found it easy to secure access to interview people like this, who ran or worked in establishments that catered to local demand, without his help. Dan also subsequently introduced us to a number of other people who were able to provide us with information that was extremely useful for our research.

Dan not only helped to facilitate our research in brothels, but also gave us many insights into the phenomenon of sex tourism. He described himself as a former sex tourist and spoke quite openly about his experiences in Thailand, the Philippines and the Caribbean, as well as talking at length, and very articulately, about his own biography, sense of self and his views on gender, race and sexuality. We did exchange contact details at the end of our trip, but have never been in touch with Dan since.

The TSM crew

On another field trip to the Dominican Republic in 1998, we visited a bar in a tourist resort that was advertised on the website of a club run by and for male heterosexual sex tourists called 'Travel and the Single Male'. We sat down at a table and ordered drinks, and got talking to a group of white American men sitting next to us. The most voluble of the group were an expatriate, aged 57, and two tourists, aged 71 and 48, who had visited the resort many times before. Our conversation was tape recorded by a radio documentary maker who had accompanied us on this field trip, and an extract from the transcript is provided below.

EXPATRIATE: Women's lib in America in the United States has killed marriage in America for any man who has brains. I wouldn't even marry a rich woman.

O'CD: But is it not the same here then?

EXPATRIATE: No. They're raised different. Women's lib hasn't hit here …

SEX TOURIST A: In the States, [women] hire folks with cameras. They go to bed with cameras. If they wake up with a bruise, they take a picture of it. Call it abuse. Possible abuse.

EXPATRIATE: In the United States, if you grab your wife like that, and you yell at her, put a little black blue mark, just a little one, she'll …

SEX TOURIST A: When you've got a goddamn female announcing the NBA basketball game. These females go into the men's locker rooms, but the males cannot go into the ladies' locker rooms. Most of these girls are dykes anyways …

EXPATRIATE: Oh yeah. She can call the police and say 'He hit me. Didn't leave a bruise, but he hit me'. And he never even punched her and he goes to jail. She can take a knife to him, and nothing.

SEX TOURIST B: Yeah, no marks, nothing …

O'CD: So is it completely the opposite here?

EXPATRIATE: The difference here is she'll beat the shit out of you. You go for a Dominican girl and she'll go for a knife.

O'CD: Do you speak from personal experience?

EXPATRIATE: Oh yes.

SEX TOURIST A: The difference is the cops are never called.

O'CD: Is it here like it was forty years ago in the States?

SEX TOURIST A: Fifty years ago. The worst thing that ever, ever happened in the States was they gave women the right to vote.

EXPATRIATE: The right to vote and the right to drive …

O'CD: Is this what people mean when in England people say that in America there's political correctness, that people can't say certain things?

EXPATRIATE: You can't use the N word, nigger. Always when I was raised up, the only thing was the F word, you can't use the F word. Now you can't say cunt, you can't say nigger … There's just so many words I could use against women in the United States … I don't like white women … Every time you meet a woman in the United States, she wants to know 'How much do you make?' …

O'CD: What about black women in the States?

EXPATRIATE: They're Americanized. They've all got their lawyer's number tattooed on their wrist just like the white women.

The men continued to discuss their own and other male American acquaintances' sexual 'adventures' in the Dominican Republic, listing experiences that included paying third parties to have sex with girls as young as eleven years old. Again, this data was extremely useful for developing analyses of sex tourism which we have subsequently written up and published (O'Connell Davidson and Sanchez Taylor 2001; O'Connell Davidson 2001, 2005).

Talking about identity

As noted above, when we first attempted to write about the methodological issues associated with our research on sex tourism, our efforts were informed by a growing literature on reflexivity. This literature stressed that social researchers should reflect on how the data they gather and the way they analyse it may be affected by their own gender, class, race, national and sexual identity. It challenged orthodox assumptions about researchers as abstract, disembodied professionals who produce universal and objective knowledge, and talked instead of the need to situate knowledge through reference to the researcher's personal biography and particular and embodied standpoint (for example, Harding 1987; Haraway 1988; Katz 1994; Nast 1994; Wolf 1996).

It also paid attention to the fact that the researcher not only sees, but is seen by the research subject, and that this too impacts on the research process. Ethnographers, for example, do not enter the field merely as 'professionals', but also as men or women, as bearers of specific racial and ethnic identities, as persons of a given nationality, and as individual emotional and sexual beings (Kulick and Willson 1995; Lewin and Leap 1996). As active participants in the research process, their research subjects will, to a greater or lesser degree, respond to them as such (Padfield and Procter 1996). The management of self as an embodied, emotional and sexual being is thus an inescapable feature of the process of social research (at least that which entails interaction with people).

It is one thing to recognize, in the abstract, that researchers come to their research with particular histories and that the way their bodies are socially marked has implications for the process of research, but not so easy to write about this in relation to specific pieces of research. To begin with, gender and race are not undifferentiated categories, nor are they the only systems of classification that are used to locate individuals socially or that individuals use to locate themselves in the social world. If we want to understand how a researcher was positioned in relation to the subject matter of her research or how her research subjects were likely to have seen her, is it clearly not enough for her to tell us that she is, for example, a black, Asian or white British woman. But how many other aspects of her social identity should she reflect on? Age, class background and sexuality are generally mentioned in reflexive accounts of research. However, researchers do not routinely provide a detailed description of their bodies. Instead, we are only told whether, for example, a white researcher is blonde-haired or dark-haired, or a black researcher is light-skinned or dark-skinned, or whether the researcher is fat or thin, athletically built or scrawny, hirsute or hairless, tall or short, able-bodied or with disabilities when these features of embodiment are deemed by the researcher to have been significant for the research process and/or her reading of the data.

Likewise, although as Gallagher (2000: 67) observes, '[r]eflecting on how personal biography influences the research process is a well travelled road', the type and degree of detail about an individual's personal history and experience provided in reflexive accounts varies. And again, researchers only provide the snippets of biography that they subjectively perceive as being relevant to understanding their interactions with research subjects and/or their engagement with the research topic (see, for example, Chapkis 1986; Wacquant 2005; Brooks-Gordon 2006; Yip 2008). Whether their research subjects would agree that the physical, social and biographical details researchers choose to provide in reflexive accounts of their research were actually salient to their interactions is another matter.

Why did we find it so difficult to present and discuss aspects of our social and personal identities that would help to situate our research on sex tourism? One immediate problem arose from the fact that there were two of us. Liz Stanley (1993: 50) argued for the use of an 'autobiographical I', one that recognizes that knowledge differs 'according to the social location (as a gendered, raced, classed and sexualized person) of the particular knowledge producer'. But can there be an 'autobiographical *we*'? And if so, how can this 'we' be analytically and critically placed in the text if both the individuals concerned have very different social identities and personal histories?

At first undaunted by this challenge, we started by noting we were two female researchers in their thirties, one black one white, both British born, but one with Jamaican and Spanish migrant parents (Jacqueline Sanchez Taylor), the other with white British parents (Julia O'Connell Davidson), one middle class and one working class, one single and childless and one divorced with children. We talked briefly about how useful it was to the research that Jacqueline is bi-lingual in English and Spanish, and discussed how and why her knowledge of Jamaican culture was important when we conducted research in Jamaica. We further observed that our multiple and simultaneous identities made it difficult for people to 'fix' us in any given social location, and that this was probably helpful in terms of enabling us to enter into a wide range of different social interactions in different places with different types of people.

But the more we tried to write about the impact of our social identities on the field relations we established and the data we gathered, the more uncomfortable we became. It felt as though we were implicitly claiming some kind of causal link between our bodies' social markings and the data we had collected. And yet what difference would it have made to the episode with Dan if we had been two white male researchers? We had the impression that Dan decided to help us because he liked us and because he was bored by the people he came into contact with in his everyday life. We cannot know certainly that this was his motivation, but if it was, and if two white male researchers had shared his sense of humour and been sympathetic to him, isn't it possible that he would have been equally willing to assist them?

Would two middle-class male researchers have felt any more able to insist that Dan honoured his promise to take Dolores out for dinner with them, or any less guilty about leaving her behind in the dark? If they were conducting the same research in the same setting, would their whiteness or their maleness have led them to ask her different questions or to interpret her responses differently? And what of the TSM crew? Since the same racist, sexist and homophobic attitudes are regularly expressed in the club's publications and internet chat room, we can fairly confidently state that the fact we were two British women, one white, one black, did not encourage these particular white American male interviewees to either play up or play down their hostility towards social groups they deem to be inferior. Meanwhile, as several of the chapters in Twine and Warren's (2000) edited collection on researching race show, there is no reason to suppose two white male researchers would have found it any easier to listen to these men's racism without challenging it.

Getting people to assist you and to open up and talk about their attitudes and experiences demands the performance of emotional labour no matter what your social identity. Dwelling on the possible (yet ultimately unknown and unknowable) effects of our social identity on our research subjects seemed somehow to downplay the skill and effort that we brought to the fieldwork.

Though we could not talk with certainty about what our social identities meant for the people we researched, one thing we could confidently discuss was what they meant for our own experience in the field. For example, when researching in Latin America and the Caribbean, tourists (sometimes also local people) assumed that Jacqueline was a local woman and this allowed us to observe directly the difference that race and assumed nationality made to women's lived experience in sex tourist resorts. Police officers, hotel security guards and sometimes even hotel receptionists who were polite and respectful to Julia frequently behaved in a suspicious, rude, hostile or intimidating manner towards Jacqueline. And though Julia was sometimes the recipient of unwanted sexual attention from local men and much more rarely from male tourists, Jacqueline was constantly sexually harassed by male tourists as well as by local men. In places where tourist-related prostitution was most extensive and visible, male tourists would sometimes even physically grab hold of Jacqueline as she walked along a beach or stood in a bar, and try to kiss her, or pull her over to their table to sit with them. Jacqueline was exposed to many other indignities and insults whilst conducting field research, not least of which was having to accept, without challenge, the TSM member in the interview extract above look her squarely in the face as he made his complaint about not being allowed to use the word 'nigger'.

Though for reasons discussed below we did not mention this in our unfinished papers, the fact that we were partners, as well as co-researchers, added another layer of unpleasantness to all of this. It was also difficult to spend so much time working in contexts that were so profoundly homophobic.

As evidenced by the work of Moreno (1995), Gearing (1995) and Twine (2000), describing the experiences of racism and/or sexual harassment or assault during fieldwork can make a valuable contribution to a literature on methods that helps researchers to prepare for fieldwork and/or to come to terms with their own experiences after conducting fieldwork. But describing such experiences is not necessarily the same thing as providing a reflexive account of the research process, and as soon as we had written down our stories from the field, we wondered what they were really for. We worried that they sounded like a form of special pleading, as though we were trying to claim that our 'suffering' made our accounts of sex tourism somehow more authentic than accounts that might be produced by other researchers, a claim that neither of us actually support. We also worried that the real impulse for telling stories like the one about Dan was confessional. The guilt we felt about abandoning Dolores was just one small contribution to an extensive catalogue of guilt built up in the course of research that constantly required us to form intimate but temporary relationships with women, men and children living in extremely difficult circumstances, people who, despite our enormous first-world privilege, we were powerless to assist in any meaningful way.

We also recognized that to truly situate the research in the context of our own identities and biographies, we would have to do more than simply talk about how unpleasant it had been to conduct the fieldwork. Research on male sex tourists has painted different pictures of their motivations (for example, Odzer 1994; Kruhse Mount Burton 1995; Seabrook 1996), and this is partly because data is interpreted through the lens of different personal, as well as political and theoretical preoccupations. To give a reflexive account of the knowledge we produced about male heterosexual sex tourism, then, we would also need to explore our standpoint in relation to gender, heterosexual sexuality and sex commerce, and this presented us with much more intractable problems.

Let's not talk about sex

In one of our unfinished papers we wrote:

> Our research is concerned to achieve an interpretive understanding of the phenomenon of male sex tourism … The interpretive researcher's human capacity for emotion is implicitly acknowledged as a research tool when methodologists discuss empathy as central to achieving *verstehen*. Empathy is an essentially reflexive process – we are capable of grasping another person's moral and emotional universe only through a kind of hermeneutic process of shifting back and forth between our own emotional experience and moral stance and those of our research subjects, constantly examining the gaps and the similarities between us.

What we did not mention was sex. We did not speak of the need for some kind of dialogue between our own *sexual* experience and that of our research subjects, or discuss how people's *sexual* desires and practices might (or might not) connect to the moral and emotional universe they inhabit.

The fact is that during the research process we did consider our research subjects' life stories and accounts of their practices in relation to our own personal histories – sexual as well as emotional. We did think back to incidents and relationships in our own lives that had some parallels with those we encountered as 'professionals' researching sex tourism. We also drew on our own experience of the emotions that can be connected to, or expressed through, sexuality (excitement, desire, self-affirmation, love, affection, betrayal, jealously, anger, boredom, depression, loneliness, frustration, humiliation, etc.) in order to identify with those expressed by our research subjects. But we did not mention any of this, and it still seems to us that there were good reasons for keeping silent.

The first concerns the particular and powerful stigma that attaches to any form of sexual practice that is popularly regarded as deviant, and the way this stigma can extend to those who research such practices (see Hayward and Mac An Ghaill 2006). A white middle-class male ethnographer can add to the perceived authenticity of his research by telling tales from the field that show how he got close to the black working-class boxers he studied without his academic distance from the research topic, or his gender, class and race identity, being called into question (see Wacquant 2005). But those who research sex walk a fine line between claiming authority by showing how deeply they have immersed themselves in the field and/or demonstrating their 'insider' status, and jeopardizing their professional reputation by revealing that have come *too* close to a stigmatized form of sexual activity.

Indeed, merely providing a detailed description of the research setting might be enough to trigger suspicions that there was insufficient distance between the researcher and the others she or he observed. This is a particular problem for those who conduct ethnographic research on commercial sex, since such researchers will almost inevitably see and hear things in the course of that research which some would regard as a sexual experience to see or hear. For example, simply entering a brothel, visiting a red-light area, being in the company of a sex worker or hearing about the details of her or his work, would be a source of voyeuristic sexual pleasure for some people.

Prostitution occupies a troubled and troubling space between two very different symbolic domains – the public world of market relations, and the private domain of sexual and domestic life – and 'the ambiguities and boundary loss implied by prostitution may help to explain the hugely negative stigma that is commonly attached to female prostitutes' (O'Connell Davidson 2005: 26). Researchers who enter this space are often conscious that they too may be perceived negatively, that their academic peers may suspect them of having failed to maintain clear boundaries between their 'public' professional selves, and their 'private' sexual selves. One response to this is to follow the tradition of ethnographic writing that presents the researcher as having undergone a process of self-mortification in order 'to achieve ethnographic discovery', thereby setting up 'a version of fieldwork premised on the self evident distance between a self and an other' (Coffey 1999: 20). Accounts that follow this tradition have to present the researcher as though she was sexually naïve or unmarked by previous sexual experience when she first entered the field, which is not only normally untrue, but also implicitly sustains the very

Madonna/whore dualism that most feminist researchers want to challenge (see, for example, Ackers 1993; Sanders 2006). And yet what is the alternative? How many researchers would be happy to write openly and seriously about their own sexual history or their own sexual responses (or even lack of sexual response) in the field?

All researchers (not just those who do research on sex) enter the field as sexual, as well as gendered, raced and classed, beings, and their real or perceived sexual identity has an effect on all their encounters in the field. However, straight male academics very rarely publish reflexive discussions of how their sexuality or their mode of relating to other people as sexual beings may have impacted on their research, and the furious attacks on the morality and professionalism of some gay men who have dared to do so illustrates why – so far as one's career is concerned – it can be dangerous to talk about sex (see Bolton 1995 and 1996).

But there is another reason why we are relieved that we never published any reflections on how our personal sexual and emotional biographies positioned us in relation to the research. Caplan (1993: 24) may be right to observe that ethnographers often 'use the field to work through other parts of their lives'. However, it takes time, sometimes a very long time (and sometimes also the assistance of a therapist), before people can begin to understand the relationship between their own biographies and the research that they conduct, especially when that research focuses on such difficult and emotionally charged territory as sex tourism. Even if ten years ago we had been willing to publish what seemed like a truthful account of how we came to the research and how we managed to successfully achieve an empathetic identification with the emotional and moral universe of men like Dan or the TSM crew, this account would almost certainly now appear to us as analytically and factually flawed.

For all these reasons, we feel that so far as reflecting on our research on sex tourism is concerned, silence has been golden.

Acknowledgements

The support of the ESRC which funded our research on tourist-related prostitution in Jamaica and the Dominican Republic (award no: R000237625) is gratefully acknowledged.

References

Ackers, H. (1993) 'Racism, sexuality and the research process of ethnographic research', in D. Hobbs and T. May (eds) *Interpreting the Field: Accounts of Ethnography*, Oxford: Oxford University Press.

Bolton, R. (1995) 'Tricks, friends and lovers: erotic encounters in the field' in K. Kulick and M. Wilson (eds) *Taboo*, London: Routledge.

——(1996) 'Coming home: the journey of a gay ethnographer in the years of the plague', in E. Lewin and W. Leap (eds) *Out in the Field*, Chicago: University of Illinois Press.

Brooks-Gordon, B. (2006) *The Price of Sex: Prostitution, Policy and Society*, London: Willan.

Caplan, P. (1993) 'Introduction', in D. Bell, P. Caplan and W. Karim (eds), *Gendered Fields: Women, Men and Ethnography*, London: Routledge.

Chapkis, W. (1986) *Beauty Secrets: Women and the Politics of Appearance*, Boston: South End Press.

Coffey, A. (1999) *The Ethnographic Self: Fieldwork and the Representation of Identity*, London: Sage.

Gallagher, C. (2000) 'White like me? Methods, meaning and manipulation in the field of white studies', in F. Twine and J. Warren (eds) *Racing Research, Researching Race*, New York: New York University Press.

Gearing, J. (1995) 'Fear and loving in the West Indies: research from the heart (as well as the head)', in D. Kulick and M. Willson (eds) *Taboo*, London: Routledge.

Haraway, D. (1988) 'Situated knowledge: the science question in feminism and the privilege of partial perspective', *Feminist Studies*, 14 (3): 575–600.

Harding, S. (ed.) (1987) *Feminism and Methodology*, Bloomington: Indiana University Press.

Hayward, C. and Mac An Ghaill (2006) 'Knowing sexuality: epistemologies of research', in D. Hobbs and R. Wright (eds) *The Sage Handbook of Fieldwork*. London: Sage.

Katz, C. (1994) 'Playing the field: questions of field work in geography', in *The Professional Geographer*, 46 (1): 67–72.

Kruhse-Mount Burton, S. (1995) 'Sex tourism and traditional Australian male identity' in M. Lanfont, J.B. Allcock and E.M. Bruner (eds) *International Tourism: Identity and Change*, London: Sage.

Kulick, D. and Willson, M. (1995) *Taboo*, London: Routledge.

Lewin, E and Leap, W (1996) *Out in the Field*, Chicago: University of Illinois Press.

Moreno, E. (1995) 'Rape in the field: reflections from a survivor' in D. Kulick and M. Willson (eds) *Taboo*, London: Routledge.

Nast, H. (1994), 'Opening remarks on " women in the field"', *The Professional Geographer*, 46 (1): 54–66.

O'Connell Davidson, J. (2001) 'The sex tourist, the expatriate, his ex-wife and her "Other"': the politics of loss, difference and desire', *Sexualities*, 4 (1): 5–24.

——(2005) *Children in the Global Sex Trade*, Cambridge: Polity.

O'Connell Davidson, J. and Sanchez Taylor, J. (1996) 'Child prostitution and sex tourism', Research Papers 1–7, Bangkok: ECPAT.

——(2001) *Children in the Sex Trade in the Caribbean*, Stockholm: Save the Children Sweden.

Odzer, C. (1994) *Patpong Sisters: An American Woman's View of the Bangkok Sex Industry*, New York: Blue Moon.

Padfield, M. and Procter, I. (1996) 'The effect of interviewer's gender on the interviewing process: A comparative study', *Sociology*, 30 (2): 355–66.

Sanders, T. (2006a) 'Sexing up the subject: methodological nuances in researching the female sex industry', *Sexualities*, 9 (4): 449–68.

——(2006b) 'Researching sex work: dynamics, difficulties and decisions', in D. Hobbs and R. Wright (eds) *Sage Handbook of Fieldwork*, London: Sage.

Seabrook, J. (1996) *Travels in the Skin Trade: Tourism and the Sex Industry*, London: Pluto.

Stanley, L. (1991) 'Feminist auto/biography and feminist epistemology', in J. Aaron and S. Walby (eds) *Out of the Margins: Women's Studies in the Nineties*, London: Falmer.

——(1993) 'Auto/biography in sociology', *Sociology*, 27 (1): 41–52.

Stanley, L. and Wise, S. (1993) *Breaking out Again: Feminist consciousness and feminist research*, London: Routledge.

Twine, F. (2000) 'Racial ideologies and racial methodologies', in F. Twine and J. Warren (eds), *Racing Research, Researching Race*, New York: New York University Press.

Twine, F. and Warren, J. (eds) (2000) *Racing Research, Researching Race*, New York: New York University Press.

Wacquant, L. (2005) 'Carnal connections: on embodiment, apprenticeship and membership', *Qualitative Sociology*, 28 (4): 445–74.

Wolf, D. (ed.) (1996) *Feminist Dilemmas in Fieldwork*, Boulder, CO: Westview.

Yip, A. (2008) 'Researching lesbian, gay and bisexual Christians and Muslims: Some thematic reflections', *Sociological Research Online*, 13 (1) http://www.socresonline.org.uk/13/1/5.html.

4 The desire to talk and sex/gender-related silences in interviews with male heterosexual clients of prostitutes

Sabine Grenz

In commercial sexuality, sex is exchanged for money or other goods and the biggest prostitution market is the heterosexual market for men. As such, prostitution is a highly sexed and gendered field. Moreover, the history of sexuality and gender results in an ambivalence of visibility and secrecy of prostitution. On the one hand, the sex-industry is very present in daily social life through, for instance, magazines, sex-shops, and sex-clubs, all of which draw on traditional gendered stereotypes including both that of the strong male sexual drive as well as the division between the 'holy' and the 'whore'. Prostitution is also the daily work and experience of various people working in the sex-industry and/or consuming sexual services. On the other hand, prostitution is wrapped in secrecy for the very same reasons, i.e. traditional assumptions about sex and gender. Usually, sex-workers do not talk about their work to persons outside the industry in order to avoid stigma (cf. Sanders 2005: 116f.; Day 2007). Similarly, clients of prostitutes only rarely talk about going to a sex-worker. Thus, 'prostitution is still a sensitive social taboo area' (Kleiber and Velten 1994: 46; my translation).

Despite the stigma and the related shame, in spring and summer 2001 I managed to interview twenty-six male heterosexual clients of prostitutes in Germany, mostly in Berlin. These interviews were used for a study aimed at unravelling the secrecy surrounding these men and investigating the ways in which masculine identity is discursively reproduced through (or performed in) commercial sex (cf. Grenz [2005] 2007). Power relations caused by gender as well as other power axes, such as my being the researcher and them being the research object, were complex and fluid (cf. Grenz 2005). Reading about this process, one could wonder how my sex/gender has influenced the answers and whether participants would have been more open if they had talked about their sexual experiences in commercial sexuality to a male interviewer.[1]

Gerheim (2007) recently published the preliminary results of his study of heterosexual clients of prostitutes in Germany. Whereas the actual content does not appear to be very different from the material I collected,[2] the power dynamics as well as the specific ways in which masculinity was reproduced visibly differ in both studies. In order to outline these discrepancies, I will first discuss issues of secrecy as well as the 'desire to talk' in research on sexuality in more general terms. Then, my discussion will move on to the question of how interviews can be influenced by the particular gendered relations that work through them, what kind of silences as well as challenges heteronormativity might produce and how this situation can be made productive for knowledge about qualitative empirical research.[3] I will analyse the differences between the two interview settings (male-to-male vs. male-to-female) and interpret their specific silences as well as articulations by taking into account culturally produced and historically grown constructions of femininity and masculinity.[4]

Conflicts between secrecy and the desire to talk

Even though prostitution is not illegal in Germany, only a few of the participants in my and other studies have ever talked about their experiences with prostitutes (cf. Hydra 1991; Kleiber and Velten 1994). The danger of being ridiculed, of losing their partners or of both appears to be too great (cf. Hydra 1991). Consequently, in my research as in other studies, participants were 'anxious about being able to preserve their anonymity'[5] (Kleiber and Velten 1994: 46; cf. Gerheim 2007: 150). Furthermore, I observed that it was not always the fact of actually going to prostitutes that male clients concealed, but rather the particular sexual practice carried out with a prostitute or – as in one case – the inability to have sex with a prostitute. Participants kept these details secret not only from women, but also from other men.

If prostitution is so closely related to stigma and shame one wonders why clients of prostitutes would participate in a study at all. According to Plummer, 'people may tell their sexual stories as a relief from tension' (1995: 34). This aspect is very obvious in my study as well as Gerheim's (2007) study. Some participants joined the project, because talking helped them to find some clarity about themselves. They found themselves in conflict between living out what they thought of as their desires and the low social value of being a punter, on the one hand, and, on the other hand, their own moral values such as faithfulness. The interview released them[6] and was thus a 'positive sanction' (Rothe 1997): Because sex-purchase is something participants would rather not talk about openly, a level of secrecy is created and it is this very secrecy which in turn creates the need to talk about it. Dieter, [7] one of my participants, expressed this quite clearly: 'For me it is a psychological necessity that I can just get it off my chest, and at home I obviously can't do this.'

Subsequently, they made use of the interview process 'as part of a therapeutic encounter for "redemption and social reincorporation" through a desire to help science' (Plummer 1995: 34). Or, perhaps they told their tales 'through a desire for immortality, a desire for order, as special pleading or simple exhibitionism' (p. 34). Moreover, it should not be forgotten that 'for many the telling of a tale comes as a major way of "discovering who one really is"' (p. 34).

If the historical context that inevitably influences research on prostitution is considered, namely the development of sexual sciences that have led to a culture of constant public as well as private confession (Plummer 1995), the interpretation that telling one's sexual story can serve as 'a voyage to explore the self' (Plummer 1995: 34) reveals more complex implications. In *The History of Sexuality* ([1976] 1990), Michel Foucault argues that *scientia sexualis*, which was developed during the eighteenth and nineteenth centuries in Europe, 'concerned itself primarily with aberrations, perversions, exceptional oddities, pathological abatements and morbid aggravations' ([1976], 1990: 53). It was not concerned with intensifying pleasure, with drawing 'truth … from pleasure itself' (p. 57), but with finding the truth about sex. As such, *scienta sexualis* was 'subordinated in the main to the imperatives of a morality whose divisions it reiterated under the guise of a medical norm' (p. 53); it 'declared the furtive customs of the timid, and the most solitary of petty manias, dangerous for the whole society' (pp. 53–54). In order to find these 'dangerous' sexual practices, *scientia sexualis* used a secularized version of confession. According to Foucault, confession is one of the major tools of power, indeed 'the truthful confession was inscribed at the heart of the procedures of individualization by power' (pp. 58–59). Confession has become an everyday and compelling cultural practice that 'has spread its effects far and wide. It plays a part in justice, medicine, education, family relationships and love relations' (p. 59). Furthermore, it is so common that it is no longer regarded as a tool of power:

> The obligation to confess is now relayed through so many different points, is so deeply ingrained in us, that we no longer perceive it as the effect of a power that constrains us; on the contrary, it seems to us that truth, lodged in our most secret nature, 'demands' only to surface; that if it fails to do so, this is because a constraint holds it in place, the violence of a power weighs it down, and it can finally be articulated only at the price of some kind of liberation (p. 60).

In this sense, concealment is not only a means of disclosure, but also the necessary condition for confession. This is especially true in research where the scientific frame provides a sense of anonymity, supposed neutrality and contact with experts.

Both aspects – the secrecy as well as the desire to confess – play an important role in probably all interview processes on prostitution. In *The Sociology of Secret Societies,* Georg Simmel (1908) describes this interactive process as follows: We do not give a complete account of what is happening in our consciousness when we tell each other something. Instead, we communicate only what we believe are the 'useful bits', those bits that we believe will be understood. Thus, certain details might remain undisclosed during interviews, because participants tell their stories according to what they believe is relevant information. [8]

Ken Plummer (1995) also regards stories as 'joint actions' (p. 20). One actor is the storyteller; the other is the coaxer who '[brings] people to the edge of telling a story they might never have told before, and [coaches] them to tell it in a certain way. … Coaxers can play a crucial role in shifting the nature of the stories that are told' (p. 21). As a consequence, one has to consider the interactive character of storytelling in any research project and keep in mind the fact that participants alter their stories according to: a) what they think the interviewer expects to or can bear to hear; b) how they believe s/he is going to interpret what is said; and c) how what is said will be perceived by the wider public when the study is published.

Heteronormative masculine self-assertion in interviews

Neither Simmel, Plummer nor Foucault distinguish between the different outcomes of this interactive process caused by different gender settings. However, because sexuality is highly gendered one can assume that heterosexual men tell their stories differently than, for instance, gay men, lesbian or straight women. One can further assume that they tell the story differently depending on the sex/gender of their listener. Michael Schwalbe and Michelle Wolkomir's (2001) study of men's behaviour in interview situations concludes that for male participants an interview can be both 'an opportunity for signifying masculinity' as well as 'a peculiar type of encounter in which masculinity is threatened' (p. 92).

It is important to note here that the way Foucault theorizes confession does not happen only as the result of an outside force such as a person conducting the interview. It also arises from an internal wish to speak, to articulate feelings, deeds, and so on, in order to clarify one's own identity, of which sexuality has become one of the most important aspects (cf. Halperin 1993). As Plummer points out:

> No longer do people simply tell their sexual stories to reveal the truth of their sexual lives; instead they turn themselves into *socially organised biographical objects*. They construct … tales of the intimate self, which may or may not bear a relationship to a truth. Are their stories really to be seen as the simple unfolding of some inner truth? *Or are their very stories something they are brought to say in a particular way through a particular time and place?* And if so, where do they get their stories from? Once posed this way, the sexual stories can no longer be seen simply as the harbingers of a relatively unproblematic truth.
>
> (1995: 34, emphasis in the original)

Thus, masculinity is not to be seen as the 'real' or 'inner' truth of the interviewees, but as something constantly reproduced in the interview setting through the content of their stories as well as through the interaction between the interviewer and the interviewee. Thus, in the interviews (in

Gerheim's as well as my study) masculine heterosexual identity was in the making. This 'making' includes insecurity that might lead to the perception of a *threatened masculinity*. Masculinity cannot be understood as a stable entity men can rely on, without questioning the existing power relations between men and women. However, the interview process can be interpreted as an irritation to socially dominant perceptions of masculinity. The 'looker' is commonly constructed as being male. Being looked at and/or being investigated may, thus, make a man feel uncomfortable because in the position of the looked-at, one becomes an object and might perceive oneself as outside of a norm.

Furthermore, in the constellation of a man being interviewed by a woman, the sense of the male 'looker' and the female 'looked-at' is subverted, as is the related notion of active versus passive. In my research project this subversion was intensified because I was asking the men about their sexuality, an important aspect of identity in the Western world, and they might have been afraid of being rejected. [9]

However, because stories are not only told for the listener, but also for one's own 'self-assertion' (Schütze 1987: 39), the situation can also be interpreted in the opposite sense, as signifying masculinity (Schwalbe and Wolkomir 2001: 92). Sexual stories, in particular, are at once informative for the listener and a relief for the storyteller in his (or her) search for redemption (Plummer 1995: 34). Here, the cultural assumption that women are better listeners and enhancers of a man's speech plays an important role. Moreover, talking about one's sexuality can also be a pleasant and seemingly innocent turn-on (as one of my participants admitted). However, this happened in a heterosexual setting. As I will show, in Gerheim's study erotic emotions appear to be less present. Thus, heteronormativity, including homophobia, male bonding and female 'othering' in the interview process need to be interrogated.

Even though these discussions are not new to sexual research, they need to be further developed in feminist as well as mainstream social studies on dominant (as opposed to marginal) positions. The fact that researchers are involved in their research and, hence, also in the interview situation is something feminist theorists in particular have pointed out. However, this has usually happened from the perspective of research on marginalized people. In the context of research on privileged positions such as heterosexual men who pay for sexual services, the researcher cannot remain outside either. S/he joins the discursive reproduction of gendered identity to a certain extent, even if s/he would rather stay innocent. In the remainder of this essay I will show the distinct involvement that might occur in either woman-to-man or man-to-man interview settings of this kind.

Establishing homosociality and heterosexuality

Carol Smart regards the activity of interviewing as 'intrinsically female' (1984: 155), because of the empirical 'fact' that 'women frequently operate as facilitators to male speech. That is to say that women do tend not to interrupt but rather to encourage and help the flow of men's talk' (Smart 1984: 155).

This belief is shared by Janet Finch, who interprets listening as a female strength. She argues that 'practice in research teams does suggest that research directors often regard women as especially suited to this task' (1993: 170). Thus, there exists a widespread assumption that women are better listeners than men. These ideas are based on associations of feminine identity with nature, the sexual, and the irrational, and thus with emotions, feelings, desires, and so on. As a consequence, based on these assumptions women appear to be much better suited to listening and particularly talking about sexuality than men.

In my study, these assumptions about particular feminine qualities were reproduced by the clients.[10] I asked all prospective participants whether they preferred to be interviewed by a man or a woman. None of them wanted to be interviewed by a man and many indicated that they preferred to discuss this particular topic with a woman.[11] Participants also mentioned this preference during their interviews, saying, for instance, 'well, with men it's like this ... that everybody wants to boast somehow' (Dieter). Or, 'to be frank, I would rather discuss this with a woman instead of a man' (Christian).

The desire to disclose can also be related to the relationship between the prostitute and her client, since it is frequently mentioned that clients make use of prostitutes also as listeners to their personal problems. The interviewees themselves often compared talking to me with talking to a woman working in prostitution. Dieter, for instance, told me the following about going to massage parlours:

> But one can also talk about a lot of things, because one will never meet the girl or woman again, or one doesn't have to, if one doesn't want to. It's like I'm coming to you now and just want to talk about it.

However, not all potential interviewees share these preferences. Udo Gerheim (2007) advertised his research on prostitution and his search for clients with his full name (p. 150). Thus, his participants contacted him knowing that he was a man. In these interviews gender relations were established in a different way, operating on an assumption of sameness rather than difference.

The effects of sameness in interview processes where a woman interviewer conducted interviews with women participants have been stressed by feminists (e.g. Mies 1978; Finch 1993; Oakley [1981] 1997). As a female interviewer speaking to male interviewees I could not relate to these theories. Rather, I was treated as the 'other', as a representative of the opposite sex and, thus, as having quantitatively as well as qualitatively different sexual desires. In a man-to-man interview setting the dynamics are again reversed. Consequently, in Gerheim's study such notions of sex-sameness were present during his interviews with male heterosexual clients of prostitution. Even though the power structures were different to the situations described by feminist authors, he was still considered the outsider within. Interviewees would tell him about prostitution as a potential peer, similarly to the interviewees Janet Finch (1993) talked to as a woman. Thus, homosociality and with it male bonding appears to be an important dynamic in the interview process.

To give an example: in one interview passage a man talks about being lonely and desiring sexual experiences from time to time and explains this desire as a consequence of male biology. I was told the same logic by several interviewees who were mostly referring to the myth of the strong male sexual drive. However, these statements showed a significant difference: The interviewees in my study would regularly explain it to me as somebody with a different sexuality, whereas Gerheim was told: 'I believe it is like that for everybody, including you' (Gerheim 2007: 152). Or in a different passage the same interviewee explains his decision to remain single. Partly, he does not want to be burdened or have his freedom taken away from him because of a relationship to a woman. In this context, he addresses the interviewer, saying: 'you know that too [what it means] to be bound'. To give yet another example, a different participant, who is a regular user of internet portals where punters give each other tips and write reviews about clubs, etc., explained the difference between sex in and outside of prostitution to Gerheim (2007). In this context he said: 'The point of time when you penetrate is not so critical [in prostitution]. Whether you wish to do so after 2 min or 20 min does not matter' (p. 159). He continued by telling him further technical advantages. Thus, he addressed Gerheim as a peer, as someone who understands his feelings and who potentially shares his desires.

With such observations, general social assumptions – for example that women are better listeners – cannot be transferred uncritically to the interview setting; the interviewer, Gerheim, functions as facilitator of male speech as well. However, since the interviewees create their stories according to their assumptions of what might be interesting for him, his listening generated discourses of homosociality and heterosexuality in a way that was very different from that which was established in my interviews. One could argue that both of us became involved in the interview and made accomplices, but in very distinct ways. Whereas Gerheim was perceived as a peer and thus a potential client of female prostitutes (a fear that he expressed himself; cf. Gerheim 2007: 148), I was perceived ambivalently as both the potential sex-worker as well as the potentially asexual woman.

Homophobia and eroticism

It is common knowledge that when one talks about one's experiences, the related emotions may become vivid again (Schütze 1987: 41). In the case of research on the consumption of sexual services this obviously would be dominated by sexual emotion. One participant told me about the erotic kick he got just from thinking about talking about his sexuality. For him either the research situation or I myself as a still-anonymous person was already sexualized. For other participants sexual feelings might have come up during the interview, not necessarily in response to me, but in response to the process of narration itself. Alternatively, desire surfaced and I became its object just because I happened to be there.

Another option might be that for ethical or other reasons participants avoided making me their object and tried to normalize the situation. Just to give an example, Rolf, who at the time of the interview was unable to fully control muscles in his lower abdomen because he still had not recovered from back surgery, explained to me:

> Yes, well to be frank, ehm, it can happen, you just have to look at me, and then I get – I orgasm … Yet, it can also happen that we 'torture' ourselves for two hours and nothing will happen. … Well every normal human can control their sexual drives or their orgasm, I can't. … It can happen to me that while we are sitting here, I suddenly orgasm, yes, because I can't control it … without me thinking or imagining, seeing anything, it suddenly happens and I can't do anything about it.

Rolf explains a medical fact that obviously has nothing to do with our relation to each other and uses a very common procedure of including a listener in one's explanation. During the interview I was astonished that he mentioned it in this way. However, thinking back on it, this quote could signify attempts to neutralize emotions in this situation by indirectly saying, 'Don't worry. I don't feel attracted to you, even though there are some sexual feelings operating.' Or, 'Please do not feel attracted to me.' Nonetheless, the statement points to the fact that this interview setting inherited the sexualization of the encounter similar to the passage I described above about Gerheim's study – when a participant told him about the advantages of having sex with a sex-worker. It could also have been a mere general statement, using 'you' as a general form. However, it is unlikely that he would have used this form with a male interviewer. Thus, such a statement brings the researcher into one's own experience. As a result, the coaxing process described by Plummer (1995) is not only about actively asking the right questions that make interviewees talk. It is also about being brought into their stories and being placed as a particular and sexed/gendered listener. As a result, one constantly experiences an interference of the learned aspects such as the neutrality of an interviewer.

In one case I very obviously became the object of desire of one participant. Christian told me that sometimes he would ask shop assistants whether he could kiss their feet. Because at the time of our interview none of them had agreed, he told me he would like to know how a woman might feel when being asked this favour. I replied that I would find it quite awkward. Instead of giving up he then asked me: 'I would really like to know, if I asked you, could I maybe kiss your feet, Sabine, let's say, how would you react to this?'

Similar cases are mentioned in a study about clients by Hydra, a Berlin organization which advocates for the rights of prostitutes (1991): 'The men assumed our understanding of their form of sexuality; some, for instance, took the opportunity to give the interview in a woman's dress' (Hydra 1991: 24). Furthermore, O'Connell Davidson (1994: 217) discovered that one of her participants was actually masturbating during the interview. In my situation, the interviewee's request was no surprise as he had given such a lengthy introduction to it that I somehow was expecting it. Thus I did not feel overpowered.

Schwalbe and Wolkomir (2001) interpret the sexualisation of the woman-to-man interview situation as an attempt by the man to exercise control. It can take different forms: 'flirting, sexual innuendo, touching, and remarks on appearance' (2001: 94) can be made. All of them may appear innocent, but they point to gendered power relations (Schwalbe and Wolkomir 2001). On the one hand, one could argue that this is particularly the case here, because in the heterosexual context women frequently operate as sexual objects. Representations – as well as acceptance – of women as sexual subjects are still exceptions (e.g. Ussher 1997). On the other hand, he displayed his desire and took the risk of being rejected. Thus, my rejection through which I implicitly established myself as sexual subject in addition to my position as a researcher, and hence the 'looker', undercut this dynamic.

In summary, sexualization of the interview situation is linked to what I described before as the different ways of involving a man or woman researcher into one's story. As I demonstrated above, Gerheim was included into the interviews via homosociality. Homosociality is closely linked to homophobia, the neglect of erotic relationships between men (cf. Messner 2001: 259). While socially homogenous relationships are created, sexually the opposite happens. According to Michael Kimmel, 'Homophobia is a central organizing principle of our cultural definition of manhood' (2001: 277). The development of a heterosexual identity includes the rejection of being potentially homosexual, because homosexuality is linked to emasculation, and men and women are constructed as being oppositional within normative heterosexuality. Whereas men have been constructed as rational and in sexual and emotional terms rather selfish, women have been increasingly constructed as responsible for relationships, endowed with the ability to love (Wolf 1995). Furthermore, during the course of the nineteenth century the exchange of intimacy between men became a sign of being homosexual and became increasingly tabooed (Eder 2002). This can be observed in the interview passages published by Gerheim (2007), since participants appear to include the interviewer (Gerheim, in this instance) as a peer in their perspectives on feminine identity. As a result, the erotic emotion is never directly operating between the two persons, but is instead always channelled via a sex-worker or another woman between them. Hence, both interview settings display heteronormativity, but in distinct ways.

Conclusion

To sum up, the secrecy surrounding prostitution makes confession an important part of the interview process. Without secrecy, the disclosure would have less weight, but with secrecy a social research interview setting builds a perfectly ritualized form for it. Moreover, this confession does not happen in a gender neutral space, but rather is related to the sex/gender of the interviewer as well as the interviewee. The story told by the interviewee differs in relation to what he imagines the interviewer would like and can bear to hear. As a result, co-axing (cf. Plummer 1995) is not only an active procedure, but also entails passive aspects due to the social positioning as man or woman. Similarly, the wish to confess takes on very distinct forms (cf. Foucault [1976] 1990). The researcher, nonetheless, has only limited influence on how the interviewee reacts to this social position and how s/he structures his/her story accordingly (Simmel, 1908).

However, in the settings discussed here for Gerheim's (2007) and my ([2005] 2007) study this appears to influence not so much the actual content, but the way the content is spoken about. Just to give a final example of the necessary difference, Schwalbe and Wolkomir advise interviewers not to use flirting as strategy to establish rapport, because this may include 'the distinct disadvantage of encouraging a participant to try to create an impression of himself as sexually desirable' (2001: 94). In my case doing so could have had serious consequences. The participants, however, flirted with me and thus created the same effect: they tried to appear sexually desirable. Additionally, some men had a bad conscience for using sexual services. If this is taken into consideration along with the possibility that in a disputed area such as prostitution it is very likely that clients will want to appear as politically correct as possible, it is not surprising that, the general undertone of all interviews was, 'Even though I pay for sexual services, I am a normal man and I am not as bad as you as a woman might think of me'. In the case of Gerheim's study, clients were no less defensive. The underlying politics in his study resemble the statement: 'You might claim not to be a client, but I will show you that because of this you are not a better person. And, who knows, maybe afterwards you will pay for sexual services, too.' As I have shown, either of the underlying statements causes different silences in the interview and either of them results in selective disclosure.

Consequently, the challenges for a man or woman interviewer differ significantly. Even though it appears that as a woman one is far more in danger of being integrated into the sexuality of the interviewee, I have demonstrated that this is only true superficially. In a man-to-man interview the same power dynamics are present and it is far more likely that they – as well as the silences they create – are going to be overlooked, because in the man-to-man interview erotic emotions are silenced. Thus, this setting creates more distanced social relations and, hence, appears to be more suitable to mainstream standards of social research. Whereas a woman interviewer is confronted with sexual emotions, a man interviewer is perceived as a potential peer. Both positions appear to be exclusive in this particular heterosexual space.

This very concrete meta-level of the interview, reflecting the social positioning of both interview parties therefore needs to be included into one's methodology. In other words, homosociality as the creation of a supposedly neutral form of closeness between heterosexual men needs to be questioned just like the supposedly less neutral sexualisation created in a woman-to-man interview. Both interview settings display the same social relations that, first of all, create the desire for commercial sexuality and, second of all, create the particular forms of secrecy surrounding it.

Notes

1 This assumption is of course in itself problematic as it assumes a sexual truth of a person that only needs the right circumstances to come out.
2 This observation is true for all of the studies conducted thus far on male heterosexual clients of prostitutes (Hydra 1991; Kleiber and Velten 1994; Velten 1994; Ahlemeyer 2002).
3 Since I have discussed the complexity and fluidity of power relations in the interview situation elsewhere (Grenz 2005), they will only be marginally treated in this essay.
4 These constructions do not only play a part during the interview, but also in the decision-making process for the participation in such research. Some participants in my study clearly stated that they would never discuss such issues with a male interviewer. Other potential participants never turned up; perhaps they would have preferred to talk to a male interviewer.
5 I translated all quotes from German studies into English.
6 Andrea Rothe (1997), who studied sex tourism in Thailand, also notes that after the interview participants appeared to be calm and relaxed.
7 All participants' names were anonymized.
8 Some interviewees might have hidden things intentionally. For instance, when I assured people (in writing) that all locations and personal names would remain anonymous, some answered that 'one would not say anything identifiable in such research, anyway'. Thus, even though they talked freely about their experiences, my impression was that some interviewees concealed issues quite consciously. They may have also done so in order to avoid situations they felt would be too shameful for them as well as for me.
9 This might be a reason for some participants: being hesitant to talk; not giving information of any depths; needing more assurance and opening up only slowly. For instance, one participant would wonder aloud 'if I should say it' (Michael). Others just told a bit and then waited for – or even asked for – new questions: 'Well then, next question' (Paul). One interviewee criticized me for asking detailed questions, for instance asking, 'Um, do we become precise again?' (Peter). However, all these difficulties can also be related to the fact that participants were not necessarily used to social scientific research methods, did not know how to articulate sexual issues, or felt ashamed to do so, which was consistently expressed through phrases like 'how can I put it' (Peter), or 'it's difficult to analyse' (Peter).
10 The consequences of these relations are explained in more detail in Grenz (2005).
11 Graaf et al. (1996) reported a similar experience in their quantitative study about the transmission of HIV in which they interviewed male heterosexual clients of prostitutes.

References

Beier, K.M., Bosinski, H.A.G., Hartmann, U. and Loewit, K. (2001) *Sexualmedizin*. Munich: Urban and Fischer.

Braun, C. von (1999 [1985]) *NichtIch – Logik, Lüge, Libido*, 7th edn. Frankfurt: Verlag Neue Kritik.

Cronin, A.M. (2000) *Advertising and Consumer Citizenship: Gender, Images and Rights*. London: Routledge.

Day, S. (2007) *On the Game. Women and Sex Work*. London/Ann Arbour, MI: Pluto Press.

Eder, F.X. (2002) *Kultur der Begierde. Eine Geschichte der Sexualität*. Munich: Beck.

Foucault, M. (1990 [1976]) *The History of Sexuality: An Introduction*. 2nd edn. London: Penguin.

Finch, J. (1993) 'It's great to have someone to talk to: ethics and politics of interviewing women', in M. Hammersley (ed.) *Social Research. Philosophy, Politics and Practice*. London: Sage.

Gerheim, U. (2007) 'Freier. Ein sich windender Forschungsgegenstand. Projektskizze einer qualitative-empirischen Untersuchung zu habituellen Mustern heterosexueller Prostitutionskunden', in E. Mitrovic (ed.) *Arbeitsplatz Prostitution. Ein Beruf wie jeder andere?* Hamburg: Lit.

Graaf, R. de, Zessen, G. van, Vanwesenbeeck, I., Straver, C.J. and Visser, J.H. (1996) 'Segmentation of heterosexual prostitution into various forms: A barrier to the potential transmission of HIV', *Aids Care*, 8 (4): 417–31.

Halperin, D.M. (1993) 'Is there a history of sexuality?', in H. Abelove, M.A. Barale and D.M. Halperin (eds) *The Lesbian and Gay Studies Reader*. London: Routledge.

Hydra (1991) *Freier – Das heimliche Treiben der Männer*. Hamburg: Galgenberg.

Kimmel, M.S. (2001) 'Masculinity as homophobia: fear, shame, and silence in the construction of gender identity', in S.M. Whitehead and F.J. Barrett (eds) *The Masculinities Reader*. Cambridge: Polity.

Kleiber, D. and Velten, D. (1994) *Prostitutionskunden – Eine Untersuchung über soziale und psychologische Charakteristika von Besuchern weiblicher Prostitutierter in Zeiten von Aids*. Bonn: Bundesministerium für Gesundheit.

Messner, M.A. (2001) 'Friendship, intimacy and sexuality', in Whitehead and F. J. Barret (eds) *The Masculinities Reader*. Cambridge: Polity.

Mies, M. (1978) 'Methodische Postulate zur Frauenforschung. Dargestellt am Beispiel der Gewalt gegen Frauen', *Beiträge zu feministischer Theorie und Praxis*, 1: 41–63.

Oakley, A. (1981) 'Interviewing women: a contradiction in terms', in H. Roberts (ed.) *Doing Feminist Research*. London: Routledge.

O'Connell Davidson, J. and Layder, D. (1994) *Methods, Sex and Madness*. London: Routledge.

Plummer, K. (1995) *Telling Sexual Stories. Power, Change and Social Worlds*. London: Routledge.

Queen, C. (1997) 'Sex radical politics, sex-positive feminist thought, and whore stigma', in J. Nagle (ed.) *Whores and Other Feminists*. New York: Routledge.

Rothe, A. (1997) *Männer, Prostitution, Tourismus. Wenn Herren reisen …* Münster: Wachs Verlag.

Sanders, T. (2005) *Sex Work: A Risky Business*. Devon: Willan Publishing.

Schütze, F. (1987) *Das narrative Interview in Interaktionsstudien I*. Hagen: Department of Educational and Social Science and Arts, Gesamthochschule, Fernuniversität.

Schwalbe, M. and Wolkomir, M. (2001) 'The masculine self as problem and resource in interview studies of men', *Men and Masculinities*, 40 (1): 90–103.

Sedgwick, E.K. (1990) *Epistemology of the Closet*. London: Harvester Wheatsheaf.

Simmel, G. (1908) 'Das Geheimnis und die Geheime Gesellschaft', in G. Simmel, *Soziologie – Untersuchungen über die Formen der Vergesellschaftung*. Leipzig: Duncker und Humboldt.

Smart, C. (1984) 'Doing the research: practices and dilemmas', in C. Smart, *The Ties that Bind: Law, Marriage and the Reproduction of Patriarchal Relations*. London: Routledge and Kegan Paul.

Ussher, J.M. (1997) *Fantasies of Femininity: Reframing the Boundaries of Sex*. London: Penguin.

Wolf, M. (1995) *… quasi irrsinnig' Nachmoderne Geschlechter-Beziehung*. Pfaffenweiler: Centaurus.

5 Silencing accounts of silenced sexualities

Meg Barker and Darren Langdridge

In this chapter we explore occasions when we as researchers have grappled with questions of whether to silence aspects of already silenced sexualities. By silenced sexualities we mean those which fall outside taken-for-granted heteronormativity, or other aspects of Rubin's (1984) 'charmed circle' of sexual behaviour. Specifically our research has focused on gay men's sexual practices; on bisexuality, which is largely invisible in popular culture (Barker and Langridge, 2008); on openly non-monogamous relationships, which are generally deemed unworkable in popular culture (Ritchie and Barker 2005); and on sadomasochism which remains pathologized, criminalized and largely unknowable (Langdridge and Barker 2007). During our time serving on the Lesbian and Gay Psychology Section committee of the British Psychological Society and working together on many research and writing projects, there have been several occasions when we have been confronted by our uneasiness about including certain participant accounts or academic narratives.

Particular examples of such times include our mutual concern over the proliferation of academic and therapeutic writing on 'barebacking', which may give the impression that the practice is far more common than it actually is and stigmatize gay men more widely with the kinds of pathologising explanations that are put forward (Barker et al. 2007; Langdridge and Flowers 2005; Flowers and Langdridge 2007).[1] We have also discussed the opportunities and limitations afforded by both 'identity politics' and 'queer' discourses in relation to bisexuality (Barker and Langdridge, 2008) exploring the possibility that queer theory perspectives are in danger of continuing the erasure of a sexuality which is already invisible. Finally, we have entered into an ongoing dialogue about the academic representation of openly non-monogamous relationships. These can broadly be divided into those which celebrate such relationships as potentially feminist, queer or otherwise radical ways of structuring and managing relationships (e.g. Pallotta-Chiarolli 1995; Robinson 1997; Heaphy et al. 2004) and those which highlight the limitations of non-monogamous relationships and the ways in which they may reproduce and reinforce hetero- and mono-normativity in various ways rather than challenging them (e.g. Jamieson 2004; Finn 2005; Klesse 2006). Whilst we are sceptical of uncritical acceptance of the former view, we also worry that the latter perspective might reinforce dominant societal discourses which position such relationships as fundamentally unworkable or 'nothing new' (Ritchie and Barker 2006).

In this chapter we will focus on one particular debate which we have returned to several times over the last few years during our editorship of one journal special issue and one edited book on sadomasochism (Langdridge and Barker 2005, 2007). We found ourselves conflicting over the question of whether we should include narratives of sadomasochistic practices as 'healing' and 'therapeutic' in our writing. During the chapter we will include excerpts of our ongoing discussion of this issue to highlight broader questions which qualitative researchers need to reflect upon when considering how to report their research. We are in agreement that the reporting of research can never be a neutral or value-free activity, and that the personal, political and theoretical agendas of the researchers inevitably colour the work and influence which stories are told and not told. As part of an ongoing reflexive project (Finlay and Gough 2003) we feel it is important to scrutinize the process of deciding how to write and disseminate research.

The theoretical frame of this chapter is Ken Plummer's work on the telling of sexual stories (Plummer 1995). Plummer believes that we all tell stories about ourselves: narratives about who we are and how we came to be that way, which we repeat to ourselves and others to make sense of our lives and to present ourselves in certain ways. Often these draw on the stories that are in the media and the communities we inhabit. Plummer further argues that today 'sex' has become the 'big story', with people presenting tales of their sexual behaviour and identity (such as the 'rape survivor' or 'coming out' story) in talk shows, magazines and newspapers, over telephone help lines and in support groups. This means that such stories often take on similar structures and contain the same key elements. For example, coming out stories often begin with somebody recognising that they were 'different' in some way as a teenager and progress through their realisation that there were others like them and them putting a name to their difference.

Plummer argues that stories can be seen as joint actions with different individuals, groups or organisations involved in the stories in various ways. These include the story-tellers who produce accounts, for example the interviewees in research projects or participants on talk shows. Also involved in the production of stories are the 'coaxers, coachers and coercers' (ibid.: 21) who have the power to elicit stories from the tellers, for example the therapist or newspaper journalist. Then there are the consumers of the story who include the television viewers and readers of newspaper reports about research. Of course some of these consumers will also be story-tellers themselves and the stories they read and hear will influence the stories which they, themselves, tell. As Plummer says, 'stories get told and read in different ways in different contexts. The consuming of a tale centres upon the different *social worlds* and *interpretive communities* who can hear the story in certain ways and hence not others and who may come to produce their own shared memories' (ibid.: 22). In this chapter we reflect on the difficulties, and indeed discomforts, involved in selecting which stories to present and how to present them in our research, knowing the potential political implications this may have for a set of sexual identities and practices which remain pathologised and criminalised (Langdridge 2006). Through a dialogical presentation of our own arguments on this topic we hope to extend understanding about the potential and peril in researching and writing about silenced sexualities.

Before presenting and reflecting on three key moments from our dialogue on these issues, it is necessary to provide a brief introduction to the sexuality under consideration and the stories in question.[2] SM is a broad term used for sexual identities and practices involving pain play, bondage, dominance and submission, and erotic power exchange (Langdridge and Barker 2006). Langdridge and Butt (2004) argue that SM is having its time at the beginning of the twenty-first century: There are communities of support for telling stories of SM identities and practices, and these are becoming more visible in popular culture. Whilst there has been a proliferation of SM imagery in advertisements, pop music, fashion, television and movies (Weiss 2006; Sisson 2007) we would argue that SM is still largely unknowable, with the majority of people struggling to comprehend it. Depictions of SM can be divided into three main categories: safe kink, dangerous deviance, and the ridiculous. The first category includes common exhortations for heterosexual women to 'spice up' their love life with a pair of fluffy handcuffs or a sequined riding crop. As Storr (2003) found, such representations police strongly against people straying 'too far' into 'real' SM, and Gill (2007) sees this as part of a general move from sexual objectification of women to a kind of subjectification where messages of 'get and keep your men' hide beneath a veneer of post-feminist sexual liberation. The second category of dangerous deviance includes common depictions of SMers as serial killers and SM as a slippery slope towards criminal and harmful activities (Barker 2003) that may result in trauma or be the result of traumatic psychopathology. The third category portrays SMers as objects of ridicule in cruelly humorous depictions of the neighbour who turns out to be a dominatrix, or the businessman who wears a gimp suit at the weekend. As Billig (2005) argues, such ridicule is used as a strong disciplinary means to uphold social norms.

All three of these representations clearly position 'real' SM as other and unknowable, and this is reflected in current laws and psychiatric nosologies which continue to criminalize SM practices beyond the 'transient and trifling' (Weait 2007) and to pathologise their practitioners (Kleinplatz and Moser 2007). However, in recent years a new story has emerged in both SM communities and mainstream media which has sparked our heated debates in its potential to offer an alternative possibility to the stories mentioned above, *or* to further reinforce stigmatising and pathologising views of SM. This is the story of SM as a 'healing' or 'therapeutic' practice which might take a person from a position of mental illness to psychological health (as in the film *Secretary* 2002), from powerlessness to control over their own bodies (as in the documentary *Sick* 1997), or from fear and victimization to excitement and a movement away from past trauma (as in the SM book *Radical Ecstasy* by Easton and Hardy 2004). Stories along these lines have emerged in our own qualitative research with SMers and online SM communities (e.g. Langdridge and Butt 2004; Ritchie and Barker 2005) as well as those of other researchers (Taylor and Ussher 2001). This leaves us with the question of how, if at all, to include such stories in our research.

Broadly speaking, in our discussions, Meg has taken the position that these 'healing' and 'therapeutic' narratives are important and interesting and should be included, in some way, in writing on SM. Darren, on the other hand, has expressed serious concerns over how such stories may be taken up by wider audiences if 'coaxed' by us – 'us' being broadly supportive of such marginalised sexualities – and 'consumed' by them – 'them' being the consumer who presently sees such marginalised sexualities as mad or bad.

First moment of dialogue: how dare we censor our participants' experiences?

MB: I'll kick off then. I think my main concern is that people are *saying* these things. They're saying that they find their SM practices to be therapeutic and healing. So how can you possibly justify not including these stories?

DL: Well they're saying a lot of things: this is just one of many stories and to my mind a dangerous one at that.

MB: But it *is* in there: it's part of the lived experience of many people. Doesn't neglecting to mention that go against everything we're aiming to do as phenomenological researchers and as people who come from a strong background in feminist research? Shouldn't we be all about giving people a voice, not silencing people?

DL: I agree that it requires enormous justification to warrant the silencing of any narrative, but I think that there may be such justification in this case. This story has the potential to be perverted by the social world quite unlike the others. There is a real danger inherent in a story which may lead to a very particular reception by those less amenable to SM identities/practices.

MB: We do have to be aware of the political implications of our research for the communities we're researching; you're right about that.

DL: I would also add that all new social movements require consciousness raising, and research can be a part of that, but I think that there are some discourses which may be helpful in the everyday life of participants which, if re-produced, may be twisted, tainted and used in damaging ways by people and institutions antagonistic to the very people voicing such stories. Such stories may inadvertently give people something with which to further pathologise and even criminalise SMers. This is a particular problem with SM because of the degree to which these people and communities remain disenfranchised. Perhaps other minority communities could survive similar stories – the gay community can probably survive stories about crystal meth, for example, because it is established – but the SM community is still incredibly vulnerable.

Here we are torn: as academics are we simply facilitating the telling of stories regardless of their implications? Surely, we do much more than this: we tell our own stories when we engage in academic writing and, in the process, we have the opportunity to select and/or prioritize some stories over others. At the very least we tell stories through our particular personal and theoretical lens, such that it better serves our own political agenda. We feel it is particularly important to recognise this aspect of the research process in qualitative research when we perceive the stories we hear and re-produce as potentially harmful for the very same people who voice them. This is clearly problematic for researchers – such as us – who are steeped in the history of feminist research and phenomenology. We share the desire to encourage the oppressed to move from 'silence to voice' and, through this, work with the liberatory potential of such politically informed research practice. But there is a naivety in simply saying 'I'm just giving voice to … ': a failure to recognise our power and an abrogation of responsibility. If we care about the communities we research then surely we must care about the way in which our research might inadvertently hurt the subjects of our research. But this is, of course, complex, especially if we choose to silence a story that is clearly and honestly being told. What of our duty of care as researchers here when choosing to silence the voices of our participants?

Part of our accountability as researchers (Banister et al. 1995) is to consider carefully how the stories that we 'coax' or 'coach' from people are presented. It might seem arrogant to assume that our research papers will make much of an impact on the widely circulating sexual stories available to people. However, the areas we work on are written about by relatively few academics and so we often find ourselves being two of a very small number of academics who are asked to comment on these issues by journalists, film-censors, therapist-trainers and so on. Also, as Meg learnt the hard way when several national and international newspapers reported on her conference presentation on non-monogamy (Ritchie and Barker 2006), it is not always easy to determine how research will be received and re-produced. There is a responsibility, as a researcher, to try – as far as possible – to predict how the media and wider social world are likely to take up the accounts that are produced, especially when the sexualities we write about are largely silenced with available narratives either non-existent or stigmatising.

Second moment of dialogue: what's the problem with this narrative anyway?

MB: I still don't understand quite why you perceive such a problem with narratives of SM as potentially therapeutic though. It's not as if the therapy industry is so wonderful, particularly when it comes to SMers. What's wrong with people taking things into their own hands? You could see it as empowering.

DL: It's not just SM. When it comes to major trauma I wouldn't recommend someone to do anything which involves reliving the trauma, most especially in situations and settings where things might get dangerously out of hand. Things like psychodrama, or even acting classes, can be risky too. Obviously I respect people's right to do whatever they feel works for them. But if I was offering advice concerning serious mental health difficulties and sexualities, I would urge caution and probably advise people to see a *good* mental health professional, whilst taking your point that therapy in general doesn't have a great history with SM, or other minority sexualities.

MB: Are we not getting into dangerous territory though if we try to distinguish between people with little problems who can use their own methods and people with big problems who need professional help? And I'm uncomfortable reifying the medical and psychiatric profession as the only places people can work through 'big stuff'.

DL: Yes, fair enough, I think there is a difficulty drawing hard and fast boundaries.

MB: Why the squeamishness about SM in particular? What's the difference between me confronting my fear of heights by taking a cable car up a mountain and waiting for my terror to turn into excitement, and an SMer using a word they were bullied with in a scene to take away its power, or using needle play to return to a powerless experience of being in hospital in a positive context.

DL: I guess my problem here is one of boundaries. Psychotherapy has clear boundaries. A *good* therapist is deliberately trying to help you and nothing else: their own needs are secondary. SM doesn't work like this. On some level it is about your own needs, accepting that aftercare is commonplace and many people engaged in these practices care deeply for each other.

MB: But I disagree. What's the difference between the businessman who finds it healing to go to a pro-domme once a week to let out their stresses and strains and the person who pays a therapist to listen to their problems once a week?

DL: Hmm, interesting point. I agree that there *is* no real difference in terms of outcomes although the process is clearly different. For me here (writing as an academic rather than as a psychotherapist) my concern is that what we *call* this process, how we name it, is potentially problematic. My main worry is the notion of 'healing' – as we see with the businessman visiting the pro-domme – and 'cure' – where someone engages in a scene to work through trauma – being conflated. As soon as you start naming something as healing there is an implication that a person can be cured by it. This should not necessarily be the case but – probably due to the dominance of the medical model – that is what tends to happen. Two implications follow: first, that SMers have a need for healing and second, that once 'cured' people will stop doing SM. It seems a pretty negative way of storying SM practices. And putting aside the question of whether such practices heal or not, what happens once you're healed?

SM and mental health have a particularly difficult and complex history and, as such, represent continuing concerns for those of us who seek to wrest the story of SM from the psychiatric profession (see Langdridge and Barker 2007, for more on this). In facilitating the telling of a story so clearly located in psychiatric and psychotherapeutic language there is a real danger of such research furthering the oppression of SMers rather than offering emancipatory potential. SM is still classified as a mental health problem in both the standard psychiatric nosologies (DSM-IV-TR and ICD-10) and through the UK Mental Health Act this means there is a real danger of forceful psychiatric intervention into people's private lives, without there actually being any issue of harm to self or other. Even within SM communities there is a common discourse suggesting care when playing with people with mental health problems. By encouraging a story of SM as healing we may also be serving to support the continuing notion of SM as pathological, rooted in trauma. The worry is that outsiders might draw on such stories to justify brutally policing these worlds, as we have seen with the impact of the criminalisation of HIV transmission on gay and bisexual men (Monk 2004).

Furthermore, as with any community, there is a very real power in the discourses that media representations do and do not make available to impact on the self-monitoring and self-policing of individual identities and practices. We have both noticed, in our research and therapeutic work with lesbian, gay and bisexual people, that there has been a shift in recent years from knowledge and identity possibilities coming through communities, to people drawing on media stories to make sense of their experiences. Such media-isation is part of the wider self-surveillance culture where media stories have become hugely influential in how people understand themselves and live their everyday lives (Gergen 2000). If the only stories available are those of trauma and pathology there is a real danger that SMers will monitor and police themselves in negative ways, potentially further fuelling these very limiting and pathologising discourses. Media stories have the power both to offer up new potentialities and to twist and pervert them.

Third moment of dialogue: shouldn't we be putting out multiple stories?

MB: One thing I do agree with you about is that the therapeutic narrative is just one story amongst many. I've talked to people who felt excluded by it because for them SM was about fun, or sex, or doing something transgressive. My question now is why not just ensure that we keep emphasising that there *are* multiple stories and putting them all out there. That's better than a lot of mainstream psychology and therapy which assumes that all SMers do it for the same purposes on all occasions.

DL: That's a fair point, and it seems like a good solution on the face of it although there is still the possibility of one story eclipsing all others. There's also an aspect of our personal experience and background in here as we discuss these issues. I think that the 'therapeutic' use of SM is really uncommon in a gay SM context and perhaps that is part of my difficulty with this story.

MB: Whereas it's something that I'm quite familiar with in the literatures and communities I'm involved with. Sounds like it's back to the debates we had about 'barebacking': the concern that it's such a minority activity so it's not great if people talk about it as if it isn't.

DL: That's right: 'healing' SM, like 'barebacking', is minority practice. We shouldn't ignore either of them, but equally we shouldn't encourage the dominance of those stories at the expense of other stories, especially when working within oppressed minority communities. I'm also concerned that once we present a range of stories, other consumers and producers of such stories – such as the media – may well hear and re-produce only one tale and that will be the most salacious one or one which fits with their existing stereotype of SMers as damaged people. On some media training that I've just been on there was a strong suggestion that, as qualitative psychologists, we should just pick one theme – if possible, the most 'exciting' one – when engaged with the media. That, for me, reflects the reality of the social world in which we live.

MB: Okay, so you're saying that if qualitative work which highlights multiple accounts is produced and communicated, there is a risk that one story will be taken up and re-produced disproportionately?

DL: Exactly. And there's another aspect to it as well: a kind of McDonaldisation of narrative. From the research on SM, we know that there is an alternative, related way of making sense of SM which talks of transcendence. That goes back to an older story which clearly involves healing through extraordinary peak experiences. But this more subtle and nuanced story has been eclipsed by the therapeutic narrative because there is a preference for stories that are simple, new and about personal conflict.

MB: I see, so perhaps a story of SM as a way to transcendent states or enlightenment, or a more humanistic one of personal growth rather than recovery from trauma, might be ways of coaching the story which doesn't reinforce dominant, pathologising discourses, and which also taps into existing understandings in the social world that sexual experiences can be transcendent or generally good for people.

DL: Yes. The therapy story comes out of medical discourse and is still in it. We'll have to wait a long time until it's not. Whereas other stories offer greater potential, for example, the transcendence story has always been outside Western medical discourse.

MB: It's like there's a kind of loop with people drawing on dominant discourses and putting stories back out there which reinforce them.

DL: Yes, and perhaps one of our roles as coachers is to offer perspectives that rupture that feedback loop.

MB: But whilst we might seek to advance more subtle and nuanced stories that still leaves us with the dilemma of what we do with stories inflected with the medical model. We have an ethical responsibility to be true to the stories as told and relatively limited opportunity to nuance these if aspects of potentially less risky stories are not present in the accounts we elicit.

The dangers of multiple narratives becomes particularly clear if we compare this story of SM with the story of 'barebacking': the deliberate act of engaging in unprotected anal intercourse most commonly associated with gay and bisexual men, which is currently in the ascendancy in the academy. In a controversial paper by Michele Crossley (2004) on 'barebacking' in the *British Journal of Social Psychology*, the casual and arguably careless presentation results in an easy conflation of a minority activity – 'barebacking' – with a very real and pressing concern about increasing unprotected anal intercourse amongst gay and bisexual men (Flowers and Langdridge 2007). Whilst the paper has been strongly criticised, it is highly cited and provides easy justification for reduction in proven health promotion strategies, as well as a return to the image of the gay or bisexual man as pathological. Furthermore, the story of 'barebacking' is growing – in spite of it being a minority practice – with other stories of gay and bisexual male sex becoming eclipsed in the process. Because we do care about the subjects of our research we do not want to engage in work which facilitates a minority story of 'healing SM' to be conflated with other stories of SM, such that SM becomes solely the story of healing trauma through sexual practice. There is a real danger of it becoming a dominant narrative due to the perception of 'strangeness' that SM evokes, as was once the case with lesbian, gay and bisexual people and practices. Perhaps until SMers have full citizenship (see Langdridge 2006) that is not just about rights and responsibilities but also wider public acknowledgment (Phelan 2001) then there will always be such a risk with stories which engage with the more complex and difficult aspects of SM identities and practices.

A convincing and appropriate social psychological explanation for the process in which such stories might be taken up and re-produced comes from *Social Representations Theory* (Moscovici 1981). In this theory social representations – such as the representation of SM – are thought to be taken-up by individuals as they 'anchor' these stories into existing representations. Here, a new experience is assigned to an element of an existing representation to enable it to seem more familiar and so be understood better. As researchers we feel we have a duty to think about the way stories from pathologised people and communities will be anchored into people's representations. Within such communities a story of healing may be a story that can be used constructively within existing representations of health and illness in a personally productive way. But the danger lies in the way in which outsiders may engage in such a process of anchoring such that this particular minority discourse becomes dominant and brings with it much more than was intended, in terms of the mental health and motivations of SMers.

Social representations of healing tend to be – in the West at least – medical and curative. Understandings of SM tend to see it as pathological and rooted in trauma: this can be seen in popular manuals for therapists such as Hudson-Allez (2005) who also writes for popular magazines on the topic (e.g. *Bizarre*, December 2007). Might it not be better – politically speaking – to encourage the telling of stories of growth and transcendence which might be anchored into representations other than the traditionally Western medical model? The stories in Barker et al.'s (2007) chapter, for instance, are mostly not really stories of healing in a medical sense but rather stories about the psychological and spiritual good that may occur through sex, and, in particular, SM. Similarly, Taylor and Ussher (2001) divide the small number of their participants who draw on pathologising narratives from the larger number who position SM within a mystical or spiritual framework, rather than proposing a wider 'therapeutic' narrative which might encompass both types of narrative.

Our own positions vis-à-vis this issue complicate our own hearing of such stories and we recognise that anchoring occurs for us as researchers just as it does for people in the social world who read our writing. This probably accounts for some of the difference in how we each hear and anchor such stories and the disagreement which fuelled this chapter.

In conclusion, we think it worth noting the difficulties that qualitative research with oppressed people and communities raises and how this presents real and pressing difficulties for the research process. We hope that this chapter has alerted other researchers to some of the difficulties that may arise when engaged in phenomenologically grounded research with oppressed people and communities. Indeed, we hope even more that our discussion of the issues may enable others to better think through this dilemma. Richard Feynman (1985), the renowned physicist involved in developing the atomic bomb (who deeply regretted his involvement in the project), argued that sometimes scientists should not ask certain questions or go certain places, for the eventual use of their endeavours may not be what they hoped. In many ways, the social sciences are learning this lesson, most particularly as a result of feminist criticism, with quantitative researchers less often asking inappropriate questions, for instance, about differences between men and women, and instead re-framing the object of their work to better enable the social sciences to produce knowledge that offers positive potential. But, perhaps ironically, things are more difficult for qualitative research since things emerge – without warning – and we may find ourselves confronted with stories later in the research process which present us with the very difficult dilemma of how we should treat this knowledge. We do not have the luxury of learning from Feynman in this particular case about whether we should have gone there since, as qualitative researchers, we have so often *already* gone there with the very best of intentions.

Notes

1 We have chosen in this chapter to reference critical writing on these articles and presentations rather than the original pieces in an attempt to silence this story. We do not want to contribute to the already worryingly high citation count for the work in question.

2 For a much more detailed explanation and discussion see Barker et al. (2007).

References

Banister, P., Burman, E., Parker, I., Taylor, M. and Tindall, C. (1995) *Qualitative Methods in Psychology: A Research Guide*, Buckingham: Open University Press.

Barker, M. (2003) 'Rewriting the sexual script? Constructions of sexuality in the bi, poly and S/M communities', *Presentation to the Fifteenth Annual International Congress on Personal Construct Psychology*, Huddersfield, July 2003.

Barker, M. and Langdridge, D. (2008). Bisexuality: working with a silenced sexuality, *Feminism & Psychology*, 18(3), 389–94.

Barker, M., Gupta, C. and Iantaffi, A. (2007) 'The power of play: the potentials and pitfalls in healing narratives of BDSM', in D. Langdridge and M. Barker (eds) *Safe, Sane and Consensual: Contemporary Perspectives on Sadomasochism*, Basingstoke, UK: Palgrave Macmillan: 197–216.

Barker, M., Bowes-Catton, H., Iantaffi, A., Cassidy, A. and Brewer, L. (2008) 'British bisexuality: a snapshot of bisexual identities in the UK', *Journal of Bisexuality*, 18 (3): 389–94.

Barker, M., Hagger-Johnson, G., Hegarty, P., Hutchinson, C. and Riggs, D. (2007) 'Responses from the lesbian and gay psychology section to Crossley's "Making sense of 'barebacking' ", *British Journal of Social Psychology*, 46: 667–77.

Beckmann, A. (2007) 'The "bodily practices" of consensual "SM", spirituality and "transcendence"', in D. Langdridge and M. Barker (eds) *Safe, Sane and Consensual: Contemporary Perspectives on Sadomasochism*, Basingstoke, UK: Palgrave Macmillan: 98–118.

Billig, M. (2005) *Laughter and Ridicule: Towards a Social Critique of Humour*, London: Sage.

Crossley, M.L. (2004) 'Making sense of "barebacking": gay men's narratives, unsafe sex and the "resistance habitus", *British Journal of Social Psychology*, 43: 225–44.

Dick, K. (1997) (Director) 'Sick: The Life and Death of Bob Flanagan, Supermasochist' [Film]. Distributed by Lions Gate Films.

Easton, D. and Hardy, J.W. (2004) *Radical Ecstasy: SM Journeys to Transcendence*, Eugene, OR: Greenery Press Ltd.

Feynman, R. (1985) *'Surely You're Joking Mr. Feynman!' Adventures of a Curious Character* New York: W.W. Norton.

Finlay, L. and Gough, B. (2003) *Reflexivity: A Practical Guide for Researchers in Health and Social Sciences*, Oxford: Blackwell.

Finn, M. (2005) 'The discursive domain of coupledom: a post-structuralist psychology of its productions and regulations', PhD thesis, University of Western Sydney.

Flowers, P. and Langdridge, D. (2007) 'Offending the other: deconstructing narratives of deviance and pathology, *British Journal of Social Psychology*, 46 (3): 679–90.

Gergen, K. (2000) *The Saturated Self*, New York: Basic Books.

Gill, R. (2007) 'Supersexualise me: advertising and the midriffs', in F. Attwood, R. Brunt and R. Cere (eds) *Mainstreaming Sex: The Sexualization of Culture*, London: I.B. Tauris.

Grenz, S. (2005) [2007] 2nd edition '(Un)heimliche Lust. Über den konsum sexueller dienstleistungen', Wiesbaden: VS Verlag für Sozialwissenschaften.

Heaphy, B., Donovan, C. and Weeks, J. (2004) 'A different affair? Openness and non-monogamy in same sex relationships', in J. Duncombe, K. Harrison, G. Allan and D. Marsden (eds) *The State of Affairs: Explorations in Infidelity and Commitment,* Mahwah, NJ: Lawrence Erlbaum Associates.

Hudson-Allez, G. (2005) *Sex and Sexuality: Questions and Answers for Counsellors and Therapists.* London: Whurr Publishers.

Jamieson, L. (2004) 'Intimacy, negotiated nonmonogamy, and the limits of the couple', in J. Duncombe, K. Harrison, G. Allan and D. Marsden (eds) *The State of Affairs: Explorations in Infidelity and Commitment*, Mahwah, NJ: Lawrence Erlbaum Associates: 35–57.

Kleinplatz, P. and Moser, C. (2007) 'Is SM pathological?' in D. Langdridge and M. Barker (eds) *Safe, Sane and Consensual: Contemporary Perspectives on Sadomasochism,* Basingstoke, UK: Palgrave Macmillan: 55–62.

Klesse, C. (2006) 'Polyamory and its "others": contesting the terms of non-monogamy', *Sexualities*, 9(5): 565–83.

Langdridge, D. (2006) 'Voices from the margins: SM and sexual citizenship', *Citizenship Studies*, 10 (4): 373–89.

Langdridge, D. and Barker, M. (eds) (2005) 'Contemporary perspectives on sadomasochism (S/M)', Special Issue of *Lesbian & Gay Psychology Review.* 6 (3).

—— (2007) *Safe, Sane and Consensual: Contemporary Perspectives on Sadomasochism*, Basingstoke, UK: Palgrave Macmillan.

Langdridge, D. and Butt, T.W. (2004) 'A hermeneutic phenomenological investigation of the construction of sadomasochistic identities, *Sexualities*, 7(1): 31–53.

Langdridge, D. and Flowers, P. (2005) 'Resistance habitus and the homophobic social psychologist, *Lesbian & Gay Psychology Review*, 6(1): 48–52.

Monk, D. (2004) *Criminalisation of HIV Transmission*, presentation to the Changing Tomorrow Conference, Leicester, 4–7 September 2004, Accessed from http://www.ukcoalition.org/amidoingsomething/criminalisation.htm on 2/2/08.

Moscovici, S. (1981) 'On social representation' in J.P. Forgas (ed.) *Social Cognition: Perspectives on Everyday Understanding*, London: Academic Press: 181–209.

Oakley, A. (1981) [1997] 'Inter viewing women: a contradiction in terms', in Helen Roberts (ed.) *Doing Feminist Research*, London: Routledge, 30–61.

Pallotta-Chiarolli, M. (1995) 'Choosing not to choose: beyond monogamy, beyond duality', in K. Lano and C. Parry (eds) *Breaking the Barriers of Desire*, London: Five Leaves Publication.

Phelan, S. (2001) *Sexual Strangers: Gays, Lesbians and Dilemmas of Citizenship*, Philadelphia, PA: Temple University Press.

Plummer, K. (1995) *Telling Sexual Stories: Power, Change and Social Worlds*, London: Routledge.

Ritchie, A. and Barker, M. (2005) 'Feminist SM: a contradiction in terms or a way of challenging traditional gendered dynamics through sexual practice?' *Lesbian & Gay Psychology Review*, 6(3): 227–39.

—— (2006) '"There aren't words for what we do or how we feel so we have to make them up": constructing polyamorous languages in a culture of compulsory monogamy', *Sexualities*, 9 (5): 584–601.

Robinson, V. (1997) 'My baby just cares for me: feminism, heterosexuality and non-monogamy, *Journal of Gender Studies*, 6 (2): 143–57.

Rubin, G. (1984) 'Thinking sex', in C.S. Vance (ed.) *Pleasure and Danger: Exploring Female Sexuality*, Boston: Routledge and Kegan Paul: 267–319.

Shainberg, S..(2002). (Director). *Secretary* [Film]. Los Angeles: Slough Pond.

Sisson, K. (2007) 'The cultural formation of s/m: history and analysis', in D. Langdridge and M. Barker (eds) *Safe, Sane and Consensual: Contemporary Perspectives on Sadomasochism*, Basingstoke, UK: Palgrave Macmillan: 10–34.

Storr, M. (2003) *Latex and Lingerie: Shopping for Pleasure at Ann Summers,* Oxford: Berg.

Taylor, G.W. and Ussher, J.M. (2001) 'Making sense of S&M: a discourse analytic account', *Sexualities,* 4(3): 293–314.

Weait, M. (2007) 'Sadomasochism and the law', in D. Langdridge and M. Barker (eds) *Safe, Sane and Consensual: Contemporary Perspectives on Sadomasochism,* Basingstoke, UK: Palgrave Macmillan: 63–82.

Weiss, M. (2006) 'Mainstreaming kink: the politics of BDSM representations in U.S. popular media', in P. Kleinplatz and C. Moser (eds) *SM: Powerful Pleasures,* Binghamton, NY: Haworth Press: 103–32.

Part II

The unspoken in the research process

6 Silencing differences

The 'unspoken' dimensions of 'speaking for others'

Christina Scharff

Introduction

'The investments, dilemmas, and implications of researchers' ethical decisions and moral choices are usually secreted away, buried, concealed, and hidden from public scrutiny […]' (Halse and Honey 2005: 2142). Seeking to explore difficulties and insecurities openly, this chapter focuses on the methodological issues and ethical dilemmas arising from qualitative research by adopting an explicitly feminist methodological framework. Feminist researchers have drawn attention to ethical dilemmas involved in doing qualitative research. Making a range of contributions, feminist critics have focused on the power-dynamics in the research process and the dilemma of representation, especially where feminists are researching across difference. In this chapter, I would like to shed light on a further ethical issue, namely the 'unspoken' dimensions and 'silences' that can occur in the qualitative research process.

My interest in silences has emerged from the qualitative interviews I conducted for an empirical study of feminist consciousness amongst a diverse group of young British and German women. Researching feminist (dis-)identification, I interviewed 40 women aged between 18 and 35 in Berlin, London and Birmingham in 2006/2007. Half of the interviews were conducted in Berlin and I sought to obtain a diverse group of research participants in both countries. The identity characteristics of the women I interviewed varied across multiple axes of differentiation – such as sexual orientation, ethnic and socio-economic background. This chapter draws on my experience of conducting research with a particular group of young women: six young white Germans who were comparatively uneducated, mostly unemployed welfare recipients. Written from my perspective as a white, educated, middle-class feminist researcher, I will demonstrate various instances of silences in the interviews with the aim of drawing attention to emerging ethical and methodological issues.

In order to contextualise my argument about the unspoken dimensions of research within feminist methodological debates more broadly, the first section of this chapter will review feminist debates on research ethics. Specifically focusing on the researcher-researched dynamics and the dilemmas of representation, I will illustrate that the multifaceted nature of social research implies that there are no generally applicable solutions to ethical concerns raised in research. Rather than attempting to 'solve' the problems involved in speaking to, for and about others, we should seek to critically reflect upon them.

In this vein, the second section of this chapter points to a way of improving ethical practice by also investigating the unspoken dimensions of research. We should not only critically examine the problematic issues arising from the spoken aspects of research, but should also analyse the silences in the research process. Silencing practices (in terms of silencing oneself and/or others) constitute one means through which differences are negotiated which raises specific ethical dilemmas that have to be explored. Consequently, the third and final section will argue that the analysis of silences can improve our understanding of interpersonal dynamics in the research process and thereby enhance reflexive practice. Drawing on the feminist notion of 'reflexivity', I will end the chapter by advocating reflexive analysis. Although I am aware of the shortcomings of 'reflexivity', I will emphasise its analytical potential, especially if it involves the investigation of 'silences' within research.

Ethical dilemmas in qualitative research

When adopting a feminist methodological framework, it is crucial to bear in mind that feminist research is a 'perspective' (Reinharz and Davidman 1992: 241) rather than a clearly defined set of methods. However, feminist theorists identify recurrent themes in the literature on feminist methodology (Ramazanoglu and Holland 2002; Letherby 2003). Maynard (1994: 21), for example, argues that feminist methodologies focus on women's experiences and are concerned with ethical questions that guide research practices. In particular, feminist researchers have drawn attention to ethical issues arising from face-to-face interviews. Feminist researchers have theorised the research process extensively, emphasising that it does not represent an equal encounter, but is characterised by power-imbalances (Opie 1992; Phoenix 1994; Luff 1999; Grenz 2005).

Describing power-relations during the research process, Letherby (2003: 78) emphasises the authority of the researcher in selecting and rejecting data at the different stages of the research. In the pre-fieldwork stage, for example, the researcher determines the questions and further selects data during analysis and writing-up. Moreover, after leaving the field, the researcher has ultimate control over the material. Highlighting the powerful position of the researcher in the research relationship does not, however, imply that the researched is always in a powerless position. Research participants have the power to deny or gratify access (Phoenix 1994). In addition, research participants can exercise power *during* the research process: they can refuse to answer, decide what to talk about and not tell the truth (Letherby 2003: 116). Furthermore, the circumstances that the interview takes place in can give power to the participant (Phoenix 1994: 59) and Opie (1992) argues that interviewees potentially experience the research as empowering.

Reflecting upon the powers of the researcher and the researched respectively demonstrates that power-relationships in the research process are not fixed, but changing: 'it becomes evident that there is not an either/or power relation between the researcher and the researched' (Grenz 2005: 2111). Differences between the locations of the researcher and the researched, such as 'race', gender and socio-economic background enter the interview but they do not do so in a predictable way (see Phoenix 1994: 49). As Brah (1996: 125) points out, it is a contextually contingent question whether difference pans out as inequity, exploitation and oppression or as egalitarianism, diversity and democratic forms of political agency.

How are researchers to ensure that research is conducted ethically if the power-relationships between the researcher and the researched are complex and changing? Acknowledging the shifting dynamics of power within the research process seems to imply that there can be no universally valid approach to solving the ethical dilemmas in research. The need to reflect on ethical dilemmas becomes even more obvious when recalling the dilemma of representation. According to Alldred (1998: 150–51), research is frequently regarded as providing a space in which hitherto silenced people can 'be heard' in the public sphere through the dissemination of findings. However, as the feminist debate in recent years has demonstrated, there are dangers involved in speaking for others, particularly if these are members of a group that we do not belong to and that is oppressed in ways we are not (Wilkinson and Kitzinger 1996: 1).

As early as 1979, Lorde called for feminists to examine women's differences (2001: 106). Feminist theory and research should seek to include the diversity of women's experiences; 'yet the dangers of speaking across difference of race, culture, sexuality, and power are becoming increasingly clear' (Alcoff 1995: 98). The location of the researcher is epistemologically salient and more privileged positions can be discursively dangerous by, for example, reinforcing the oppression of the group spoken for (Alcoff 1995: 99). Acknowledging differences and seeking to avoid exploitation in the process of knowledge production seems to suggest that we should limit research to relationships between those who share as much as possible. However, as Ramazanoglu and Holland (2002: 115) emphasise, the complex nature of identities and the ways in which they intersect with social divisions make such an aim difficult to achieve. The recognition of multiple intersecting axes of differentiation implies that various 'solutions' to the dilemma of representation, such as silence, retreat or engagement, all pose ethical questions (Fine 1994: 81). Even if we were able to clearly demarcate what constitutes the 'other', the 'declaration that I "speak only for myself" has the sole effect of allowing me to avoid responsibility and accountability for my effects on others; it cannot literally erase those effects' (Alcoff 1995: 108). Conducting research on feminist consciousness, it was my aim to obtain a diverse sample in order to explore how and whether feminist (dis-)identification is mediated by young women's locations. However, I was acutely aware of the dangers of speaking across difference. Alcoff's argument on the problematic effects of speaking solely for oneself nevertheless encouraged me to include the voices of a diverse group of women in my study.

In order to offer ways of dealing with the dilemmas of representation,[1] Alcoff (1995: 111) develops several interrogatory practices that researchers should get involved in when speaking across difference. For example, she states that the '*impetus to speak* must be carefully analysed and, in some cases (certainly for academics) fought against' (ibid.). It is this interrogatory practice that I would like to focus on the next section of this chapter. In my opinion, the impetus *not* to speak should be critically investigated as well. Developing Alcoff's reflections further, I think it is crucial to also inquire into the motivations for remaining silent. When and why do silences occur and what do they potentially tell us about the research process? The theoretical explorations of the dilemma of representation seem to centre around the spoken dimensions of 'speaking for' and silences are predominantly theorised as 'lack' of representation and therefore not always focus of the debate. Silences are mentioned in relation to the continuing silencing of the voices of the subaltern (Spivak 1988), signalling oppression (Lugones and Spelman 1983: 573), and are said to be a consequence of the refusal to speak for others (Wilkinson and Kitzinger 1996: 12). However, my research made me aware that silences can constitute a crucial feature of research across difference and should be explored to potentially enhance ethical and reflexive practice.

Silences in the qualitative research process

According to Letherby (2003: 109), '[s]ilences are as important as noise in research and the interpretation of silence is as important as the interpretation of what is being said'. When reflecting upon the dilemmas of representing difference, I became aware that my experience of researching others involved numerous unspoken dimensions. I would like to illustrate this in relation to my research with the six socio-economically disadvantaged women I met in Berlin. The interviews with this group were characterised by a number of silences which centred around our different socio-economic backgrounds.[2] These differences in terms of socio-economic status seemed to be salient in the interviews and yet remained 'unvoiceable'. Consequently, I started to wonder whether silencing practices were one means of negotiating our differing locations and whether my research shows that there can be a lot of 'non-speaking' in the process of 'speaking for and to others'. I think that this is not only an interesting paradox but also points to the need to interrogate the ethical dimensions of the silences that occurred.

For instance, I asked myself whether it was ethical not to voice the fact that these six women were being interviewed because of their lower socio-economic status. As I mentioned before, I made a conscious effort to obtain a diverse sample in my research and generally recruited participants through snowballing. In this case, however, I had contacted an acquaintance of mine who is a street worker in Berlin. She helped me to make contact with young women from disadvantaged socio-economic backgrounds and thereby enabled me to obtain access to a group of women I would not have been able to approach otherwise. Importantly, neither I nor the street worker had told these research participants explicitly why they, and not others, had been selected. I went with my intuition and felt that it would have been inappropriate to disclose that I wanted to interview these women because of their less privileged socio-economic backgrounds. However, this raises the question of whether they gave me fully informed consent.[3] I told them about my study, the kinds of questions I would pose, that everything would be treated confidentially and then asked them for their oral or written consent. However, would these women have consented had they known that I wanted to interview them primarily because of their socio-economic positioning? But how could I have communicated my desire to interview them in a way that was not offensive, did not reinforce my more privileged socio-economic status and essentialised the differences between us?

The second instance of practising silence in the research process emerged from the fact that none of these women knew what the term 'feminism'[4] potentially means. In order to illustrate this, I would like to draw on an interview with a 26-year-old single mother of three:

Have you ever heard of the term feminism? This is also one of those questions that I ask everybody – anything that you can think of … or what it could mean?

No, that doesn't mean anything to me.

Or somebody being feminist, or something like that –?

No, nothing at all, no, because, at the moment, I hardly have any time to deal with something like that.

Okay, it's also – it was a bit similar to the women's movement, you know, women, who advocated women's rights and so on, one often calls them feminists –

Uh, okay, but no, the word, I didn't know it, no.

This interview extract supports the findings of Aronson's study on feminist consciousness which shows that the space to think about feminist issues might be a luxury that not all women can afford (2003: 917). The fact that none of the six socio-economically disadvantaged women knew the potential meaning of feminism illustrates that it is important to take diversity into account when researching feminist consciousness. However, what I would like to focus on in this chapter is the fact that I mainly remained quiet about feminism in all the six interviews. I tended to briefly explain what prevalent understandings of 'feminism' are and alluded to the history of the women's movement. On the whole, I felt very uncomfortable 'lecturing' research participants, specifically if I had the impression that the interviewee was not showing much interest in the subject. Hence, I avoided talking about feminism at length. I also did not correct two research participants who confused the meaning of 'feminism' with 'femininity'. But do the silences around the meaning of feminism indicate that I did not take the women seriously by not having a proper dialogue with them?

A third example that equally illustrates silences within the research process focuses on one participant who made a very xenophobic statement during the interview. The interviewee was a 19-year-old white German who had just started vocational training as a cook. Since she had had difficulties finding a job, I had asked her about her views on unemployment:

And, if you like think about unemployment, or so, how do you feel about it, or what is your opinion about it?

Well, I think that they should create more jobs (*Yeah*) – yeah, that's my opinion about it. And all the foreigners should leave Germany and – go where they belong and they should also stay there, I mean –

[Pause] Uhm, have you ever heard of Alice Schwarzer? Does anything come to mind when you hear her name?

No. …

As the pause in the transcript indicates, I was shocked to hear such an outright xenophobic remark. I felt very uncomfortable and was not sure how to react. In the end, I did not challenge her xenophobia which left me feeling guilty and ashamed. I immediately shifted the focus of the conversation by asking about the well-known German feminist activist Alice Schwarzer. I felt that I could not criticise the political views of the research participant because it could have negatively impacted on our rapport. More importantly, I did not want to present myself as someone who knows better, occupying moral high-ground. I continue to feel guilty about not challenging her xenophobia and explaining to her that the presence of 'foreigners' does not account for the high unemployment rate in Germany. I now ask myself whether I should have argued against her xenophobic remark in order to speak for groups that are in an arguably less powerful position than this white German woman. This raises the question of where to draw the line between respecting 'others', i.e. this woman's views on the one hand, and 'speaking for other others', i.e. 'foreigners' on the other hand, who are oppressed in ways that the researcher and the researched are not.

According to Luff (1999: 698), '[l]istening to, nodding or saying simple 'uhms', or 'I see', to views that you strongly disagree with, or ordinarily, would strive to challenge, may be true to a methodology that aims to listen seriously to the views and experiences of others but can feel personally very difficult […]'. Letherby (2003: 112) points to a similar dilemma, but argues that listening to views that we, as researchers, disagree with, might help us to better understand and more effectively confront them in the future. Similarly, Islam (2000: 51) defends his strategy of not challenging anti-black comments during his field research because he feared it would create a distance between himself and the research participants. Overtly critiquing racists remarks could have generated hostility and easily led to his being expelled from his research community (ibid.).

Even though there may be good reasons for not criticising interviewees' prejudices directly (indeed, research participants do not consent to having their political views challenged upon signing the consent form), the question remains of whether it is ethical to write about such instances. Focusing less on the conduct of research, I would like to draw attention to the presentation of the findings. Because: what are the effects of representing racist accounts made by members of a comparatively powerless group in relation to education and socio-economic privilege? Does it contribute to fostering a negative or bad image of disadvantaged communities (Bourgois 2000: 207)? Sharing my dilemma of not having challenged a xenophobic remark with friends and colleagues, I had the impression that most were not surprised that less educated women would exhibit racist tendencies. However, only *one* research participant reproduced xenophobic ideology and I felt uneasy about validating common prejudices which hold that socially disadvantaged communities are racist (see Armstead 1995: 635). I sensed that there was an expectation in middle-class and/or educated circles that women from less privileged backgrounds would be xenophobic. Reporting the incident therefore raised issues about reproducing stereotypes of lower-class participants in the presentation of data.

According to Becker, there is no right solution to dealing with prejudices in the research situation (2000: 248). The dilemmas around the xenophobic remark shed light on the ethical dimensions of silences in research and demonstrate that these should be explored. The three silencing practices that I referred to above raise ethical questions about 'full consent', 'having a proper dialogue', or 'taking seriously the voices of others'. Moreover, they are all instances in which I, as the researcher, was silenced[5] by choosing not to voice specific issues. Consequently, I would like to ask what these silences can tell us about the nature of the dialogue that is taking place in the interview, the research relationship and the positioning of the individuals that are involved?

Attending to the silences in research might offer us an enhanced understanding of the interview situation and can potentially make us more aware of the power-relations in the research process. What do repeated silences on my part expose, for example in relation to the second instance of the silence around the meaning of 'feminism'? My decision not to 'lecture' the interviewees on the potential meaning of feminism mainly arose from the consideration that I did not want to perpetuate the inequalities between the researched and I, specifically with regard to the vast differences in our educational backgrounds. Seeking to ensure rapport, this silencing practice also constituted a strategic means to maintain a good relationship with the participants. In this sense, my silence around feminism was productive in that it potentially contributed to the maintenance of rapport, highlighting that silencing practices are not intrinsically constraining or negative. However, I also held back from telling these interviewees about the women's movement because I mostly sensed that there was no interest. Body language, such as looking away when being asked questions around feminism, as well as expressions of boredom by giving very brief answers indicated to me that this topic was not appealing. In this particular instance, the participants silenced me by not responding to my attempts to engage them in a conversation about feminist consciousness. There was some resistance to discussing issues around gender which is perhaps indicative of the broader phenomenon of young women's repudiation of 'feminism' (McRobbie 2004). Similar to the instance of the racist remark that remained unchallenged, the research participants had the power to set the agenda several times and to avoid the discussion of certain topics. I am not sure whether these aspects about the strategic maintenance of rapport and the occasional power of the researched would have come to light if I had not reflected upon these silences.

Silences and reflexivity

Feminists have invited researchers to explore the space between the researcher and the researched. According to Finlay (2002: 533), '[h]aving come to understand that the researcher, the world, and the researcher's experience of the world are intertwined, the challenge is to identify that lived experience that resides in the space between subject and object'. Similarly, Probyn (1993) calls for researchers to investigate the space between my self and another self. In my opinion, silences can be regarded as residing between the researcher and the researched. The critical investigation of silencing practices potentially helps us to occupy this space and become more aware of commonalities, differences and potentially shifting power-relationships.

Paying attention to silences can also increase our understanding of the extent to which 'difference' impacted on the research process. What does it mean when certain issues remain unvoiced such as the selection criteria for participants? Or that none of the socio-economically disadvantaged women in my study mentioned the differences that existed between us? I believe that our different socio-economic backgrounds were dramatically obvious because the research participants, for example, knew that I was living abroad to pursue a degree at university. Consequently, I would argue that the silences around our different life experiences and opportunities potentially expose the impact of our differences on the research. This is not to claim that there are no other reasons which explain why we refrained from openly talking about our different locations: 'differences' are not usually openly addressed, specifically in a neo-liberal climate which claims that inequalities have ceased to persist (see Walkerdine 2003; Gonick 2004). Thinking about the interviews with this group of young women, however, I was struck by the number of silencing practices I could detect. In these interviews, differences between the researcher and the researched surfaced and the simultaneous occurrence of silences raises the question of their function in relation to 'difference'. In this instance, the silences seemed to have constituted a central means to negotiate the different locations of the researcher and the researched; silencing practices facilitated negotiation. Consequently, the analysis of the silences in the interview potentially highlights the pertinent role of difference in the research process, shedding light on issues that might have otherwise remained unexplored.

Both Finlay's (2002) and Probyn's (1993) claims on exploring the space between the self and the other have emerged from their discussions of 'reflexivity', raising the question of whether attending to silences in research can improve reflexive practices. Fonow and Cook (2005: 2219) claim that reflexivity has come to mean 'the way researchers consciously write themselves into the text, the audiences' reactions to and reflections on the meaning of the research, the social location of the researcher, and the analysis of disciplines as sites of knowledge production'. Critical reflection takes place at different stages in the research and also entails being accountable for the knowledge that is produced (Ramazanoglu and Holland 2002: 119). This involves reflecting upon how knowledge is authorised, the community that the researcher produces knowledge within, and why certain stories are told rather than others (ibid.). Reflexivity attends to the 'hidden' or unexamined stages of the research process (Fonow and Cook 1991: 5) which is why an exploration of the silences within research lends itself to reflexive practice. According to Finlay (2002: 532), reflexivity involves an examination of 'subjective responses, intersubjective dynamics, and the research process itself'. I would argue that we should also regard the attention to silences as a crucial part of reflexive analysis. Being clear about the nature of the research process (Maynard 1994: 25) should involve a critical investigation of the unspoken dimensions of the research and a reflection on the possible functions that these silences fulfil as well as the ethical issues arising from them.

Advocating reflexive analysis involving the investigation of silences within research, I am however aware of the problems associated with 'reflexivity'. Critical reflection is limited because a high degree of self knowledge cannot be easily obtained. We cannot free ourselves from the social constraints on our knowing and a high level of self-awareness might only be possible through intense psychoanalysis (Finlay 2002: 542). Moreover, the focus on self-reflexivity risks muting the voices of the participants (Ribbens and Edwards 1998: 204). According to Kobayashi, reflexivity gives rise to a dilemma:

> While reflexivity is an important, and some may say essential, aspect of recognising the difference between the studier and the studied and even in some cases of taking moral responsibility for that difference, indulgence in reflexivity is ironically the very act that sets us apart.
>
> (Kobayashi 2003: 348)

Although I broadly agree with Kobayashi's claim, I would argue that reflexive analysis does not always have to be 'indulgence' and that the alienating potential of reflexivity might depend on the degree to which it is practised.

Drawing attention to another way in which reflexivity may contribute to reinforcing differences, Skeggs (2004: 129) points out that the ability to be reflexive is a privilege, representing a position of mobility and power. Reflexivity is made possible through access to resources, and the technique of telling for the middle class depends on accruing the stories of others, of those less privileged. 'Yet, if research is judged to be legitimate on the basis of self-telling, we can see how research methods themselves constitute class difference' (ibid.: 134). By advocating reflexivity, researchers engage in a classed practice and potentially reinforce unequal power relationships. However, Skeggs (ibid.) does not offer a deterministic account, but claims that some reflexive practices could maintain inequalities while others might be more subversive.

As Finlay (2002: 542) argues, reflexivity can be viewed as only one way of analysing the complexities of intersubjective dynamics, and is certainly not the only way. However, reflexive analysis can provide a good first step to obtaining more insight into how the location of the researcher and the researched impact on the research relationship and facilitate specific personal dynamics (ibid.: 542). Moreover, reflexivity enables public scrutiny because it provides detailed information about the research decisions and the various dynamics that took place during the research process (ibid.). If we include the analysis of silences in the process of reflexivity, reflexive thinking does not only offer insight into the spoken dimensions of research and the dilemmas arising from them. Attending to the silences in research also sheds light on the unspoken aspects, providing an enhanced understanding of the complex interpersonal dynamics and the opportunity to deepen our understanding of the multiple ways in which 'difference' is played out in the research situation.

Conclusion

In this chapter, I sought to explore a specific aspect of the qualitative research process: namely its unspoken dimensions and silences. Contextualising my reflections within broader feminist methodological debates, I started by demonstrating that the face-to-face contact in the interview raises specific ethical issues that are complicated by the dilemmas of representation. Qualitative research can exhibit unequal power-relations and issues around 'speaking for others' and the complexity of social life mean that there are no generic solutions to dealing with the multifaceted nature of power-relationships in the research process. Drawing on my experience of conducting research with a group of comparatively uneducated women from a disadvantaged socio-economic background, I attempted to show that silencing practices were a crucial means for negotiating uncomfortable power relationships in the research process. Raising ethical questions about the specific silences that occurred in my research, I have highlighted the need to attend to the unspoken dimensions of research. The investigation of silencing practices in research potentially offers a more refined understanding of the research-relationship and the way 'difference' is negotiated in the process. Claiming that the analysis of silences in research should constitute an important aspect of reflexivity, I am hoping that an increased awareness of the interpersonal dynamics within the research process enhances ethical practice. Even though I believe that there is no standard solution to the dilemmas in research, my claim is that reflexive analysis can raise our awareness of the complexities in research. Reflexivity should be a central component of qualitative research and, crucially, also involve the exploration of the 'unspoken' dimensions of 'speaking for others'.

Notes

1 See also: Fine 1996; Wilkinson and Kitzinger 1996 (esp. chapters by Bell and Burman).
2 I deliberately refrain from using the term 'class' in relation to the German context. According to Knapp (2005: 257), alternative terms, such as 'Schicht' (strata) tend to be used in German scholarship. The use of the term *Klasse* is associated with Marxism as the only field where this term, as opposed to the more commonly used *Schicht* (strata), is employed (Knapp 2005: 257).
3 Concerning the concept of consent, one has to bear in mind that the line between informed and uninformed consent is blurry (Thorne 1980; for a further problematisation of the concept see Halse and Honey 2005).
4 Referring to the terms 'feminism' and 'women's movement', I am aware that feminism represents many different theories and that there is no one women's movement with a unified set of goals (Whelehan 1995: 1). For these reasons, this essay refers to 'feminism' and the 'women's movement' as *discursive* categories to signify the multiple, individual as well as cultural, understandings of the concepts.
5 I would like to thank Ros Gill for pointing this out to me.

References

Alcoff, L. (1995) 'The problem of speaking for others', in J. Roof and R. Wiegman (eds), *Who can Speak? Authority and Critical Identity*, Urbana: University of Illinois Press.

Alldred, P. (1998) 'Ethnography and discourse analysis: dilemmas in representing the voices of children', in R. Edwards and J. Ribbens (eds), *Feminist Dilemmas in Qualitative Research: Public Knowledge and Private Lives*, London: Sage.

Armstead, C. (1995) 'Writing contradictions: feminist research and feminist writing', *Women's Studies International Forum*, 18 (5/6): 627–36.

Aronson, P. (2003) 'Feminists or "postfeminists"? Young women's attitudes toward feminism and gender relations', *Gender and Society*, 16 (6): 903–22.

Becker, H.S. (2000) 'Afterword: racism and the research process', in F.W. Twine and J.W. Warren (eds), *Racing Research, Researching Race': Methodological Dilemmas in Critical Race Studies*, New York: New York University Press.

Bourgois, P. (2000) 'Violating apartheid in the United States: on the streets and in academia', in F.W. Twine and J.W. Warren (eds), *Racing Research, Researching Race: Methodological Dilemmas in Critical Race Studies*, New York: New York University Press.

Brah, A. (1996) *Cartographies of Diaspora: Contesting Identities*, London: Routledge.

Fine, M. (1994) 'Working the hyphens: reinventing self and other in qualitative research', in N.K. Denzin and Y.S. Lincoln (eds), *Handbook of Qualitative Research*, London: Sage.

Finlay, L. (2002) '"Outing the researcher": the provenance, process and practice of reflexivity', *Qualitative Health Research*, 12 (4): 531–45.

Fonow, M.M. and Cook, J.A. (1991) 'Back to the future: a look at the second wave of feminist epistemology', in M.M. Fonow and J.A. Cook, *Beyond Methodology: Feminist Scholarship as Lived Research*, Bloomington: Indiana University Press.

—— (2005) 'Feminist methodology: new applications in the academy and public policy', *Signs: Journal of Women in Culture and Society*, 30 (4): 2211–36.

Gonick, M. (2004) 'Old plots and new identities: ambivalent femininities in late modernity', *Discourse: Studies in the Cultural Politics of Education*, 25 (2): 189–209.

Grenz, S. (2005) 'Intersections of sex and power in research on prostitutes: a female researcher interviewing male heterosexual clients', *Signs: Journal of Women in Culture and Society*, 30 (4): 2091–2113.

Halse, C. and Honey, A. (2005) 'Unravelling ethics: illuminating the moral dilemmas of research ethics', *Signs: Journal of Women in Culture and Society*, 30 (4): 2141–62.

Islam, N. (2000) 'Research as an act of betrayal: researching race in an Asian community in Los Angeles', in F.W. Twine and J.W. Warren (eds), *Racing Research, Researching Race: Methodological Dilemmas in Critical Race Studies*, New York: New York University Press.

Knapp, G.A. (2005) 'Race, class, gender: reclaiming baggage in fast travelling theories', *European Journal of Women's Studies*, 12 (3): 249–65.

Kobayashi, A. (2003) 'GPC ten years on: is self-reflexivity enough?', *Gender, Place and Culture*, 10 (4): 345–49.

Letherby, G. (2003) *Feminist Research in Theory and Practice*, Buckingham: Open University Press.

Lorde, A. (2001) 'The master's tools will never dismantle the master's house', in C. Moraga and G. Anzaldua (eds), *This Bridge Called My Back: Writings by Radical Women of Colour*, Berkeley, CA: Third Women Press.

Luff, D. (1999) 'Dialogue across the divides: "moments of rapport" and power in feminist research with anti-feminist women', *Sociology*, 33 (4): 687–703.

Lugones, M.C. and Spelman, E.V. (1983) 'Have we got a theory for you! feminist theory, cultural imperialism and the demand for "the woman's voice"', *Women's Studies International Forum*, 6 (6): 573–81.

Maynard, M. (1994) 'Methods, practice and epistemology: the debate about feminism and research', in M. Maynard and J. Purvis (eds) *Researching Women's Lives from a Feminist Perspective*, London: Taylor & Francis.

McRobbie, A. (2004) 'Post-feminism and popular culture', *Feminist Media Studies*, 4 (3): 255–64.

Opie, A. (1992) 'Qualitative research: appropriation of the "other" and empowerment', *Feminist Review*, 40: 52–69.

Phoenix, A. (1994) 'Practicing feminist research: the intersection of gender and "race" in the research process', in M. Maynard and J. Purvis (eds) *Researching Women's Lives from a Feminist Perspective*, London: Taylor & Francis.

Probyn, E. (1993) *Sexing the Self: Gendered Positions in Cultural Studies*, London: Routledge.

Ramazanoglu, C. and Holland, J. (2002) *Feminist Methodology: Challenges and Choices*, London: Sage.

Reinharz, S. and Davidman, L. (1992) *Feminist Methods in Social Research*, New York: Oxford University Press.

Ribbens, J. and Edwards, R. (1998) 'Epilogue', in *Feminist Dilemmas in Qualitative Research: Public Knowledge and Private Lives*, London: Sage.

Skeggs, B. (2004) *Class, Self, Culture*, London: Routledge.

Spivak, G.C. (1988) 'Can the subaltern speak?' in C. Nelson and L. Grossberg (eds), *Marxism and the Interpretation of Culture*, Urbana: University of Illinois Press.

Thorne, B. (1980) '"You still takin' notes?": fieldwork and problems of informed consent', *Social Problems*, 27 (3): 284–97.

Walkerdine, V. (2003) 'Reclassifying upward mobility: femininity and the neoliberal subject', *Gender and Education*, 15 (3): 237–48.

Whelehan, I. (1995) *Modern Feminist Thought: from the Second Wave to 'Post-feminism'*, Edinburgh: Edinburgh University Press.

Wilkinson, S. and Kitzinger, C. (1996) 'Theorising representing the other', in S. Wilkinson and C. Kitzinger, *Representing the Other: A Feminism & Psychology Reader*, London; Thousand Oaks, CA: Sage Publications.

7 Not telling it how it is

Secrets and silences of a critical feminist researcher

Bipasha Ahmed

What has always made working as a critical feminist psychologist appealing to me has been its overt political standpoint and the focus on challenging oppression, particularly within the discipline of psychology and in the way psychology is researched, theorised, applied and practised. Critical psychologists broadly speaking seek to challenge oppressive power relations that tend to be perpetuated and sustained within and by Psychology, both as a discipline and as an institution (Fox and Prilleltensky 1997). However, equally important to me is the question as to how such ideas may be taken up and have influence outside academia. For example, critical and feminist psychologists have worked hard to discuss and challenge oppressive practices against particular groups; those who may be affected by psychology but on the whole exist outside the institution. There is often debate about how influential our work as critical psychologists can be on 'real people'. However, this particular debate comes into sharp focus when interacting with 'real people' as part of fieldwork outside academic contexts where it becomes very apparent how difficult it can be to convey the aims of the various forms of critical psychology to the very people whom we are hoping will benefit from our research.

This chapter will discuss some of the tensions and contradictions I have encountered whilst trying to conduct research from a feminist critical psychological approach. I will focus on the collaborative research[1] I have been conducting on South Asian women's experiences of sexual violence and of the services they may or may not access to deal with such experiences. My interest in this research has stemmed from my own personal interests, as a South Asian woman, on South Asian women's issues. Having been involved in South Asian women's activism in a variety of forms, I became involved with particular groups that worked with women who had experienced various forms of violence and abuse. It felt appropriate therefore, that as a critical feminist psychologist, I could and should consider these issues within my work as a researcher. The research I am focusing on for this chapter was conducted with agencies and organisations within both the statutory and voluntary sectors that have experienced working with South Asian women survivors of violence. All participants were accessed via these organisations (rather than say, as individuals via personal contacts). I will discuss the dilemmas and issues I have encountered which led me to be either secretive or silent with regard to my identity as a critical feminist psychologist. I do this by focusing on what I consider are important critical psychological principles which, I argue, nevertheless become difficult to uphold at certain points in the research process. I often found that describing myself as a critical feminist psychologist researcher became inadvertently paradoxical. Sometimes it felt difficult to do 'good ethical research' whilst still adhering to the values of being a good critical psychologist during the process of conducting research. Part of the problem when trying to apply these principles or 'tenets' in non-academic contexts is that they have primarily emerged within academic contexts rather than developing from real research practice. Difficulties emerge in trying to apply these tenets when interacting with people who are not only unfamiliar with them, but are also unfamiliar with the academic cultural contexts where such ideas are discussed and debated.

Important tenets of critical psychology: challenging power and assumptions

As I have alluded to already, I believe there are two particular 'tenets' of critical psychology that are crucial in conducting research and developing theory (e.g. see Parker 1992; Parker and Spears 1996; Fox and Prilleltensky 1997). I have tried wherever possible, to be guided by these principles at all stages of my research. I understand these tenets as:

1 Challenging oppressive power relations (including during research between the researchers and participants)
2 Challenging taken for granted assumptions which may have particular negative consequences (for example, stereotypical assumptions which may be made about South Asian women and South Asian communities in the case of my research).

However, I have found my ability to uphold these particular commitments has been compromised. I feel that at times I have been silent, or silenced about what I do and what my beliefs are as a researcher, critical psychologist and feminist, but also as a South Asian woman concerned for other South Asian women. Decisions to 'hold back' for a number of reasons (which I discuss below) could be deemed as unethical in research terms in that the approach taken is not fully conveyed to those taking part. In other words, there is a lack of transparency about the approach being taken, which could be considered as a form of 'deception'. Additionally, the silences and secrecy which are considered necessary at times, partly for pragmatic reasons (e.g. the need to be able to continue with the research), lead to the important tenets of critical psychology not being upheld, which again questions the ethical bases of doing critical psychological work.

I will discuss my experience of these problems by outlining a variety of non-academic contexts where I have encountered people as part of the research process. These are particularly those moments at the first stages of research, such as attending non-academic conferences, making initial contact with a variety of organisations to ask them to participate and the negotiations with such organisations that occur when trying to 'access' participants. Very little attention has been given to these stages of the research process. Although the importance of being reflexive about the research process when analysing and writing up, or even at the stage of 'collecting data', has been discussed (Altheide and Johnson 1998; Finlay and Gough 2003), I feel that these earlier stages are just as important and pose considerable challenges when trying to maintain an identity as a critical psychologist conducting research in the best way possible.

'You're a psychologist? Why?': reactions when attending practitioner conferences

When I first became involved in studying South Asian women's experiences of sexual violence, I attended a number of practitioner conferences to get a sense of how practitioners worked directly with such women, what their practices were and the kinds of policies that were being developed. However, this was one of the earliest contexts within which I found that there was a challenge to my identity as an academic researcher, as a psychologist but also as a critical feminist psychologist. The reactions I experienced from delegates at practitioner conferences are very different from those at academic conferences. Academics in general tend to be frowned upon, and psychologists are viewed even more negatively. Admitting to either or both of these 'identities' led to very particular perceptions and opinions about who I was and what people believed I did or who and what I represented. For example, in my initial interactions I found that when introducing ourselves to each other inevitably questions were asked about why we were all there, what we did, what organisation or institution we were from. I would reveal that I was an academic psychologist and if pushed I would say a little about my research interests. The initial reaction to this was to question why I was doing research rather than, say, working directly with South Asian women, almost as if they felt I was misguided in some way. I did not have a problem with this reaction, as it is often a question I asked myself anyway. However, this particular reaction seemed to resonate with me as, for the most part, the practitioners I would talk to were also South Asian women. There was a sense that on the one hand I was considered an 'insider' (a South Asian woman, interested in issues regarding the welfare of other South Asian women). On the other hand, I was simultaneously considered an 'outsider' in that I was an academic researcher and a psychologist. This began to set up a particular background that would affect what I then felt I could or could not reveal about myself and what I did. I found that many of those I interacted with immediately began to criticize the work of psychologists, for example, expressing the feeling that psychology as a discipline colluded with stereotypical perceptions about South Asian communities and the view that psychologists are responsible for perpetuating stereotypes about the mental health of South Asian communities. I was being made aware that people's perceptions of me as an individual was based on their perceptions of psychologists more generally, as if taking the opportunity to off-load their frustrations on me as a representative of the discipline. What was particularly interesting was the way in which part of the negative response (not necessarily nasty, sometimes in jest) related to what they believed was my power, as a researcher and a psychologist. My perceived power as a psychologist and even my potential abuse of it was at issue. Although I agreed with what was being said, I did not feel powerful and as a critical psychologist in that context. I did not feel I fitted the description of 'powerful psychologist' more generally.

What then often followed from these interactions and reactions were vain attempts on my part to allay the fears of those I was talking to. I would try and explain that I agreed with much of what they said, and that I am a critical psychologist who wishes to challenge the very kinds of power relations and stereotypes they were criticising. However, such explanations did not seem to provide reassurance. I was often faced with a response of suspicion and scepticism. They did not quite believe that I was a psychologist who was critical of my own discipline, or that it was possible to be an academic psychologist and to do truly critical, feminist work. Indeed, there was a sense that my intentions in being at that conference were suspect and that I was not necessarily 'on side'. What I found particularly frustrating was that what might have been useful about claiming an identity as a critical psychologist suddenly became use*less*. Why was this happening when critical feminist psychologists had worked so hard at making explicit our challenges to mainstream psychology, exactly the kind of psychology I now seemed, ironically, to be lumped in with? The knowledge, awareness and critical tools I have acquired in my development as a critical psychologist, suddenly seemed to become things that were 'private', un-shareable, and opaque. It also emphasised how such knowledge, awareness and criticality are attributes I have acquired through my privileged position as an academic working in an academic context. Therefore, it became very unsatisfactory when I felt that I was unable to convey my ideas to those people I felt I really wanted to make understand. I felt as if I was inadvertently forced to keep a secret. This, therefore, became a clear indication of the problems that occur when those I am trying to engage with as part of my research do not have access to the academic culture within which the values of critical psychology have been articulated. In the end, I found myself talking about my research and my approach to it in very simplistic terms, not fully disclosing what I actually did in terms of the 'critical' approach I was taking. The tenet of trying to transcend power relations in our research in this context became a difficult one to uphold. What was considered to be my power as a researcher was what was explicitly the issue.

'So you are here to slag us off then?': reactions when making initial contact with organisations

A secondary reason for attending practitioner conferences was that I hoped to meet and talk to people about my research with the possibility that this may lead to making contacts with organisations that might eventually participate. This brings us to another stage in the research process that raises problems for the identity of a critical psychologist, or at least my experience in this research. That is, the stage at which you make initial contact with organisations in order to persuade them to take part in the research and those early negotiations where, if you are lucky enough to gain contact in the first place, you are then invited to explain your research and discuss your intentions for conducting it. These are the kinds of negotiations that are required before those organisations make a final decision about whether they will participate or not. In these situations I initially felt relatively powerless. There was a sense that those in charge within these agencies are the gatekeepers of your research at that point in that it is in their hands whether or not the research will continue, albeit for good ethical reasons that we would want them to be able to make such decisions. These interactions brought to light another response when trying to identify as a critical psychologist. As well as having my explanations treated with suspicion, I also felt *mis*understood. Once I got past the initial information about being an academic/researcher/psychologist, I was often asked to elaborate about what I planned to do with regards to, for example, methodology. Sometimes (though not always) at the point of trying to explain my critical approach I would make what I thought was an exceptional effort to explain exactly what we were doing with our research and the approach that we took in what I thought was non-academic language. However, a common assumption made was that we were there simply to be critical of the agencies themselves and their practices ('you're here to slag us off then', as one of the workers in one of these organisations once commented). In other words, a more basic understanding of the word 'critical' is understood and in those negotiations it is difficult to continually try and correct people's understandings, as it can feel awkward and ultimately patronising towards those I am negotiating with. It is also at this stage that the issue of dissemination is often flagged up and that the issue of my power as researcher is made explicit again. Often it was pointed out that researchers ultimately have the power to say whatever we wish at the end point of the research. The issue of dissemination, therefore, was treated cautiously. In fact it felt as if trying to convey a particular idea of 'criticality' that was sometimes misunderstood actually led people to be even more cautious than usual. This interaction revealed a further problem for the privileged position of the critical psychologist. The question I became faced with was: 'who are you to be critical?'

Thus, again I became alerted to my own power as a researcher and how difficult it is, in the eyes of those I am approaching in my research but also from my own viewpoint at that time, to transcend. There was an acute awareness that researchers in many respects have the 'final say' in the dissemination of their research, regardless of the approach that they take, and the power to do so is often what is focused on rather than how we may use that opportunity to do something better.

Colluding with stereotypes – negotiating 'access' to research participants

If we were successful in managing to persuade agencies and organisations to take part, the next stage of the process was to enter into negotiations about gaining access to participants. In the case of our research, this involved asking to interview people working for the organisations who had experience of working with South Asian women survivors, but also the much more sensitive issue of asking to talk to the women survivors themselves. It was this latter request that led to another instance where I felt one of the 'tenets' of critical psychology became difficult to uphold. When negotiating access to survivors, there is much discussion about their 'vulnerability'. Obviously, there are good ethical practices we would want to follow as researchers which ensure that we treat these particular participants sensitively and considerately. Similarly, the organisations themselves will feel they have a duty to protect their clients from potentially insensitive researchers. However, a particular construction of 'vulnerability' is used in order for us to adhere to such ethical practices. Yet, a consequence of this was the way discussions about how we would conduct research with this particular group of women would lead to the homogenising effect of talking about them in very generic terms. Instead, this approach led to further constructions of them as vulnerable in ways that seemed to reproduce stereotypes that critical feminist researchers like myself and organisations alike would wish to challenge. It posed a particular problem for me as a critical psychologist in that I found that I was in effect colluding with the reproduction of these stereotypes about South Asian women and South Asian communities. For example, we seemed to be colluding with the idea that South Asian women were more vulnerable than other women and this was because Asian communities or Asian 'cultures' are more oppressive and patriarchal than others. This left me feeling very uncomfortable. On the one hand, I was betraying my own deeply held beliefs. On the other, I felt that two central principles of critical psychological work were forced into conflict: I sought to challenge precisely these kinds of stereotypes yet in order to negotiate access I had to – implicitly or explicitly – collude with them. What made this even more paradoxical was the fact that the organisations themselves were equally vehemently opposed to such constructions of South Asian women, yet they too mobilised them. This was a very strange, uncomfortable and dilemmatic situation for a number of reasons. It is as if an artefact of conducting this kind of research forced us to reproduce these stereotypes between us in order for us to develop satisfactory criteria to be able to conduct the interviews with this particular group of women.

So where does this leave us? Critical psychologists or hypo/critical psychologists?

It could be argued that these contradictions, or our compromised credentials as good critical psychologists, could leave us prey to the criticism of being hypocritical rather than critical, that we are not upholding important principles whilst conducting our research. The first question one may ask is: does it matter? As long as the overall 'bigger message' is that we challenge oppressive practices and power relations, should we be concerned that there are moments on the way to doing this where we sometimes turn a blind eye, compromising our aims and principles? I think it does. I particularly think it does because these moments highlight problems in the way we disseminate our ideas and make them accessible. I certainly believe that as good feminist or critical psychologists this should be an aim of what we do, or rather if we did not, that in itself is contradicting one of the main aims which is to question our privilege and challenge problematic power relations. Failing to make our ideas accessible may perpetuate rather than challenge our privilege and bolster rather than transcend such power relations. How best to make our ideas accessible, however, is not a simple matter and needs further consideration and urgent debate.

Reflexivity as a solution? Still talking to ourselves?

Reflexivity is a concept which has been developed mainly within feminist and social constructionist academic research but which can equally be applied to professional practice (Wilkinson 1988; Ahmed 1997; Anderson and Ahmed 2003). It refers to a recognition and self-awareness of who we are, what we are doing and how our actions might affect those with whom we are working. It is also understood as the need to reflect critically on research and professional practice so as to reveal taken-for-granted assumptions that are often overlooked. It may, therefore, seem an apt critical tool to apply in thinking about the very tenets of critical psychology I have tried to discuss here. In other words, we should critically reflect on how our actions might affect our research participants. This may reveal taken-for-granted assumptions that are overlooked whilst conducting our research. But to what end? There has also been much criticism of a reliance on reflexivity as a 'get out' clause, in that it allows us to seem like we are tackling such things in our research, when actually all we are doing is reflecting on ourselves, possibly in an over indulgent narcissistic way (Patai 1994; Pillow 2003; Burman 2006). For me, the only way reflexivity may be useful is to move beyond this kind of introspection and at best should only be a first step which allows us then to consider how our work is affecting those we are working with, in particular where we disseminate our ideas, to whom we disseminate and how we might do so in an accessible way. In my opinion, when we are debating and developing our ideas, including important political ones about oppressive practices, taken for granted knowledge, and how these might lead to, for example, colluding with stereotypes about oppressed groups, we are still falling into the trap of doing so in essentially elitist ways. In particular, we still only write for very particular academic audiences, rather than for those whom we are trying to empower, and we write in ways that are arcane and jargonistic, thereby obscuring the very kinds of debates and ideas that need to be more widely accessible. As someone who should be familiar with the academic culture in which these ideas are discussed and the kinds of language used, I still often find myself struggling to understand the work of my peers. It constantly makes me wonder how such work comes across to those who are not familiar with the culture or the language. I am not suggesting some kind of 'dumbing down' approach, or suggesting that our work should be less complex or intellectual. However, we are clearly not being reflexive enough on the issue of disseminating our ideas beyond academic audiences or thinking about the accessibility of our work. This is another irony as grass-roots movements and activism influence many of us, yet we seem to have trouble with how we then work on those ideas and feed them back. This is certainly something that becomes clear when trying to teach our ideas to undergraduate students, let alone write for different audiences. The issue of disseminating widely and accessibly needs our time and thought. We still have work to do before comfortably being able to claim that we truly are critical and/or feminist psychologists and for that claim to be taken seriously.

Note

1 I have been conducting this research with Paula Reavey and Anamika Majumdar (London Southbank University).

References

Ahmed, B. (1997) 'Feminist psychology and professionalism: Some comments on theory and method', Proceedings of BPS Annual Conference, Edinburgh, British Psychological Society.

Altheide, D. and Johnson, J. (1998) 'Criteria for assessing interpretive validity in qualitative research', in N. Denzin and Y. Lincoln (eds) *Collecting and Interpreting Qualitative Materials*, Thousand Oaks, CA: Sage.

Anderson, I. and Ahmed, B. (2003) 'Sexism in psychology and how to end it: feminist and critical debates in applied contexts', in R. Bayne and I. Horton (eds) *Applied Psychology*, London: Sage.

Burman, E. (2006) 'Emotions and reflexivity in feminised education action research', *Educational Action Research*, 14 (3): 315–32.

Finlay, L. and Gough, B. (eds) (2003) *Reflexivity: A Practical Guide for Researchers in Health and Social Sciences*, Oxford: Blackwell.

Fox, D. and Prilleltensky, I. (1997) *Critical Psychology: an Introduction*, London: Sage.

Parker, I. (1992) *Discourse Dynamics: Critical Analysis for Social and Individual Psychology*, London: Routledge.

Parker, I. and Spears, R. (1996) *Psychology and Society:Radical Theory and Practice*, London: Pluto Press.

Patai, D. (1994) 'When method becomes power', in A. Gitlen and Y. Lincoln (eds) *Power and Method*, New York: Routledge.

Pillow, W.S. (2003) 'Confession, catharsis, or cure? Rethinking the uses of reflexivity as a methodological power in qualitative research', *Qualitative Studies in Education*, 16 (2): 175–96.

Wilkinson, S. (1988) 'The role of reflexivity in feminist psychology', *Women's Studies International Forum*, 11 (5): 493–50.

8 Critiquing thinness and wanting to be thin

Karen Throsby and Debra Gimlin

The body is a prime site for silences and secrets. Its weights and measurements are coveted as confidential and communicated in whispered tones, and magazines and make-over TV shows tutor us in the art of hiding and disguising our 'problem areas'. It is also a site of intense, and profoundly gendered, bodily work – through the careful surveillance of the body, and the management of its size and shape through a multiplicity of technologies of dieting, surgery, exercise regimes, etc. The extent to which these demands to work on the body, especially in relation to size and shape, fall upon women means that it is not surprising that issues surrounding the management of body weight, size and shape have long been a central concern for feminist social scientists. Indeed, the gendered nature of bodily norms and the gendered distribution of risk, responsibility and work relating to body size have been explored at length by feminists since the late 1970s (see Bell and McNaughton 2007). While employing a range of theoretical perspectives, writers such as Orbach (1978, 1986), Millman (1980), Chernin (1981, 1986), Spitzack (1990), Wolf (1990), Bordo (1993), MacSween (1993), LeBesco (2004) and others have drawn critical attention to social constructions of body size that link thinness to moral worth (as well as health, self-control and beauty) while equating fatness with immorality, low self-esteem, illness and self-indulgence – constructions which have profound social consequences, especially for women.

The considerable stigmatisation experienced by large women has led many feminist researchers to write critically about the proliferating practices and technologies of weight loss that can be seen as both produced by, and productive of, the social repudiation of the fat body (Spitzack 1990; Wolf 1990). Furthermore, by conceptualising slimming as only one of a number of gendered technologies targeting women's bodies (see Stinson 2001), feminist authors have linked it to practices as diverse as fertility treatment and cosmetic surgery. While these technologies differ in their goals, they share both an objectification of the female body and the hope of transforming it, with (arguably) limited regard to the physical and emotional risks involved. Reflecting a core conviction within feminist research and politics, one of the central features of feminist work in this area is the incorporation of women's own accounts of their experiences and perceptions of these practices (Reinharz 1992) – a methodology which we have both engaged in extensively in our own research careers (Gimlin 2002; Throsby 2004). The act of creating spaces for women to narrate their own stories is conceptualised within feminism as a political act, breaching normative silences and forcing us to rethink what we 'know'.

Feminist sociologist Kathy Davis' interview-based study of women's experiences of cosmetic surgery is a good example of this, and she narrates frankly the transformation of her own view of cosmetic surgery:

> After listening to women's stories about their suffering with their appearance as well as their struggles to overcome this suffering, I began to feel dissatisfied with the assumption that women have cosmetic surgery in the interests of conforming to the current ideals of feminine appearance.
>
> (2003: 74)

While we laud the efforts of Davis, and other feminist writers, to reflect upon her own perceptions and feelings, and how they may shape (and be shaped by) both the collection of data and its analysis, we also want to draw attention to the largely *disembodied* form that these reflections often take. Despite efforts to 'bring the body back in' to social scientific analysis, we actually find a striking paucity within the feminist literature on women's body-related practices (including our own work), not so much of the bodies of those researched, but rather, those of the researchers themselves (see, for example, Joanisse and Synott 1999; Ogden et al. 2005; Ogden et al. 2006; Gimlin 2007; Throsby 2007). For us, this raises a question: given the feminist goal of reflecting upon our own part in 'producing' social scientific findings, where do researchers – and more specifically, their bodies – fit into critiques of women's body management? In particular, how can we, as feminist sociologists writing critically about the technologies and ideologies of body size and shape, account for our own bodily desires and practices, both in conducting the research and writing it up? In short, how is it possible to critique the ideologies and practices of slimness while wanting (and trying) to be slim?

As a starting point, we want to suggest that the exclusion of the embodied self of the researcher does an injustice, not only to social scientific understandings of female bodily experience, but also to our research participants. That is, privileging researchers' thoughts and beliefs over their bodily desires and practices ultimately reifies the same mind–body dualism that feminists have long been trying to overcome. Furthermore, we would argue that acknowledging that researchers' own bodily wishes and practices are shaped by the same processes that mould those of our respondents, better enables us to walk the fine, but crucial, line of remaining respectful of participants' desires while simultaneously criticising ideologies pertaining to body size.

However, behind this somewhat idealised statement lies the very real puzzle about how to do this effectively – that is, how can we acknowledge our own embeddedness in the ideologies and practices of body management that we are exploring without losing the focus on the research participants and upstaging their narratives with our own, while at the same time avoiding having to make revelations about our own bodies and practices that we would prefer not to place in the public arena? This constitutes another fine line – that of striking a balance between solipsistic self-reflection and a disembodied authorial stance that allows the researcher to position herself outside of the technologies and practices that she is studying, and often critiquing.

While we have argued that there is a relative paucity of researchers' bodies in the literature on weight loss, there are some notable exceptions which illustrate both the possibilities and pitfalls associated with writing the embodied self into our research. Significantly, however, in raising and critiquing these examples, we are not suggesting that we have any better solutions; indeed, our own strategies of categorically not discussing our own bodies in our work suggest that we are far from having answers to these questions. Instead, in this chapter, we are trying to explore *why* the researchers' body is so hard to place, even (or perhaps, especially) in research to which bodies are so central.

The one area of the literature where the authorial body is unabashedly placed centre stage is in the size-acceptance literature (Cooper 1998; Wann 1998), where the fat body is reclaimed as a site of celebration and beauty in direct resistance to the prevailing repudiation of fatness. However, the vast majority of the feminist literature, while sharing the critical perspective of these authors in relation to gendered norms and practices of the management of body size and shape, is far less forthcoming about the authorial body. Instead, the researcher's own embodiment gets written into texts in two key ways: first, instrumentally, through the body as a means of accessing a research site; and second, as illustrative of the complexity of dealing with issues of body size and shape, prior to making the critique of weight management ideologies and practices. Cressida Heyes' insightful paper 'Foucault goes to Weight Watchers' (Heyes 2006) is a good example of both (see also Stinson 2001 for an illustration of the former). Heyes attended Weight Watchers as a customer and a researcher for 10 months, frankly describing her motives for joining as 'a complex mix of the personal and the professional' (ibid.: 127). She suggests that she was 'interested in losing weight, embarrassed by that desire, and curious about institutionalised weight-loss programmes', producing writing from what she potently describes as a 'fraught standpoint', encapsulating the dilemmas inherent in being a 'critical and engaged feminist' (ibid.). Heyes herself asks the rhetorical question, 'How can I speak from my normalized position as a dieter simultaneously with my critical position as a diet resister?' (ibid.), but she defers the 'ethical and ethnographic questions' that are raised by her participation. Indeed, the specificities of her own engagement with Weight Watchers, and of her own body sink into the background of the paper, locating herself implicitly within the community of 'dieters' and 'members' to which she belongs.

Susan Bordo, on the other hand, offers a more confessional account of her own weight loss in her highly influential contribution to the feminist literature on the management of body size and shape, *Unbearable Weight* (1993). She announces in the introduction that in 1990 she 'lost 25 pounds through a national weight loss programme', noting that this was 'a choice that some of my colleagues viewed as inconsistent and even hypocritical, given my work' (ibid.: 30). Arguing that the goal of feminist cultural criticism is 'edification and understanding', rather than to provide a 'blueprint for the conduct of personal life' (ibid.), Bordo nevertheless reflects that her own weight loss, while benefiting herself, 'has also diminished my efficacy as an alternative role model for my female students' (ibid.: 31). The somewhat defensive tone of this discussion highlights the difficulties which feminists face in the task of juggling competing convictions and desires in relation to their bodies, and Bordo quickly directs attention away from her own body and its management towards the book's focus on the 'complexly and densely institutionalized *system* of values and practices within which girls and women – and increasingly, men and boys as well – come to believe that they are nothing (and are frequently treated as nothing) unless they are trim, tight, lineless, bulgeless, and sagless' (ibid.: 32, emphasis in original). However, the commentaries offered by both Bordo and Heyes are ultimately *dis*embodied, and their own engagements with the practices that they are studying fade quickly from the centre of their work.

In what is arguably a more embodied analysis, Victoria Pitts-Taylor's book *Surgery Junkies* (2007) includes an entire chapter devoted to a discussion of the author's decision to undergo rhinoplasty. Pitts-Taylor highlights a number of personal aspects of that decision and the process itself – the pain and suffering involved, the importance of her economic advantages in enabling her to make such a decision in the first place, and the frequently negative reactions she received from students and colleagues who learned about her procedure. One interesting aspect of Pitts-Taylor's account is the often defiant tone that it takes. For example, by stressing the lengthy research she engaged in prior to selecting a surgeon, her unwillingness to undergo additional procedures recommended by some physicians, and the fact that her decision to have rhinoplasty was motivated in part by a recent skiing accident, Pitts-Taylor presents herself as a thoughtful, self-conscious subject who might take part in heteronormative beauty practices, but is not enslaved by them. It is also interesting that, while this discussion is left until nearly the end of the book, Pitts-Taylor's participation in cosmetic surgery is flagged up at the very beginning, almost as a challenge to the reader to question her analysis of cosmetic surgery because of her complicity with the practice.

While useful in understanding researchers' experiences, what is missing from all of these accounts is a consideration of the ways in which the body itself impacts on the production and analysis of data. Lee Monaghan's research on men's understandings and experiences of weight and its management offers a good example of an attempt to write the authorial body in this way. In the methodology section of his paper 'Body Mass Index, Masculinities and Moral Worth: Men's Critical Understandings of "Appropriate" Weight-for-height', Monaghan (2007) – a body builder – describes his own commitment to lifting weights in order to 'gain and retain lean muscular weight'. He also refers to his (non-weight lifting) research associate as '"thin" verging towards an "average build"' (ibid.). These descriptions are mobilised later in the paper during a discussion of men's 'muscle talk', which centres around the idea that someone could be heavy but fit as a result of muscularity (for example, in rugby players) (ibid.: 594). Speculating on the possible influence of his own body size and shape on the interviews, Monaghan concludes that this talk 'was not an artefact of my interactions with men and how they may have perceived my body build', since his research associate 'generated similar data' (ibid.). Instead, he argues that 'muscle or athlete talk' provides a means for men to 'deflect possible moral opprobrium' whilst preserving and protecting 'appropriate masculinities' (ibid.: 595). However, while Monaghan's reflexivity around his own body (and its practices) in his research adds a welcome (and, within this field, unusual) dimension to the analysis, it is also evident that the effect of our own bodies on the research process is always extremely hard to 'know' and account for.

Particularly in relation to ethnographic and interview research, then, what difference does it make when the interviewer is slim? Or fat? What difference does it make to the analysis and writing-up process? We want to suggest that there is a silence surrounding the acknowledgement of the role of our embodied selves on the research process and products, and that there is considerable discomfort around the fact that bodily appearances and practices matter in the research process in ways which are impossible to escape, but very difficult to write about. While we have no solutions to offer, we want to suggest that the acknowledgement of this difficulty is a crucial element to the critical appraisal of those practices (and those who engage with them).

The rest of this chapter will focus on our own experiences of researching technologies and practices of the management of body size and shape in order to explore the effect, first, of our own bodies on the research itself, and second, the difficulties that we have confronted in articulating those in our writing. In the first section, Karen discusses her ongoing research on obesity surgery, where her body size positioned her as an outsider to the community that she was studying; and in the second section, Debra explores her interview research into dieting practices and considers how expectations of similarity and difference impacted on both the interviews themselves and the work of analysis and writing up. In the concluding section, we argue that these should not be seen as resolvable problems, but rather as resources for thinking reflexively about these complex and challenging issues – as sociologists, and as feminists.

Karen

In 2005–6 I conducted interviews with 29 women and 6 men, all of whom had either had, or were waiting to have, obesity surgery. Obesity surgery refers to a constellation of interventions which aim to reduce stomach capacity and/or intestinal length in order to limit the body's capacity to consume and absorb food. It is a weight-management technology of last resort which carries the risk of chronic and acute side effects and complications, but which also offers the possibility of dramatic and sustained weight loss for those for whom all other attempts at weight loss have proved unsustainable (see, for example, Ackerman 1999; Janeway et al. 2005). Obesity surgery is a highly contested technology, and those who undergo surgery are necessarily cautious about how they will be seen (and judged) by others – both for having become visibly large in the first place (something for which individuals are routinely held morally responsible), and for the decision to turn to surgery (Throsby 2007).

I recruited the participants for this study through the online discussion forums of one of the only organisations in the UK providing information and support for those wanting, undergoing and living with obesity surgery. After the first few interviews, a discussion thread opened on the forums enabling members who were waiting to be interviewed to get feedback on the process, and on me, from other participants. One of the first questions asked on the thread was whether I was fat – a question which was clearly oriented towards gauging how sympathetic I might be, but which also highlighted the (potential) significance of my own body (and its size) to the process of data production. In the discussion thread, and at various points during the research, I was described by the participants as 'slim', 'normal', and in one case, 'skinny'. This is a description which by any standard does not reflect my actual body size and shape, which hovers stubbornly on the borderlines of medicalised categories of 'normal' and 'overweight'. But more significantly, the epithet 'skinny' (along with 'slim' and 'normal') signals the presumption of a 'natural' state of non-fatness that requires limited effort to maintain. In this sense, therefore, I was cast by the participants as an obvious outsider who could have no understanding of the problems that they faced.

In one sense, this was true; I have no personal experience of extreme obesity, or of obesity surgery, and was not a member of the online community. Nor was this a problem in terms of conducting the research; in fact, the strong desire of the participants to 'teach' me in my role as a sympathetic outsider about their experiences generated a wealth of rich data. However, this presumption also rendered unspeakable my own ongoing frustrations and desires in relation to body size, and the practices that I engage in in order to manage my weight (for example, distance running, sporadic dieting, as well as the familiar gamut of feelings of guilt and shame around food and the body associated with female embodiment). Early on in the interviews, I made misplaced interjections of solidarity with the participants which were intended to demonstrate shared understanding, but which, in fact, disrupted what I later understood as the construction of the obesity surgery patient's situation as unique (and therefore, requiring extraordinary intervention) – a case that could not be made if the participants and I were seen as experiencing similar 'problems' with food or dieting. One participant, for example, described how an opened packet of biscuits would 'call' her in the night, but my response – 'I know what you mean' – was quickly set aside by an emphatic reiteration of the potency of her compulsion to eat and the excesses that this had led her to. Others noted that it was impossible for someone *like me* (i.e. someone who was presumed to easily maintain a not-fat body) to imagine their struggles in relation to their own bodies, and with food. These observations were always amicably made, and in discursive terms simply served to emphasis the suffering that had driven them towards surgery. However, this highlighted to me the extent to which my own body was imbricated in the interview process in ways that I felt did not reflect my own embodied experience and practice, but which were also hard to identify and articulate in writing up the research. This rendered me complicit in assumptions about my own body and 'body work' (Gimlin 2002) that went unchallenged, both in the interviews themselves, and in the papers arising out of the research – an outcome that is problematic given the troubling assumptions underpinning the contemporary 'war on obesity' that we can 'know' the body and its practices from its appearance and size (see, for example, Murray 2005).

Debra

During the last 15 years, I have conducted research in a range of body-management sites: in aerobics classes and a hairstyling salon some years ago and, more recently, in a commercial slimming group. I have personal experience of these and many other forms of 'normative' body modification, including restrictive dieting, which I have engaged in many times since around the age of 10. My goal in taking part in these slimming regimes, at least until my last encounter with commercial dieting, was to lose weight rather than to conduct research. Yet because I have always been interested in studying other women's experiences of group slimming, I decided in April 2005 to begin a study of one (all-female) meeting of a multi-national weight-loss corporation. Being aware of the low rates of long-term success in restrictive dieting, my intention was to better understand the organisational and other discursive resources that dieting women draw upon in accounting for the failure to lose weight and/or their re-gaining weight after an initial period of successful weight loss.

As an ethnographer, I wanted very much to participate in the dieting programme alongside my potential respondents. However, I knew that I would face certain obstacles in gaining access to the site. First, because my body reflects my involvement in long-distance running, I suspected that it would not meet the organisation's minimum (over-)weight requirements for my height. Therefore, in preparation for my first meeting, I dressed in baggy jeans, a large leather belt and heavy-soled boots. I layered on two thick shirts topped by a bulky sweater (living in a part of Britain that is often chilly in April, my attire went unnoticed). I did not correct the group leader when she estimated my height at two inches less than it actually is. After stepping on the scale (as is required for all members each week), the leader and I agreed to a goal that was about six pounds lower than my actual weight. Second, while I wanted to experience the same challenges that other dieters faced, and hoped that doing so would encourage my full acceptance in the group, I was concerned that revealing my research interests would distance me from the other members. However, after announcing my intentions, I noticed little change in my interactions with the other dieters, perhaps because my status as a fellow slimmer overshadowed my role as a researcher.

That identification was made possible in part, I believe, by the group leader's tendency to draw attention to me as a particularly 'successful' dieter. During my second weigh-in (after a week of hunger so significant that it disrupted both my sleep and my concentration), I learned that I had lost over seven pounds. As was customary during the weekly discussions, the leader asked some of the women present to report our weight loss to the group. After I did so, one member turned to me, clapping, and declared, 'now that deserves a round of applause'. The other members joined her. I was thrilled, not only because my suffering had paid off in terms of weight loss, but also because I hoped that my success would help to solidify my place in the group. I continued to nurture my acquaintanceship with other members by taking part in the meetings for coffee and other brief social gatherings that frequently followed weekly classes.

Still, being identified as a 'model' dieter drew attention to the many ways that my feelings and desires about my own body and its size were made unspeakable throughout the research and writing-up process. For example, because I was viewed as someone who could lose weight successfully, other members wanted to learn my 'secret' and so asked me for advice. Among the variety of responses that came to mind, some (e.g. 'stay hungry constantly') were politically very problematic, while others (e.g. 'stop dieting') would have seemed disingenuous or at least unhelpful. However, while neither could be spoken, these responses represented my own long-term experience of dissatisfaction with a body that, while thin, was never thin 'enough'. At the same time, that dissatisfaction exists alongside my feeling unable to talk about it, both because I am sufficiently slender by most medical and aesthetic standards, and because I nonetheless remain critical of gender structures that encourage women to strive for unattainable body ideals.

My status as a successful dieter also foregrounded my body itself, making it a focus of attention and a topic of discussion. For example, during conversations and interviews, respondents regularly made comments such as 'I'd like to get down to a size 12 … though that probably seems big to you', and (referring to my involvement in running), 'if you like to exercise, it must be easier to lose weight'. Such comments silenced any acknowledgement of those many physical features (e.g. encroaching crows' feet, weak nails, a flat chest and so on) that cause me considerable insecurity and that are, if anything, exacerbated by weight loss. At the same time, such statements both aligned me with my fellow dieters, in so far as they assumed a shared effort to lose weight, and distanced me from them, given that they presented me as having certain qualities (a liking for exercise) that made my struggle with weight a relatively easy one.

Even more significantly, the foregrounding of my (successfully dieted) body also served to produce data and so, ultimately, to problematise the analytic process. Specifically, it created just the sort of phenomena that I set out to investigate; because I was a 'better' dieter than my respondents, many of them highlighted their relative 'failings' (such as slow or temporary weight loss) and 'weaknesses' (e.g. a disliking for exercise) during our conversations and interviews. In effect, my body served in part to produce those failings and, arguably, many of my research findings. Coming to realise the effect that my body had on the data I collected, I opted to omit such commentary from the writing-up of my analysis. This omission was motivated in part by what I now see as a feminist ideological pressure not to 'come out' as thin in authorial texts, because to do so is to distance oneself from the oppression experienced by research participants in ways that, in this case at least, further reinforce the stigma of fatness. Yet this choice came with a price for me personally – a price that is for the most part unmentionable in the context of contemporary expectations about the detachment researchers should maintain from their subject matter. That is, by presenting myself in publications as a member of the slimming group, and omitting reference to my own (comparative) slenderness, I allow readers to imagine me to be overweight. I therefore run the risk of associating myself with all of the negative constructions of fatness that I have long worked hard not to embody.

Conclusion

In this chapter, we have tried to demonstrate difficulties of writing the researcher's body into research on the experiences and understandings of body size and its management. As an outsider to the collective culture of the obesity surgery patients she interviewed, Karen found that her own ongoing discomfort with, and attempts to change, her body size were (necessarily?) silenced by assumptions on the part of her participants about her body as easily and comfortably not-fat, relative to their own extreme and often debilitating levels of obesity. Undisrupted, this outsider status prompted the generation of a rich body of data, as the participants sought to explain the particularity of their situation to someone who was judged to be sympathetic, but unknowing. As an insider to the dieting culture of her participants, Debra's status as a successful dieter rendered her own weight loss method, and her political concerns about the act and context of weight loss, unspeakable, even while she was being held up as exemplary to others in the group. In both cases, the participants made reference to people 'like you' in their accounts. In Karen's case, this pertained to people who did not know what it was like to worry about weight, or to struggle to maintain it; in Debra's case, this referred to those who were deemed fortunate enough to be successful slimmers. This momentary visibility of our own bodies and practices in the interviews signals the fact that bodies matter (for researchers and participants) in the research process in ways that are occasionally apparent, but more commonly elusive. Furthermore, even those moments where the researchers' bodies and practices *are* evident are profoundly difficult to write into publications – despite a feminist commitment to reflexivity – in part as a result of the desire not to engage in self-revelation on a personal issue, and in part because it is not always clear what the utility of that revelation would be. Indeed, we both remain unsure as to *how* to write our own bodies in.

Consequently, and perhaps frustratingly for readers (and ourselves), we have no answers to offer to the questions that were raised at the beginning of the chapter, except to note that this dilemma – how to incorporate the researcher's body into research on the body – is one that reflects more broadly the tense relationship that many feminists experience between the ideology of accepting our bodies as they are, the critique of normative body ideals and practices, and the desire for them. This tension, however uncomfortable and inexpressible, serves as a useful qualifier to the critiques of ideologies of slimness, the 'war on obesity' and the diet industry that are so politically appealing, but which ultimately fail to account for the complexity of people's engagements with those ideologies and practices. It also suggests that feminist epistemology or politics should be understood not so much as a standard that we must compel ourselves to conform to, but instead as an effort to balance our own integrity with that of the research data.

References

Ackerman, N.B. (1999) *Fat No More: The Answer for the Dangerously Overweight*, New York: Prometheus Books.

Bell, K. and McNaughton, D. (2007) 'Feminism and the invisible fat man', *Body & Society*, 13 (1): 107–31.

Bordo, S. (1993 [2003]) *Unbearable Weight: Feminism, Western Culture and the Body*, Berkeley, CA: University of California Press.

Chernin, K. (1981) *The Obsession: Reflections on the Tyranny of Slenderness*, New York: Harper.

—— (1986) *The Hungry Self: Women, Dieting and Food*, New York: Random House.

Cooper, C. (1998) *Fat and Proud: The Politics of Size*, London: The Women's Press.

Davis, K. (1995) *Reshaping the Female Body: The Dilemma of Cosmetic Surgery*, New York and London: Routledge.

—— (2003) 'Surgical passing: or why Michael Jackson's nose makes "us" uneasy', *Feminist Theory*, 4 (1): 73–92.

Gimlin, D. (2002) *Body Work: Beauty and Self-Image in American Culture*, Berkeley, CA: University of California Press.

—— (2007) 'Discourses of ageing and narrative resistance in a commercial slimming group', *Ageing & Society*, 27 (1): 1–19.

Heyes, C.J. (2006) 'Foucault goes to Weight Watchers', *Hypatia*, 21 (2): 126–49.

Janeway, J.M., Sparks, K.J. and Baker, R.S. (2005) *The Real Skinny on Weight Loss Surgery: An Indispensible Guide to What You Can Really Expect*, Onondaga, MI: Little Victories Press.

Joanisse, L. and Synott, A. (1999) 'Fighting back: reactions and resistance to the stigma of obesity', in J. Sobal and D. Maurer (eds) *Interpreting Weight: The Social Management of Fatness and Thinness*, New York: Aldine de Gruyter.

LeBesco, K. (2004) *Revolting Bodies? The Struggle to Redefine Fat Identity*, Amherst, MA: University of Massachusetts Press.

MacSween, M. (1993) *Anorexic Bodies: A Feminist and Sociological Perspective on Anorexia Nervosa*, London: Routledge.

Millman, M. (1980) *Such a Pretty Face: Being Fat in America*, New York: W.W. Norton.

Monaghan, L. (1999a) 'Challenging medicine: bodybuilding, drugs and risk', *Sociology of Health & Illness*, 21 (6): 707–34.

—— (1999b) 'Creating 'the perfect body': a variable project'. *Body & Society*, 5 (2–3): 267–90.

—— (2000) *Bodybuilding, Drugs and Risk*, London: Routledge.

—— (2007) Body Mass Index, masculinities and moral worth: men's critical talk about appropriate weight-for-height. *Sociology of Health & Illness*. 29 (4): 584–609.

Murray, S. (2005) '(Un/be)coming out? Rethinking fat politics', *Social Semiotics*, 15 (2): 153–63.

Ogden, J., Clementi, C. and Aylwin, S. (2006) 'The impact of obesity surgery and the paradox of control: a qualitative study', *Psychology and Health*, 21 (2): 273–93.

Ogden, J., Clementi, C., Aylwin, S. and Patel, A. (2005) 'Exploring the impact of obesity surgery on patients' health status: a qualitiative and quantitative study', *Obesity Surgery*, 15 (2): 266–72.

Orbach, S. (1978) *Fat is a Feminist Issue*, New York: Berkeley.

—— (1986) *Hunger Strike*, London: Faber and Faber.

Pitts-Taylor, V. (2007) *Surgery Junkies: Wellness and Pathology in Cosmetic Culture*, New Brunswick, NJ: Rutgers University Press.

Reinharz, S. (1992) *Feminist Methods in Social Research*, New York: Oxford University Press.

Sobal, J. (1999) 'Sociological analysis of the stigma of obesity', in J. Germov and L. Williams (eds) *A Sociology of Food and Nutrition: Introducing the Social Appetite*, Melbourne: Oxford University Press.

Sobal, J. and Maurer, D. (eds) (1999a) *Weight Issues: Fatness and Thinness and Social Problems*, New York: Aldine De Gruyter.

—— (1999b) *Interpreting Weight: The Social Management of Fatness and Thinness*, New York: Aldine De Gruyter.

Spitzack, C. (1990) *Confessing Excess: Women and the Politics of Body Reduction*, Stony Brook, NY: SUNY Press.

Stinson, K. (2001) *Women and Dieting Culture: Inside a Commercial Weight Loss Group*, New Brunswick, NJ: Rutgers University Press.

Throsby, K. (2004) *When IVF Fails: Feminism, Infertility and the Negotiation of Normality*, London: Palgrave

—— (2007) "How could you let yourself get like that?": stories of the origins of obesity in accounts of weight loss surgery', *Social Science and Medicine*, 65: 1561–71.

Wann, M. (1998) *Fat! So? Because You Don't Have to Apologise for your Size*, Berkeley, CA: Ten Speed Press

Wolf, N. (1990) *The Beauty Myth: How Images of Beauty are Used Against Women*, London: Vintage.

9 Inside 'doorwork'

Gendering the security gaze

Kate O'Brien

Club Fusion is a 2000-capacity city-centre venue owned by one of the largest leisure companies operating in the UK. On weekend nights the venue attracts locals, especially white working-class young people aged 18–25 years into the high-energy dance music scene. It is 12.50 a.m. I have been taken off the front doors where I have been searching women with no respite since opening at 10.00 p.m. I am standing with Ian in the bar 3 area. I need to use the toilet (there are no staff toilets) and this is my first visit to the female toilets since I started my shift. I inform Carl, the doorman responsible for supervising the ground floor, where I am heading and make my way down the stairs to the main toilet area. I follow a young woman down the stairs who reminds me of Jodie Marsh, the glamour model and reality TV celebrity. She is wearing a short black skirt, calf-high black-leather boots with chrome buckles, and a sexy stripy top. She isn't aware that a member of the security team is behind her as she flashes her breasts to a group of males who pass her as they walk up the stairs. They glance at me, smiling in recognition that the young woman is unaware of my presence.

As she enters the ladies toilet area her knees appear to stop functioning. She holds on to the chip-wood sink unit to stop herself from collapsing on to the floor. The toilet area is shabby and unkempt – toilet rolls are strewn on the damp and sticky carpeted floor. The space is noisy with conversation and is congested with similarly dressed female bodies, some of them using the mirrors above the grimy sinks to reapply make-up. I help her to a standing position and say, 'You need to sort yourself out or you are going to have to leave' (ejection of customers exhibiting the signs of being 'too drunk' is club policy). I am watched by some of the other women in the toilet area as they wait for a free cubicle. Her dilated pupils tell me that the cheap drink on offer in Club Fusion tonight is not the only source of her intoxicated state. Like the vast majority of customers in here, she has taken ecstasy and the effects are causing her to behave flirtatiously and momentarily to lose balance and coordination. Upright again, she struggles to open her bag and then when she does, the contents fall out and onto the floor. Her knees give way once again as she attempts to retrieve her make-up and mobile phone. I tell her that she has to leave the venue and I escort her out of the toilet area, up the stairs and towards the doors that lead to the exit area. I walk behind her again, this time with one of my hands on her back, the other on her arm to keep her upright. She resists my hold, she doesn't want to leave and I struggle to keep her under control. She tells me that she wants to find her friend and repeats her friend's name as she tries to head back on to the rammed dance floor.

I radio for assistance and Carl, who is closest to my position, arrives quickly. He immediately assumes a leadership role and takes command of the situation. Within seconds, another doorman arrives. I try to inform Carl of the situation and stress that we should attempt to find her friend but he doesn't hear me. The volume of the music is so high and the venue so dark that he is unable to hear me or read my facial expressions. Carl goes into auto-pilot – 'drugged up' and 'fucked up' punter – 'shovel them out'. He takes a more forcible approach with her and walks her out of the venue using his left hand to hold her in an arm lock behind her back. I express my concern to the other doorman about Carl's aggressive approach as we follow them out of the main club space and into the entrance area. I can be heard in this part of the club. I explain to Carl that she is not in a state to get herself home safely; she is vulnerable, so if we have to eject her from the club then we need to find her friend. He replies, 'No, just leave it. She's not our problem now. They're not our problem when they're outside.' She is escorted out of the building alone and I am sent back to my position.

(Field notes, Club Fusion, April 2005)

Introduction

So there I stood, a female member of a nightclub security team breathing in the nocturnal culture of Britain's drinking environment, its excesses of fleshy sexuality, hedonism and intoxication. As a feminist ethnographer, I was simultaneously learning the tacit rules and discrete occupational codes underpinning the masculinist occupational culture of 'doorwork'. One of the first 'codes of the door' I learn is that you must always back up your colleagues and at Club Fusion[1] regular customer-service rules do not apply – the customer is never right. I had played a pivotal role in the outcome of the evening for the young woman we had ejected. She was so intoxicated that she was unable to stand upright and yet she was made to leave the venue by the door team without her coat and a friend to help her home safely. I recall a feeling of being destabilised. In the name of academic research I was occupying a cultural environment underpinned by moral codes that conflicted with my own and consequently being provoked to think and behave in ways I was not accustomed. Moral tangles such as this define the murky world of the fieldwork endeavour, and are arguably most revealing in studies of deviant groups and illegal settings (see, for example, Polsky 1967; Hobbs 1988; Maher 1997), yet they are frequently concealed from the ethnographic text. However, the emotional and the personal underpin the fieldwork endeavour (Coffey 1999), and importantly, their exposure has the potential to offer valuable insights into the ordinary everyday spaces of moral processes that embed local worlds (Kleinman: 1999: 413; see also Ferrell and Hamm 1998).

The opening to this chapter is illustrative of the moral tangles I faced whilst adopting a 'complete participant role' (Adler and Adler 1987) and conducting covert research[2] in licensed venues whilst working as a nightclub bouncer, an occupation also referred to as a 'door supervisor'. The ethnographic fieldwork described in this chapter contributed to a larger study, with Louise Westmarland and Dick Hobbs, which was concerned with exploring the role of female bouncers within the context of Britain's bourgeoning night-time leisure markets.[3] Our project was carried out between 2004–6, focused on five major UK cities and included interviews with fifty female bouncers and interviews with key stakeholders including police and local authority licensing officers, night club operators and security firm directors. We have presented the substantive findings of our study elsewhere, which to date have drawn primarily on interview data and hinged on an analysis of femininities and violence in recounting how women 'working the doors' deal with violence and aggression (Hobbs et al. 2007; O'Brien et al. 2008). Connecting with the theme of this book, and indeed acknowledging the significance of secrecy and silences to cultural settings (Simmel 1906), social interaction (Goffman 1969) and the research process, this chapter contributes a further layer of understanding to our study of female bouncers.

The main concern of this chapter is a methodological and epistemological one, where I focus on the significance to the research enterprise of the personal and the emotional self. This is especially pertinent with ethnographic fieldwork, a research practice that involves emotional engagement with those under study 'on their turf', with the purpose of discovering and understanding social practices and situated meanings from the perspectives of those being researched. Situated within a feminist ethnographic framework (see Reinharz 1992), which among other goals embraces the emotional dimensions of the research enterprise, situating the 'the self as a gendered, embodied, sexualized and emotional being' (Coffey 1999: 12) in the fieldwork endeavour, I draw on my observations and personal experiences of conducting fieldwork in licensed venues, whilst employed to work as a door supervisor. This role involved me performing the routine tasks of door security work, including vetting customers at point of entry and managing violent and disorderly customers inside venues. I was also required to undertake the gender specific tasks performed by female bouncers such as searching female bodies, monitoring female toilets and performing first-aid tasks.

Accordingly, this *confessionary* (Van Maanen 1988) presents a selection of ethnographic episodes that serve to uncover some of the ethical and moral tangles I negotiated during the course of fieldwork. Underlying this reflexive account of the field research process is an analysis of how I negotiated gender, not least because I occupied a work setting where female co-workers are coded as 'other' (see Westmarland 2001). My female gender, bodily capital (a female body, 5 foot 6 inches tall and of a slight build) and cultural capital (middle class, academic) was at odds with the attributes of those who occupy this work setting – an occupational culture demarcated by working-class heterosexual masculinity and forceful bodies suggestive of potential violence (Winlow 2001; Monaghan 2002a, 2002c; Hobbs et al. 2003).

The second concern of this chapter is with the 'hidden' aspects of 'door culture', or 'back regions' (Goffman 1959), where I offer insights into the cultural aspects of night-time security work, and the spaces of control that tend to be concealed from the public gaze. Recent British ethnographic studies of male bouncers have described an occupational culture defined by pragmatism and 'unofficial' rules of engagement (Winlow 2001; Monaghan 2002d; Hobbs et al. 2003), where work practices and a set of occupationally discrete codes are 'learnt informally within the enacted environment' (Hobbs et al. 2002: 358). In their recent study, Hobbs et al. (2003) have argued that controlling and maintaining order within Britain's alcohol-fuelled night-time leisure markets requires a specialised form of commercial control, occupied by personnel able to utilise violence and intimidating techniques in order to deal with the aggressive disorder that flows from mass intoxication. My own immersion in this occupational setting was limited; I worked only twelve shifts in five different venues. However, engaging in participant observation *from within* allowed me to experience firsthand, and construct an emotional and embodied understanding of the cultural specificities of night-time security work through a gendered lens (see also Monaghan 2002b). In other words, my status as a female 'rookie bouncer' provided me with experiential knowledge of the moral codes and informal work practices underpinning this occupational culture from the epistemological standpoint of 'the other'. For the purposes of this chapter, I draw in particular on fieldwork carried out in nightclub venues and give particular attention to the methodologies utilised by door staff to control the consumption and supply of illegal drugs.

Background

The study from which this chapter draws was concerned with exploring a diverse range of issues such as gendered working bodies, femininities and violence, the changing needs of the night-time economy in the UK and the experiences of women engaged in 'non traditional' occupations. Specifically, we were interested in examining how women perform an occupational role where authority is derived from local reputation and the potential physicality of their bodies (Hobbs et al. 2003: 144), and to document women's experiences and behaviours from their perspectives. Attentive to the significance of gender as embodied and performative and also acknowledging that gender is a situated accomplishment, where gender is (re)produced during interaction and shaped by organisational structures (West and Zimmerman 1987: 127; West and Fenstermaker 1995; Miller 2002), our study was underpinned by an analysis of how female door staff *do gender* within this highly embodied and masculinist occupational culture (see Hobbs et al. 2007).

The responsibility for governing and gate-keeping Britain's night-time leisure markets has for some time been the domain of males, especially the category of men I refer to above who are equipped with the cultural and bodily resources suited to navigating the potentially violent worlds they occupy. Although women comprise only 11 per cent of door staff in England and Wales (SIA 2005), and so mirror both public policing and the private-security industry generally (Erickson et al. 2000; Wakefield 2003), we found that the demand for female personnel was increasing during the study period. We have explained this development as a consequence of the increase in the number of young women engaging with the night-time economy in the UK. The sheer number of young women now consuming night-time leisure spaces has created new commercial and legal demands for the 'gender specialist', authorised to control, search and monitor the 'deviant' female body (O'Brien et al. 2008). The Licensing Act 2003 is significant here in that guidance accompanying it has intensified the demand by operators for female personnel since section 182 of the Act stipulates that the employment of women can be a condition of a venue's licence, especially nightclub venues where a search policy is normally required (DCMS 2007). As I will describe later in the chapter, like many of the female bouncers in our study who regularly worked in nightclub venues, my primary role in Club Fusion was to search women's bodies and their handbags for drugs and to monitor female-only spaces.

Concealment and disclosure

The decision to immerse myself into the cultural milieu of night-time security work was not taken lightly, not least because I was aware from my observations and interviews with female bouncers of the volatile and potentially violent environments they occupy. I was also attuned to my personal and professional responsibilities and sensitive to the criticisms of those who adhere to a more orthodox methodological position and warn of the dangers of being an active agent in the field. Central to these methodological debates is the issue of concealment where critics emphasise the ethical problems inherent in conducting covert research (see Bulmer 1982). Although I did not set out to conceal my identify from those I engaged with in the field, it was an inevitable outcome of this particular study. As Lugosi (2006: 542) concludes from his ethnographic observations of the nuances of hospitality in a UK gay bar, licensed venues are inhabited by 'fragmented groups, with discontinuous membership'. Consequently, my interactions with customers, and in most cases venue staff, were sporadic and momentary and therefore most were unaware of my research identity.

I made efforts to establish open relationships with the security staff I worked with and make explicit my academic interests. However, it was often not practical or possible for me to 'come clean' and disclose my research role to all my colleagues; in some venues, I worked as a member of such a large team that I often had little, if any, physical interaction with my co-workers. For example, Club Fusion employs a door team of eighteen staff who are strategically deployed at key observation posts inside the venue. The interior space of Club Fusion is vast and dominated by a first-floor gallery that overlooks the main dance-floor area and the four dancing podiums located around its perimeter. There are a total of five bar areas in this venue, including a VIP area, and so a large door team is required to provide adequate surveillance. Interaction with some of my colleagues in this venue was limited to radio contact and during moments of chaos, typically, episodes where door staff were called *en masse* to manage violent incidents.

Amongst those I worked with most closely and who were aware of my identity, I was surprised by how unsuspecting they appeared to be of my academic interests. I was savvy enough in the practice and politics of doing ethnography to understand the importance of refraining from behaving like an observer; I only asked questions appropriate of a new recruit and never attempted to record my observations and conversations whilst I was 'on the job'. However, door-work subcultures are closed groups, demarcated by a high degree of in-group solidarity and masculine displays of loyalty, such as the 'obligatory firm handshake' on arrival and departure (Monaghan 2002c), and so I expected to be treated with suspicion and with some degree of hostility. I discovered that contrary to my preconceptions, the majority of the men I worked alongside were intrigued by the focus of the research and wanted to share with me their experiences of the job and to offer their views about women working the doors. My female gender signalled minimal threat and helped forge field relations where I was assigned the status of 'acceptable incompetent' (Lofland and Lofland 1995), and my male co-workers assuming the status of experts. Nonetheless, throughout my time working at Club Fusion I was never invited into the underbelly of this occupational culture which, in this venue, is defined by inclusion into the post-shift drinking session where events of the evening are dissected, debated and celebrated.

Playing the rookie

My transition during the study period from playing a peripheral membership role (Adler 1993), which involved me shadowing female bouncers 'on the job',[4] to an active membership role, where I actually became one of the women we were studying, occurred when I agreed to work as a door supervisor for one of our key informants, a director of a large security company operating in the north of England.[5] I began working for the company on a temporary basis, providing cover, often at short notice, for female employees who called in sick. This meant that during a relatively short period of the fieldwork, I worked in a variety of licensed venues including two large-capacity nightclub venues, an 'up-market' high-street-style bar, a city-centre pub and an independent DJ bar. These venues differed significantly, most notably because they operated quite distinctive 'house rules' in order to target, and therefore manage specific markets. For example, in contrast to the DJ bar, which on weekend evenings operates a membership-only policy in order to attract the 'trendy crowd', Club Fusion caters for the 'rough crowd', a market coded by its members' attachment to 'problem estates' and who are excluded from the majority of city-centre venues. I was therefore required to adapt to a range of different styles of private governance (see Hadfield 2008), which in Club Fusion, for instance, demanded a hostile and forceful approach in order to effectively induce compliance amongst those located on the bottom rung of the night-time leisure market (Van Maanen 1978; Choongh 1998).

As a new member of the door team at Club Fusion I was regularly advised by doormen that I was behaving 'too nice', 'too soft' and 'too caring'. Referring to customers as 'the scum of the earth', one doorman (MB8) warned me: To get on in Club Fusion you need to toughen up, you need to learn not to trust them. They'll take you for a ride. You need to learn to not care about them' (field notes, April 2005, Club Fusion). Such displays of hostility towards Club Fusion patrons often extended to acts of violent aggression, intimidation and humiliation. For instance, on one occasion, I was required to attend an incident involving a young male customer whom the doormen suspected was dealing ecstasy tablets inside the venue. It is club policy for a female member of the door team to be in attendance and witness intimate searches of male customers. He was taken into a concealed space located at the rear of the venue which serves as a fire exit and is hidden from the gaze of CCTV cameras. He was then subjected to a strip search by two doormen where he was instructed to undress, leaving on only his underwear. The young man's resistance to this order and verbal aggression directed at the two doormen resulted in the following response from the larger of the two doormen (MB5): 'Shut the fuck up. You don't know who I am, fuck off you little twat, fuck off you little prick, I'll find out where you live you fucking little cunt' (field notes, May 2005, Club Fusion). His clothes were searched and no drugs were found. Dressed only in his underwear and carrying his clothes and shoes, he was then forcibly escorted out of the venue by the two doormen. This incident is illustrative of the methodologies employed by door staff to control and discipline, which in this venue are governed by a masculine culture of threat and intimidation. Displays of public humiliation have symbolic meaning (Garfinkel 1956; Hobbs et al. 2003) which, in the example above, signal to the policed populace, and young men in particular, the retribution that will come if drugs are traded without sanction, on this door team's watch. On a methodological note, this episode is indicative not only of the ethical tangles I was forced to confront adopting an active membership role, but also of the ways in which I was required to emotionally adjust to 'feeling and display rules' (Hochschild 1983), in order to engage effectively in the emotional labour required of door staff (see Martin 1999). I found it difficult to manage my feelings and to switch to 'hard emotion' mode (Kleinman and Copp 1993) but refusing to comply with these door rules and protocols signalled failure to my colleagues and those I was responsible for policing.

Extending these arguments, I discovered an exception to the emotion work rule outlined above in that some doormen capitalized on the 'overtly sexual nature of their work environment' (Monaghan 2002b) in their preferential treatment, flirtations and, in some instances, sexual encounters with selective female customers (Winlow 2001). Such displays of heterosexual masculinity are pervasive within this occupational setting, as they are in other male-dominated work settings such as policing (Heidensohn 1995; Westmarland 2001, Silvestri 2003) and the coal industry (Padavic 1991; Yount 1991). I found that maintaining rapport required me to modify my own standpoints during interaction with my male colleagues. For example, within the social context of 'door banter', where sexual references, joke, and innuendoes are the main currency of exchange, I was required to 'play the game' and make light of the 'sexual hustling' that was sometimes directed at me (Gurney 1985). I felt in some situations that doormen used overtly sexualised behaviours towards me as a means of testing my suitability to perform the role of female bouncer. At one venue, the head doorman (MB3) responsible for my induction to the venue and its door policies suggested to me after only thirty minutes of my shift that I 'would look good in a bullet proof vest and thigh high boots' (field notes, June 2005, Destiny Bar). Operating within this heterosexual masculinist domain *par excellence* required me to negotiate gender with tact and when responding to such comments, I felt it was important to strike a balance between resistance and compliance (Daniels 1983). Mirroring the sentiments of many of the female bouncers we interviewed in our study (see Hobbs et al. 2007), I found that it was important to show my male colleagues that I was capable of 'handling myself', in other words, to engage in impression management (Goffman 1959) in order to be taken seriously. At the same time, I was required to conform to male-imposed definitions of femininity and the sexualising practices of doormen. In the next section I will develop this point where I focus on 'search work', a body-intensive work task that is highly gendered and a form of interaction with customers that encompasses screening for potential 'deviant' bodies, and conducting intimate and often intrusive searches.

Searching female bodies

I arrive at Club Fusion just before 10 p.m. I peer inside and see one of the doormen walking towards the front doors to let me in. He pushes the door open, grunts at me and walks back to the cashier booth and resumes his conversation with two other doormen. I am not encouraged to join them. I feel excluded and uncomfortable. These men are huge, bald headed and thick necked. Similar-sized doormen arrive, including Darren, the head doorman who is at least 6 ft 4 ins tall. He reminds me of a life-size transformer toy: rigid, square jawed and ready for battle. I have met Darren before. He is expecting me and says, 'I'll get somebody to fix you up', and then proceeds to explain my role and responsibilities: 'Women don't really do the same as men. You are not expected to do the same as men. There are a lot of kick-offs in this venue and you're not expected to get stuck in. You will be doing a lot of the searching tonight.' (field notes, Club Fusion, March 2005). As Darren, the head doorman of Club Fusion illustrates here, sex-stereotyping of female bouncers by male colleagues is based on normative conceptions of femininity and perceptions of women's lesser capacity to 'handle violence' and is a pervasive feature of door work (O'Brien et al. 2008). The allocation of work tasks is based on a highly gendered division of labour that assigns some women to traditional feminine practices, for instance, 'fronting' venues, performing first-aid tasks, and searching and laying their hands upon other women's bodies (see Hobbs et al. 2007). As I have outlined above, the Licensing Act 2003 has served to intensify the gendering of door work in this way because only female security personnel are permitted to search female customers. In Club Fusion, the majority of searches take place at point of entry. Customers are selected by door staff and their bodies, clothes and personal items are searched for illegal drugs, weapons and other contraband items such as alcohol as they enter the venue.

Within the context of 'search work' at Club Fusion, male and female customers are controlled differently and their bodies are screened for potential disorder in highly gendered terms. Male customers entering the club are vetted by male door staff and, if requested to do so, they are instructed to empty the contents of their pockets onto a table. Their bodies are then inspected for metal weapons with a search wand. The search wand is a remote form of body surveillance in that it does not involve physical contact with the body and is only used with males. Women's bodies, in contrast, are searched more meticulously and intrusively, with the objective of checking their bodies for illicit substances rather than weapons. At Club Fusion I was required to frisk female bodies in intimate areas, for instance around the waistband area, underneath the breasts and, if necessary, inside shoes and boots and underneath hats. I was also expected to check the contents of handbags and purses and search items such as mobile phones and lipstick cases where small quantities of illicit substances, like ecstasy pills, can be hidden.

The following extract from my field notes provides further insights into these observations where I reveal the tacit and unspoken rules that underpin the gendering of body surveillance, and provide a reflexive account of how I engaged in search work:

> There are two tables positioned in the entrance area and I am instructed to position myself at one of these tables and search women as they enter the venue. I am immediately introduced to the politics of random

> selection: I ask Dave, who is responsible for searching male customers, if I should select every third or fourth female. He tells me to, 'Pick out girls who [I] think are trying to get drugs in, it's up to [me]'. The front doors are opened. I can see and hear a long queue of customers outside. I have only seconds to take in the significance of the task I am given. What would a young woman who carries drugs into clubs look like? How would she dress? How would she behave? I hesitate for too long. Dave is watching me. I nervously select a young woman who arrives with another female and two males. The only criterion I use to make this first selection is that I notice Dave searching one of the males she is with. I feel uncomfortable placing my hands on her body, touching her flesh and delving into the secret domain of her handbag. As the night progresses, I find confidence. I learn from observing my colleagues to use my body strategically; I block access to the cashier booth using my body; I feel a sense of authority by standing astride; I don't smile or welcome customers, I use limited eye contact.
>
> (Field notes, Club Fusion, March 2005)

Tasked with performing a disciplinary and control role over other women I discovered the power of non-verbal cues as a strategy to induce control, which I found I deployed instinctively. I also realised the symbolic value of my uniformed body and found that my masculine apparel, badge and radio supplied me with a sense of authority and power (see also Manning 1997). As the fieldwork progressed I also became assimilated into the finely tuned occupational rules governing the vetting of customers and learned how to read signs of 'trouble', which in my role as a 'gender specialist' required me to make judgements about potential 'unruly' female customers. Unlike my male colleagues, however, I did not possess local knowledge or previous encounters with Club Fusion patrons that would help inform my decision-making. Instead, I drew on my experiential knowledge of clubbing cultures and familiarity with the embodied signs of ecstasy induced intoxication. More significantly, however, I found that I was making judgements based on a subcultural style and deportment I associated with the white, female 'chav' (Tyler 2008) and selecting women wearing a distinct style of clothing and hair style and accessorized with heavy gold jewellery. I was coding young women's bodies on the basis of cultural signifiers of class, conforming to populist representations of a particular category of British youth (Nayak 2006), and upholding misconceptions about class-based connections with drug taking. In essence, therefore, I was operating in ways not dissimilar to the public police when categorising social groups they associate with threat and disorder (Choongh 1998). When writing up my field notes and reflecting on the night's events after a shift, I found it difficult to reconcile my actions in relation to search work. As I describe in the following sections, this was especially acute when during the course of searching women I discovered illegal drugs.

With the primary function of representing commercial interests, door staff are required to operate strategically and pragmatically when controlling the use and supply of illegal drugs inside venues. This is especially pertinent for venues competing for advantage within the dance-orientated nightclub sector where the consumption of illegal drugs usually represents a core component of their commercial appeal (Hobbs et al. 2003: 224–31). Previous studies of British dance clubs have indicated that security staff working in some venues will regulate drug distribution inside venues by sanctioning particular drug-retail enterprises, and this can often involve taxing profits made from drug sales (see Measham et al. 2001, Chapter 6). My position as rookie, and in all likelihood my status as an 'outsider', meant that I was not introduced to the club-drug-dealing enterprises that may have been operating in the venues where I worked. It was strikingly apparent, however, that ecstasy use and in-club trading was pervasive in both nightclub venues I observed. In fact, its consumption was integral to the music genre on offer and the club ambience being promoted more generally. I observed that door staff seldom found drugs when searching customers' bodies at point of entry. This type of search, as opposed to the more aggressive search that can occur inside the venue, represents a strategy limited in its capacity to 'catch' or deter miscreants. Rather it can be seen as a staging ritual that achieves two important objectives: first, it represents a public display to the police and licensing officials that the venue operates responsibly, which in turn prevents unwanted attention that may threaten the venue's licence. Second, searching customers as they enter the venue, and the manner in which the search is conducted, has symbolic value, establishing lines of authority and setting the tone of the culture of control inside the venue. I discovered drugs at the entry point on only three occasions; each of them involved young women. In two cases I found a single ecstasy pill, and on one occasion a small quantity of cannabis resin. In the example I provide below, my discovery resulted in an 18-year-old woman being taken into police custody for possession of a Class A drug.

I worked only two shifts in Club Cuba, a venue also popular with Club Fusion regulars and where I observed the head doorman routinely, and knowingly, permit under-age female customers entry into the venue. It was an unusually quiet post-midnight period during a Friday evening shift when I stopped and searched a young woman entering the venue alone. I found an ecstasy tablet, somewhat unimaginatively hidden, in the bottom of her cigarette packet. Drawing on Goffman's (1969) insightful observations of individuals' capacity to acquire, reveal and conceal information, the young woman in question was not skilled in techniques of concealment. I sensed from her nervous disposition as she entered the venue that she had something to hide and wanted to be inside the club as quickly as possible. My action to search the young woman's handbag signalled to her that I was suspicious and instead of playing the 'expression game' and diverting my attention away from the location of the ecstasy tablet, she panicked and focused her gaze on the cigarette packet. Goffman states that 'the arousal of suspicion in another so that he suspects he is being suspected can be a strategic loss' (ibid.: 52). Without time to think through the consequences, I emptied out the contents of her cigarette packet onto the table. The confined entrance area of this venue meant that my actions could also be observed by venue staff and doormen positioned in this area and so I had no option but to follow through with the inevitable discovery. The head doorman took command of the situation and contacted the police.

This incident represented a token 'catch', important for dance venues like Club Cuba and Club Fusion because they demonstrate to agents of state control that security staff are operating effectively and responsibly. On a personal and emotional level, I felt as though I had crossed the line and that I was no longer simply researching the field. Playing an active member role meant that on this occasion I was instrumental in criminalising an easy target; a young female recreational user detached from legitimised urban networks.

Conclusions

Ethnographic fieldwork has the potential to penetrate beneath the surface of our social worlds and to uncover the secrets and silences that organize and bind cultures, relationships and interactions. As I have argued in this chapter, operating beneath the public façade of nightclub security work and concealed from the public gaze are a set of occupational codes and work practices that are learnt informally within the enacted environment. I have also illustrated how participant observation allowed me to construct an emotional and embodied understanding of the gendering of night-time security work. As a woman occupying this highly masculinist work setting, I was required to comply with the existing gendered order, for example, via the specific roles that I was tasked with such as searching and laying my hands upon other women's bodies, and to accommodate the overtly sexual nature of this work environment. It may be tempting to consider the recent demand for female bouncers as signalling a dismantling of traditional gender arrangements; however, by situating myself 'inside the interaction' (Ferrell 1998) I discovered that I was reinforcing traditional 'feminine practices' and actualising and reproducing normative gender expectations.

In the final ethnographic episode I describe above, and others that I confess in this chapter, I have illustrated that fieldwork is an embodied enterprise that demands a physical and emotional connection to the field (Coffey 1999). Moreover, the fieldworker's participation can have significant consequences for those being researched, especially when the fieldworker takes on an active membership role. From my perspective as a female fieldworker employed to work as nightclub bouncer, I was particularly sensitive to the ways in which my actions affected the young women I was tasked with controlling. My ethnographic gaze was also preset to observe the behaviours of doormen towards female customers and, in a more general sense, to focus on the construction and performances of femininities and masculinities within these liminal night-time environments. In offering a reflexive and autobiographical account of the field research process, this chapter connects with important methodological debates about epistemology, the researcher and the researched relationship, and subjective experiences of the researcher. These debates have been driven by feminist scholars (see for example, Stanley and Wise 1993), and are currently being energised by current criminological field researchers who call for a more embodied, emotional and reflexive understanding of crime and transgression (Ferrell et al. 2008, Chapter 6; Measham and Moore 2006; Kane 1998). Revealing the secrets and silences that embed the field research process can contribute important layers of understanding about situated meanings and emotions of those we study and the environments they inhabit.

Notes

1 The names of venues and individuals have been changed to maintain anonymity.
2 The majority of doorstaff I worked with were aware of my academic interests; however, as detailed later, I did not disclose my researcher identity to customers and venue staff.
3 This chapter results from an ESRC-funded study entitled 'Women on the door: female bouncers in the new night-time economy' (Award reference number RES-000-23-0384).
4 In some cases permission was required from security firm directors or licensees.
5 As part of the fieldwork I had participated in door supervisors' courses and so I was licensed to work as a door supervisor.

References

Adler, P.A. (1993) *Wheeling and Dealing: An Ethnography of an Upper-Level Drug Dealing and Smuggling Community*, New York: Columbia University Press.

Adler, P.A. and Adler, P. (1987) *Membership Roles in Field Research*, London: Sage.

Bulmer, M. (1982) 'Ethical problems in social research: the case of participant observation', in M. Bulmer (ed.) *Social Research Ethics: An Examination of the Merits of Covert Participant Observation*, London: Macmillan.

Butler, J. (1990) *Gender Trouble: Feminism and the Subversion of Identity*, New York: Routledge.

Choongh, S. (1998) 'Policing the dross: a social disciplinary model of policing', *British Journal of Criminology*, 38: 623–34.

Coffey, A. (1999) *The Ethnographic Self: Fieldwork and the Representation of Identity*, London: Sage.

Daniels, A. (1983) 'Self deception and self-discovery in fieldwork', *Qualitative Sociology*, 6: 195–214.

DCMS (Department of Culture, Media and Sport) (2007) *Guidance Issued Under the Section 182 of the Licensing Act 2003 and Guidance to Police Officers on the Operation of Closure Powers in Part 8 of the Licensing Act 2003*, London: DCMS.

Erickson, B.H., Albanese, P. and Drakulie. S. (2000) 'Gender on a jagged edge: the security industry, its clients, and the reproduction and revision of gender', *Work and Occupations*, 27 (3): 294–318.

Ferrell, J. (1998) 'Criminological verstehen: inside the immediacy of crime', in J. Ferrell and M. Hamm (eds.) *Ethnography on the Edge: Crime, Deviance and Field Research*, Boston: Northeastern University Press.

Ferrell, J. and Hamm, M. (1998) *Ethnography on the Edge: Crime, Deviance and Field Research*, Boston: Northeastern University Press.

Ferrell, J., Hayward, K. and Young, J. (2008) *Cultural Criminology: An Invitation*, London: Sage.

Garfinkel, H. (1956) 'Conditions of successful degradation ceremonies', *American Journal of Sociology*, 61 (5): 420–24.

Goffman, E. (1990 [1959]) *The Presentation of Self in Everyday Life*, London: Penguin.

—— (1969) *Strategic Interaction*, Oxford: Basil Blackwell.

Gurney, J. (1985) 'Not one of the guys: female researcher in a male-dominated setting', *Qualitative Sociology*, 8 (1): 42–62

Hadfield, P. (2008) 'From threat to promise: nightclub "security", governance and consumer elites', *British Journal of Criminology*, 48 (4): 429–47.

Heidensohn, F. (1995) *Women in Control? The Role of Women in Law Enforcement*, Oxford: Oxford University Press.

Hobbs, D. (1988) *Doing the Business*, Oxford: Clarendon.

Hobbs, D., O'Brien, K. and Westmarland, L. (2007) 'Connecting the gendered door: women, violence and doorwork', *British Journal of Sociology*, 58 (1): 21–38.

Hobbs, D., Hadfield, P., Lister, S. and Winlow, S. (2002) 'Door lore: the art and economics of intimidation', *British Journal of Criminology*, 42 (2): 352–370.

—— (2003) *Bouncers: Violence and Governance in the Night-time Economy*, Oxford: Oxford University Press.

Hochschild, A. (1983) *The Managed Heart: Commercialization of Human Feeling*, Berkeley: University of California Press.

Kane, S. (1998) 'Reversing the ethnographic gaze: experiments in cultural criminology', in J. Ferrell and M. Hamm (eds) *Ethnography on the Edge: Crime, Deviance and Field Research*, Boston: Northeastern University Press.

Kleinman, (1999) 'Experience and its moral modes: culture, human conditions, and disorder', in G.B. Peterson (ed.) *The Tanner Lectures on Human Values*, Salt Lake City, UT: University of Utah Press.

Kleinman, S. and Copp, M.A. (1993) *Emotions and Fieldwork*, Beverly Hills, CA: Sage.

Lugosi, P. (2006) 'Between overt and covert research: concealment and disclosure in an ethnographic study of commercial hospitality', *Qualitative Inquiry*, 12 (3): 541–61.

Maher, L. (1997) *Sexed Work: Gender, Race and Resistance in a Brooklyn Drug Market*, Oxford: Oxford University Press.

Manning, P.K. (1997) *Police Work: The Social Organisation of Policing* (2nd edn), Cambridge, MA and London: MIT Press.

Martin, S.E. (1990) *'Breaking and Entering': Policewomen on Patrol*, Berkeley, CA: University of California Press.

—— (1999) 'Police force or police service? Gender and emotional Labor', *The Annals of the American Academy*, 561 (1): 111–26.

Measham, F. and Moore, K. (2006) 'Reluctant reflexivity, implicit insider knowledge and the development of club studies', in B. Sanders (ed.) *Drugs, Clubs and Young People, Sociological and Public Health Perspectives*, Aldershot: Ashgate.

Measham, F., Aldridge, J. and Parker, H. (2001) *Dancing on Drugs: Risk, Health and Hedonism in the British Club Scene*, London: Free Association Books.

Lofland, J. and Lofland, L.H. (1995) *Analysing Social Settings: A Guide to Qualitative Observation and Analysis*, Belmont, CA and London: Thomson Wadsworth.

Miller, J. (2002) 'The strengths and limits of "doing gender" for understanding street crime', *Theoretical Criminology*, 6 (4): 433–60.

Mitchell, (1993) *Secrecy and Fieldwork*, London: Sage Publications.

Monaghan, L. (2002a) 'Hard men, shop boys and others: embodying competence in a masculinist occupation', *The Sociological Review*, 50 (3): 334–55.

—— (2002b) 'Opportunity, pleasure and risk: an ethnography of urban male heterosexualies', *Journal of Contemporary Ethnography*, 31 (4): 440–77.

—— (2002c) 'Embodying gender, work and organisation: solidarity, cool loyalties and contested hierarchy in a masculinist occupation', *Gender, Work and Organisation*, 9 (5): 504–36.

—— (2002d) 'Regulating unruly bodies: work tasks, conflict and violence in Britain's night time economy', *British Journal of Sociology*, 53 (3): 403–29.

—— (2003) 'Danger on the doors: bodily risk in a demonised occupation', *Health, Risk and Society*, 5 (1): 11–31.

Nayak, A (2006) *Race, Place and Globalisation: Youth Cultures in a Changing World*, Oxford: Berg.

O'Brien, K., Hobbs, D. and Westmarland, L. (2008) 'Negotiating violence and gender: security and the night time economy in the UK', in S. Gendrot and P. Spierenburg (eds) *Violence in Europe: Historical and Contemporary Perspectives*, New York: Springer.

Padavic, I. (1991) 'The re-creation of gender in a male workplace', *Symbolic Interaction*, 14 (3): 279–94.

Polsky, N. (1967) *Hustlers, Beats and Others*, Chicago: Aldine.

Reinharz, S. (1992) *Feminist Methods in Social Research*, New York: Oxford University Press.

Silvestri, M. (2003) *Women in Charge: Policing, Gender and Leadership*, Cullompton, Devon: Willan Publishing.

Simmel, G. (1906) 'The sociology of secrecy and secret societies', *American Journal of Sociology*, 11: 441–98.

Stanley, L. and Wise, S. (1993) *Breaking Out Again: Feminist Ontology and Epistemology*, London: Routledge.

Tyler, I (2008) 'Chav mum chav scum: class disgust in contemporary Britain', *Feminist Media Studies*, 8 (1): 17–34.

Van Maanen, J. (1978) 'The asshole', in P.K. Manning and J. Van Mannen (eds) *Policing: A View from the Streets,* Santa Monica, CA: Goodyear.

—— (1988) *Tales from the Field,* Chicago: University of Chicago Press.

Wakefield, A. (2003) *Selling Security. The Private Policing of Public Space*, Cullompton, Devon: Willan.

West, C. and Fenstermaker, S. (1995) 'Doing difference', *Gender and Society*, 9: 8–37.

West, C. and Zimmerman, D.H. (1987) 'Doing gender', *Gender and Society*, 1 (2):125–51.

Westmarland, L. (2001) *Gender and Policing: Sex Power and Police Culture*, Cullompton, Devon: Willan.
Winlow, S. (2001) *Badfellas: Crime, Tradition and New Masculinities*, Oxford: Berg.
Winlow, S. and Hall, S. (2006) *Violent Night*, Oxford: Berg.
Yount, K.R. (1991), Ladies, flirts, and tomboys: strategies for managing sexual harassment in an underground coal mine', *Journal of Contemporary Ethnography,* 19 (4): 396–422.

10 Raising the curtain on survey work

Rebekah Wilson

In this chapter, I use a theatrical metaphor to discuss my experience of face-to-face survey work. The plot seems simple: PhD student visits London streets to survey 450 passers-by on the topic of marital surnames. She performs the same routine each time, neatly collects her questionnaires and returns home. Or so a typical textbook might say. But what *really* happens when the curtain is raised? Who is the researcher behind the lead role? Does she perform the same character each time she meets people? Is she comfortable being on stage? How is her performance shaped by those watching? Do they ever heckle and jeer? Does she fall flat? These questions are seldom asked of survey work. We are given just basic details about the central characters, and learn nothing about their research experiences. How did they act and how did others react? This chapter draws attention to the unspoken realities of survey work to reveal what (and who) hides behind this seemingly silent approach to data collection.

My recital of survey work calls for a reflexive approach. This act of self-reference is usually avoided within quantitative arenas. What would be gained, in my case, by revealing that the face-to-face delivery of questionnaires cannot be standardised? It would appear to limit the validity of my findings. But is this really the case? Ryan and Golden (2006: 1198), for instance, when discussing their quantitative study, suggest 'a reflexive approach would not undermine the value of the research study but would add a depth of understanding about how, where, when and by whom data were collected'. My reflexive account is guided by Goffman's dramaturgical model (1959). This framework helps to explain my role within the research process, for example the characters I played and how these were managed. It is also used to highlight some of the dilemmas I faced in carrying out face-to-face survey work that would go unspoken in a conventional textbook account.

Taking to the stage

Goffman's dramaturgical model suggests that social interaction is a theatrical performance. People (known as actors) perform 'front stage' behaviours to convey a particular impression of themselves to others – although this might be contradicted when an actor is 'backstage'. The frontstage behaviours I performed (and was consequently fatigued by) were mainly showcased at libraries, pubs, medical centres and cafés across London. The corners of these sites became backstage areas. My performances were regulated by what Goffman calls 'impression management' (i.e. my appearance and manner was controlled to convey particular impressions). Yet, adding a feminist perspective, my age, gender, size and ethnicity were not stage-managed.[1] Certainly, as we know from authors such as Phoenix (1994), such markers can play a major role in research relationships.

Showcasing my behaviour required certain props that my audience could identify as belonging to a particular performance (my 'personal front', in Goffman's terms). But, which character should I play? Student in jeans? Academic wearing glasses? Market researcher with clipboard? How should I walk? What should I say? Such debates typically go unheard in quantitative accounts. Nothing would be said about the rehearsals I staged in front of my bathroom mirror ('dramaturgical discipline', as said by Goffman). 'Hi there, have you got a minute?' Nothing would be said about my anxiety as I headed off to ask complete strangers to do me a favour. Readers wouldn't know that I longed to stay on the bus when I had arrived at fieldwork sites. They would be oblivious to the sleepless nights I endured before heading out and the tired muscles I suffered on my return home.

While I have interrupted strangers before, requesting the time or directions is hardly the same as asking someone to engage with a research instrument. Not only did I need to enter their personal space but also call for their time. Both of these are precious commodities within a culture that emphasises personal ownership and individual choice. It soon became clear that potential participants were entirely private beings even though they were using public spaces. My reluctance to perform in front of these people may result from my Englishness, as cultural standards on physical intimacy differ. Fox (2004), for instance, claims the English are obsessed with privacy. But perhaps my reluctance also speaks of extreme individualisation within neo-liberal society and its effects on social interaction.[2]

Judging the performance

My desired audience was those people who would agree to complete a questionnaire. I had intended to reach such people on the street. They would be asked to stop and answer a series of questions which I would read out loud. But this took too long when piloting and I decided that people needed to be sitting. This led me to cafés, pubs, libraries and waiting rooms, and it seemed polite to ask permission before approaching customers and patients. Those standing behind counters became judges who presided over my performance. I shouted over coffee grinders and mimed the ticking of boxes. They replied: 'What's it for? Which university? How long will it take?' They often checked with managers who lurked behind office doors. Some asked me to write letters or call back another day, while others let their customers decide.

Even with prior permission, access remained a problem. I queued with a group of sales reps at a medical centre to speak to a receptionist. She wanted to check my credentials with the doctor despite seeing an email he'd sent. I was asked to wait on her side of the desk, so sat for 15 minutes among semen sample assessments listening to complaints from patients. They had been up all night with aches and pains, yet I would soon be asking them to complete a questionnaire. I listened to private conversations like: 'Has your mother had this cream before?' It was in settings like this that my situation did not fit the dramaturgical model. Goffman suggests that, like an actor's personal front, her setting needs to be identifiable as belonging to a particular performance. My settings gave no clues about my role. Behind a desk at a medical centre, I might be seen as a receptionist rather than an outsider waiting to hand out questionnaires.[3]

The panel of judges played a crucial role in gaining access to my audience. It was in these situations that the power-dynamic that usually exists between researcher and researched was reversed (as in work by, for example, Smart 1984; Phoenix 1994; Grenz 2002). The judges were performing their own show of managerial authority by allowing or disallowing access to their customers or patients. Yet, once given access, I took the role of judge. I decided who to interrupt through 'unfocused interaction' (Goffman 1963). That is, while flicking through books or ordering coffee, I constantly glanced at those around me. Nothing was said. No eye contact was made. But all the time, while trying to look anonymous, I was scanning their appearance wondering who would be next. Did they want that coffee to go? I hoped for the sake of my project that they didn't.

The aim of such unfocused interaction was to gauge the age and gender of potential participants for two quotas. This called upon my knowledge of cultural standards (or perhaps stereotypes). Like me, each person had their own personal front that, on the basis of current norms, enabled me to identify certain performances. I found myself asking: How is their hair styled? What colour is it? How much hair do they have? I listened for footsteps and voices. Were they heavy or soft, high or low? The two quotas encouraged me to approach people who I might have normally avoided. But still, I was out of my comfort zone. Should I interrupt the male builder doing a crossword, the veiled woman reading to her children, the middle-aged man using his laptop or the elderly woman empting biscuits from her shopping trolley to eat with her mug of tea in the library?[4]

Behind the curtain

My unfocused interactions required a hiding place, or at least somewhere I could blend into the background. So, I lurked behind bookcases in libraries and racks of leaflets in medical centres. These places also served as a retreat. I was constantly entering other people's personal space and was fully exposed to their remarks be they polite or rude, friendly or hostile, joking or serious. My hiding places, be they bookcases, toilets or back-row seats, offered me protection from such encounters. Added to this, searching for people, approaching them, performing a routine, answering questions, being accepted or rejected, made me feel tired. Thus, I relished having an hiding place or an 'escape hatch' (Murray 2003: 391) to which I could withdraw.

The feeling of exposure may have been something to embrace, as it was a chance to uncover more about my audience. Indeed, surveying face-to-face gave me an insight into people's lives not usually achievable by just using a questionnaire.[5] Those who felt their stories deserved more than a tick-box gave me access to their lives. I became their audience rather than they being mine. They told me how marriage, divorce, remarriage, giving birth, adoption and immigration had caused problems with regards to surnames. One woman explained that she, her 18-year-old son and six-year-old daughter each used different surnames. She had requested, during court proceedings with her daughter's father some years ago, that the girl be given her surname. But, having heard nothing since, she asked me how to take action, requiring a shift in character that I felt unable to enact.

Once people had agreed to take part, I handed over a questionnaire and retreated. I was no longer performing at this point, but was usually still on view. It was an interval that made me uncomfortable. Was I pressurising people by being around? What if they took issue with my questions? So, I exited stage left, read leaflets on meningitis, made frequent toilet trips or scribbled in my notebook. Such awkwardness intensified as I sat among those who had refused to take part or those who had given up. I hoped they would leave so they wouldn't watch my routine again. I was keen to avoid eye contact as this could prompt questioning, as was the case when sitting with two women in a waiting room. One remarked that her doctor was very attentive and quite aware that she didn't take her medicine or quit smoking. The other agreed. This prompted the following tirade which was intended for my ears:

What do they know about smoking, drinking, eating? They didn't live through the war. How dare they tell us what to do? Like this study. Are they paying me? People in the government know nothing. They just read books. They haven't experienced the real world. They are all boys. Not like the old days when they were men. They need experience. Are you going to tell us what to think? It's a bloody nanny state. Why would you want to know how people live? What's the point? People just do what they want to do.

The backstage areas I used needed to be well calculated. They couldn't encroach upon the day-to-day workings of the site and needed to be good vantage points. At a library, I would take regular tours through bookcases, each time returning to a desk surrounded by dictionaries and street atlases. Yet, at a medical centre, I had to settle for the furthest chair from the door. These areas lessened my sense of exposure, as did one item requested by a library – a badge showing my name and institution. This became part of my personal front and I felt naked without it. I felt it took the emphasis off me as people would focus on its wording rather than my face. It also seemed to legitimise my performance.[6] People could see my 'student' character was genuine and had a better idea of what to expect from my performance. Indeed, a few people only took part because of my scholarly role or because they had a fondness for my institution.

Observing people required a hiding place, and this presented me with an ethical dilemma. Did it matter that I was watching people as a researcher rather than a member of the public? Was I misleading them into thinking I was someone else? Did they think I was an ordinary member of the audience unaware that I was watching their actions (a 'Shill' in Goffman's terms)? Was it reasonable to note down private conversations, such as the woman who told me about her attempt to change her daughter's surname? Similar to Birch (1998) and Murray (2003), I asked myself if I was being honest with people. I certainly felt uncomfortable secretly noting their reactions and comments as I sat among them, but less so when I was backstage. Yet, just because I was out of view, were my actions more ethical?

And......action!

At each fieldwork site, my performance revolved around the same plot: to persuade people to complete a questionnaire. However, this was not tackled in the same way each time. Indeed, as Goffman suggests, society is not a homogeneous creature and we act differently according to time, place and audience. So, in the context of my survey, I might energetically approach people in the morning, but by late afternoon simply ask: 'Can you fill this out before you go?' My performance also depended on the rules and dynamics of the places where people were surveyed. The libraries, for instance, had strict policies about noise, but it was quite normal to strike up conversation with people in pubs. The people using public spaces also impacted on my performance, as I negotiated different positions of status and power.

Looking back, my audience had a major impact on my performance. I would observe their gestures, moods and predicaments and construct my opening line accordingly. I might say: 'I can see you are busy' or 'I know it's early'. I would seek out commonalities: 'Which university did you go to? Such performances correspond with Grice's (1989) 'co-operative principle'. That is, I tried to ensure that the purpose of my conversation was continued by others. Also, using cultural norms for appearance, I tried to ascertain which performance would elicit a positive response. Murray (2003: 391) summarises this scenario as follows:

> Just what action is taken in any given situation depends upon the definition the researcher holds to be relevant to the particular situation. Definitions held, and therefore actions taken, shift and change in response to

the participants who are present and the various statuses and identities they invoke.

Using Murray's explanation, there were other actions I took in response to the participants who were present. I would make apologies for my questionnaire, despite it being a prized piece of work that I had spent months perfecting and reflecting upon:[7] 'Sorry it is so long', 'Thanks for sticking it out', 'If you get bored, you can always fill out one of these'. This performance leads me to Hochschild (1983; 2003). She draws on Goffman's dramaturgical model, but suggests we control our emotions not just the surface of our performance. It is on the basis of 'feeling rules' that we know which emotions to exhibit in particular settings. This idea and her thoughts on 'emotional labour' are particularly instructive when considering the emotions that I displayed to my audience in order to promote the completion of my questionnaire, such as displays of humour, sympathy and even self-deprecation.

The most successful of my performances were watched by an audience of one. It was particularly difficult to present my routine to people in groups, as they were often engaged in conversation. So I mainly relied on people sitting alone, sometimes with children in pushchairs. This excluded several clusters like mothers in libraries and teenagers chatting over text messages. At times, it was difficult to know who was alone. I might approach someone in a café, only for them to be joined by someone else later which meant they gave less time to the questionnaire. They occasionally discussed questions with their companion, or tried to hide their answers from their spouse. I overheard one woman ask her husband if he could finish her questionnaire because she didn't feel like doing the rest. Other women said they would pass it to their husbands when they arrived, suggesting that their views were identical or that his were more relevant.

In contrast to my successful performances, my actions were less effective when dealing with my oldest age quota, the over-70s. It became apparent that, in planning my research strategy, I had failed to fully consider the physical condition of these audience members. They were just one group within my sample who could be easily reached as they went about their daily lives. Yet I became deeply embarrassed as they strained to read my questions. A woman who had just had a cataract operation and was waiting for new glasses asked me: 'Am I ticking the right boxes?' The hand of a man who had suffered a stroke shook furiously as he tried to grip the sides of the questionnaire. There were similar encounters elsewhere and I tried to offer assistance by ticking boxes or turning pages. I might skip some of the questions though, reducing it from four pages to two, if the task seemed like too much hard work.

My survey work called for a multitude of identities and Goffman's dramaturgical model helps to disentangle these. It is when applying this theatrical metaphor that I have noticed the difficulty I faced in staying loyal to my role as a feminist researcher. Take, for instance, the characters I played when dealing with men in pubs: desperate female student and tolerant female patron. These roles were assigned to me on entering the pubs, again showing how the balance of power shifted within my research. A pub manager introduced me to some of his regulars: 'Could you help this young lady?', 'Could you spare a second for a lovely lady?' The men joked with the manager that he only wanted help when it involved a woman. They laughed about always having time to help 'a lady'. I smiled through gritted teeth, annoyed at myself for accepting such gendered power relations.

The avoidance of seriousness is a common feature of English pub talk, according to Fox (2004). Not only that, but pub banter is often based on sexist humour. I listened to several jokes about nagging wives: 'My wife drove me to drink, but I still haven't thanked her for it', said one man quoting W.C. Fields. He got divorced 20 years ago. 'She took everything.' He was not alone in his cynicism. Another man had been married and divorced three times. He was much happier with his meals-for-one. His co-drinker was only at the pub to get away from his wife. There was no way he was answering questions about marriage customs. These remarks emphasise the broader social context in which my research is placed. I was annoyed by the men's comments, yet they were so familiar. Likewise, my conversations with participants show that some people are frustrated and even angered by the custom of marital surname change. Yet, they go along with the practice because it is so familiar.

As a tolerant female patron, I listened to a pub manager tease his friend: 'He's going to pop the question soon.' I smiled. It was a 'tolerant-but-slightly-superior smile' that is 'characteristic of females listening patiently to male pub-goers' (Fox 2004: 103). His soon-to-be engaged friend took a questionnaire and muttered his way through it as I sat beside him: 'Feminism is a bad thing', 'Women are going to take over the world', 'It won't be long before they get the top jobs'. I found myself laughing. His girlfriend had more qualifications than him and he was happy for her to earn the cash. He'd be a lazy house husband. A female colleague objected: 'What do you think women do at home all day?' He made a few jokes about watching daytime TV. He asked: 'What's my relationship status?' 'Am I dating?' 'More like shagging', the manager said. 'We go on dates', he insisted. 'Only if you can get a shag at the end', a colleague sniggered. Again, I laughed along, despite feeling uncomfortable. I silenced my usual rebukes to avoid conflict and get my questionnaires completed. But this raises questions: Is such collusion ever acceptable? When, where and for what purpose?

All quiet on the set

The pub encounters show the ways in my audience attempted to silence my performance. There were in fact many more men who waved me away or declined to take part without making eye contact. They often appeared too busy to be interrupted. Several laughed on learning the survey was about marriage, as if the subject didn't concern them. They certainly seemed less accustomed to being approached than women and less agreeable to my line of questioning. Their main concern was that my survey had a 'strong female bias' which made it 'sexist' in their opinion. A few pointed to their heads to show that my 'sexism test' had been found out, despite this being imaginary. One man bawled: 'What's the point of me, or any other man, filling this out?'

The men above seemed unsympathetic to the questions I was raising. One man said it was 'just traditional' for married women to take their husbands' surnames, but if he married me, and if I was the main wage earner, then I would be in charge. Thus, he could take my surname and I could 'beat him up' if he didn't do so. Others, including women, were defensive in their replies, assuming that I was picking fault with their lives. Such reactions correspond with Ingraham's (1999) work on weddings and heterosexuality. She argues that critical examinations of sacred or valued practices and institutions (in my case surname change by married women) are 'frequently resisted and suppressed' by researchers because their readers might view such discussions as 'personal attacks on themselves or on heterosexuals as a group rather than as institutional analyses or inventories' (ibid.: 9).

The hostile reactions of some women to feminist-led research have been noted by researchers such as Millen (1997), Luff (1999) and Andrews (2002). Such encounters can produce, as I discovered, uncomfortable feelings and much frustration. One woman, whom I was unfortunate to meet twice at a library, was particularly critical of my research. She 'didn't agree' with my questions and thought the questionnaire was 'meaningless'. But, sitting next to me a week later, she seemed to have acquired an interest in my work and asked about my response rate. Such interest was short-lived though as she began to wax lyrical about 'traditional families' where '*men* knew their roles'. She expressed the view that 'children suffer when mums work and leave them with childminders'. Then she asked: 'Wouldn't I be satisfied just to see my children grow?' Surely I wouldn't have spent weeks handing out questionnaires if I thought it unnecessary.

The outbursts above angered me immensely, but my reactions to them varied. Replying to the woman, I spoke generally about opportunities now available to women (only to be asked if we really needed these). But, the man who bawled is the only participant to whom I gave details about myself. It was only by presenting a compelling front ('dramatic realisation', as said by Goffman) that I could stress why the research was so important to me. My usual reaction, however, resonates with Grenz's (2002: 21) account of interviewing male clients of female prostitutes, where she 'responded with "feminine" politeness to avoid insults and keep the interview going'. She refers to this as 'obedience to power'. Yet, she also describes her silence as an 'exercise of power' since it enabled her to collect a particular discourse. Perhaps I was exercising power by accepting the conditions that would return the largest number of questionnaires?

The criticism I encountered sometimes occurred in the form of whispery moans ('staging talk' in Goffman's terms, i.e. gossiping about the technical aspects of a performance). The two women who complained about government interference muttered to each about the length of the questionnaire: 'Especially for this time in the morning', 'Isn't it awful?' I joked with them saying they didn't look too busy, but they weren't amused. One said: 'I've come to visit the doctor, not go to school.' One woman waved a questionnaire in the air and pointed in my direction as she spoke to a group of women about why she was delayed. One man prolonged the completion of his questionnaire, over-dramatising the effort involved each time I walked past. He said: 'This must get the prize for the most boring questionnaire.' I thanked him. He later revealed that he hadn't meant anything personally. He's 'always like that', apparently.

There were also ways that other people, not just me, were silenced in the research process. They had better things to do with their time and I couldn't force them to take part. Some took issue with surveys in general: 'I don't do surveys.' Some thought the topic was a waste of time: 'What's the point?', 'What use does it have?' Some might have taken part but were too busy: 'I have to get to the osteopath in Kingston.' And, others thought themselves exempt: 'I'm not married', 'I'm not a woman', 'I'm getting divorced' or 'I've been married too long'. Others thought the task was 'beyond them' or that they were 'too old-fashioned'. One elderly man returned an incomplete questionnaire saying: 'We don't know about all these things like living together and swapping partners.' It is difficult to draw inferences from such comments. Were my actions the cause of their refusal or were they simply performing their right to silence?

Aside from what was expressed through visible traits, my performances were rather quiet. Most people were simply told that the survey was for 'a university project' and this was also written on the questionnaire. The badge I wore gave some details about me, but these were minimal. One trait that remained hidden was my sexuality and relationship status. Such 'mystification', to use Goffman's phase, was enacted to avoid any damage to my performance. Exposing that I was married might draw me into conversations about my surname decision. Not only this, revealing that my surname remains unchanged, was likely to label me as a feminist (Embleton and King 1984; Atkinson 1987; Murray 1997; Suter 2004). Fearing this might turn people away, I attempted to pass as single, helped by not owning a wedding ring. These were acts of temporary rejection that I hoped would ultimately enable me to understand more about feminism and marriage during my PhD write-up.

Final curtain falls

In writing this chapter my audience has changed. I am no longer standing before strangers in the street, but am facing an academic audience who will judge my performance in a different way. Later on, such readers will also critique the findings of my PhD research in a certain way because of the reflexive approach taken in this chapter. Aside from this front stage area, no longer does my backstage involve bookcases and toilets, but the desk where I planned my research strategy many months ago. My experience of surveying, and the responses contained within the pages of my questionnaires, now sits alongside 31 follow-up interviews through which questionnaire participants told me their personal stories of marital naming. I have begun to consider the ways people reacted to these methods and the processes that enabled me to hear their opinions and experiences. Both were interactive processes that required specific performances.

The application of Goffman's dramaturgical model shows that both my survey and interviews were based on relationships that involved an interaction between me and my audience. Like the survey, I needed to enter the personal space of my interviewees and also call for their time. When interviews were taking place, I had to think about when to speak, when to be silent, when to make eye contact and when to take notes? There was a need to consider my responses too. Should I be amused by or sympathetic to their stories? Like the survey, I was also confronted with anti-feminist remarks and was unsure if and how to challenge these. It is apparent, therefore, that there are commonalities between the collection of quantitative and qualitative data when using a face-to-face method. But, it is only when taking a reflexive approach that these became apparent.

To conclude, in this chapter, I have made clear some aspects of survey work that typically go unheard. I have shown the face-to-face delivery of questionnaires to be a highly interactive process requiring many different performances. I have also drawn attention to some of the dilemmas I faced when interacting with my audience. Yet, revealing these aspects has not been easy. I wrestled with traditional ideas about how quantitative research should be written. Were there aspects of my work that *really* should remain hidden? Would I appear incompetent even with several years of research training? Would my actions be seen as exploitative despite my endless worries about ethics? No, for these concerns are common to all researchers. The problem for those of us using quantitative techniques, however, is that we face greater pressure to conform to 'normal' scientific procedures. Breaking the silence that surrounds quantitative work is challenging, but has the potential to transform both research practice and the knowledge gained from our research endeavours.

Acknowledgements

I would like to thank Sarah Blake, Alice Gavin, Nick McGlynn, Aliya Rao and Miloney Thakrar for helping to distribute questionnaires. Thanks also to Hazel Johnstone for her assistance with printing.

Notes

1 Social class is not included here as I became conscious of changing my north of England accent to a more southern and perhaps 'educated' voice as I performed my role as a PhD student. Also, as I explain later, I attempted to pass as single rather than (heterosexually) married.

2 Thanks to Alice Gavin for her comments on this point.
3 A small number of people took a questionnaire thinking it was connected to the location in which they were being surveyed and looked somewhat bemused when it was collected. As Goffman suggests, social establishments (to which his model was originally applied) are places 'surrounded by fixed barriers to perception in which a particular kind of activity regularly takes place' (1959: 231). The activity I was carrying out was irregular even though most people were familiar with the conventions of survey work.
4 Items such as books, laptops and mobile phones were used as 'barrier signals' (Fox 2004:85). They indicated that a person was unavailable and also marked their personal space.
5 Perreault (2002) gives an excellent account of information that is missed when using questionnaires.
6 However, in wearing a badge, I was asked how to work the photocopier, find a book or turn on a computer. One man asked me to make sense of letter he had received about incapacity benefit, and another asked me to write a letter to the Driver and Vehicle Licensing Agency about his stolen car.
7 Questionnaires are often presented as unproblematic instruments that appear as if from nowhere. But my experience shows that creating a questionnaire can be a highly complex and time-consuming process. No doubt I could write a paper about how I agonised over my questionnaire's content, design and length: 'Should I split this question into two?' 'Should I move this question further down?' I was so pleased to finally see it printed that I hesitated about writing identification numbers on each copy for fear of spoiling them.

References

Andrews, M. (2002) 'Feminist research with non-feminist or anti-feminist women: meeting the challenge', *Feminism & Psychology* 12(1): 55–77.

Atkinson, D. L. (1987) 'Names and Titles: Maiden Name Retention and the Use of Ms', *Journal of the Atlantic Provinces Linguistic Association* 9: 56–83.

Birch, M. (1998) 'Re/constructing research narratives: self and sociological identity in alternative settings ', in J. Ribbens and R. Edwards (eds) *Feminist dilemmas in qualitative research: Public knowledge and private lives*, London: Sage

Embleton, S. M. and King, R. (1984) 'Attitudes towards maiden name retention', *Onamastica Canadiana* 66: 11–22.

Fox, K. (2004) *Watching the English: The Hidden Rules of English Behaviour*, London: Hodder.

Goffman, E. (1959) *The Presentation of Self in Everyday Life*, Hammondsworth Penguin Books.

——(1963) *Behaviour in Public Places. Notes on the Social Organisation of Gatherings*, New York: Free Press.

Grenz, S. (2002) 'Power relations in interviews with sex-workers' clients – or how a research situation can parallel prostitution', in S. Chopra, S. Grenz, C. Hemmings, C. Mclean, S. Mullassery, L. Narayanaswamy, C. Pedwell, L. Perreault, A. Willey and J. Wilson (eds) *Marginal Research: Reflections onLlocation and Representation*, London: London School of Economics, Gender Institute: Research in progress series.

Grice, H. P. (1989) *Studies in the Way of Words*, Cambridge, MA, London: Harvard University Press.

Hochschild, A. R. (1983) *The Managed Heart: Commercialisation of Human Feeling*, Berkeley, CA: University of California Press.

——(2003) *The Managed Heart: Commercialisation of Human Feeling*, 20th anniversary, with a new afterword Edition, Berkeley, CA: University of California Press.

Ingraham, C. (1999) *White Weddings: Romancing Heterosexuality in Popular Culture*, New York: Routledge.

Luff, D. (1999) 'Dialogue across the divides: moments of rapport and power in feminist research with anti-feminist women', *Sociology Volume* 33(4): 687–703.

Millen, D. (1997) 'Some methodological and epistemological issues raised by doing feminist research on non-feminist women', *Sociological Research Online* 2(3): http://www.socresonline.org.uk/socresonline/2/3/3.html.

Murray, S. B. (2003) 'A spy, a shill, a go-between, or a sociologist: unveiling the 'observer' in participant observer', *Qualitative Review* 3(3): 377–95.

Murray, T. E. (1997) 'Attitudes towards Married Women's Last Names: Evidence from the American Midwest', *Names* 45: 163–83.

Phoenix, A. (1994) 'Practising feminist research: The intersection of gender and 'race' in the research process', in M. Maynard and J. Purvis (eds) *Researching Women's Lives from a Feminist Perspective*, London: Taylor Francis.

Ryan, L. and Golden, A. (2006) "Tick the box please': a reflexive approach to doing quantitative social research', *Sociology* 40(6): 1191–1200.

Smart, C. (1984) *TheTties that Bind. Marriage and the Reproduction of Patriarchal Relations,* London: Routledge & Kegan Paul.

Suter, E. A. (2004) 'Tradition never goes out of style: the role of tradition in women's naming practices', *The Communication Review* 7: 57–87.

Part III

Silence, secrecy and telling research stories

11 Avoiding the 'R-word'

Racism in feminist collectives

Kathy Davis

This chapter focuses on some of the methodological problems which I have encountered in writing a history of one of the first, most famous, and most respected feminist collectives in the US – the Boston Women's Health Book Collective (BWHBC) – based on interviews with its founding members.[1] As I was beginning my research, the collective had just gone through a particularly turbulent period of conflict centring around the issues of power inequalities within the organization, and racism. Like many feminist groups which began in the early seventies, the founders of the BWHBC were predominantly white, middle-class, college-educated women. As their project grew, they hired staff members – often women from different class, educational, and ethnic or racial backgrounds than the founders. This led to a series of conflicts and ultimately resulted in the staff resigning *en masse*. To the consternation of the founders, former staff members publicly accused the BWHBC of racism and, more generally, of 'unsisterly' behaviour in an open letter to a leading feminist journal under the title 'It happened here, too!' (Sojourner 1997).

Confronted with the accusation of racism in their midst, the founders as predominantly white feminists found themselves stuck between the urge to talk about racism (thereby displaying their commitment to anti-racism) and the desire to be silent (thereby avoiding personal guilt or collective responsibility). To be accused of racism by the staff was obviously painful and confusing for a group that had prided itself on its commitment to fighting class discrimination, racism, and homophobia, not only on the pages of *Our Bodies, Ourselves*, but within the organization as well. The founders were frustrated after years of negotiation and saddened by their inability to resolve the problems in their own midst. Moreover, the public accusation of racism evoked a shock wave in the larger 'feminist community' in the US. For many feminists, it was hard to reconcile their image of the feminist group which had brought *Our Bodies, Ourselves* into so many women's lives with accusations of elitism, unwillingness to share power with newcomers, and racism.

The public charge of racism automatically placed the founders before a painful dilemma. On the one hand, their ideological commitment to universal sisterhood and the abolition of all forms of social inequality, including racism, made it essential that racism be addressed and combated within their group. On the other hand, the merest whiff of racist practices, let alone displays of insulting or discriminatory behaviour on the part of white women towards women of colour would not only be ideologically unacceptable and morally repugnant. They would be shameful, something to be pushed away, dismissed, or banned from conscious awareness. Thus, they found themselves compelled to both confront and deny the issue of racism, to talk about it and to silence it.

It goes without saying that this made my undertaking as researcher considerably more complicated than I had expected. I had envisioned writing a history of a feminist project – that is, a history which would recognize the important achievements of one of feminism's most favourite projects. While I did not assume that the collective would be perfect and was prepared to engage with its inevitable shortcomings and mistakes, I had not anticipated a public accusation of racism in a group which I had regarded as exemplary for feminism.[2] I was, thus, faced with the problem of how to write about the group in a way that preserved the significance of their work as an important feminist project, while providing an honest and critical account of the recent storms, particularly around the thorny issue of racism.

From the outset, I rejected trying to take an 'objective' stance or just sticking to the 'facts,' thereby setting myself up as neutral arbiter in the recent conflicts. In addition to the epistemological problems such a position would entail, it was untenable for practical reasons as well. I had insufficient access to information that would allow me to understand both 'sides' of the story. The staff members who had left the organization suspected me as a white woman doing research 'for' the founders and were, therefore, reluctant to speak with me – or, at least, to speak to me about the events in question. The founders were willing to speak to me, once they had decided that I was not just another 'muckraker looking for dirt', but their willingness was undoubtedly also shaped by their perception of me as a white, European woman (close enough to give them the benefit of the doubt, but far enough removed not to be emotionally involved). However, I could hardly rely on them to provide 'objective' accounts, since their version of events would inevitably be shaped by their social locations, not to mention their partial – and, of course, biased – perspectives on the conflicts in question.

In addition to worrying about how to find out what had 'really' happened, I struggled with how to position myself as white researcher. As a white feminist with a long-standing commitment to the struggle against racism, I assumed that the women of colour on the staff would be the underdogs in any conflict involving racism. Nevertheless, simply taking their side in the recent conflicts was not without its problems. It would require me to position myself as a white feminist, who, in contrast to the founders, was an exception to the rule of white racism – one of the 'worthy white few' (Simonds 1996: 190). I seriously wondered upon what grounds I could claim such moral superiority in view of the long-standing ideological and practical struggle, which the founders had waged against racism. Why should I be any less implicated in white privilege or any less susceptible to colour blindness than they were? Ultimately, I decided that if neutrality or taking sides were not options, my best bet was to tackle the issue head on, using my ambivalences as a white feminist researcher talking to white feminist activists about racism as an analytic resource.

In this chapter, I explore the evasions and silences which emerge when white feminists try to make sense of the difficult, painful and shameful business of racism in their midst. I show how I learned to 'hear' these silences as providing information about the conflicts in question and how they helped me to understand how such silences can undermine a feminist commitment to anti-racism, thereby reproducing precisely the racialised inequalities feminists are committed to transforming. I then draw conclusions about what these interviews reveal about whiteness (as identity, structural privilege, and everyday practice) and why this, in the final analysis, is the biggest silence of all.

Listening to silences

Because my interviews were conducted against the backdrop of the recent conflicts – conflicts which had been aired and discussed publicly within the feminist community – my informants could not fall back on a canned version of their history, a version which simply glorified their triumphs and successes. The shadow side of their history had already become a public secret. Without exception, they were all deeply troubled by recent events which were at the forefront of their minds. As one founder put it: '[t]here's a cloud hanging over the Collective now and it will never be the same.' After an initial period of deciding whether or not they could trust me, most seemed to welcome the interview as an opportunity to talk about these events, including the mistakes that they had made and how they hoped to do things differently in the future.

I was, of course, anxious to hear what 'really' happened and hoped with the help of my interviewing skills and some empathetic listening to get the story from the 'horse's mouth', so to speak. However, while my informants clearly wanted to talk about what had happened – and, indeed, throughout their interviews referred to it constantly – they rarely did so explicitly. In particular, the painful (and shameful) issue of racism was rarely mentioned in so many words. While they went to considerable lengths to describe recent events, they did so without ever mentioning what I came to think of as the 'R-word'.

In this context, I found that I could not simply concentrate on what my informants *said*, but also what they did *not say*. I began to pay attention to what was noticeably absent from their narratives, what was avoided, repressed, or even intentionally left out. In other words, I embarked on what Mazzei (2003) has aptly called, the 'pursuit of the muffled sub-text' as the only way I could discover and begin to understand the 'truth' of what had happened in the collective.

I will now look at three examples which required listening for silences – all involving a precarious mixture of both talking about and, at the same time, avoiding talking about racism.

'A lot of conflicts could have been helped by having a really good policy ... '

One of the issues which had been particularly contentious within the organization involved the hiring of new staff. Most of my informants admitted that they had made many mistakes in the past. They had continued to operate under the old motto 'we're all equal' and 'everyone can do everything' without realizing that this might not work with newcomers from different class and educational backgrounds and that 'more mentoring' might be necessary. Nor had they given sufficient thought to how the organization should be restructured so that it would be attentive to the (unintentional) effects of racialized structures of inequality (for example, the need for procedures for addressing and redressing grievances). Although their intentions to make the organization more diverse and representative were good, they all felt that they had not been successful in opening up the organization to a broader diversity of women. As one founder put it, '[w]e were trying to do something very hard and were not doing it'.

My informants talked about racism in general terms. They also freely acknowledged that in a racially divided society like the US, racism would hardly come to a halt at their own front door, no matter how committed they were to combating it. All agreed that a structural analysis of racism was required if their organization were to be inclusive and free of racialized hierarchies. However, as tensions mounted and staff members accused the founders of dragging their feet when it came to instigating fundamental changes in the organization, the founders increasingly reacted evasively or defensively. Whereas many of the staff, particularly women of colour, saw covert racism and subtle exclusions at all levels, the white founders seemed to be less able – or less willing – to reflect on their privileges and more concerned with protecting their vision of the collective history from a critique that was too unpalatable to bear.

Many looked for ways to explain the present state of affairs while downplaying the significance of 'race' and reframing it as a more general 'organizational problem':

> A lot of the conflict that happened around race, I feel happened because there weren't uniformly agreed on standards of evaluation and accountability. And so the rules weren't all evenly applied and certain founders felt like they didn't have to obey certain rules, like to get there on time. And so if you try to get other people to get there on time, it feels unfair to the newer staff to be held to an accountability that the founders aren't. Because they're used to the going and coming. They've

> been here 25 years. So a lot of the staff conflicts, I think could have been helped by having a really clear, good, universally agreed upon personnel policy.

This informant begins with an acknowledgement that the conflicts were about 'race'. However, she quickly moves on to the 'real' problems – namely, inadequate organizational standards of evaluation or uniform rules concerning accountability. While these aspects certainly captured one level of the recent conflicts, they also deflect attention from racialized structures of privilege within the organization as well as the resentment that differential treatment is likely to evoke in the context of a racialized society like the US.

Reframing racism as an organizational problem is a form of 'avoiding the R-word'. It both acknowledges that race has been an issue, while simultaneously, subsuming it under more 'urgent' matters – like, for example, developing better 'personnel policy'. The foregrounding of other issues has been dubbed 'liberal racism' (Gordon and Newfield 1995) or 'reasonable racism' (Billig et al. 1988; Billig 1999). This is not about the overt expression of racist sentiments – something that has become increasingly taboo in many parts of the population – and, indeed, can easily go hand in hand with a discursively held commitment to anti-racism. However, by framing discriminatory practices in a discourse of 'universal equality' or 'fairness' or 'rationality', the outcomes of endemic racism are left unaddressed. It evades the invisible privileges and forms of social and cultural capital to which white people have automatic access, as part and parcel of what 'being white' in the US means. A more equitable policy or some additional 'mentoring' of newcomers suggests that a level playing field is – with a little more effort – well within reach, thereby eliminating the more difficult – but crucial – task of the sustained and ongoing analysis of how white privilege intersects with power at all levels of an organization, sabotaging even the most well-meaning attempts to eliminate structured and sedimented forms of inequality and exclusion (Frankenberg 2001; Zajicek 2002).

'It became totally irrational'

One of the most troubling events of the recent history of the collective – at least for the founders – had been the staff's decision to bring in a union.[3] In the midst of what seemed to be interminable discussions about how to restructure the organization, the staff decided that they needed to bring in a union to represent their interests. They no longer had confidence that their problems could be resolved without outside help. It was clear that they did not – or no longer could – view the white founders as being 'on their side'. The white founders responded to this turn of events with consternation and disbelief. As one put it, '[w]e had always been feminists – you know, anti-capitalist and all that – and suddenly we were managers'. The staff's desire to bring in a union was not only frustrating, but many founders found it difficult to see their action as being in 'good faith'. After all the 'hours and hours' they had spent meeting together and talking, trying to create 'an organization that makes sense', it felt to many as a 'betrayal'.

As one informant put it:

> I mean, I'm not anti-union ... (but) the whole thought was that we could really communicate and work out whatever it was, blocks or whatever, and ... no, they were going to unionize and it was the only way. They felt that since things were so unclear about the founders and privilege ... that that was the only thing they could do. It was beyond discussion. It became totally irrational, I think. ... The other thing that made it even more complicated is that everything was also being discussed in racist terms, which is also crazy. So it was like people who knew the collective said, '[o]h, it's so frustrating and sad' ... But that was what was going on.

She presents the staff's decision to bring in the union as linked to the issue of racism. However, rather than exploring how the two were linked, she simply characterizes the situation as 'crazy' and 'irrational'. Although she is quick to point out that she is not ideologically opposed to unions ('I'm not anti-union, but ... ') and acknowledges that there were some grounds for complaint ('founders and privilege'), she makes no attempt to explore the staff's side of the story. Not only is any other version of events omitted, but the events themselves are deliberately kept vague and incomprehensible ('things were so unclear'). The staff's actions are made to appear as 'irrational' and unconstructive ('beyond discussion'). In contrast, the actions of the founders were perhaps a bit slow, but, nevertheless, constructive and geared toward the greater good – the creation of an organization that would 'make sense' for everyone. She draws upon a generalized feminist community who can be counted upon to share her view that is, to regard the events as 'frustrating and sad' rather than, say, 'justifiable and necessary'.

Through this excerpt, the informant is both talking and not talking about 'race'. It enters her narrative as an implicit sub-text. The conflict itself is reframed as a matter of who can speak in the name of reason and good faith. One of the features of whiteness is that one's actions can be construed as unquestionably rational rather than ideologically or personally motivated (Gordon and Newfield 1995). 'We don't get it' is a luxury which only whites can enjoy, allowing the privilege of not even having to attend to the advantages it affords unless one chooses to (Mazzei 2003: 365) The emphasis on 'confusion' absolves herself, but also the other founders, from responsibility for the events in question ('If we had understood, we could have done something about it') and leaves unaddressed to what extent they really tried to understand the reasons for the staff's behaviour – reasons which might have made their actions seem less 'irrational'.

'Things we had done so naturally at the beginning. ... '

Like many other social movement groups interested in developing strategies for confronting racism, the collective organized anti-racism workshops, sometimes for founders alone to 'work on' their own internalized racism, sometimes for staff members to express their experiences with everyday racism in the organization, and sometimes together with the intention of exploring new ways to work together and make the organization work for all its members. While most of my informants were convinced that such workshops were necessary, their narratives displayed some of their misgivings as well. As one explained, she was often torn between feeling 'proud' of the other (white) members of the collective for being so 'honest' and 'trying so hard' to work on racism, while the workshops themselves involved meaningless and often ridiculous games which seemed to bear little relationship to the problems at hand. Describing one such workshop, she recalled:

> It always seemed to me that things we had done so naturally, at the very beginning got turned into kind of *hokey*. Eventually, we always had to have facilitators ... to help us analyze what was wrong with us, to help us try and get along and understand each other in the enlarging group we were becoming. (But) when we started in the seventies, we did it all ourselves, because we *could* do it ourselves. That was part of it, taking that power.

The reason for these workshops was to bring the group members together and it is clear from her language how polarized they had become. The lines of demarcation are firmly in place, yet without having to mention explicitly that the 'we' refers to the white founders while the 'enlarging group' refers – at least in part – to the women of colour in the staff. While the informant expresses the commitment of the founders to 'work on' making the group more inclusive, the racially inflected 'we' and 'them' undermine this intention.

She also expresses her undisguised longing for the 'good old days' when 'we' did things 'naturally'. The term 'natural' seems innocent, describing an organic way of dealing with conflicts in the group. However, it avoids the fact that the composition of the former group was anything but 'natural'. Its homogeneity as a group of predominately white, middle-class women may well have accounted for a less conflictuous collaboration, but it was hardly a coincidence. The juxtaposition of 'natural' and 'hokey' glosses over the fact that the group had always been 'about race'. From the outset, its composition, its structure, and the interactions among the members had been racialized, whereby doing things 'naturally' simply meant engaging in 'doing whiteness' (Lewis 2004).

And, finally, her words indicate how powerless she feels in the face of the seemingly intractable conflicts within the organization. Her narrative reflects a kind of 'power reversal', whereby the powerlessness of the (white) founders is emphasized, while the women of colour are endowed with power to determine what happens in the organization. Such power reversals are frequently employed when white people talk about 'race'. They allow them to position themselves as the victims of the anger, manipulation, or aggression of minority groups, while the powerlessness of minorities is downplayed and their efforts to change their situation redefined as divisive or – in this case – 'hokey' (Zajicek 2002: 165). This frequently employed repertoire of power reversal is exacerbated by what Wendy Brown (2001) has aptly called 'left melancholia'. Upon discovering their inability to effectively combat the sources of racism, poverty, violence in their midst, many feminist activists may find themselves propelled into a state of mourning. Their sense of progress in history disappears, resulting in a nostalgia for a glorified past and a painful political paralysis in the present.

In conclusion, did listening to silences allow me to discover what 'really' happened concerning the issue of racism in the BWHBC? On one level, it did not. I was never able to reconstruct the actual events, let alone sort out which individuals were to blame for the problems around racism and the eventual disintegration of the collective. Most informants had difficulties coming up with concrete examples of racist practices and, when they did, the occurrence were often so decontextualized that it was difficult to reconstruct what they had meant for all parties concerned.[4] Criticisms of individuals on either side tended to be assiduously avoided or attributed to an unnamed individual.[5] The evasions and silences – what was not said – told a story of their own, however. The silences, first and foremost, told a story about the difficulties white feminists have in sustaining their ideological commitments to feminism, while, at the same time, shouldering their complicities in the historical legacies of a racially divided society. But, they also allowed me, with a little imagination, to understand what the situation might have been like for the women of colour working in the organization. It is not difficult to comprehend that when the organization is presented as the most pressing concern, it places the onus of bringing up the subject of racism on those members who are most affected by it. It is their job to get – and keep – racism on the agenda. Moreover, if bringing up racism is treated as irrational, disruptive, or a sign of 'bad faith' against the common interests of the organization, it is easy to see that the concerns and complaints of individuals will be unlikely to receive a serious or empathetic hearing. And, if the early days of the collective are regarded as the 'natural' and best way of doing things, it is clear that newcomers will have their work cut out for them if they want to eke out a space for themselves in the organization or feel that they belong.

So far, I have been dealing with the ways that my informants talked and did not talk about race. At this point, the reader may have the impression that my informants were all engaged in avoidance while I, as interviewer, was simply listening to the silences and valiantly employing my critical faculties to ferret out the hidden sub-text in their narratives.

While this was, to some extent, true, I was, by no means, an innocent bystander. Together with my informants, I was an active participant in the evasions and silences. I was complicit in avoiding the R-word.

Complicities of the white researcher

At the outset of this chapter, I described the difficulties I had as a white interviewer talking to white feminists about racism. My ideological commitment – and, in this sense, I was no different than my informants – is to combat racism and white privilege wherever they rear their ugly heads, including in feminist thought and practices. However, looking back at my interviews, I found myriad instances where I, too, participated in the silencing of the issues of race and racism. For example, I actively encouraged my informants to expound on the 'organizational' difficulties. I expressed sympathy at the 'confusion' of recent years. And, I became circumspect and tactful when the charges the staff had made were mentioned. At the first sign of discomfort in my informants, I would 'instinctively' look for a 'safer' topic and direct the interview into more uncontroversial conversational waters.

The following example is an illustration. One of my informants recalled a meeting which took place during a particularly difficult period, noting that, much to her surprise, it was 'a really positive event … in spite of the turmoil'. It involved picking out photographs for the new *Our Bodies, Ourselves* and, in the interests of 'celebrating women's diversity', considerable effort had gone into the selection of photographs. The informant remembered how exhilarating it had been, going around tables looking at photographs and deciding which ones would reflect the spirit of the book. I found myself as interviewer becoming optimistic as well, thinking that, perhaps, after all, they had managed to come together despite all the recent conflicts around racism. However, my hopes were shattered when, in answer to my question of how the initial selection of photographs had been made, she gave the names of two members of the collective (a white founder and a black staff member). But, she added:

> L. [the staff member] didn't show up because she was having such difficulties at the time … I was sad … but she was just too hesitant to be amongst too many of the founders. But it was an absolute pleasure to do that. It was an occasion that brought us together. That's what I liked about it.

I immediately understand that if L. did not feel comfortable 'with too many white founders', this was obviously a reflection of the conflicts about racism in the group. While I could see that my informant was troubled by her absence, labelling it as 'sad' also absolved her of any responsibility, transforming it into something to be sorry about, but not accountable for. More importantly, however, by describing this particular meeting as a (rare) occasion of togetherness, I wondered whether it had not been so pleasant and congenial precisely because the absence of women of colour allowed white women to avoid the thorny problem of race.

While I was aware that this was going on during the interview and elicited information about L.'s absence at the meeting, I did not comment on these silences. Nor did I openly question the informant's depiction of the situation as a moment which 'brought us together'. In short, I let it slide.

It could, of course, be argued that, as an interviewer, I had no other choice. I needed to establish rapport with my informants so that they would speak freely to me about a subject which they found painful and potentially incriminating. Calling them on their evasiveness might well have upset the interview relationship, causing them to watch their words or even refuse to talk to me. In his essay on doing research on 'race', the well-known methodologist Howard Becker (2000) argues that although critical researchers may feel uncomfortable with their silence, it is better for your research to keep quiet than to 'get into an argument with someone from who you want information' (ibid.: 249). Applied to my research, this suggests that I did well to go along with my informants' silence because this was the only way I could get them to talk to me. Becker's recommendation leaves an important issue unaddressed, however. The interviewer cannot disassociate herself from what is happening in the interviews. By keeping quiet, she is not simply passively listening to her informants, but she is actively involved in the construction of meaning, including meanings that remain implicit or silent.

Thus, avoiding the R-word was not simply a matter of my not wanting to rock the boat (although that was certainly part of the story). I was also actively engaged in producing the very silences around race and racism which were the subject of my research. Moreover, I was intimately involved in what was, in hindsight, the most notable feature of the interviews – namely, the fact that 'we' – interviewer and informants – were all white feminists engaged in the activity of talking about race and racism by not talking about it. It is this remarkable silence which – as I will argue in the next section – any white feminist researcher who is sensitive to the issues of race and racism – needs not only to confront, but also to analyze.

Constructing white-ness

In her perceptive study on the culture of avoidance among white people, Eliasoph (1999) argues that many white people are more than willing to voice anti-racist sentiments in private or 'backstage' settings, but are reluctant to do so in more public arenas. Confronting racism in public is treated as 'making a scene' or 'trying to get attention', something which is discouraged in the interest of maintaining the interaction. 'Whites perpetuate racism ... as passive bystanders ... (who) notice the action and do not actively support it but do not do anything to oppose it, either (1999: 486).' While Elisasoph's study refers to interactional behaviour among white people in everyday settings, her insights seem equally applicable to the kinds of avoidance that occurred in my interviews – evasions and silences that allowed the interaction to remain intact through the construction of a shared white identity. By not behaving as a 'race traitor' (Magrest 1994; Alcoff 1998) – that is, as a person who publicly and vocally distances herself from the privileges of whiteness – both my informants and I engaged in the reproduction of whiteness. The desire to avoid a conflict which might disrupt our interaction transformed me into a passive bystander – someone who notices the action, but does not actively oppose it in the interests of keeping the peace. White people do not avoid talking about race because they necessarily share a bond of racism, but because they collectively put race-talk into the category of 'topics to be avoided by polite people'.[6]

As many critical theorists of whiteness have argued, studying whiteness involves, first and foremost, exposing the silences upon which 'whiteness' rests.[7] This means showing how whiteness is constructed as racially unmarked. Whiteness needs to be analysed as a distinctive social location, a standpoint, a set of cultural practices, and a position of structural advantage, which is embedded in processes of inequality and exploitation at all levels of social life (Frankenberg 1993). The invisibility of whiteness is its most salient feature. It is extraordinarily difficult for most white people to acknowledge that they are white. White people insist – as many do – that they do not 'have' a race or that 'race is not an issue for them' precisely because whiteness is the unmarked norm against which all other identities are defined and racialized. Obviously, this invisibility is a delusion as any person of colour will attest for whom whiteness is only all too visible (Frankenberg 2001). However, it is a delusion which allows white people to indulge in a fantasy of being 'just ordinary people' that is unavailable to most people of colour. Many white people can go through life without ever having to think about race and racism unless they choose to. It is the person of colour, as 'racialized other', who bears the burden of 'playing the race card'.

Thus, 'whiteness' is per definition about avoidance. By avoiding naming itself, whiteness becomes 'power evasive', silently reproducing dominance rather than subordination, normativity rather than marginality, and privilege rather than disadvantage (Frankenberg 1993: 237). It allows white people to remain comfortable rather than taking a closer look at the assumptions upon which their comfort rests (Rasmussen et al. 2001: 13). Whiteness sets itself up as the centre, relegating all that is non-white to the periphery. It portrays itself as universal, the voice of propriety and reason, so ubiquitous and entrenched that it requires no explanation or defence. The actions, experiences, and interactions of white people to seem natural and normal, while the actions, experiences, and interactions of people of colour can be labelled as irrational, manipulative, or detrimental to the common good.

Conclusion

At the outset of this chapter, I raised the issue of the methodological problems which a researcher encounters when informants are not able or willing to talk about subjects which they find painful, shameful, or ideologically dilemmatic. When confronted with their silences, the researcher will need to find ways to listen to and interpret what her informants say as well as what they do not say – in so many words. One way to do this is for the interviewer to remain silent herself and to analyze – after the fact – what has been implied, but not said by her informants in the hopes of getting an accurate portrayal of the events in question.

It will become clear that evasions and silences are often not simply obstacles to discovering what 'really' happened. On the contrary, they have their own story to tell. Silences speak to the anxieties and fears of the informants. They provide insight into those aspects of informants' experience which are taken for granted – as natural as the air they breathe and, consequently, unavailable for spoken discourse. Silences can indicate what informants in specific contexts deem unacceptable to be told and, therefore, require censorship. And, finally, silences allow informants to veil unacceptable power and privilege, whose exposure could challenge their legitimacy, their sense of self, or their world view.

Silences are not simply sources of information to be plumbed in the interests of a more nuanced and sophisticated understanding of informants or the context in which they are involved, however. As we have seen, the researcher is actively implicated herself in the production of silences – silences which are often complicit with racialized relations of power. Whether she likes it or not, she is not an innocent bystander. She, therefore, has no other recourse than to acknowledge and reflect upon her participation in the very silences she has set out to analyse. It is only by probing these silences for their meanings, their motivations, and their sources that the researcher can develop a more 'truthful' understanding of what happened than any mere rendition of the facts could ever provide.

Acknowledgements

I would like to thank Willem de Haan and Helma Lutz and the editors of this volume for their helpful and constructive suggestions.

Notes

1 Emerging in the wake of second-wave feminism, the BWHBC authored the well-known classic on women's health, *Our Bodies, Ourselves*. Since the first edition in 1970, this book has gone through more than 12 revisions, sold more than 4 million copies, and been translated in more than 25 languages. It changed the way generations of women felt about their bodies, their sexuality, and their health. In addition to being a catalyst for the international women's health movement, it has had an important impact on the organization and provision of health care within (and outside) the US as well as on medical research and legislation. See Davis (2007).

2 This was, in hindsight, a bit naïve as similar conflicts were occurring in other feminist organizations – something that has been written about at length (see, for example, Simonds 1996; Ruiz and DuBois 2000; Scott, 2000; Morgen 1998, 2002).

However, this attests to the popularity, credibility, and, indeed, almost mythical status of this particular group – issues which I discuss at length in Davis (2007).

3 While the public image of the group was that of a collective, in reality, it had evolved into an organization run by paid staff and a few founders and a board (consisting of founders and several additional women from the community). Many of the founders were only marginally involved in the organization and as board members tended to 'rubber stamp' decisions which were made by the staff and those founders active in the organization. While many of the tensions were played out between the board and the staff, they often involved conflicts between the staff and the active founders who were extremely powerful in terms of experience, expertise, and their dual position as staff members and board members.

4 An example was related by one of the staff members (white) who complained about the 'everyday racism' in the collective. When I asked her to give an example, she described how one of the staff members (an African American woman) came to work in a turban and a dress made from Kenti cloth. She remembered guiltily that she blurt out, 'Wow, you look so exotic today'. Whether this remark is heard as racist or as friendly depends on the context, the relationships between the members of the collective, the degree of tension within the organization, and, of course, who is making the joke and who is its object.

5 See Scott (2000) for an analysis of different meanings given to (anti-)racist practices in feminist organizations.

6 See also Roediger (1994) for an interesting discussion of how politically progressive whites shun the whole enterprise of talking about race.

7 See also Winddance Twine and Warren (2000), Best (2003) and Lewis (2004) for some good examples of how silences around 'whiteness' can be analysed.

References

Alcoff, L. (1998) 'What should white people do?' *Hypatia*, 13 (3): 6–26.

Best, A.L. (2003) 'Doing race in the context of feminist interviewing: constructing whiteness through talk', *Qualitative Inquiry*, 9 (6): 895–914.

Becker, H.S. (2000) 'Afterword: racism and the research process', in F. Winddance Twine and J.W. Warren (eds) *Racing Research, Researching Race*, New York: New York University Press.

Billig, M. (1999) *Freudian Repression. Conversation Creating the Unconscious*, Cambridge: Cambridge University Press.

Billig, M., Condor, S., Edwards, D., Gane, M., Middleton, D. and Radley, A. (eds) (1988) *Ideological Dilemmas: A Social Psychology of Everyday Thinking*, London: Sage Publications.

Bonilla, A., Taylor, A., Canetti, M. and Yanco, J. (1999) 'An open letter to the board of directors, Boston Women's Health Book Collective', *Sojourner*, 23 (4): 4.

Brown, W. (2001) *Politics out of History*, Princeton: Princeton University Press.

Davis, K. (2007) *The Making of Our Bodies, Ourselves. How Feminism Travels Across Borders*, Durham: Duke University Press.

Eliasoph, N. (1999) '"Everyday racism" in a culture of political avoidance: civil society, speech, and taboo,' *Social Problems*, 46 (4): 479–502.

Frankenberg, R. (1993) *White Women, Race Matters: The Social Construction of Whiteness*, Minneapolis: University of Minnesota Press.

—— (2001) 'The mirage of unmarked whiteness', in B. Brander Rasmussen, E. Klineberg, I.J. Nexica and M. Wray (eds) *The Making and Unmaking of Whiteness*, Durham, NC: Duke University Press.

Gordon, A. and Newfield, C. (1995) 'White philosophy', in K.A. Appiah and H.L. Gates (eds) *Identities*, Chicago: Chicago University Press.

Lewis, A.E. (2004) '"What group?" Studying whites and whiteness in the era of "color blindness"', *Sociological Theory*, 22 (4): 623–46.

Magrest, M. (1994) *Memoirs of a Race Traitor*, Boston: South End Press.

Mazzei, L.A. (2003) 'Inhabiting silences: in pursuit of a muffled subtext', *Qualitative Inquiry*, 9 (3): 355–68.

Morgen, S. (2002) *Into Our Own Hands. The Women's Health Movement in the United States, 1969–1990*, New Brunswick: Rutgers University Press.

—— (1998) 'The dream of diversity, the dilemma of difference: race and class contradictions in a feminist health clinic', in J.B. Cole (ed.) *Anthropology for the Nineties. Introductory Readings*, New York: The Free Press.

Rasmussen, B.B., Klinenberg, E., Nexica, I.J. and Wray, M. (eds) (2001) *The Making and Unmaking of Whiteness*, Durham, NC: Duke University Press.

Roediger, D. (1994) *Towards the Abolition of Whiteness*. New York: Verso.

Ruiz, V.L. and DuBois, E.C. (eds) (2000) *Unequal Sisters: a Multicultural Reader in U.S. Women's History*, New York: Routledge.

Scott, E.K. (2000) 'Everyone against racism: Agency and the production of meaning in the anti-racism practices of two feminist organizations', *Theory and Society*, 29: 785–818.

Simonds, W. (1996) *Abortion at Work. Ideology and Practice in a Feminist Clinic*. New Brunswick, NJ: Rutgers University Press.

Sojourner, T. (1994) *Ain't I a Woman?* Canada: Scholastic.

Winddance Twine, F. and Warren, J.W. (eds) (2000) *Racing Research, Researching Race*, New York: New York University Press.

Zajicek, A.M. (2002) 'Race discourses and antiracist practices in a local women's movement', *Gender & Society*, 16 (2): 155–74.

12 Suppressing intertextual understandings

Negotiating interviews and analysis

Ann Phoenix

Feminist researchers have made enormous contributions to understandings of the ways in which the research process is not innocent, but is riven with power relations. For example, Ann Oakley (1981) pointed out in the beginning of the 1980s that research interviews could not simply be conducted as if researchers could follow a well-worked out recipe. Instead the research interview had to be understood as an interaction and, in her research, one where two women were in relationship and shared comfortable understandings. Black researchers have also explored the ways in which power relations are negotiated in situations where they are interviewing and analysing data from black and white research participants. They often have to engage with uncomfortable power relations in the research team as well as in the interview situation and in analysis (e.g. Phoenix 1994; Gunaratnam and Lewis 2001; Gunaratnam 2003). Such explorations have, however, tended to focus predominantly on what is said. Yet, any researcher knows that the success of the research process is partly dependent on what is not said as, for example, where researchers feel angry with a participant (e.g. Hubbard et al. 2001) or where they make decisions about what to disclose or not disclose about themselves in order to build rapport with participants (Song and Parker 1995; Abell et al. 2006). Although silence can result because some things cannot be spoken because they are unconsciously repressed (Hollway and Jefferson 2000; Frosh 2002), silences often arise because the researcher and participant(s) are negotiating understandings and meanings from other areas of their lives and from their multiple intersections. They thus involve the suppression of some aspects of intertextuality.

Julia Kristeva (1980) coined the term 'intertextuality' in recognition that the meaning of any text is affected by the meanings established in other previous or contemporary texts. Following Saussure, Kristeva considered that the author of a text and its reader are connected and that each text is connected to other texts (as in Bakhtin's dialogism[1]). The two axes are linked because there is no straightforward transfer of meaning from writer to reader. Instead, every text and every reading depends on prior codes which mediate meaning. This is an idea that underpins the notion of texts being socially constructed.

Current uses of intertexuality include verbal as well as written discourses that form 'intertextual chains' (Solin 2004). Since research interviews are concerned with the construction of meanings, interview accounts are always necessarily intertextual in that modes of telling and what is considered worthy of telling come from wider social understandings that involve intertextuality (Fox 1995). However, intertextuality has to be negotiated in that the interviewer and interviewee are always already practised at speaking and interpreting and are likely to make different allusive links and unconscious associations to what each says. Silences and secrecy are likely to arise when either of the participants fear either that they will be 'misread' or want to defend themselves against possible readings that they would rather not be made or are hurt or embarrassed about readings they can see being made. Considering silence and secrecy can, therefore, allow us to understand the psychosocial impulse (Irwin 2004) for particular things being said or not said and difficult to say, i.e. Kristeva's 'structuration' (or how particular ways of structuring talk and silence come into being) and so deepen understandings of what generates 'troubled subject positions' (Wetherell 1998).

This chapter aims to explore the ways in which the intertextuality can lead to uncomfortable dynamics and silence, secrecy and erasure in the research process, but can also be used to make implicit disclosures and to illuminate psychosocial processes that serve to construct normative everyday practices and silence what is constructed as 'non-normative'. The chapter draws on accounts produced in three research projects over the last 15 years to discuss the complexity, impact and meanings of secrets and silences for the research process and participants (including the researcher) and the knowledge that is produced.

Silence and secrecy as performative

Interest in silence and secrecy has grown in recognition of their ubiquity and that they serve multiple functions for human development and identities. For example, the development of secrecy in childhood is argued to be crucial to the development of identity. Manen and Levering (1996) argue that to have a secret gives children a feeling of inwardness, privacy and inner invisibility, and so of personal identity. As a result, they argue, this makes what is kept secret valuable (so that some people will go to great lengths to uncover a secret). Keeping secrets thus helps children to develop a degree of autonomy, independence and powerfulness and is always simultaneously an experience of self. According to Manen and Levering (1996) there is a developmetal trajectory to the keeping of secrets. Young children are unsure whether to divulge secrets, but older children (by the age of about 12 years) feel that divulging secrets would threaten their friendships. Secrecy thus becomes linked with the forbidden and with fear and punishment.

Studies of adults find that silence often results from the negotiation of difficult dynamics and so is context specific. From a study of sexual minorities in the workplace, Ward and Winstanley (2003) suggest that silence can be viewed as a multifaceted and metaphorical 'negative space'. They identified five forms of silence in the research process: reactive silence and the absence of response; a form of suppression, (self) censorship, self-protection and resistance. Mazzei (2008) found that white students training to be teachers in her class in a small liberal arts university in the midwest USA were silent on race because they were fearful of giving offence, being wrong, appearing stupid, being marginalised by peers and losing privilege. Using her own experience, Mazzei suggests that many white people are brought up 'not to notice' people's colour. According to Leonardo (2004), white people support a 'color-blind discourse' because it maintains their privilege by continuing to normalize their whiteness.

It has become commonplace to recognise that silence can be unconsciously motivated. The idea of repression has passed into popular discourses so that speakers themselves sometimes mention that they may have repressed something that happened to them (Phoenix 2004). In doing so, they implicity suggest that their silence is beyond their control and so is not due to secrecy. More consciously employed silence and secrecy perform a number of functions in interactions ranging from smooth maintenance of interaction through politeness to the management of shame. Secrecy can also be deliberately displayed in order to signal that there are things that are too terrible to be said and so to prevent further probing. This indicates that power relations can be played out through the negotiation of silence and secrecy. In a research interview, where there is an implicit contract for the research participant to be self-revelatory and engage in free and frank discussion, the power relations of silence and secrecy are potentially complex. The sections that follow address three sets of interactional dynamics where silence and secrecy become salient in the research process because of intertextual understandings.

Negotiating contradictory intertextual understandings: smoothing over minor epistemic violence

As a result of feminist research that interrogated the interviewing process as an interactional site, it became clear in the 1980s that many research participants (particularly women since they are more often research partipants in interview studies) enjoy the interview process and find talking about their lives 'therapeutic' (Oakley 1981; Brannen 1988). In such research, talking at length and easily is often considered to be indicative of good rapport between researcher and participant and researchers are generally considered largely responsible for establishing and maintaining that rapport. Yet, since interviewing is a process and a range of topics are often the focus of conversation, fluency and rapport may both fluctuate in unpredictable ways as, for example, when racialisation and racism are interview topics (Phoenix 1994). In some interview situations, interviewers and participants can sometimes be engaged in struggle for the interview space because, for example, the interviewee is more powerful than the interviewer and is intent on putting over particular versions of self-presentation, regardless of what the interviewee wants to talk about. Ball (1994) and Puwar (1997) both discuss the ways in whch interviewing Members of Parliament in the UK can pose difficulties that serve to silence some of the issues with which the researcher is concerned.

What appears to be missing from this literature, however, is the silence produced when the interviewer makes an unwitting gaffe in the interview situation. In the extract below, a 14-year-old young woman was being interviewed at her school for a study of social identities in young people (Tizard and Phoenix 2002). As part of the exploration of identities, young people were asked whether they had ever thought about being another colour or the other sex.

Q. Have you ever thought you would rather not be a boy?
A. A girl!
Q. Oh sorry. Have you ever thought you would rather not be a girl?
A. No.

In this context, I spoke not as a listener, as should be the case in interviews, but as an author, bringing into being something that originated with me, rather than the interviewee. In Lyotard's (1985) terms, I violated the language game then in play. What I brought into being was the fact that I found the interviewee's gender presentation ambiguous and, feeling forced by the demands of the interview, to commit myself to indicating what I considered to be her gender, made the wrong choice. It is indicative of the centrality of gender in most societies that this mistake should matter at all. However, as the interview progressed and I realised that I would have to ask the question, I had felt increasingly stressed, racking my brain for cues. Her name gave no clue, nor did her clothing. I found myself surreptitiously scrutinising her shoes, trousers, jumper, hair, looking for signs of breasts and at her top lip for signs of an incipient moustache. The situation made explicit the sorts of bodily readings that many of us regularly do.

I found myself thinking that the young person in front of me seemed to accord with Jessica Benjamin's (1996) theory of gender over-inclusiveness and that bi-gender and bisexual positions are products of healthy development. Benjamin argues that there are complementary relationships between categories often constructed as binary opposites such as male and female. These polarities produce tensions that can disrupt rigid identities and allow ambivalence and multiplicity. In adolescence, this ambivalence can produce gendered commonalities where young people of both sexes can dress in ways that blur differences between them as well as emphasising difference and recognising themselves as unique (Benjamin 1998). Nonetheless, while this theoretical resource seemed potentially helpful, other textual understandings that gendered identities are central to young people's performativity and identities made it impossible for me to feel sanguine. This was particularly the case since any interview dynamic requires maintenance of a flow of interaction, which limits opportunities to think about those dynamics.

It may seem that my assumption was simply bizarre, but justifiable and unproblematic given that this research participant made choices to perform herself in a sexually ambiguous way. However, I made explicit something that would usually remain part of a normative silence between people who have just met – that I found her gender ambiguous. An indication that it was not a trivial event is provided by the fact that, aside from correcting ourselves, neither of us used familiar cultural devices for repairing a rupture in talk, e.g. joking, smiling, self-deprecation or explanation. We each smoothed over the event because it placed us in troubled subject positions (Wetherell 1998). In my case, I made my troubled subject position explicit since I had already been anxious about getting the question 'right'. We colluded in what Ward and Winstanley (2003) call reactive silence. Our very collusion in keeping my gaffe silent closed down discussion of gendered identities. Although I tried hard to be upbeat in the rest of the interview, it was not clear what the impact was on the participant. At the end of the interview, when asked how the interview had been for her, she simply said 'It was fine' and added nothing further. It is impossible to tell whether this short interchange had any impact on how she felt or behaved outside the interview or indeed, whether it was a surprise to her or something that she had experienced previously. However, it can be argued that this was a minor instance of epistemic violence in that I imposed my understandings on her.

Unlike the above example, the second example in this section was difficult to foresee and was an unwitting error of judgement that produced silence, was detrimental to the longitudinal element of the research I was conducting and highlighted a family secret that outsiders could not have guessed. The incident involved occurred in a longitudinal study of 16–19-year-old first-time mothers and their babies, followed from later pregnancy until the children were 21 months (see Phoenix 1991). I had met the participant, who was white, at an antenatal appointment and interviewed her at her parents' house in late pregnancy. Relations there were very friendly and I felt relaxed when I went to her newly allocated council flat to interview her for the first time after birth, when her baby was six months old.

Q. Have you experienced any racism because you have a black baby?
A. (Said indignantly) She's not black! She's Italian. She only looks dark because my grandmother's Italian.
Q. Oh sorry.

I was surprised by this response because, as a black researcher, I had no doubt that the baby was of mixed parentage. She had 'Afro' hair and her skin colour was as dark as that of some children with two black parents. My intertextual understandings included knowing what a range of people of mixed parentage look like, that people of mixed parentage are subject to racism and that the mothers of children of mixed parentage are sometimes subjected to racist abuse.

I felt very awkward as I continued with the interview. Soon after this exchange, the participant said that she had to go to collect her child benefit before the post office closed. She agreed that I could return to complete the interview and said that I should telephone to arrange a time. I was so disturbed by this interchange that I played it to the research team and discussed the implications for a baby growing up in this context of denial, silence and secrecy. I was concerned to see how this mother–infant dyad would be faring at the next interview (at 21 months). I repeatedly telephoned in the next few days, but got no reply. I therefore called her parents' house in case she was staying there. Her mother answered the telephone and said in a harsh and determined voice: 'She doesn't want to see you any more.' I asked if she knew why, but her mother simply said, 'She just doesn't want to see you.'

In this instance, I made audible something I thought was self-evidently visible. In not maintaining silence, I brought to light something that was being kept secret and may have been deeply repressed by one or more members of her family. I felt that the participant reacted as if it was deeply insulting to be 'accused' of having a black child and struggled with concern about how her six-month-old daughter would be treated as she grew up. At the same time, longitudinal studies are deliberately and necessarily intertextual in that understandings from one interview can often inform what is asked in the next. I was aware that I did not believe the quick riposte that the baby was dark because her great-grandmother is Italian. I knew from the previous, interview that the participant was one of only two members of the sample who had said that she did not know who the father of her baby is. She explained that she had been drunk when she conceived and had not even been aware that she had ever had sexual intercourse.

In order to heal the violent breach in rapport that I had caused, I had consciously to suppress such intertextual understandings and to move on to the next area of the interview. The participant also apparently smoothed over the rupture in the interview in that she answered questions politely, if coolly. However, her refusal to see me or even to speak to me again suggests that she was both upset by what I said and unwilling to be faced with the possibility that I had forced to her attention that her child's father is black. In wanting to keep blackness silent, the participant moved to get out of the extreme troubled subject position that I put her into by making the father of her child irrelevant to her certainty that her daughter is not black and, instead, locating her daughter's dark skin colour in her own grandmother's origins. In doing so, she used prolepsis to avoid my potential charge that since she does not know who the father is and so that he could well be black by giving a potentially plausible explanation for her daughter's colouring that serves to fix her as 'white' in a twentieth-century context. A reasonable explanation for the complexity of the interactions produced by my question is that the participant was simultaneously doing two sets of intertextual work. She seems to me to have drawn on her intertextual understanding that I knew that she does not know who the father of her daughter is while suppressing this and drawing on intertextual understandings that mixed parentage is disapproved of and blackness is a non-preferred option. As a result, she vehemently rebutted the possibility that her daughter has any black parentage. In doing so, she silenced me and then maintained a permanent and resistant silence (Ward and Winstanley 2003) in the research project by refusing to take any further part. That silence makes experiences of motherhood like hers less available to, and so less visible in, the research project and disrupted her longitudinal element in it. Twenty years on, I still wonder how that family handled the (inevitable) reflection from the rest of society that the baby was of mixed parentage. I occasionally feel a faint anxiety that this might have been a source of difficulty for the child involved and hope that there was some satisfactory resolution to these identity issues in what was clearly a network of supportive and loving relationships.

For both the participants quoted above, the negotiation and contestation of silence (and secrecy) have potential consequences for their identity positions in that both episodes challenged their positioning and potentially, their views of themselves – as positioned in relation to gender or racialisation. However unintentional were my interventions, my breaching of silence nonetheless involved epistemic violence in that they produced knowledge that potentially could have violent impact on their social understanding and lives. Spivak (1988) uses the concept of epistemic violence to indicate the ways in which colonial discourses attempt to constitute the colonial subject as 'Other'. Arguably, in these two interviews my interventions served to constitute the research participants as Other in ways that may (in the first case) or are likely (in the second case) to have been experienced as damaging employment of power relations. It is not surprising that the interplay of voice and silence produced self–other distance (Fletcher and Watson 2007). As Fox (1995) suggests, 'intertextual approaches break the distinction between researchers and researched, in as much as the researcher becomes part of the social which is being explored'.

Doing identity through partial revelations: using silence, secrecy and intertextual understandings

It is not unusual for participants in research to say that their lives are so ordinary that they have nothing of interest to tell. This concern is perhaps not surprising given that in everyday interaction narratives only become 'tellable' if they are new, reportable, unusual, funny or shared stories (Ochs and Capps 2001). However, Norrick (2005: 323) proposes that as well as this 'lower boundary' of tellability, there is also an 'upper boundary' in which 'some stories, though eminently tellable in their extra-ordinary content, are not tellable for many tellers under most circumstances, because they are too personal, too embarrassing or obscene'. As a result, narrators avoid or hedge risky story topics 'to preserve their own reputation as well as to avoid offending listeners … [And] to avoid transgressing norms of propriety, embarrassing their listeners and losing face' (Norrick 2005: 329). What is told is, therefore, both about the construction of speakers' identities and their reading of what their listeners expect (Bamberg 2004).

The negotiation of whether or not to tell 'risky stories' in an interview illustrates how silence and voice are both always present in the interview situation since not everything can be told and narrators, including researchers, have to make decisions about what to tell and what to leave silent (Hubbard et al. 2001; Abell et al. 2006; Riessman 2008). This negotiation allows participants to do identity by deciding not only what not to say, but whether and, if so, how not to say it. Norrick (2005) suggests that 'Interlocutors exhibit characteristic behaviors orienting to the upper boundary of tellability and marking narratives threatening to encroach upon it, and they negotiate transgressions beyond it … in the pursuit of intimacy and for mutual enjoyment.' However, in research interviews, participants also transgress the upper-bounds of tellability because they want to contribute to the research and sometimes because, in telling new stories, they sometimes lead themselves into other stories that they do not want to tell before they have had the opportunity to censor what they are saying. What they construct as constituting the upper- or lower-bounds of tellability is intertextual in that it is produced from multilayered cultural experience and knowledge. The two examples presented in this section both appear to have this quality of a story emerging somewhat unexpectedly because the participant is in full flow of telling their story. The first comes from the study of mothers less than twenty years mentioned above (Phoenix 1991) and the second from a study currently being conducted of the ways in which adults who have had non-normative childhoods transform their experiences over time in dealing with them.

Q. So did your father mind that you moved to London when you got married?
A. He couldn't, not after what he done to me.
Q. What did he do?
A. What he shouldn't have. [Silence]

A. Because by the time I turned 21 (inaudible) was getting, he was getting funny with himself because that wasn't easy either, being the eldest, being the girl, living with your step-father. In many ways you're assuming the role of wife, the role of mother, carer, you know, and he started to get ideas in his head you know and er – [Ten-second silence while the participant wipes her eyes]
Q. Would you like me to turn that off for a while?
A. Yeah. [Recorder off]
A. [Recorder on] Not going down that road again.

In both quotes, the participants do not name the sexual abuse they hint at and say nothing further about it. However, it is understood between us that they are hinting at sexual abuse because we all have intertextual understandings from the wider culture that sexual abuse occurs and that it is a 'shameful' subject that are difficult to talk about. Both, therefore, demarcate the upper-bounds of tellability (Norrick 2005). In refusing to continue with the subjects they have raised, the participants relegate the subject to silence and simultaneously make it an area of secrecy. Manen and Levering (1996: 100) suggest that 'secrecy is always simultaneously an experience of self, of personal identity' and that the development of self is related to the development of secrecy. They suggest that it is helpful to ask how the self is concealed or revealed in the practice of secrecy and what the consequences are for the formation of identity. The two women in the quotes above perform different identities through their silences. In the first example, the participant constructs for herself a shameful identity that provokes anger and a sense that her father needs to make reparation for what he has done. She does not appear deliberately to display secrecy in order to be in control of power relations, but does use it agentically to signal that some things are too terrible to be said and so to foreclose further discussion. Her silence can be read as both self-censorship and self-protection (Ward and Winstanley 2003).

In the second quote, however, the participant appears to be displaying self-protection, but while she weeps (and the woman in the first quote does not), she does not appear to be engaging in self-censorship, but to be repressing her memories through the process of talking (cf. Billig 1999). In a short extract, she also manages to perform herself as both having been overwhelmed with bad memories and in control of the practice of secrecy. One feature of the interview was that the participant felt that it was an opportunity to tell her story in ways she had not told it before. It can, therefore, be seen as an opportunity for development that allowed her to try out identities around disclosure and secrecy. The interview can thus be seen as a space for the reworking of her identity and, apparently paradoxically, for gaining a sense of herself as a powerful person, in control of a secret and different from other people interviewed in the same study. So successful was she at signalling this that it was clear to me as the researcher that this was not a site for encouraging further revelations or to attempt to engage in open discussion.

In both cases, the women signal that they have 'tellable' stories, but resist telling them and so avoid transgressing normal boundaries of propriety and intimacy (Norrick 2005). Establishing and negotiating the limits of tellability requires the deployment of intertextual understandings about shame, what can and should be told, the therapeutic possibilities raised by secrecy and disclosure in interviews, given that research participants often find the opportunity to talk about their experiences to an interested researcher helpful (Lowes and Gill 2006). Since these intertextual possibilities were implicit, the fact that both interviews continued with no apparent loss of rapport for at least a further hour, it is likely that researcher and participant in each case were drawing on complementary intertextual understandings that made the suppression and silencing of particular accounts a preferred ethical option. The relational processes involved in negotiating silence, secrecy and disclosing talk appeared to produce connection in this instance (Fletcher and Watson 2007).

The next section shifts from silence and secrecy resulting from the dynamics of the interview situation to silence and secrecy reported in the interview situation.

Subscribing to intertextual normativity: (re)producing and disrupting silence and secrecy

Since interviews, particularly research interviews, are about disclosure, it is not surprising that participants often reflect on their lives and identities and talk about issues that have been previously kept secret or silent. An examination of such issues necessarily reveals a great deal about what participants and those in their social networks consider shameful, acceptable and normative and so illuminates participants' identities and everyday practices. In the following quote, from the 'Transforming Experience' study, the interview uses current technologies in that the participant contributed her account from Sweden and was only asked to say what her experiences of having been a language broker for her parents had been.

> H: When we were newly arrived and none of us spoke Swedish, translators usually addressed my mother when translating, even if the topic was about school and us kids. I didn't need to take responsibility and my mom handled the information. After a while I had to tell my mom what had happened in school and what the teachers told us to prepare for the next day. This was my first encounter with translating for my parents and I found it quite amusing. I was also rather proud of myself for knowing things that my parents didn't. At the same time, I didn't want people to know that my parents didn't understand Swedish or that their language skill was poor. To me, it was kind of a family-secret that I usually enjoyed but did not want to reveal to others.
>
> (Language brokers study)

In the above example, Husniyah herself orientates to what she considers to be a family secret, although it is not clear from her account that any other member of the family considered it so. This is invaluable in helping to construct what she considers to be normative family positioning. As a child in an Arab family, recently migrated to Sweden, she did not want her family to appear deficient in Swedish society. This suggests that she perceived Swedish society as negatively judgemental about migrants who do not speak Swedish. Children's feelings, that stigma attaches to language brokering and their parents' lack of facility in the language of the country in which they live, accord with findings from research done in other countries on children as language brokers. For example, Orellana et al. (2003) found that Latino/a children who were language brokers for their parents in the USA found shopping expeditions to be embarrassing, humiliating, or shameful 'because their identities as poor, working-class or immigrant families were made salient and exposed for public judgment' (p. 518). In a similar way, children who are language brokers frequently do not have their accomplishments in language and as agents who act in their social worlds as they 'para-phrase' for their parents and others (Orellana et al. 2003).

The fact that Husniyah talks of herself as having learned soon after arriving in Sweden (aged eight years) that people who are not able to speak Swedish are devalued indicates her disapproval of her parents' lack of facility in Swedish was probably highly visible. Her account also suggests that she viewed her family as in some ways vulnerable in Swedish society and constructed herself as on the family side of the family/society boundary. She considered that her identity as loyal to her parents overrode pleasure at the power language and culture brokering gave her. In a few sentences, Husniyah suggests that at eight she was able to reconcile intertextual knowledge about how linguistic minorities were seen in Sweden gleaned from the wider culture with knowledge of how teachers, for example, viewed her language brokering and her parents' views and needs. It provides an indication that it is not only personal identity that develops from the learning to keep secrets in childhood (Manen and Levering 1996), but that the keeping of secrets also fuels familial and ethnicised identities. The narrating of her secret thus provides psychosocial insights into her microsocial and macrosocial positioning as well as her retrospective intertextual social understandings.

Just as the reporting of secrets during a research interview can illuminate psychosocial processes, the reporting of areas of silence can illustrate the complexities of differential positioning within families and that what is remembered depends on the emotions associated. In the following example, also from the 'Transforming Experiences' research programme, the participant is talking about her family's experiences of serial migration.

Q. Right. And does that mean that it wasn't talked about in the family?
A. No it definitely wasn't talked about.
Q. So you never talked about it with your parents at all?
A. No, no. It was never ever talked about. Um (.) you know if you asked a question obviously the question was answered, and I actually ... I did my degree very late in life, I only done it I think 6 or 7 years ago. And one of the first pieces of work that I had to do was to write (.) it was a module called Cultural Influences, and was to write about my (.) you know my earliest experiences. So at that time you know I opened up almost a huge can of worms by going back and asking you know my mum and dad and my siblings about you know how things had happened. You know I discovered at that time who was born at home, who was born in hospital – I

found out all sorts of things. That everybody sort of you know participated, and that was really really interesting, but I think we found out more through that than through anything else. And that's why I think this is so important. Because it was at that stage that I (.) I think I'd grown up thinking that wow, mum and dad were amazing, you know they've done all of these things. They came here because (.) we were quite well off in [the Caribbean] (.) um, and that you know they left all that they knew and they (.) you know and came, and I always thought that that was amazing. But when I actually thought about it, like I say doing my own degree, I opened up almost a huge can of worms by going back and asking you know my mum and dad and my siblings about you know how things had happened … But when I actually thought about it … and I thought about as a mother myself how do you leave your children and where do you leave your children. And as a wife myself, how (.) you know how (.) you know I couldn't cope without my husband – all of those aspects came into play for the first time ever. Because up until that point I just accepted that that was our experience and that was the first time I challenged it.

In the extract above, Vadne deliberately employs intertextuality as her way into breaking the silence she explains that her parents maintain about serial migration and her family's experience of it. Indeed, intertextuality in the form of her degree study gives her probing of her family story legitimacy to 'open up a huge can of worms', apparently by questioning how her parents could have done what they did in spending time apart and leaving their children. However, when asked (immediately after the last extract) how she knew the story of the serial migration if it was never talked about, Vadne's story becomes more complex.

Q. Right, okay. So when you say you accepted that it was your experience, how did you know about it then if it was something that wasn't talked about in the family and you were … very little?

A. Um, well it must have been talked about in little dribs and drabs, but it you know wasn't um (.) that's quite an interesting question, I don't know, so it must have been talked about. But I think it was (.) it was amongst us – mum and dad didn't really talk to us, you know, about what they would see as private things, grown up things. Maybe you know things that are painful, I don't know. It wasn't something (.) I think it was more through us talking about things. And by us actually I mean the girls, because like there's … girls and there's … boys, and the boys don't really get involved in anything, you know not to do with emotions …

Q. Anything you'd like to ask me?

A. Um (.) no I just think it's really important that this work gets out there. I really can't tell you how important it is. Like I say not in academic circles, I don't really care about academic. Now I mean that, I just think it should be accessible in straight English for people to just look at you know, um (.)

not look at, do you know what I mean, to access. Um (.) I just think it's really really important. Because I know, I'm fully aware that my parents have got a story to tell, and that every (.) and my aunts and my uncles and everybody else. And that's obviously not just in my family, it's everybody, you know. Um (.) and that's why I was so pleased to do this.

In the above extract, the participant clearly feels that the experience of serial migration was both a profound one for her family and one that is difficult to understand, but needs to be told. It is commonplace for the participants in the serial migration study to say that their experiences were never talked about and that there are generational differences in preparedness to talk as well as gendered differences. However, her account also shows the constructive and contradictory nature of memory in that she gives a precise account of events that happened when she was a toddler, while maintaining that serial migration was 'never ever' talked about. However, the 'accuracy' of her account is not at issue in the research process in that her desire is to disrupt what she sees as the family silence about serial migration. The importance to her of having the story told suggests that bringing the story into the open is one way for her to claim a 'liveable life' by constituting themselves within the norms of personhood as intelligible subjects (Butler 2004). The ways in which speaking out is used to claim intelligibility are produced from intertextual sources about what normative family life looks like and what everyday practices should be like in contemporary western societies (Phoenix 2007).

Conclusion

This chapter has explored some of the ways in which the intertextuality is inextricably linked to the dynamics of silence and secrecy in research interviews in ways that illuminate the construction of normative and 'non-normative' everyday practices and families. The chapter discussed three ways in which intertextual understandings are negotiated in the research process: to smooth over the epistemic violence that results when the interviewer makes explicit an understanding that contradicts that of the participant; where participants use silence to signal secrecy and what cannot be said or further probed and where their orientation to silence and secrecy illuminates their positioning in 'non-normative' family practices. In each example presented silence and secrecy are performative; being about the 'doing' of identities and positioning.

It would, however, have been possible to discuss numerous other instances of how silence and secrecy are central to the construction of narratives in research interviews, in interviews and in analysis and publication. The very ubiquity of such examples lends support to Manen and Levering's (1996) suggestion that secrecy is crucial to development of identities in childhood and extends this to adult identities; personal, familial and ethnicised. This suggests that consideration of everyday negotiations of 'tellability' (Bamberg 2004; Norrick 2005) and its relationship to the construction of identities and the claiming of 'liveable lives' (Butler 2004) would repay further close examination. The examples discussed in the chapter demonstrate that researchers and participants are interlinked in intertexual chains (Solin 2004) which, because they are implicit, are generally silent and have to be negotiated. These intertextual chains provide fruitful sites for analysis.

Notes

1 Bakhtin (1981 [1930s]) suggested that thought and language are dialogic. In other words, all language is produced in relation to things that have been said before and in anticipation of a response. In turn, what has been said produces responses. This means that language and thought are part of the process of re-describing the world and are always in dynamic interaction with previous and future thought and language (rather than standing alone as new and disconnected) (see Maybin, 2001).

References

Abell, J., Locke, A., Condor, S., Gibson, S. and Stevenson, S. (2006) 'Trying similarity, doing difference: the role of interviewer self-disclosure in interview talk with young people', *Qualitative Research*, 6 (2): 221–44.

Bakhtin, M. (1981 [1930s]) *The Dialogic Imagination: Four Essays*, ed. M. Holquist, trans. C. Emerson and M. Holquist. Austin, TX and London: University of Texas Press.

Ball, S. (1994) 'Political interviews and the politics of interviewing', in G. Walford (ed.) *Researching the Powerful in Education*. London: University College London Press.

Bamberg, M. (2004) '"I know it may sound mean to say this, but we couldn't really care less about her anyway": Form and functions of "slut-bashing" in 15-year olds', *Human Development*, 47: 331–53.

Benjamin, J. (1996) *Shadow of the Other: Intersubjectivity and Gender in Psychoanalysis.* London: Routledge.

Billig, M. (1999) *Freudian Repression: Conversation Creating the Unconscious.* Cambridge: Cambridge University Press.

Brannen, J. (1988) 'The study of sensitive subjects', *Sociological Review*, 36 (3): 552–63.

Butler, J. (2004) *Undoing Gender.* New York: Routledge.

Fletcher, D. and Watson, T. (2007) 'Voice, silence and the business of construction: loud and quiet voices in the construction of personal, organizational and social realities', *Organization*, 14 (2): 155–74.

Fox, N. (1995) 'Intertextuality and the writing of social research', *Electronic Journal of Sociology*, http://www.sociology.org/content/vol001.002/fox.html.

Frosh, S. (2002) *Afterwords: The Personal in Gender, Culture and Psychotherapy.* New York: Palgrave.

Gunaratnam, Y. (2003) *Researching 'Race' and Ethnicity Methods, Knowledge and Power.* London: Sage.

Gunaratnam, Y. and Lewis, G. (2001) 'Racialising emotional labour and emotionalising racialized labour: anger, fear and shame in social welfare', *Journal of Social Work Practice*, 15 (2): 131–48.

Hollway, W. and Jefferson, T. (2000) *Doing Qualitative Research Differently: Free Association, Narrative and the Interview Method*. London: Sage.

Hubbard, G., Backett-Milburn, K. and Kemmer, D. (2001) 'Working with emotion: Issues for the researcher in fieldwork and teamwork', *International Journal of Social Research Methodology*, 4 (2): 119–37.

Irwin, W. (2004) 'Against intertextuality', *Philosophy and Literature*, 28 (2): 227–42.

Kavanaugh, K. and Ayres, L. (1998) '"Not as bad as it could have been": assessing and mitigating harm during research interviews on sensitive topics', *Research in Nursing and Health*, 21 (1): 91–97.

Kristeva, J. (1980) *Desire in Language: A Semiotic Approach to Literature and Art*. New York: Columbia University Press.

Leonardo, Z. (2004) 'The color of supremacy: beyond the discourse of "white privilege"', *Educational Philosophy and Theory*, 36: 137–52.

Lowes, L. and Gill, P. (2006) 'Participants' experiences of being interviewed about an emotive topic', *Journal of Advanced Nursing*, 55 (5): 587–95.

Lyotard, J.-F. (1985) *Just Gaming*, translated Jean Loup Thebaud. Minneapolis: University of Minnesota Press.

Manen, M.V. and Levering, B. (1996) *Childhood's Secrets: Intimacy, Privacy, and the Self Reconsidered*. New York: Teachers College Press.

Maybin, J. (2001) 'Language, struggle and voice: the Bakhtin/Volosinov writings', in M. Wetherell, S. Taylor and S.J. Yates (eds) *Discourse Theory and Practice: A Reader*. London: Sage.

Mazzei, L. (2008) 'Silence speaks: whiteness revealed in the absence of voice', *Teaching and Teacher Education*, 24 (5): 1125–36.

Norrick, N. (2005) 'The dark side of tellability', *Narrative Inquiry*, 15 (2): 323–43.

Oakley, A. (1981) 'Interviewing women: a contradiction in terms', in H. Roberts (ed.) *Doing Feminist Research*. London: Routledge.

Ochs, E. and Capps, L. (2001) *Living Narrative: Creating Lives in Everyday Storytelling*. Cambridge, MA: Harvard University Press.

Orellana, M.F., Dorner, L. and Pulido, L. (2003) 'Accessing assets: immigrant youth's work as family translators or "para-phrasers"', *Social Problems*, 50 (4): 505–24.

Phoenix, A. (1991) *Young Mothers?* Cambridge: Polity.

—— (1994) 'Practising feminist research: the intersection of gender and "race" in the research process', in M.A. Maynard (ed.) *Researching Women's Lives from a Feminist Perspective*. London: Taylor & Francis.

—— (2004) 'Extolling eclecticism: language, psychoanalysis and demographic analyses in the study of "race" and racism', in M. Bulmer and J. Solomos (eds) *Researching Race and Racism*. London: Routledge.

—— (2007) 'Claiming liveable lives: adult subjectification and narratives of "non-normative" childhood experiences', in J. Kofoed and D. Staunaes (eds) *Magtballader*. Copenhagen: Danish Pedagogical University.

Puwar, N. (1997) 'Reflections on interviewing women MPs', *Sociological Research Online*, 2(1), http://www.socresonline.org.uk/socresonline/2/1/4.html.

Riessman, C.K. (2008) *Narrative Methods for the Human Sciences*. London: Sage.

Solin, A. (2004) 'Intertextuality as mediation: on the analysis of intertextual relations in public discourse', *Text*, 24 (2): 267–96.

Song, M. and Parker, D. (1995) 'Commonality, difference and the dynamics of disclosure in in-depth interviewing', *Sociology*, 29 (2): 241–56.

Spivak, G.C. (1988) 'Can the subaltern speak?' In C. Nelson and L. Grossberg (eds) *Marxism and the Interpretation of Culture*. London: Macmillan.

Tizard, B. and Phoenix, A. (2002) *Black, White or Mixed Race: Race and Racism in the Lives of Young People of Mixed Parentage*, 2nd edition. London: Routledge.

Ward, J. and Winstanley, D. (2003) 'The absent presence: negative space within discourse and the construction of minority sexual identity in the workplace', *Human Relations*, 56 (10): 1255–80.

Wetherell, M. (1998) 'Positioning and interpretative repertoires: conversation conversation analysis and post-structuralism in dialogue', *Discourse and Society*, 9 (3): 387–412.

13 Dirty work

Researching women and sexual representation

Feona Attwood

This chapter examines the policing of speech and the silences that have resulted from this in academic work on sexual representations. In particular, it focuses on the examination of women's relationships with sexual representation, drawing on the accounts of researchers in the field, as well as my own experiences of working in this area. My work focuses on sex and the media – particularly on pornographies, sexuality online, and researching and teaching sexually explicit media. This last area of interest is taking on new urgency in the current context where sex education and media literacy are claimed as central to citizenship, yet remain underdeveloped, and where misconceptions and myths about sex media continue to be reproduced in public debates and in legislation. It is this strand of my research which prompted me to start collecting the accounts of researchers who work in this area, as part of a broader project on contemporary groups who produce public knowledge about sex media.

Despite a belief that in late modern societies we are 'incited' to speak about sex, tensions and silences still persist and some types of speech and speakers are strongly discouraged. This is the legacy of an earlier set of shifts in which artistic and scientific modes were established as the 'proper' forms for speaking sex and were associated with middle-class male scholars who built 'secret museums' (Kendrick 1996 [1987]) to house sexually explicit art and artefacts and developed a 'science of sexuality' – sexology. Secular confession, with its attendant baggage of shame became a primary mode of sexual speech and some groups of people – notably women and children – became the objects of sexual enquiry whilst being excluded from speaking authoritatively about sex.

These restrictions have made talking about sex a difficult business. Even today in our 'sexualised' culture, explicit sexual speech is marked as 'crude', indirect and disparaging forms of sexual speech such as innuendo persist, and sex education continues to be a notoriously embarrassing experience for everyone involved. And although women are often the *object* of sex talk, their own speech continues to excite considerable disquiet and suspicion. As Linda Williams has argued (1991), women are seen as unreliable sexual narrators, and sexual representations produced by women are frequently accused of ventriloquising male desires. Because of this, women are doubly silenced – forbidden to speak, disbelieved when they do.

Sex and scholarship

While a scholarly approach has historically been one way of legitimating speech about sex, sex is a problematic area for academics today. This is particularly true of despised forms of sexual representation such as pornography, towards which, as Linda Williams writes, 'it is difficult to strike a proper attitude' (ibid.: xi). Certainly, admitting to any pleasure in the object of study is taboo. As Alan McKee notes:

> The only researchers who have actually admitted in print that they enjoy porn are those who have identities outside of the academy as well – as sex therapists or educators. I can't recall an example of an academic employed at a university acknowledging in their research that they have a personal interest in the genre. Porn consumers are still, always, them – not us.
>
> (McKee 2007)

This is not surprising, given that talking about sexual representation is fraught with difficulty and sometimes danger. As Henry Jenkins (2004: 2) notes, academics have had 'their reputations destroyed, lost their jobs, and faced legal sanctions for teaching or researching porn'. As a result, research into sexually explicit media is underdeveloped, and as a recent report in the *Times Higher Education Supplement* notes, there is an 'urgent need for more critical engagement with pornography' (Attwood 2007: 1).

These difficulties help to explain the many gaps in our knowledge about women's relationships with sexual representations. That an interest in sex still signifies awkwardly in relation to norms of femininity, and that feminism is still popularly associated with an anti-porn stance, may also contribute to the difficulty of speaking about sexually explicit media. Yet women's engagement with porn appears to be growing. Reliable figures on pornography consumption are notoriously hard to come by, but it is widely claimed that women use porn in increasing numbers. This is echoed in collections of 'ordinary' women's views on sexuality, such as Abby Levine's account 'Better Living through Porn' (Damsky 2000). The account documents Levine's relationship with feminism and pornography in a changing political climate in which her porn eventually moves 'from a bag hidden in the top of the closet, to a few books in a bedside drawer, to an entire bookcase in the bedroom … just more books on the shelf, mixed in with some poetry and wedding planners' (ibid.: 330).

But despite the burgeoning of accounts which celebrate porn for women, women's relationship to pornography continues to be marked as difficult, as some recent popular texts demonstrate. Even books which are positive about porn are based on the premise that it is a problem. Violet Blue's *The Smart Girl's Guide to Porn* starts from her own search for porn that is 'hot, and not scary or disappointing' (2006: viii), while Ayn Carrillo-Gailey's *porn-o-logy* (2007) recounts the quest of her protagonist, 'a good girl', to overcome her ignorance and fear about porn. Pamela Paul's *Pornified* (2005) describes women's engagement with porn as entirely problematic, damaging to their relationships with men and to their own self-esteem.

This awkwardness around pornography carries over into academics' experience of researching sexually explicit media. A number of researchers reported in their accounts that their work is often regarded by others as 'thrilling', 'taboo' or 'a joke', or that it is 'somehow heavy, difficult and unpleasant'. One described being regarded as 'not very bright and sexually available' when she began to work in the area. As researchers, we may be subject to 'inappropriate' remarks, 'puerile' responses and even personal abuse. Our work carries little cultural capital and it is often not taken seriously or accorded the same kind of status as other forms of media research. Our disciplinary home may have a bearing on this: researching pornography is more acceptable in cultural and media studies and less so elsewhere. All the same, wherever we work, we sometimes find that what we research is not deemed *worthy* of study; hence the astonishing view, still held by some academics, that it is possible to write about sexually explicit media without having viewed any. It is often difficult, if not impossible, for us to teach or research our subject 'at work', that is, on university premises. The responses of others and the conditions in which we work function to enforce, if not silence, then a great deal of self-consciousness about the work we do and how we can speak about it, marking our knowledge as a kind of 'dirty secret'.

The lack of status carried by sex research and the suspicion that surrounds it can make working in this area problematic in other ways. For example, in instances where researchers have been harassed and upset in the course of their work, it may be particularly hard to report this or to ask for support, and reporting uncomfortable or ambiguous findings may involve political dilemmas for us. Sex research may also result in a lack or loss of professional status and make career progression difficult for us, a very obvious form of silencing. However, it's important to note the differences in the experiences of researchers. For example, one spoke of a 'certain street credibility' that porn studies can carry amongst students and noted that issues of regulation, funding and status vary quite dramatically from country to country. Another described 'commendable levels of support' from their institution. What typically emerges, though, is a patterning of responses – encouragement from others in the field, leg-pulling by friends and some colleagues, a certain amount of awkwardness with relatives and a mixture of amusement, condescension, suspicion and hostility from a variety of other sources. Extending research beyond the confines of the academy in more public arenas may also result in different kinds of problems, making us more vulnerable to personal attack, whilst simultaneously making it more difficult to be taken seriously in an academic context. These difficulties, all of which work to enforce silence or particular ways of speaking about sex, are compounded by the bigger silence which often meets our research in the public sphere where politicians and journalists routinely ignore work which does not reproduce the familiar view of sexually explicit media as dangerous and its consumers as 'others'. In this respect, the disciplinary bias that favours media and cultural studies approaches to sex is reversed; in public, these carry little weight. For example, the UK Justice Department's commissioning of a 'Rapid Evidence Assessment' on the 'harm' of 'extreme pornography' (2007) was obtained from academics with no background in media research and based on an extraordinarily out of date set of theoretical and methodological approaches to media consumption (Barker 2007).

Talking about sex

The difficulties of talking about sex manifest in a range of ways in academic research, in problems about the terms we use and the kinds of sentiments that are permissible. At the most basic level, terms like 'sexually explicit media', 'erotica' and 'pornography' are used in a variety of ways. In Dana Wilson-Kovacs' (2008) study of women's consumption of sexual materials, participants listed a wide range of texts that they were familiar with, including soft-porn magazines, erotic books, photography, mainstream films and more explicit films and magazines that they referred to as 'hardcore'. However, they classified these items in quite different ways – for one a text might count as 'pornography', while for another it might be 'erotica'. For some participants in a study of the audiences of the film *Crash*, erotica and pornography were 'mutually exclusive', while others used the terms 'in combination' (Barker et al. 2001: 52). This problem of terminology is derived in part from the weight that it carries; in particular, '"pornography" carries a judgement on the user – to admit to being aroused by pornography is to admit a weakness. To say that you like it is even more problematic' (ibid.: 44). Often, of course, 'pornography' may not be used as a descriptive or generic term, but reserved for texts that are considered offensive or derogatory to women. In Susan Shaw's study, women used the term for 'violent' sexual images which 'scared' and 'disgusted' them (1999: 203). Clearly, this lack of a shared vocabulary can cause enormous problems for comparing existing studies and, more generally, for making sense of the way people view and experience their consumption of sexually explicit media.

Another problem is the difficulty that many women have with speaking about sexually explicit media at all. Karen Ciclitira found that it is particularly hard for women to be open about their enjoyment of pornography, because this might mark them as unfeminine and/or unfeminist (2002, 2004). In Dana Wilson-Kovacs' study (2008), women reported that they did not talk about porn with female friends because it was not considered suitable for women. Talking about porn with partners could be equally problematic;

participants reported feeling apprehensive that expertise in this area might make them seem too sexually knowledgeable or 'cheap'. They were also concerned that this kind of knowledge might undermine their partners' sexual confidence or, on the other hand, inspire them to suggest unwanted sexual practices such as bondage or swinging. Susan Shaw (1999: 210) has noted a further aspect of silencing: women who disliked their partners' porn use felt unable to voice their objections because of a concern with 'freedom of choice and individual rights' and because of a fear of being seen as old-fashioned and anti-sex.

These problems of terminology and awkwardness have been created partly by the framing of sexually explicit media within public and academic debates as a monolithic category which is also a social problem – or, less commonly, makes them emblems of free speech and liberation. Here, silencing takes the form of allowing only a very narrow range of approaches, making a whole raft of ideas, questions and understandings invisible and unheard. Indeed, until recently the objects of debate have rarely been defined, existing generally merely to signify the way dangerous forms of media structure our responses or impact on our behaviour. The dominance of psychoanalysis and effects approaches in discussions of porn are indicative of this – both types of theoretical 'talk' which mobilise abstract views of the media, privilege 'expert' readings and have little to say about social or cultural context.

The prominence of anti-porn feminism has also been problematic for the way porn is talked about, often working to drown out the diverse viewpoints in feminist work on sexually explicit media. It has tended to focus on pornography not as a genre, but as a blueprint for violence against women, or a form of violence in itself, reproducing a discourse about the media's 'negative effects'. It has associated porn with 'feelings of hurt, anger, frustration, fear and nausea', thereby also producing a discourse of '*negative affect* ... as the acceptable reaction to pornography' (Paasonen 2007: 47). It has also promoted a view of female audiences as ignorant. Contrasting the presentational styles of anti-porn scholar Gail Dines and s/expert Susie Bright, in the porn-education road-shows at American universities during the 1980s and 1990s, Eithne Johnson (1997) has shown how anti-porn feminist rhetoric has often relied on the use of shocking and atypical imagery to enforce a relationship of feminist expertise over the incompetent understandings of ordinary women. This approach is clearly unworkable for researchers who are concerned with a wide variety of sexually explicit media and with questions of genre, and who start from the position that women are literate and capable of making informed decisions about their media consumption.

The impact of anti-porn feminism is also evident in research into women's relationships with porn. For example, Karen Ciclitira's work (1998, 2002, 2004) shows that public debates about porn have made some women 're-evaluate whether or not they want to be a part of the feminist movement' (Ciclitira 2004: 296). The combination of an anti-porn feminist stance with the use of a psychoanalytic framework for analysing media has led to a particularly intractable problem in making sense of sexually explicit media, as an example from Clarissa Smith's (2007) study of *For Women* magazine illustrates. Laura, a participant in the study, is an academic researcher and occasional reader of the magazine. By her own account she is suspicious of pornography because it is 'framed by the male gaze … or male conceptions of what female desire should be and is'. This leads her to argue that female desire ' … is still suppressed, oppressed and still subterranean … still a big taboo area' (ibid.: 143), and that women's sex lives are 'still inchoate and being formulated and transformed and mutated into something different' (ibid.: 145). The totalising notion of a 'male gaze' suggests that all existing sexual representations must be discounted as inauthentic, while the incoherence of women's sexuality prevents new forms of expression from emerging. Inauthentic or incoherent – in this view sexually explicit media is apprehended as having nothing to say to women. As Smith notes, from this perspective there can be no valid expression of women's sexuality and no concept of women's agency in the production and consumption of sexually explicit media. The linking of a 'correct' reading of porn to superior feminist and academic knowledge becomes clear in Laura's claim that 'educated women who are doing women's studies or … gender studies … or cultural studies' maintain a distance from pornography (ibid.: 143–46); a claim that reinforces a view of women's engagement with porn as *either* educated 'reading' *or* inauthentic 'response'. There is a class dimension to this approach, which is bound up with issues of taste and cultural capital. This often manifests, as one researcher put it, as 'an aesthetic revulsion' dressed up as a 'more profound moral objection', or, as another noted, in the tendency of some disciplines, to 'rescue' certain texts on aesthetic grounds, for example, by intellectualising some kinds of porn as forms of 'art' or 'avant garde' production.

My experience is that there is still an enormously strong expectation that as a female academic researching sexually explicit media I am bound to be working from a position of 'revulsion', an assumption that follows logically enough from the correlation between the imposition of 'expert' readings onto sexually explicit media in anti-porn feminism and earlier academic takes on pornography. This default position is a seriously disabling factor in developing work in the area. Yet an unwillingness to adopt it may result in researchers being viewed as lacking in empathy with other women – to take an approach which does not start by regarding pornography as a problem or a form of violence implies a lack of regard for women's well-being. In the case of 'extreme' or illegal forms of sexually explicit media, research which does not proceed from this 'concerned' starting point is virtually impossible to carry out. In traditional disciplines it also results in the reproduction of a particular stance and methodology which work to build silence around issues of desire or pleasure by focusing on large scale quantitative projects in health, resulting in the construction, as one researcher noted, of sex as 'dry, negative and problem based'.

In contrast, pro-sex feminist discourse has tended to emphasise the potential pleasures of pornography and women readers' acquisition of expertise through experimentation and experience. This approach is more useful, though it can be problematic where it slides into a crudely oppositional stance which remains focused on transgressive figures of women – real or imagined – and on less typical types of representation, ignoring '"ordinary" porn and its "ordinary" producers and readers' (Smith 2007: 49). As one researcher remarked, '[i]t's okay to be anti-porn, or pro-porn, but to have a more complex view is still something of an academic taboo'. In the meantime, the continuing prevalence of the anti/pro debate makes it difficult to articulate more complex responses to porn and enforces a structure which focuses on argument and opposition, but which fails to move forward in any significant way.

The problem is that although it's easy to see why we might take up particular positions in debates about sexually explicit media, indeed, it is incredibly difficult to avoid, the way we do this operates within an incredibly unhelpful framework. It reproduces a set of oppositions around liberation and oppression – sexually explicit media are good/liberating/woman-friendly or they are bad/oppressive/woman-hating. Although both responses appear quite different in many respects, both leave women with very little sense of how to tackle the conflicts and contradictions of sexually explicit media, or even how to begin to talk about these. What is striking in many discussions of women's relationships with sexually explicit media is how adept they are at identifying what they don't like about sexually explicit media, but much less successful in expressing what they do or would like. Clearly, given the problems of speaking about sex, discussing sexual desires with researchers will be difficult, if not impossible, for many women, but there may also be more pervasive difficulties arising from the problem of articulating both what is forbidden and what does not yet exist. As bell hooks has noted, while it is relatively easy to be critical of negative aspects of sexuality, it is 'a far more difficult task for women to envision new sexual paradigms, to change the norms of sexuality' (2006: 7).

Doing the dirty

Talking about sexually explicit media continues to be problematic for women for all kinds of reasons; because it may be both 'unfeminine' and 'unfeminist', because of the institutional pressures and frameworks within which research is conducted, because of notions of quality and worth, because of the lack of an accepted lexicon for such discussions, and because of the way that sexually explicit media are 'overburdened with significance' (Segal 1992: 65) as an emblem of women's oppression, of the dangerous power of the media, and more recently of the commodification of sex and neo-liberalist individualism.

In their attempts to move beyond these problems, researchers working on sexually explicit media use a variety of methods and draw on a range of theoretical starting points, but those I spoke to identified a particular approach as being of more importance. This begins with questions rather than assumptions and develops work from engaging with texts and interacting with people rather than from abstract assertions and assumptions about appropriate sexual practices and forms of consumption for women. Clarissa Smith's discussion of her approach to readers of *For Women* magazine, a 1990s publication targeted at straight women and attracting a great deal of media attention because of its inclusion of male nudes, sums this up well:

> To all respondents, I stressed my desire to get to the reasons why some women enjoyed *For Women*, in spite of the theory and the common-sense claim that women don't like or read sexually explicit materials. I also made clear that although I had some theoretical knowledge I had no better answers than theirs to explain why women might like pictures of naked men and explicit stories. I intended to indicate that I came to them with an open mind and a genuine interest in their *individual* engagement with sex and sexual representations. That ploy was successful because I *was* genuinely interested.
>
> (2007: 250)

There are a range of strategies that we might adopt to use this approach to develop work in the area and to combat silence around women's engagements with sexually explicit media. Experimenting with different kinds of talk might be productive in opening up possibilities for speaking freely and openly and allowing us to say new things. Another way forward might be to focus quite deliberately on the kinds of significances that sexually explicit media take for women and the consequences of both consuming and talking about them. As Deborah L. Tolman shows in her work on teenage girls and sexuality, it is the way that the relation between femininity and sex is constructed that makes it difficult to talk about. Tolman (2002) argues that when girls talk about sex they describe how they experience sexuality as a *personal* dilemma – 'a choice between their sexual feelings or their safety' (ibid.: 44). In a context where to be female is still often to walk a tightrope between being desexualised or hypersexualised, developing an acceptable sexual identity is fraught with difficulty. Sexual feelings may be experienced as a 'problem' which, if acted on, may lead to rejection, embarrassment, frustration, or violence. The construction of this as a personal problem rather than a socially constructed dilemma imposes on girls an understanding of 'the source of danger to be *their own sexuality*' (ibid.: 46).

This may be an extreme example – clearly, many women and girls do find ways of talking about sex and enjoy doing so. Yet the researchers I spoke to point out that we still do not really know much about what they think about the production, representation or consumption of sexual material. We know very little about how sexually explicit media work for their audiences. We have not discovered much that takes us very far beyond the crude concepts of shame and arousal in understanding how women feel about sexual representations. We have little idea how they are used and viewed in intimate relationships and how women and girls see their place and meaning in the context of their lives. We do not know whether women's relationships to sexually explicit media are changing or whether they are marked by generational differences. We know virtually nothing about the ways that women are experiencing new forms of porn culture and new conventions of representation, or about their experiences in producing sexually explicit media, though more material on this is beginning to emerge. Given our institutional context, we are likely to find it hard to acknowledge our own pleasures and desires – let alone the range of emotions and responses we might feel, and the difficulty of 'striking a proper attitude' is likely to increase our own lack of articulacy and our self-consciousness in carrying out our work.

Breaking the silence

The future of research into women's relationships with sexually explicit media could take a variety of directions; looking at different types of media including hardcore, softcore, erotica and 'sexy' mainstream texts; at audiences of varying ages and backgrounds; at the different ways media are used in relationships, in more casual encounters and in women's solitary practices and fantasies; and at women's engagements with producing and circulating sexually explicit media. We also need to look much more closely and critically at the methodologies and concepts that we are working with and to become much clearer about what these allow to be heard and what they also silence.

Given the difficult history of talking about sex and the particular silences that have been enforced, it might also be strategically productive to focus on instances where women *are* voluble about sexually explicit media and where they describe their relationships with sexually explicit media as pleasurable and empowering. For, while silence and silencing continue to be features of academic work in this area, women's talk about sexually explicit media is increasingly audible beyond the academy, especially online where there are a growing number of highly visible female commentators on the subject[1] and many more women openly discussing porn in blogs, chat rooms and discussion boards.

The participants in these discussions are probably most often drawn from the group interviewed in Audacia Ray's (2007) book about women, sex and the Internet; women who have 'over the last decade or so … started to remake, question, challenge, and enjoy the adult industry in a way that perhaps is only possible with the assistance of increasingly user-friendly and inexpensive technology' (ibid.: 135). This demographic, for whom browsing free porn online became 'a common pastime as a teenager' (ibid.: 137), appear to be more confident with sex toys, forms of online sex, experimenting with sexual practices and identities, and getting involved in producing sexually explicit materials themselves, whether privately as part of their own sexual development or more publicly on erotica or altporn sites.

Critics will argue that these women are merely victims of a hypersexual culture where to be engaged in sex talk is to be suitably modern and acceptably feminine, or that they are not representative of all women. But women's use of spaces to talk about sex is significant and important, particularly if we accept Tolman's view that speaking about sex is vital in sorting out feelings about 'sexual desire, sexual entitlement, and sexual subjectivity' (2002: 192). As Tolman shows, refusing a position of sexual passivity and silence is, potentially, to be rewarded with the means to develop sexual agency, confidence and power. This is not easy – it requires the development of a political understanding of the significance of sexually explicit media and a willingness to 'delve into our own psychological remedies for living in our female bodies, textured by race, class, religion, and ability, within a patriarchal society' (ibid.: 200). Despite the problems and pressures surrounding sex talk, all of us – and especially academics whose job it is to develop knowledge and understanding about this aspect of the media's place in women's lives – need to find ways to speak more openly about sex.

Acknowledgements

My thanks to the researchers who shared their experiences and views with me for this chapter: Jane Arthurs, Petra Boynton, Sara Bragg, Karen Ciclitira, Darren Kerr, Katrien Jacobs, Susanna Paasonen, Clarissa Smith and Dana Wilson-Kovacs.

Notes

1 Regina Lynn writes the popular 'Sex Drive' column for *Wired* magazine and is the author of *The Sexual Revolution 2.0*; Violet Blue is a prolific commentator, the author of numerous books on sex and hosts her own site, 'tinynibbles'; Audacia Ray is, amongst other things, a blogger, director, author, model and editor of *Spread*, a magazine by and for sex workers.

References

Attwood, R. (2007) 'Taboos stymie a frank look at porn', *Times Higher Education Supplement*, 30 March: 1 and 8–9.

Barker, M. (2007) 'Editorial introduction', *Participations: Journal of Audience and Reception Studies*, 4 (2), http://www.participations.org/Volume%204/Issue%202/4_02_editorial.htm.

Barker M., Arthurs J. and Harindranath R. (2001) *The Crash Controversy: censorship campaigns and film reception*, London and New York: Wallflower Press.

Blue, V. (2006) *The Smart Girl's Guide to Porn*, San Francisco: Cleis Press.

—— http://www.tinynibbles.com/, accessed 14.10.08.

Buszek, M. (2006) *Pin-up Grrrls: feminism, sexuality, popular culture*, Durham, NC: Duke University Press.

Carrillo-Gailey, A. (2007) *porn-o-logy*, Philadelphia and London: Running Press.

Ciclitira, K. (1998) 'What does pornography mean to women?', unpublished thesis, Manchester Metropolitan University.

—— (2002) 'Researching pornography and sexual bodies', *The Psychologist*, 15 (4): 191–94.

—— (2004) 'Pornography, women and feminism: between pleasure and politics', *Sexualities*, 7 (3): 281–301.

Itzin, C., Taket, A. and Kelly, L. (2007) 'The evidence of harm to adults relating to exposure to extreme pornographic material: a rapid evidence assessment', *Ministry of Justice Research Series*. London

Jenkins, H. (2004) 'Foreword: so you want to teach pornography?', in P. Church Gibson (ed.) *More Dirty Looks: gender, pornography and power*, London: BFI Publishing: 1–7.

Johnson, E. (1997) 'Appearing live on your campus!: porn-education roadshows', *Jump Cut*, 41: 27–35.

Kendrick, W. (1996 [1987]) *The Secret Museum: pornography in modern culture*, Berkeley, CA: University of California Press.

Levine, A. (2000) 'Better living through porn' in L. Damsky (ed.) *Sex and Single Girls: straight and queer women on sexuality*, Seattle: Seal Press: 321–30.

Lynn, R. (2005) *The Sexual Revolution 2.0.*, Berkeley, CA: Ulysses Press.

McKee, A. (2007) 'Pornography research'. E-mail (14.10.08).

Paasonen, S. (2007) 'Strange bedfellows: pornography, affect and feminist reading', *Feminist Theory*, 8 (1): 43–57.

Paul, P. (2005) *Pornified: how pornography is transforming our lives, our relationships and our families*, New York: Times Books.

Ray, A. (2007) *Naked on the Internet: hookups, downloads and cashing in on internet sexploration*, Emeryville, CA: Seal Press.

Segal, L. (1992) 'Introduction', in L. Segal and M. McIntosh (eds) *Sex Exposed: sexuality and the pornography debate*, London: Virago: 1–11.

Shaw, S. (1999) 'Men's leisure and women's lives: the impact of pornography on women', *Leisure Studies*, 18: 197–212.

Smith, C. (2007) *One for the Girls! The Pleasures and Practices of Reading Women's Porn*, Bristol: Intellect.

Tolman, D.L. (2002) *Dilemmas of Desire: teenage girls talk about sexuality*, Cambridge, MA: Harvard University Press.

Williams, L. (1991) *Hard Core: power, pleasure and the 'frenzy of the visible'*, London: Pandora.

Wilson-Kovacs, D. (2009) 'Some texts do it better: women, sexually explicit texts and the everyday', in F. Attwood (ed.) *Mainstreaming Sex: the sexualization of culture*, London: I.B. Tauris, 147–163.

14 Keeping mum

Secrecy and silence in research on lesbian parenthood

Róisín Ryan-Flood

The sociologist Kenneth Plummer once observed that researching into the subject 'sex' makes the researcher morally suspect (Plummer 1975: 4). He was writing as a gay man researching the topic in the mid-1970s and clearly the context for research on sexuality has changed enormously in the interim, thanks indeed to the efforts of pioneers like Plummer himself. Thus, sexuality is now if not entirely respectable, then certainly an established field of academic work. But this earlier association with research on sexuality and a morally questionable position is an interesting one, given that in fact most research on sexuality is inherently concerned – whether explicitly or implicitly – with questions of ethics. Social researchers in the field are typically dealing with intimate aspects of people's lives, often in relation to social inequalities, so are therefore directly addressing issues of power, vulnerability and equality. In fact, research on sexualities typically necessitates complex negotiations of these issues. Any researcher may find themselves grappling with complex dilemmas that require ethical or indeed moral decisions.

Researching sexual identities and intimate life brings a weight of responsibility. Asking people to open up about what to many will seem like intensely private experiences and perceptions, brings with it the expectation that you will treat the 'data' – and by association the participant – with tact and sensitivity. Participants may make disclosures in the interview situation that are revelations to themselves, as the act of talking encourages reflection and insight. While participants can consciously choose what to reveal and what to omit, the research process is often unwittingly seductive in that participants may enjoy the rapt attention of the researcher and find themselves opening up more than planned or expected. It is the responsibility of the researcher to treat data confidentially and to conduct research in ways that are not harmful to participants. Along the way, the researcher may find themselves considering a number of thorny issues about what it means to 'uncover' voices and the value for members of oppressed groups of 'speaking out'.

Feminist writing has traditionally highlighted questions of voice and representation. This includes calls for the inclusion of women's voices in social research, or writing women into history where previously women's experiences have frequently been ignored. Too often the universal subject presented in social research has taken the voice of the hegemonic citizen – often a white, middle-class, heterosexual man – as representative. Feminist work has uncovered women's hidden histories and incorporated them into wider accounts of the world. The feminist emphasis on voice and representation has clear intellectual and political roots and has contributed significantly to a more egalitarian epistemological climate, as well as producing vastly more nuanced accounts of social life. However, it is perhaps the case that the importance attached to speaking out and moving from silence to voice has neglected some of the unspoken aspects of the research process. Research often presents complex dilemmas for the researcher. These may be ethical, moral, epistemological or a combination of all three. Ultimately the researcher has the authority to decide what will find its way into the final account of the research. This process may involve complex decisions about what can be disclosed about the empirical findings or research encounter. It may also require difficult choices about how to represent people. Feminist work in particular is often concerned with marginal groups. A commitment to egalitarian principles informs research praxis and marks a concern with preventing harm to participants. At times, this may require omitting information that exposes the marginal group being researched to the potentially disciplining gaze of academia and beyond. This raises a number of questions. As researchers, what secrets do we keep and why? Where do we choose silence over voice? What are the epistemological implications of these choices and dilemmas? Furthermore, what about instances where we struggle to interpret and theorize participants' silences? Perhaps they may choose to resist our efforts to 'understand' or 'record' their experiences. Or silence may incorporate complex social codes that may not be immediately evident to the researcher.

Valentine (2002) suggests that the interview is always a 'joint production' as a result of the diverse intersections of identities and biographies. In her view, rather than seeking to identify a 'transparent knowable self', feminist researchers should instead focus on the 'tensions, conflicts and unexpected occurrences' that emerge in the research process (2002: 126). This approach emphasises the agency of participants, who may resist the researchers' assumptions and interpretations. Contemporary feminist researchers acknowledge that the possibility of exploitative social relations between researcher and researched are always present. Reflexive accounts of the research process help to identify power dynamics in research, contributing to greater understanding of the epistemological basis of the work. In this chapter, conflict and dilemmas in research are analysed to illustrate how the situatedness of the researcher affected the production of knowledge and epistemological terrain. The discussion draws on research with lesbian parents in two European countries, Sweden and Ireland. Lesbian and gay communities present many challenges for research (Badgett 2003; Sullivan and Losberg 2003; Browne 2008). Researchers often face difficulties recruiting a wide sample or any participants at all. My own identity as a lesbian facilitated access to the communities I studied. I carried out interviews with 68 lesbian parents in the two countries and also did some ethnographic work at LGBT events. In this chapter, I explore two research moments: my choice to hide knowledge of participants' illegal activities; and struggling to make sense of participants' silences in their interview narratives.

Feminist research ethics: power, representation and 'the field'

Qualitative research was initially posited both as an inherently 'feminist' method and as an ideal means of achieving more egalitarian relationships in research. The interactive nature of qualitative methods was considered less objectifying than traditional quantitative methods and allowed women's voices to be integrated into the research process (Bowles and Duelli-Klein 1983; Stanley and Wise 1983). However, these claims have long since been challenged by writers who argue that there is no one feminist method and who defend quantitative methods as a useful analytical tool (Kelly et al. 1992; Oakley 2000). In a discussion of feminism and ethnography, Stacey (1991) has further suggested that participants are in fact more vulnerable to exploitation in this kind of qualitative research, where social interaction facilitates manipulation on the part of researchers. Furthermore, this approach elicits intensely personal information and understandings of the world that are ultimately simply data for the research project, rather than an egalitarian and mutual exchange. Participants in my research for example often related to me as a fellow-member of a minority (lesbian) community and interview encounters occasionally developed into more sustained social relationships. While these relationships may have positive advantages for both researcher and researched, they highlight participants' potential vulnerability, as the boundary between research and friendship can become blurred.

Power is inevitably implicated in research at every level of analysis, not just during the data collection process. The researcher is always the final author of a research text and thus has ultimate power regarding whose 'voices' to portray and how. Informed by concerns regarding 'the appropriation of the voices of "others"', the heterosexual researcher England (1994: 81) opted out of continuing a study of a lesbian community in Toronto. Mohanty (1991) and Patai (1991) both address the politics of First World woman researching Third World women. The different identities of the researcher and participants in these contexts also constitute a difference in power.

Dilemmas of representation are not restricted to researchers with 'outsider' status. Zavella (1993) found that as a Chicana woman doing ethnographic research on Chicana working mothers, her status as a cultural 'insider' hindered her understanding of the complexities of the research material. She also experienced difficulties in presenting her work on these ethnographic 'others' to her peers. Being a member of a subordinated group under study creates particular dilemmas in that 'insider' researchers experience unique constraints in how they are held accountable to the community being studied. Zavella points out that along with the cooperation facilitated by one's insider status comes the responsibility to produce analyses that are sympathetic to the interests of the participant group and to share whatever knowledge is generated with them. As an Irish lesbian, my personal identity/lifestyle facilitated research access to a difficult-to-reach community (lesbian parents) and also engendered responsibilities. Particularly where participants were not known to me personally prior to an interview, advance knowledge of my sexual identity often appeared to act as a reassurance. This is not to suggest however, that I was always and everywhere an 'insider', or that such categorisations are not mediated by other facets of identity and experience. In Ireland for example, the fact that I am from Dublin, middle-class and childless were markers of my differential situatedness compared to some respondents.

Patai (1991) highlights a further dilemma that arises when researchers – consciously or unconsciously – encourage participants to hope that research will improve their personal circumstances. As McDowell (1999: 239) notes in a consideration of ethical dilemmas in feminist research: 'Researchers may inadvertently raise expectations of positive intervention on behalf of participants, leading to feelings of disappointment or betrayal.' Researchers may also experience pressure to portray communities in specific ways as a result of particular political discourses. While it is in my view important to remain sensitive to the political context of research, this should not inhibit research in ways that are intellectually stultifying. Stacey and Biblarz (2001) have argued that the climate of hostility to lesbian and gay parents has informed researchers' portrayal of these families as 'just like' heterosexual ones. The efforts of researchers to avoid pathologising the children of lesbian and gay parents has often obscured the possibility that these children may be characterised by difference in a positive way. However, it is understandable that researchers may feel sensitive to such constraints. Even when our interpretations of research findings are sympathetic to participants, our work may be subject to distortion or interpreted differently by other readers and thus the participants from marginalised groups we study are potentially vulnerable.

In a discussion of issues of representation and readership, Nast (1994: 60) writes: 'For a number of reasons, we do not attempt to make all things apparent to all people'. Katz (1994: 71) also suggests that there are potential risks in making 'the practices of the oppressed visible to those who dominate'. Ribbens and Edwards (1998) argue that some topics of research may allow us to evade the difficult negotiation of ethics and representation more easily than others. In particular, a focus on more 'public' social worlds, and established social science topics, may allow researchers to avoid confronting and exploring them. They point out that issues regarding access, interpretation and analysis have been of concern to qualitative researchers across disciplines for many years. It is the particular topics under consideration – aspects of private, domestic and personal lived experience and understandings – that in their view present researchers with difficult quandaries. As Ribbens and Edwards (1998: 13) suggest, the transformation of 'private knowledge' into 'a more publicly based resistance, or at least a diversification and undermining of hegemonic discourses' is a valuable goal for researchers. The challenge lies in successfully achieving this in ways that are not harmful to participants.

This concern with the potential impact of research beyond the immediate context of fieldwork pertains to understandings of what constitutes 'the field' in research. The concept of 'the field' as a physically bounded spatial terrain has been challenged by ethnographers. It is increasingly also acknowledged to be located and defined in terms of 'specific political objectives that (as such) cut across time and space' (Nast 1994: 57). Rather than a researcher simply returning from 'the field' after a period of intensive research, the ethical considerations and responsibilities relating to issues of representation and difference, continue to inform the research in the writing-up stage. Thus, the ongoing negotiation of such dynamics integral to the research process highlight the spatial assumptions underpinning traditional understandings of 'the field'.

The conceptualisation of 'the field' as both a social and spatial terrain, acknowledges that the situatedness of the researcher is central to the knowledge produced. Engaging in reflexivity as part of the process of critical analysis will therefore move the discussion beyond an epistemological project of ethics and representation to a consideration of the notions of spatiality underpinning such conceptualisations. I lived in Sweden and Ireland for almost two years during fieldwork. While this research is based primarily on interviews, I also attended numerous relevant events (e.g. Pride) and my embeddedness in queer communities in both countries provided contact with people and knowledge of situations that were pertinent to the research. Katz (1994) concludes that as a 'gendered, historically constituted social and political actor who works as a social scientist and teacher' her multiple identities require negotiation of the field beyond particular spatial boundaries. Thus, her political engagement and attempts to effect social change mean that she is 'always, everywhere in "the field"' (ibid.: 72). Similarly, it is the multifaceted nature of these overlapping identities, or rather, the fact that like Katz (1994), 'I am always everywhere in the field', that informs the ethical and epistemological concerns addressed my cross-national research on lesbian parenthood.

A comparative study of lesbian parenthood

The two countries represented strongly contrasting cases for a study of sexual citizenship and lesbian reproductive rights. In 1995, Sweden became one of the first countries in the world to introduce legal recognition of same-sex relationships in the form of registered partnerships, but the same legislation expressly prohibited all parenting possibilities. So lesbian and gay couples could 'marry', but not adopt, foster or access assisted reproduction services. Parenthood subsequently became the key terrain for LGBT equality rights struggles in the country. During fieldwork in 2000–2001, I was struck by the high-profile nature of the topic. Daily discussions took place in newspapers, magazines, radio and television. Indeed, this helped to recruit for my study, as there was an emphasis on participating politically and many lesbian mothers expressed a desire for more research when they volunteered for my study. Following extensive lobbying, the laws on assisted reproduction and adoption in Sweden were changed in 2003 and lesbians can now access these services there.

In contrast, although Ireland had no option of registered partnerships for same-sex couples, parenthood possibilities had not been explicitly regulated to the same extent. Thus, lesbian and gay parenthood had largely fallen under the radar of Irish public life and popular debate. Indeed, there was no legislation prohibiting lesbians from accessing assisted reproductive services via private clinics, although adoption was restricted to heterosexual couples and single women. Local health boards had even placed advertisements for foster carers in lesbian and gay community publications. This was not, however, a reflection of widespread support for lesbian and gay parents, rather a recognition that there was a chronic shortage of foster carers in general that needed to be addressed. Embarking on fieldwork in Ireland immediately after finishing the Swedish fieldwork, I noticed that there was a 'deafening silence' around lesbian parenthood in Ireland. There was little or no discussion of the topic at a popular cultural or political level. Some community groups and lesbian mothers I met spoke about this with mixed feelings. On the one hand, the invisibility of lesbian motherhood in Irish public life allowed lesbian moms to quietly go about their business and there was a small but flourishing community of lesbian mothers in the country. However, without a political platform they continued to face legal and social discrimination. Like the Irish women I met with, I had to negotiate this tricky context, walking a tense tightrope between open lesbian and circumspect researcher.

Rethinking silence

In doing this research, I became haunted by Audre Lorde's famous words, 'Your silence will not protect you', which became a slogan of the lesbian and gay rights movement in North America during the late 1980s. In her essay (1984) where this sentence originates, Lorde argues for the necessity of articulating 'what is most important to me' (1984: 40), regardless of the consequences. She discusses the particular need for an expression of what is often left to silence, no matter what the possible outcome: ridicule, violence, even death, because the act of speaking 'profits me, beyond any other effect' (1984: 40). She made this argument in the context of her experiences as a Black lesbian mother who had experienced cancer. Her words continue to hold resonance. The way in which her famous statement 'your silence will not protect you' has become a catchphrase among (particularly North American) queer activists, constitutes a broader normative strategy within a script of coming out. Silence in this context is interpreted as living a closeted existence, which can have profoundly negative connotations within Western queer communities, as opposed to being open about your sexuality in everyday life. It is interesting to contemplate the application of these words in a wider context, particularly in view of the way that this slogan is deployed as a strategy for lesbian and gay rights in the US. Or rather, to rephrase the ethical concerns of this researcher in light of the strategies of (in)visibility on the part of participants, 'What if your silence does protect you/them/us?' In this way, silence can form an agentic strategy within a complex local context, rather than a problematic stance contrary to a linear trajectory of political openness.

Necessary subterfuge

I will turn now to two moments in my research on lesbian parenthood. The first of these concerns uncovering 'illegal' activities within the research group. A small number of Swedish participants also disclosed that in desperation, they posed as heterosexual in order to utilise services such as in-vitro fertilisation (IVF). When previously writing up this research, I have omitted this information. I did not want to alert health authorities in Sweden to the fact that some lesbians pretended to be heterosexual to access assisted reproduction. Now that the laws in Sweden have changed, I can write more openly. It was not an easy path for participants and they already faced considerable monitoring of their sexuality in using these services. The case of Anita is particularly poignant. She and her partner were in a registered partnership and were attempting to conceive with a gay male friend of theirs, Sven. Anita had fertility problems and needed IVF. She and her partner Ingela describe what happened when the doctor looked at her records and realised that she was in a registered partnership with another woman:

A: Then the next time she [doctor] met me, just me and her and then she said I must ask questions about your social status because […] she found out in the papers that I was living with a woman and then I had to say that well I lived with a woman in the past and now I lived with Sven.

I: And you had to say you were bisexual.

A: […] yes she said because you know it's forbidden if it turns out that you're a lesbian and […] she looked in my eyes and said I want you to be honest now okay and I said yeah […] and I had to look into her eyes and I hated it because I had to lie and I said of course you want the truth and the truth is I'm bisexual, I have had an affair with a woman for many years and then I met Sven, blah blah blah. Shit and I felt it was, it was horrible, I hated it. But at the same time I hate, I'm forced into this thing because I can't do anything else and I need this help to understand what's happening with my body […] It's been very hard, and I hate to play this role thing, because I'm always honest

(Anita and Ingela, Swedish participants)

This account brings to light a number of issues. First, in such situations of inequitable sexual citizenship, lesbians may find creative ways of accessing assisted reproduction. What is striking here are the concomitant ramifications for individual lesbian women in this situation. Anita and Ingela's story provides a shocking illustration of the toll the subterfuge necessitated took on them. Anita described herself as a very open person who found it stressful to lie to medical staff. In addition, for lesbian, gay and bisexual people, the coming-out process typically involves a period of reconciliation to a queer identity and a challenging path to self-acceptance and openness. Anita was no exception to this. Having accepted her lesbian identity and choosing to strongly affirm it by openness in her everyday life, being forced back into the closet was painful and compromised her sense of personal authenticity. Furthermore, added to the stress of the IVF procedure and being closeted in medical contexts, was the fact that Anita was unable to use the counselling services associated with the clinic. Since she could not be open about her circumstances, it seemed pointless to meet with the specialist counsellors there. Yet Anita found her infertility difficult to cope with, partly because she was herself adopted and keen to experience biological motherhood. She regretted that she was unable to utilise the professional support at the clinic and felt that appropriate counselling would have been very helpful for her.

In my research, I have occasionally encountered situations where participants have bypassed official channels in order to achieve their aim of becoming parents. Interestingly, in discussing these experiences with me, participants would also comment that they were unsure about the best way to write this up, but left it to me to make the decision about how to present this material, if at all. The trust they placed in me is in no small part due to my obvious political sympathies with their position. I have no ethical or moral objections to the strategies used by some of the women in my study. On the contrary, I am critical of the prohibitions of state bodies that place obstacles in the path of lesbians attempting to become parents and make the journey to parenthood that much more difficult for many of them. The decision to censor myself on this point and not discuss these alternative strategies was a fairly straightforward one. But it is one example in which researchers are compelled to censor themselves in accordance with their own ethical and political responsibilities. In this instance, silence did offer a measure of protection.

Up to this point, I've focused on the repercussions of research for participants, but another aspect of the research process that in my view is somewhat under-theorised concerns personal risk to researchers themselves. Ethics review committees, for example, are centrally concerned with preventing harm to participants, which is obviously of paramount concern. However, there are many issues pertaining to personal vulnerability and safety of minority researchers researching minority communities. There is considerable awareness around risks for researchers working on issues like terrorism or other illegal activities and covert research. However, if we take the feminist and poststructuralist point about the embodied situated subject seriously, then we also have to look at repercussions for researchers involved in other kinds of work. One notable example of this is Gill Valentine's (1998) classic article 'Sticks and Stones: A Personal Geography of Harassment', which gives an account of the homophobic harassment she experienced in the form of anonymous letters and phone calls in the workplace. She was also outed to her family by her tormentor. I myself have been on the receiving end of harassing phone calls in two separate academic workplaces that were directly related to the fact that I am an openly lesbian researcher who does work on queer lives. The notion about personal risk for minority researchers is very much related to questions of power, vulnerability, ethics, gender and shame. It could be argued therefore that support networks for researchers and awareness of difficulties they may face should more often be incorporated into research design, including funding applications.

Silenced daughters?

I will now turn to the second research moment that caused me to rethink questions of secrecy and silence. This concerns Aisling's account of how she told her mother that she had become pregnant via donor insemination. Aisling was in a long-term lesbian relationship when she had a child and both she and her partner Caoimhe had been out to their families for many years. Rather than explicitly explain to her mother that she became pregnant through anonymous donor inseminate at a clinic, Aisling chose to communicate this information in a more oblique way. This example illustrates a provocative moment in which communication occurs through what is not said, rather than what is explicitly stated:

A: When I told my mother, without coming out and saying I got inseminated because I think it would have been too much for her to take in because she's in her late sixties and again she's very conservative and as well had a very sheltered life as a young woman I just said I told the doctor I wanted to have a baby and she organised it for me hoping that she'd have educated herself enough to read between the lines and know what I was saying but my mam has a habit of taking what she believes to have been said in a conversation and making up her own little story and she was convinced it was some man and still is, married or whatever but she was convinced.

R: That you'd had an affair?

A: Yeah

C: Even though Aisling actually said look I went to the doctor and I got pregnant and the first thing her mother said was god don't tell me you don't even know the man's name […] I could see quite clearly she knew exactly what was being said.

A: And chose not to believe it. She'd be educated enough to know that insemination does happen in Ireland.

(Aisling and Caoimhe, Irish participants).

As far as Aisling and her partner Caoimhe were concerned, they had clearly communicated to Aisling's mother the fact that their son had been conceived via DI at a private clinic. They viewed Aisling's mother's reluctance to acknowledge this as a wilful disavowal of their family form and the information they had disclosed. Yet in communicating with her, they had not spoken explicitly about donor insemination or clinics; they chose to articulate it in a way that allowed this information to be 'read between the lines'. This way of communicating was articulated as a way of protecting Aisling's mother, as to come out and say it directly would have been 'too much for her' as Aisling puts it. Evelyn Conlon (1985), in an article called 'Silenced Daughters', refers to this dynamic in relation to Irish mother–daughter relationships. She talks about the secrets Irish daughters keep in order to protect their mothers from social shame or the weight of knowledge. In this instance, Aisling and Caoimhe did not choose silence, but equally to articulate something directly was considered an insensitive act. Aisling's mother's decision to ignore the information and concoct her own narrative around it was also viewed as an aggressive denial of their family form that caused them considerable anger. This example suggests that silence cannot always be understood as a lack of communication, because in this instance communication has occurred, just in a rather indirect way. Foucault (1978) noted that confession is always a complex, rather than straightforward action. He suggested that repression is rather more than the suppression of simple 'truths'. Similarly, in the interaction between Aisling, her mother, and Caoimhe, we see a complex interplay of disclosure, expectation, sexual and gendered ideologies, and the boundedness of communication within a particular cultural context. It brings to light cultural specificities in interpreting interview narratives. What are the cultural norms around silences that have to be negotiated, whereby speaking out is not simply about breaking powerful taboos about claiming rights and subjectivity, but in which communication occurs through silence? In the example of Aisling and Caoimhe's case, silence is not simply a position of non-communication, but rather encompasses complex norms and modes of inter-subjectivity.

Conclusion

In this chapter, I have outlined two instances that gave me pause for thought in relation to matters of secrecy and silence in the research process. First, my decision to keep the 'secret' that lesbian women were posing as heterosexual in order to utilise assisted reproduction services in Sweden, services from which they were legally excluded. This experience forced me to rethink the narrative of silence as repressive. While a more equal sexual citizenship context would have removed the obstacle to lesbians accessing these services – and therefore my dilemma – the fact that homophobic regulation of these services existed required taking the wider context into account when writing up. When initially writing about the empirical research, I consciously chose to protect my participants by keeping their secret. The Western emphasis on voice and coming out in relation to sexual politics was inappropriate and secrecy was in my view the only ethical choice.

The second moment, involving the communication of information that was implied, rather than directly explicated, requires reinterpreting 'voice' itself. What is 'voice'? What does it mean to 'say' something? Here, Aisling and Caoimhe enact a culturally specific process of communication. That process incorporates particular social norms about a range of issues, including: interpersonal communication across generations; mother–daughter relationships; and discourses of sexuality and embodiment, which are traditionally controversial in Irish culture and society. In relation to this discussion of ethical and hermeneutic dilemmas, my point is not to document geographies of resistance on the part of either the researcher or researched. Rather, I would argue for a shift in interest to the ways in which secrecy is productive, and silences intimate new languages, valuable to study in their own right.

References

Badgett, M.V. Lee (2003) *Money, Myths, and Change: The Economic Lives of Lesbians and Gay Men*, Chicago: University of Chicago Press.

Bowles, G. and Duelli-Klein, R. (eds) (1983) *Theories of Women's Studies*, London: Routledge & Kegan Paul.

Browne, Kath (2008) 'Selling my queer soul or queerying quantitative research?' *Sociological Research Online* 13 (1/2): http://www.socresonline.org.uk/13/1/11.html

Conlon, E. (1985) 'Silenced daughters', in L. Steiner-Scott (ed.) *Personally Speaking: Women's Thoughts on Women's Issues*, Dublin: Attic Press.

England, K. (1994) 'Getting personal: reflexivity, positionality and feminist research', *Professional Geographer*, 46(1): 80–89.

Foucault, M. (1990) *The History of Sexuality vol. 1: The Will to Knowledge*, Harmondsworth: Penguin Books.

Katz, C. (1994) 'Playing the field: questions of fieldwork in geography', *Professional Geographer*, 46(1): 67–72.

Lorde, A. (1984) 'The transformation of silence into language and action', in A. Lorde, *Sister Outsider*, Freedom, CA: The Crossing Press Feminist Series.

McDowell, L. (1999) *Gender, Identity and Place: Understanding Feminist Geographies*, Oxford: Polity Press.

Mohanty, C.T. (1991) 'Under Western eyes: feminist scholarship and colonial discourses', in C.T. Mohanty, A. Russo and L. Torres (eds) *Third World Women and the Politics of Feminism*. Bloomington, IN: Indiana University Press.

Nast, H. (1994) 'Opening remarks on "women in the field"', *Professional Geographer*, 46(1): 54–66.

Oakley, A. (1981) 'Interviewing women: a contradiction in terms?', in H. Roberts (ed.) *Doing Feminist Research*, London: Routledge.

—— (2000) *Experiments in Knowing: Gender and Method in the Social Sciences*, Cambridge: Polity Press.

Patai, D. (1991) 'US academics and Third World women: is ethical research possible?', in S. Gluck and D. Patai (eds) *Women's Words: The Feminist Practice of Oral History*, London: Routledge.

Plummer, K. (1975) *Sexual Stigma: An Interactionist Account*, London: Routledge & Kegan Paul.

Ribbens, J. and Edwards, R. (1998) (eds) *Feminist Dilemmas in Qualitative Research: Public Knowledge and Private Lives*, London: Sage.

Stacey, J. (1991) 'Can there be a feminist ethnography?', in S.B. Gluck and D. Patai (eds) *Women's Words: The Feminist Practice of Oral History*, London: Routledge.

Stacey, J. and Biblarz, T.J. (2001) '(How) does the sexual orientation of parents matter?', *American Sociological Review*, 66: 159–83.

Stanley, L. and Wise, S. (1983) *Breaking Out Again: Feminist Consciousness and Feminist Research*, London: Routledge.

Sullivan, G. and Losberg, W. (2003) 'A study of sampling in research in the field of lesbian and gay studies', in W. Meezan and J.I. Martin (eds) *Research Methods with Gay, Lesbian, Bisexual and Transgender Populations*, Binghamton, NY: Haworth Press Inc.

Valentine, G. (1998) 'Sticks and stones may break my bones: a personal geography of harassment', *Antipode*, 30: 303–32.

—— (2002) 'People like us: negotiating sameness and difference in the research process', in P. Moss (ed.) *Feminist Geography in Practice: Research and Methods*, Oxford: Blackwell.

Zavella, P. (1993) 'Feminist insider dilemmas: constructing ethnic identity with Chicana informants', in D. Wolf, D. (ed.) (1996) *Feminist Dilemmas in Fieldwork*. Boulder, CO: Westview Press.

15 Silenced by law

The cautionary tale of women on the line

Miriam Glucksmann

This chapter reflects on a very particular silencing of the research process: legally imposed restrictions on publication. It takes the form of a cautionary tale and is based on my personal experience of attempting to publish a book on women's work at the height of the Women's Movement in Britain.

Various forms of silencing affect feminist research, emanating from diverse and differing sources, as demonstrated by other contributions to this volume. Some silences arise internally from with the research process itself while others impinge on it from the outside. Some are self-imposed by researchers, others are not. While some of these restrictions are gendered, or affect feminist more than other kinds of research, others are not gendered. My story is one of an explicitly feminist investigation, silenced by the externally imposed power of law as refracted through the world of publishing. Although the constraints were not in themselves gendered, they nevertheless have implications for particular forms of feminist research.

A cautionary tale

In 1977 I took leave of absence from my lecturing job at South Bank Polytechnic in London (as it then was) and set about getting a factory job. I had been involved in the UK Women's Movement since its early days, and increasingly one of the issues that concerned us was the relative absence of working-class women from avowedly feminist campaigns and activities. Young, well-educated, middle-class women comprised the majority of women's movement activists, while working-class women, although reasonably well represented in trade-union activity, were far less likely to be found in feminist circles. I was also frustrated by the apolitical character of the academy which was in sharp contrast to the tumultuous years of the student and anti-war movements in which I had been politically formed. Was there something about organised feminism that put off working-class women, or failed to appeal to them? Was there something about their lives and experiences that made the kind of feminism we promoted irrelevant to them? Naïve as these questions may now sound, they were important issues of the time. My intention was to learn about the lives of manual women workers, by experiencing some of their world myself, in the hope that understanding their experience might provide some insights. I took the factory job for political reasons rather than for sociological research. I had no illusions about 'joining the working class', but nor did I think of what I was doing as ethnography or participant observation, although that is how it was later understood. I kept a diary during the nine months I worked in the factory, but was not thinking of writing it up. This came about only after the event, and as a tool for sharing with likeminded people what I had learned. Again the book was conceived as a political contribution, primarily of interest to feminists, and it was written in as accessible a style as possible.

A left-wing publisher was keen to publish the book, and encouraged me to retain all the real details (apart of course from anonymising the names of the people involved) and also to include chapters on the local economy of the area and on the industry. The factory was in Cricklewood in north London and manufactured speedometers, so I did quite a lot of research on that part of north-west London with its high proportion of Irish and Asian migrants, and also on instrument engineering and its place in the engineering and the motor industries more generally. I retained the real name of the factory, its location, the product and its various components, and made an effort to accurately describe the various stages of work that were required to put together speedometers on an assembly line. The publisher was happy with the manuscript but thought it wise to run it past a lawyer. The late 1970s and early 1980s were times of considerable political conflict and industrial militancy in Britain, in the run-up to Thatcher's election victory in 1979 and the early years of Thatcherism. Many articles and a few books had already been written from the perspective of manual workers, but few had been about women or based on personal experience. Huw Beynon's *Working for Ford* had recently appeared (1973), causing quite a stir, and there was concern on the part of publishers that large companies would not take kindly to bad publicity of any kind.

The meeting with the lawyer was a shock for all concerned. He spent four hours going through the first eighty pages, explaining that virtually every point I made was libellous. My comment that the managers did not hold open the swing doors for workers was libellous, as was my throwaway remark that the teenage girls who worked on the same line as me seemed more sexually mature than students of the same age. Almost every observation of this kind was judged to be libellous. This was quite apart from my account and analysis of the labour process, the division of labour, the hierarchical organisation of production, the operation of the bonus and payments system, the petty authority of the chargehands, the way the supervisors gained from getting the women to work faster. The lawyer explained that in order to legally withstand a charge of libel if one was brought against the publisher, I would need to be able to prove everything I said. The only way of doing this would be by referring to already published material, or by bringing witnesses who would testify in court to back up what I had said.

Libel law in Britain was and remains extremely restrictive. The onus of proof is on the party alleged to have committed libel. In this case if the company concerned charged the publisher or myself with libel, then we would have to provide conclusive evidence that libel had not been committed. This would be a big risk to take, and the publisher got cold feet. They asked me to rewrite the book, turning it into a much more general account of women and patriarchal power in working life. Having taken great pains to get all the details right in the first place, this was something I did not really want to consider. There were enough general accounts along such lines and it would mean deleting everything that was distinctive (and I thought useful) about mine. I was also taken aback that the publisher had not been aware of the libel laws in the first place, or warned me about them, as that seemed pretty basic.

So we parted company and I put the manuscript in a cupboard where it stayed for three years. I had time to reflect on all the texts I had read on research methods during my lengthy sociology training and all the courses I had attended, and that in none of them was the issue of libel ever mentioned. The predominant emphasis was on the early stages of the research process, concentrating on issues of access and gatekeepers in qualitative methods, on modes of interviewing, and on ways of interpreting testimony. It was as if the eventual publication of research would be unproblematic, so long as it reached a certain quality standard and had appeal to a readership that warranted acceptance by a journal or publisher. I had learned the hard way about the long arm of the law, but it was nevertheless staggering that the issue of libel was absent from all research methods training. I suspect that this remains the case today.

In the next few years, after I had calmed down from the initial shock (and returned to South Bank), I wrote a couple of talks on migrant women and factory work drawing on the experience and gave them as seminar papers. One of these was at the invitation of John Rex at Warwick University, and he asked why on earth I had never published material of such sociological interest. At the time he was the Editor of Routledge & Kegan Paul's International Library of Sociology, and so in a position to offer me a contract. I had thought the book would remain permanently in its cupboard, and was in two minds about taking it out again when faced with the prospect of revisiting the whole libel issue again with another libel lawyer.

The lawyer consulted by Routledge turned out to be a real expert in this field and not so restrictive in his judgment as the previous one. The main issue remained the same, but he was prepared to recommend that if *a, b, c, d* and *e* were disguised, then they could go ahead, and I might even be able to reveal *f*. I was very concerned to retain some element of the actual reality, to be able to identify speedometers, or Cricklewood, or motor components. In the end, we came to an agreement that the product could be identified as a motor component (but not as a speedometer) so long as I disguised my name, the firm, the trades union, all other names, the location and anything else that could make the company or product recognisable. Then followed the very disheartening process of rewriting the whole book so as to make nonsense out of everything I had made such an effort to present correctly in the first place. The chapters on the local economy and on instrument engineering were cut completely. The company became UMEC (Universal Mechanical and Electrical Components Limited), after I had checked with Companies House that no such company was registered in that name. Cricklewood became West London, Park Royal became Victoria trading estate and I became Ruth Cavendish. But the major effort was to disguise speedometers and their process of production. These were renamed as UMOs, standing for 'unidentifiable mechanical object'! Many of the components were given nonsense names that I invented, and my account of the successive stages of assembling a speedometer had to be rewritten using these.

Women on the Line eventually saw the light of day in 1982 (Cavendish 1982). It included a Preface entitled 'Freedom of Speech' outlining the libel restrictions, whose interests they protected, and what I had been required to disguise. Ironically, in spite of all the precautions, I discovered quite soon after it was published that the supervisors knew of the book's existence! I was still in contact with many of the women I had worked with, and met them in Kilburn High Road or shopping in Sainsbury's. I had told them about the book and the disguise. Strangely enough one of the tabloid newspapers reviewed it, and by chance quoted part of my description of one of the trade union convenors. This was familiar to the supervisors who put two and two together, and according to the women, 'they know it's your book'. Of course nothing untoward happened: because of the disguise the company would have had to identify itself first in order to take any legal action.

On the other hand, the disguise continued to hamper me. Because of the pseudonym, I was unable to give any talks about it. People wanting to contact the author wrote to Routledge who forwarded letters addressed to Ruth Cavendish. But I could not reply to them. Nor for many years could I make public the connection between this book and my later research and publications on women's work, despite the fact that all of it had been originally stimulated by the factory experience. Twenty-five years later I still regularly come across people (three or four in 2008) who know me, and are familiar with Ruth Cavendish's book but do not realise the connection until I tell them. Only in the second edition, published in 2009 (Glucksmann aka Cavendish 2009), thirty years after I wrote the original, has it been possible to reveal the company, product and location. The possibility of doing this is not simply due to the passage of time, but also and crucially the fact that the company withdrew from manufacturing motor components and that the factory has been closed for many years (and the buildings demolished).

Gender, power and the law

Looking back, it seems almost incredible that what was intended essentially as an analysis of gender hierarchies at work, of the intersection (as it would now be known) of gender, ethnicity and class, and of the impact of low-paid and poor employment conditions on the wider lives of unskilled women workers became so bogged down by the draconian British libel laws. My intention had not been to single out this firm or point a finger at it, but rather to highlight the conditions of work confronting migrant women with few formal qualifications, and their impact and implications for feminist understanding and practice. But through the legal prism, the original text was viewed not in the way I intended but rather as a critique of a particular company.

There are many lessons to be drawn from this cautionary tale. Perhaps the most significant is the very real power of the law to impinge on this final stage of the research process. It poses an external threat potentially affecting any research that is based on ethnographic methods, or on participant observation. Or more correctly and in actual practice, it would affect research on the sorts of powerful organisations and/or dominant individuals who have access to legal backup and the predisposition to use it. Communities and people who enjoy less or little power are far less likely to resort to the law, even though they are also covered by it. In my case, the lawyer was not worried about the young women claiming that I had libelled them by suggesting that they were more sexually mature than their student counterparts. His overriding concern was the company and its reaction. For me to take on the charge of libel was hardly realistic, as I could not or would not be prepared to provide the required evidence. There were no already published sources to corroborate what I said, so no question of referring to other material already in the public domain. It is in the nature of the investigation I was conducting that none existed, a point that could apply to very many cases of qualitative research. The other alternative, to ask the women I had worked alongside to act as witnesses in court, was of course also totally out of the question. My commitment and responsibility were to them, and my overriding aim was to give them a voice or at least to highlight the inequities of their daily working life. Calling them as witnesses would have guaranteed their instant dismissal, and was never considered. Here there was a clear connection between the participant mode of observation and the particular nature of permissible legal defence. The gendered power relations between the women, myself and the company worked to protect the company through the vehicle of libel law.

It is worth stressing that the libel laws are not gendered, and there was nothing intrinsically anti-woman or anti-feminist in the threat of legal action. Its potential impact on similar research about men would be identical. The only way in which this form of silencing might affect feminist research more adversely than other kinds would be attributable to the prevalence of qualitative methods and the preference amongst feminist researchers for deploying techniques which rely on collecting personal testimonies or interacting with their research subjects. But I would not want to make too much of this point.

What is more surprising, as already indicated, is the virtual absence of attention in research methods training devoted to such externally imposed constraints. This is perhaps all the more surprising in feminist research handbooks, where so much consideration has been accorded to relations between researcher and researched, the importance of establishing egalitarian relationships within the research process, and the development of feminist-inflected codes and protocols of appropriate conduct to guide the acquisition, interpretation and use of data. Yet the end-point where the world of publishing, and the legal system meet the results of our research, remains not only out of our control but even hidden from view, and as a consequence, very difficult to challenge.

From litigation to ethical regulation?

Looked at from a broader perspective, it is clear that regimes of research vary nationally. The relative dominance of the private and state sectors in different countries seems to play a role in shaping access and openness. In Nordic countries for example, where the public sector is particularly strong, generalised norms of public accountability make it relatively easier than in the UK to gain access to public sector and not-for-profit organisations for research purposes, and these norms rub off to a certain extent on private sector organisations. By refusing access they would be giving the impression that they had something to hide. In a planned comparative project, my Swedish counterparts were surprised at how difficult it was to gain access to British shops and factories, when for them it was relatively unproblematic.

Differing legal frameworks also contribute to the particularity of national regimes of research by imposing greater or fewer constraints and laws of different kinds. The British libel law emerges as a particularly restrictive one in favouring the party alleging libel. It is almost as if you are guilty until you prove yourself innocent. In the US, the onus of proof is the other way round from the UK, so the party claiming to have been libelled has to prove that their allegation is true, by demonstrating that the 'libeller' was presenting incorrect information or making statements for which there was no evidence. If I had been publishing *Women on the Line* in the USA I would probably have had no problem. The company would have had to prove that I was telling untruths about them. When the onus of proof is this way round, the complainant would draw attention to themselves whether or not they actually win the action, and so run the additional risk of bad publicity if they lose the case. In the UK situation, by contrast, the mere potential threat of a libel action is sufficient to deter publishers, even when the likelihood of companies bringing a case may be minimal. This is not the place for it, but it would be instructive to examine further the cultural, structural and normative shaping of research regimes and the implications of diverse national regimes for what kind of research, feminist and otherwise, may be undertaken without coming up against externally imposed barriers.

Returning to the present, although the libel laws remain the same as ever, researchers may feel more immediately pressed by the recent institutionalisation of ethical audits. Feminist researchers were in the forefront of introducing ethical concerns into research conduct (see, for example, Letherby 2003). As already mentioned, the political objective of giving a voice to people who were otherwise unlikely to be heard and of treating respondents as subjects rather than objects of research (viz. Gluck and Patai 1991), gradually translated into an understanding of how research should be conducted, and the emergence of feminist norms of research practice. Prime amongst these was treating people with respect and dignity, informing them of the research questions and gaining their consent, and using material gleaned from them in a non-exploitative manner (e.g. Oakley 1979). Many feminists understood the eventual interpretation as the result of a negotiated understanding between researcher and researched (e.g. Stanley 1990). Some of the informal rules established as part of this endeavour were later more widely accepted, being recognised and indeed institutionalised as good research practice in a variety of social science and humanities disciplines. Many found their way into the ethical codes of professional bodies representing different disciplines, and even into state-funded national research councils. The code of ethics of the British Sociological Association, for example, owes much to norms and practices originally developed in the course of feminist research (BSA 2008).

In this light, the present trend towards formalistic regulation, in the name of ethics, appears deeply ironic. Informal codes of conduct developed within the research process as part of an egalitarian project are turned into formal injunctions, and welded onto rules based on the medical or psychological model, to form the basis of ethical regulation frequently imposed by research institutions themselves. Arguably such audits and their system of 'pre-emptive ethical regulation' are driven more by the aim to obviate any potential cause for litigation against the institution, than by a genuine concern with ethics (Dingwall 2008). Very many classic ethnographic studies would never have seen the light of day under the conditions of pre-research scrutiny now prevalent.

Of course there are issues in treating research subjects in an ethical manner and normal practice is to observe these without question, especially in circumstances where the researcher is more socially powerful than the people she is researching. But not all social, or feminist, research is downwards, as assumed by the medical model, and nor is it confined to individual people and their lives. Many research questions require the study of organisations and their representatives, including those in authority. Here the tables are likely to be turned, the 'respondent' holding considerably more power than the researcher, well able to look after their own interests and control what information to reveal or withhold. Researching people in power poses different issues of access and ethics than asking women and men about their personal experience. And this is especially the case where organisations are themselves engaged in unethical or illegal activities, and the requirement for total openness about the research and informed consent is unrealistic. In these circumstances, a judgement may be reached that the ethical objectives of the research override those of research practice.

Ethical regulation suppresses power relations, including gendered ones, in the research process. As outlined above, my 'participant observation' involved entering a power field: equal to equal on the line, solidarity amongst women, and relations of power upwards through the chargehands, supervisors and management, up to the company itself. The ethical issues and my ethical obligations to the women were entirely different from those to the company. In a similar situation today, ethical regulation would act as pre-emptive libel law, requiring the anonymising of the company as much as the women, treating all parties as equal, imposing confidentiality across the board. So what I had to disguise for the libel lawyers in 1982 as part of publication would nowadays be required to be disguised at the front-end of research, even to the point of obstructing it.

People attempting to conduct the sort of investigation that I undertook in 1977 would now be stopped in their tracks at the outset, rather than at the end of the process. The silencing would probably rule out equivalent research being undertaken in the first place. Informed consent, anonymity and confidentiality, the three prerequisites for initiating and funding research embodied in current ethical regulation, would block any kind of research that relies on the researcher disguising her identity and purpose from powerful gatekeepers. On the other hand it is in many ways an inappropriate comparison. Times have changed and the political context of that epoch is long gone. My 'project' was not academic and was not undertaken as research; it only 'became' sociological years afterwards. Nevertheless, despite the historically eclipsed character of my 'research process', I feel a sense of déjà vu: the wheel has almost come full circle. A cynic might say that the fear of litigation now underpinning many institutional regimes of ethical regulation is doing the erstwhile work of libel lawyers.

References

Beynon, H. (1973) *Working for Ford*, Wakefield: E.P. Publishing.

British Sociological Association (2008) Statement of Ethical Practice. http://www.britsoc.co.uk/equality/Statement+Ethical+Practice.htm.

Cavendish, R. (1982) *Women on the Line*, London: Routledge & Kegan Paul.

Dingwall, R. (2008) 'The ethical case against ethical regulation in humanities and social science research', *21st Century Society*, 3 (1): 1–12.

Gluck, S. and Patai, B. (1991) *Women's Word: the Feminist Practice of Oral History*, London: Routledge.

Glucksmann, M. aka Cavendish, R. (2009) *Women on the Line*, London: Routledge.

Letherby, G. (2003) *Feminist Research in Theory and Practice*, Buckingham: Open University Press.

Oakley, A. (1979) *Becoming a Mother*, Oxford: Martin Robertson.

Stanley, L. (1990) *Feminist Praxis: Research, Theory and Epistemology in Feminist Sociology*, London: Routledge.

Part IV

Affective dilemmas

16 Animating hatreds

Research encounters, organisational secrets, emotional truths

Gail Lewis

> Successful empirical sociology depends on understanding the ways social actors, including researchers of all sorts, manage secrecy and disclosure of their motives, identities, and practices.
>
> (Mitchell 1993: 10).

> He that has eyes to see and ears to hear may convince himself that no mortal may keep a secret. If his lips are silent, he chatters with his fingertips ...
>
> (Freud 1905: 77).

> ... the potential space of the secret for a child, where he can build up and sustain a private tradition of the maturing and growing self ... can become distorted into secretiveness.
>
> (Khan 1977: 121).

Introduction

For at least two decades, prompted and encouraged by an ever-developing feminist research praxis, the injunction to be self-reflexive in the research process has become somewhat of a commonplace for social science researchers (see editors' introduction for discussion). In this chapter, I want to take the injunction for self-reflexivity as a starting point for looking back at some research I carried out about 15 years ago and use it as an opportunity to explore – and expose – some of the secrets and silences embedded in it.

So let me begin by using the pronoun that feminists (me included) have rendered problematic – we – and ask: how do 'we' as feminist researchers reveal and come to terms with what it is that motivates the selection of particular sections of data for scrutiny – beyond that is, the dictates of the research question(s) being addressed, the theoretical and methodological approaches adopted, the argument made? Of course I have no idea of the answer to this question but I want to pose it, to myself at least, as a way of getting to a second question: that is what is the emotional truth behind or invested in the selection of particular segments of data for analysis and the development of one's argument as against other, equally illuminating, segments? I ask the question because I think that an attempted answer might help us (to use another of those problematic pronouns) tease out some of those aspects of research, understood as a professional and personal practice, that have been rendered secret. In this chapter I think there are three such secrets: the 'secret' about and the possible effect of negative emotional experience; the occlusion of the agenda partly driving the selection of data for use in publication; and the organisational context influencing what can be said, what can be heard and what made intelligible.

Let me explain a little. In what follows I return to a small section of data generated in the course of a research project aimed at exploring how 'race' and gender were constituted in specific organisational and professional contexts and the experiences of black women social workers working in local authority social services departments in the 1980s and 1990s. In that project I interviewed 22 professionally qualified black women social workers, and eight of their managers of whatever ethnicity and gender. The data I return to here is taken from a two-hour interview with a white woman area manager and I have used this material in previously published work (Lewis 2000; Lewis 2002). As I hope will become apparent the encounter with this manager was marked by moments of acute emotional intensity and strain and led to a state of mind in me that was full of rage and bent on vengeance. Yet this desire for vengeance was masked from view, sanitised by the process of writing academically for publication. The effect was to make the affective register secret and my state of mind a secretively held undercurrent pulling some of the subsequent work with the data in a particular direction. Following a lead offered by the psychoanalyst Masud Khan (1977) my use of the term 'secret' here means kept private or undisclosed whereas 'secretively' has a different inflection aimed at summoning up a degree of slyness harnessed to a desire in me for domination in a context in which the formation of some kind of real relationship became psychically impossible. This desire for domination emerged out of the *pain* of the research encounter and was, I now think, a form of psychic defence against this pain but turned into a form of concealed hitting back.

The secretiveness and its disguise were partly facilitated by the theoretical and methodological approach I had adopted for the research, i.e. Foucaultian discourse analysis. A qualifying comment is required. I do not intend this to be read as repudiating the capacity for discourse analytic methodology to produce rich and textured analyses of the complexities of social life as people attempt to make sense of their worlds, their places in it and struggle rhetorically to establish coherent and plausible narratives as they (we!) negotiate the ideological dilemmas in which they (we) find themselves (ourselves). Yet as my theoretical and methodological orientations have expanded I have come to think that discursive work can only take us so far and that its limitations preclude the capture of some of the more inchoate, subtle and enigmatic aspects of human interaction and experience that are integral to the making of psychic and social meaning. To capture something of the emotional experience of 'race' and gender as processes of inter-subjective entanglement in organisational contexts a different (or additional) theoretical frame and methodology would have been necessary. Thus, had I been concerned to capture something of the emotional truth of the encounter between myself and the social services area manager, something of the affective registers and flows between us that punctuated the interview and was interred within but not transparent in the words that were produced as we talked then the secretiveness might not have been so easily disguised and might not have been so powerfully mobilised.

In many senses then, this is a confessional and indeed reparative piece that has running through it a claim about the impact of what different theoretical and/or methodological approaches can deliver – indeed are designed to deliver – in terms of insights into the constitution of the social and the vagaries of human experience that is constitutive of and constituted by (to speak in highly social constructionist language) that social yet which also exceeds it. I recognise that this difference is related to a major difference in the theorisation of subjectivity and subject formation but I do not intend to address this issue here. Rather I attempt to illustrate and develop the former claim by looking at the way hatred was educed and deployed in one part of the encounter with the area manager and re-examine some of the data that I have previously used in publication. I do so with the aim of thinking anew the determinants of this interaction, its content and effects, paying attention to the way that the emotional states of hatred and vengeance became central in both the inter-subjective encounter and the subsequent selection of material for publishing purposes. In doing so I want to point to what was neither seen nor directly spoken and yet was powerfully present and fundamentally contextual in a complex temporal and organisational matrix.

My re-thinking has been facilitated by a systems psychodynamic approach to organisational and group process.[1] The nature of the relationship between individual, group and organisation (Freud 1921; Jacques 1955; Menzies-Lyth 1959; Bion 1961) has long been the subject of theoretical and empirical inquiry and many different ways of conceiving the relationship have developed. There are variations among those who combine psychodynamic and systems approaches but generally they share a commitment to thinking through the dynamic relation between intra-psychic and inter-subjective processes, on the one hand, and organisational systems and their effects on individuals and groups, on the other. With a debt to group relations model associated with the Tavistock the focus is the 'here and now' of group interaction mediated through conscious and unconscious processes. Lawrence has described this model as a '"living methodology" for inspecting the conscious and unconscious realities of groups and institutions and the political relatedness (authority, management, and organization) of individuals in roles' (Lawrence 1979: 4). It 'uses subjectivity' (Lawrence 1979: 5) to gauge the quality of organisational life.

In the context of this chapter two factors are particularly significant. First is the conception of organisation as an active, on-going process and field of social action, including that of meaning-making (Stein 2008). The second is that the dynamics propelling the forms and meanings of (formal and informal) relatedness among organisational members are understood as being conscious and unconscious, cognitive and emotional. Thus 'organisation' is less a reference to a pre-existing structure and more about referencing a process of human relatedness in a context of specific roles, tasks, social and professional identities and institutionalised norms of linkage and division among different units or departments. This means that the *emotional experience and meaning* of the organisation (including the meaning given by organisational members to the hierarchies of division, status and role) is a key object of enquiry since it is this that is deemed central to capturing something of the livedness of organisational life. David Armstrong (2005: 52 [1995]) captures this in his evocative reformulation of the phrase 'organisation-in-the-mind'.

The rest of the chapter is organised into five sections. I begin with a brief outline of the approach to organisation I adopted at the time of the original research and the earlier publications. I then re-present the previously published research material, hoping to capture the affective tenor of the interaction, my responses to it and point to some questions that now arise for me. I then think about this material afresh through the lens of systems psychodynamic theory harnessed to a brief discussion of theories of multiculture. My aim is to offer a psychosocial reading of the material, inviting readers to compare this with the earlier discourse analytic reading (e.g. Lewis 2002). In doing this I hope to show some of the ways that secrecy and silence operated in the work I did after the research encounter but also how organisational (public) secrets were already animating some aspects of the encounter. I end with a brief concluding section in which I suggest some of the implications of this way of approaching research – the process and the after-image. I suggest that where the aim of feminist anti-racist research is to capture aspects of the discursive constitution of the social *and* human experience, self-reflexivity requires that we take the risk of revealing the secrets and secretiveness that may be powerfully present yet have remained silent.

Organisations as sites of difference and inequality: an earlier held view

As situated structures and processes organisations inevitably reflect wider societal inequalities yet organisations themselves are sites of power and thus are productive in the Foucaultian sense (Foucault 1978). That is, in the complex dynamic of interaction between the societal context and the organisation, the organisation becomes a space in which inequalities are constituted or brought into being. This is so not just in terms of the formal hierarchies of status, authority and chains of command but also as arena in which the 'big' axes of differentiation and inequality are themselves constituted. Of course, the movement of what we might call social subjects, i.e. people already positioned within axes of inequality and differentiation outside the organisation, across the boundaries demarcating the organisation as a specific and identifiable entity, ensures that already formed social positions and identities enter the organisation from outside. However, it is my argument (both at the time of the original research and now) that organisations do not simply reflect that which is generated outside but are also places where inequalities and the categories and identities associated with them are constituted, performed and experienced. In part this means that if one is thinking about how 'race' and gender are brought into being in particular organisations, such as social services departments as I then was, the researcher is exploring how those working within them are constituted as racialised and gendered *organisational* subjects and how this subject-hood is experienced in its organisational specifics.

Taking this approach seriously would mean tracing not just how gender and 'race' operate within the organisation – as discursive production and experiential performance, but also how the organisation, as a set of inter-subjective, group and emotional processes, 'acts back' to craft dimensions of difference in its own image and which make for the quality of human experience as felt and lived (intra-psychically and inter-subjectively) in the specifics of the here-and-now of organisational life. It is this latter part that I would now argue I failed to address in the earlier work and which meant that I was unable to make sense of and work with the powerful emotional experience of that research encounter with the area manager I call Annie.[2] Let's hear something from her now.

The research encounter – I

The following is taken from the two-hour interview with Annie and is the section of transcript material that I have previously used.[3] I had arrived as the researcher who, equipped with her armoury of social theory, was there to excavate how this other woman constructed social differences of 'race' and gender through the discursive resources she drew upon. Approximately two-thirds through the interview I ask:

GL: How do you think differences of 'race' and gender reflect themselves in this area office?

ANNIE: Well, I have not been here very long, but I think there are issues around gender, certainly, in that there are two female [team] managers, Bianca and Shirley, who are both black, and a white male, team manager, and he is acting up into the deputy post, and I certainly would say I like Bianca and Shirley a lot. It is not that I don't like Richard, but I feel more comfortable with women anyway and I am conscious that as a group of three women, we combine together to somewhat undermine and get at Richard. [laughs loudly and heartily] I don't know why I am laughing, and

> it is not funny and not good. Shocking really. It's no better … em, so if you can do that to one person you can do that to another. Um, yes it's not good, but we *do* do it, and within that er both those two women are very competent, very good workers, and there is something about this that is very good for me and although this isn't my permanent job, I am able to swan around and be area manager with team managers, um, and although I haven't thought about it till just now, but there is this sense of it is like having a better possession, a better car [pause approx 3 seconds] and part of that is of course not about the fact that they are good workers, but it is an added dimension of good workers who are women and who are also black, it is like you have got the icing on the cake.

One could analyse this sequence of talk with reference to a whole range of social theory, especially feminist post-structuralist and critical race theory to 'unwrap', analyse and reveal its workings discursively. We could show how, in answer to my question, Annie constructs a narrative that is convened around organisational positions and constructs a gendered 'we' that crosses organisational boundaries of status. We could show how this reference to their relative positions within the organisation also lays the ground for her claim of 'ownership' of the two women team managers, and how in doing so she performs racial difference by constituting herself as white without ever mentioning it. We could show how the switch from a gendered 'we' (i.e. a 'we' constituted as the gendered same) to an organisationally and racially constituted 'me/them' suggests something of the ideological dilemmas with which Annie struggles and also reinstates hierarchies and we could analyse her account in terms of its constitutive effects and her performances of gender and 'race'.

Then, in an attempt to locate this sequence of talk and the specificity of the research encounter in a more 'global' social topography of gendering and racialisation we could draw, for example, on Joan Scott (1988) and Evelyn Brooks-Higginbotham (1992) to develop a theorisation of how the social as a field of interaction and a network of power is simultaneously at work and constituted in the extract. And we could show how the categories 'race' and 'gender' were deemed (by both Annie and me as researcher) to be among those at the heart of questions of 'difference', and thus how the social (understood as uneven but intersecting 'differences') enters into the corridors and meeting rooms of public-sector organisations and come out of the mouths of those of us who work in them.

And, thinking that all this would be both politically relevant and demonstrable of a competent researcher, this is what I did. I still think there is much of value in showing how social differences are constituted in these micro-social, organisational situated processes. But, and it is a big but, let's listen to a bit more of the story – bits of the story that evoke something of the emotional experiences conjured up in the course of the encounter and which gesture toward a much more layered evocation of organisational process and the inter-subjective play of power across difference, but which were held secretively in the subsequent unfolding of the research process.

The aftermath: research diary entry.

> I left that interview in a complete rage, I can't believe it!!! "the icing on the cake!? A better possession!?" Who the 'f***' does she think she is and imagine working with her, as her team manager when she is your Area manager. Slavery done long time! Well I'll get her, I'll definitely use this. Typical bloody white people, they just cannot see can they – even when they think they're being so cool and so progressive. Well you wait. I then went off to a pre-arranged meeting with a white woman friend of mine for a cup of coffee and chat. I am impossible, passively aggressive; querying her every statement or comment. Just totally closed and rejecting. I eventually make an excuse and apologise, saying I have a terrible headache and must go home. I keep saying 'Sorry, another time soon, is that ok? Great, sorry, take care though and see you soon. What? Yeah ok I'll give you a ring tomorrow to let you know how I feel.' Even when I left and went home that interview, that shit-bag woman was still with me, she is now! I think it was when she was also talking about how she thinks black women are being progressed up the hierarchy too fast – and making it seem like she cared about them being set up to fail – I think I was on the alert then. Oh god, I hate this interviewing. ...

There are a number of things I want to say in light of this widening picture. First, the switch in register from direct speech to reportage within the brief space of this diary entry is notable. In part this is because it was written three or four days after the actual interview. But I think there is more at play than this. Despite the fact that both registers conjure up the entanglement of powerful emotional experiences across two sequential inter-subjective encounters, the register of direct speech in relation to the interview with Annie hints at my inability to move with linear time as I recall it – I register it as if it is 'now'. In contrast, the account of my behaviour with my friend, though emotionally fraught, is presented as past. Yet what binds the two experiences is that they appear as equally unprocessed, more characteristic of what Bion (1962) called 'beta elements' (i.e. the sensory and/or somatic aspects of experience (Britton 1992)). It was this that I was locked into and even though they were given a form of words I was unable to process them into a form of thinking from which I could learn and mould into an analytical tool for the research I was undertaking. Instead they became harnessed to a strategy of psychic defence and vengeance disguised behind the performance of professional competence.

I am also struck by the analytical opportunity that was lost as a result of my theoretical inability to *use creatively* the emotional experience, an analytical use that *might* have contributed to a more rounded and sensitive presentation of this part of the interview and thus a more rounded understanding of the making and experience of 'race' and gender in a particular organisational context. Yet it is precisely at that junction of the micro and macro-social in the here-and-now of the inter-subjective encounter of a research interview in a given organisational context that a particular quality of emotional experience arose. And it is this situated experience occurring within the strictures of the rules of the research game as I understood them at the time and subject to the logics of the theoretical and methodological tools I adopted that rendered ground fertile for the animation of hatred and vengeance so apparent in the research diary entry. Having heard from Annie and me separately let us hear a bit more of our question and answer interaction.

The research encounter – II

The following is a much longer sequence of text from Annie's interview that occurred about fifteen minutes into the interview, i.e. earlier than that already presented. I had been asking about the public-sector reforms introduced by the Thatcher governments, especially the introduction of the purchaser/provider system of organising service provision and structuring the relationships among departments and sections. I had wanted to know whether she thought these changes had impacted on issues of 'race' and gender and if so how.

GL: Right, so tell me if you were, if you had to sort of think how this delegation of responsibility and authority, how do you think it might have impacted on black women, because as you say the point is to take it right down to basic social workers' grade?

ANNIE: Well I suppose I would look at it from the other way actually, I would look at it from, em, the bottom up I would say, the majority of the time, I mean, mean many of the service users that we work with in this borough are black and are women and black women carers of their children.

GL: Yes, um.

ANNIE: Having had more authority and responsibility, more control over budgets has meant that, em, all workers, field workers whatever their ethnicity, their gender, are able to offer a better service to that bulk of service users, and I would say that has massive impact, if you can work much more effectively in partnership with all clients, but particularly if we are talking about black women, with black women who are carers of children, then you are going to feel differently if you are a black women worker about how valuable the service is that you are providing, I would say.

GL: Right.

ANNIE: So that's on one level, I think there is an area that concerns me that I think needs to be more openly on the agenda, and people need to *feel free* to *speak* about it, and I don't sense they are, and there is this tremendous push in 'Centreville' to get women and black women into management positions, and I think sometimes that black women are not being allowed to move up this management ladder at a pace that suits them, and are being pushed up before they are ready and could get into a position of being set up to fail, and I just think that this needs to be opened up and I think this needs to go openly onto the agenda. I am not saying that there is not other ways that other people move up the ladder before they are ready, I mean white men move up that ladder before they are ready because people, you know, whatever the push to get black women into management actually take white men into management for all sorts of reasons. So they move up before they are ready too and white women move up before they are ready, but in terms of black women I think that's having an impact I would say and I don't think that's sufficiently on the agenda.

GL: Oh. On whose agenda?

ANNIE: Well, no it is not right to say it is not on the agenda [2 second pause] but I certainly would say it's on the senior management's team agenda, this is what we have got to do, we have to get black women into management.

GL: Senior management posts?

ANNIE: Yes. Em, and that is said but what isn't open for discussion, it seems, is that it may be putting unreasonable pressures on some black women to move up the system when either they don't want to, because either they want to carry on what they want to be doing, or move up before they feel ready to do so and asking them to move up into a climate where they feel, and I know from some of my black colleagues, where they will be expected to demonstrate they are better than, and can't afford to make mistakes and are not adequately supported.

GL: So what sorts of things, er how would you think this should be managed … what kind of procedures, training, policy packages, I don't know what they might be, to both ensure that women can travel up but at the same time avoid some of those pitfalls?

ANNIE: Em, well, er I mean that is something that the senior management team, and I am not part of the senior management team that I am talking about.

GL: Right.

ANNIE: Em, Janet, um mostly Tim Smith, Judith, Andrew, Bryan Brown, I think that is something that either they have to take responsibility for and say so very clearly, and I'm not saying the rest of us don't but I think they have to lead on that, and I think they have to open the debate on it and I think they have to make the debate safe mm [2 second pause] and there was an incident about two months ago now which I feel illustrates all this and I felt very upset about, where we had a joint meeting between the two divisions. Every now and then we have these joint meetings … and somewhere or other the assistant director in community care, Judith Arsenal, who is a white woman, said that she and Andrew who is a white man had been having a discussion about how to support black staff and that they, em really felt that they didn't know where to go next and didn't know what else they could do, and, oh, that provoked am absolute storm of anger from

Tim Smith who got really angry and who I felt was particularly abusive and I said so afterwards, and he said this is a load of crap and he said you cannot sit there and say you don't know what to do, it's a cop out if our black staff hear you say that, they would be disgusted. [Voice lowered] He was really prissy about it, and I thought well you know, I was really angry and very upset about it.

GL: Did you agree with the sentiment or was it that you were angry about the way they did this?

ANNIE: Well you know, I thought he was abusing his power, as a white male, very high up the system in speaking in this way and felt that the way that he had put it wasn't at all enabling and my belief is that unless people are able to keep a dialogue going.

GL: Sure.

ANNIE: Unless people are able to say and white people *have* to be able to say I *don't know* what to do next, and I don't know, my belief is that I have a right to go to my black colleagues, black counterparts and say 'I don't know what to do next here', and they may say 'No I won't' and I may have to go elsewhere, and I may have to go outside the organisation to seek support, but it seems to me to be absolute nonsense that I shouldn't be able to go to somebody like Gemma, for example, who is my counterpart, a black women, and say 'Gemma I don't know what else to do now, will you help me?' and it seems to me that what was being said [at that meeting] was that black people can't be asked to be able to take this responsibility and the responsibility must rest with white people and I don't agree with that. Em, I'm not saying that black people have to take responsibility and tell us what to do but I think it is a shared experience, and most important for me is that you must keep the dialogue open and moving and I felt that his intervention really was unhelpful and what it meant for me was that if I had something to say, er that I wanted to say um in that kind of meeting, where the people who had the most power were the most concentrated then I was going to be very frightened to open my mouth, and this is not very constructive, and I was very upset by that really, and did say something in the meeting that I felt it was important for people to say what they felt without being castigated. He came to me afterwards and said well your body language said it all. [And I said] Well you know what you were saying wasn't helpful, it was not helpful for you as a white man, in a position of enormous power to speak in that way, and he accepted that.

With reparation in mind: rethinking the research encounter

Even in the absence of a transcription convention that captures the patterns, flows, tones and hesitations of Annie's speech I think it is possible to hear/feel the passion and emotional intensity with which she delivers it, especially where she discusses the incident with Tim Smith. She clearly states that in her view certain things are 'unsayable' in the organisational environment operating at the time. That which is 'unsayable' is racialised as are those who are silenced whilst the arbiters of the 'sayable' are gendered. She makes it clear that for her patrolling the boundaries of the 'sayable' results in an atmosphere of fear and, perhaps more importantly, this in its turn erodes any possibility of *creative* thinking among the senior management team and groups of colleagues more generally. Perhaps more tellingly in the context of my concerns, Tim Smith's anger, rage and intolerance is powerfully evoked as is her own anger and fury.

All this followed from her statement and apparent concern about black women being set up to fail, i.e. one of the things that I had referred to with such rage in my diary entry. So anger, rage, offence and a sense of being silenced and abused were emotions that *both* Annie and I refer to, suggesting that these were distinguishing features of the affective register of our intersubjectivity (at least in parts of the research encounter) and *perhaps* characterizsd more generally the affective register of the organisation as it sought to respond to issues of 'race' and gender. At this point I am not in a position to pursue the extent to which this was a more general feature of the organisational atmosphere. What I can say is that encountering powerful emotional experiences is an occupational hazard of the social and human researchers' trade.

In his book *Narratives and Fictions in Educational Research* Peter Clough (2002) presents a series of stories taken from educational settings with the aim of contributing to a project which 'redefine[s] the relations between subject with object, or researcher and researched identities, and of knowing with the known' (2002: 4). Particularly striking is the way that Clough integrates emotional experience into the narrative content and structure of the stories and argumentation. In one story organised around a boy named 'Klaus', Clough writes:

> I've met my father and his sons in so many special schools. ... By the time I got to the main road I was crying. The fear that day was a simple animal fear and it was a galvanic nothing ... by the other fear that I later felt in front of Klaus's father. I was immobilized by that other fear. That was something that reached down the canal of my composure and found the ever-leaking corrosion of my father's presence.
>
> (Ibid.: 20–22).

This brief quotation is a miss-service to Clough's book, robbing it of its full texture and complexity. Nevertheless it provides a powerful and moving evocation of the way that researchers can unexpectedly encounter our emotional and long-felt demons in the course of a day's (research) work. In this it is evocative of my experience with Annie and perhaps Annie's experience with me.

Taking a lead from Clough, I can begin by asking: So who was it that stood before each other in that interview? Who did each of us meet and what did we expect of each other as we embarked on our two-hour interaction? To begin to answer these questions a brief bit of ground-clearing is warranted. I am not about to launch into a series of conjectures about things that I cannot know, i.e. conjectures about Annie's transference based on her early life experience and inner-object world. Any such attempt would be futile and within the theoretical and methodological terms of systems psychodynamic theory it is not necessary, though any research project adopting this theoretical and methodological approach would be concerned to track (via observation and/or individual and group interviews and the researcher's own experience) the movement between different states of mind among the various staff groups as manifest in the dynamics among them as they pursue their various tasks.

That said the analysis stays within the here-and-now of the research encounter but that here-and-now *is* marked by the conjunction of a number of different and asymmetrical experiential temporalities, as the quotation from Clough indicates. As the researcher I bring a temporal here-and-now but as Annie's account unfolds *my* accumulated *past* experiences of racialising gendered talk are re-animated as part of the 'now' and becomes the aural and emotional register through which I hear and respond to everything that comes after 'I think it was when she was talking about how she thinks black women are being progressed up the hierarchy too fast'. For Annie what we can say is that she feels an urgent need to break through the organisational conspiracy of silence about issues of 'race' and gender, including whether black women are being set up to fail. A silence that, in her organisation-in-the-mind, she says (feels) is rampant at least at the level of those with more organisational status and power – white men.

Yet even here nothing is simple, for if we take the two sections of her account together we see that 'white men' are a differentiated category: there are those in the senior management team like Tim Smith and there are those organisationally subordinate to her like Richard. In relation to Tim Smith black women cannot be called upon as colleagues in a gesture of creative thinking (about anything) but in relation to Richard they can be incorporated into a kind of gang and, as Canham (2002) suggests, a key characteristic of the gang as opposed to the group is the inability to bear difference. Moreover, with an implicit nod to those beyond the Area Office, black women 'gang' members can be 'owned' as a token symbolizing what Annie had told us was seen as the organisational good: black women in some kind of management position. And there I am before her as a receptacle into which she can pour her views (anger, frustration, vengeance?). And I am ripe.

For if it was not my father and his daughters whom I met in that social services department office, who was it – for as my research diary entry suggests, I knew this 'kind' of white woman very well and here she was before me again! And she was surely, sorely well known. It was this debilitating and frightening familiarity that animated the vengeance and rage and hatred that was itself of a product of earlier hurts – at individual and collective level. The question is how to make sense of the links between these familiar hurts and the unfolding research process. I want to try to address this in a number of ways.

First, as I look back over this material I am struck by two things. One is the point already made about the prevalence of rage, hatred and vengeance in the organisation, at least as narrated by Annie. Thus we can wonder whether *all* the rage, hatred and desire for vengeance that I felt was *my own* or whether I was also expressing that felt by other people who had unconsciously communicated it to me by a process of projective identification. In this context projective identification can be thought of as a (defensive) communication animated by the organisational inability to facilitate and contain the difficulties of and foster creative thinking about matters of 'race' and gender among a staff group fractured by these forms of difference and hierarchies of grade and status. I am also struck by the sense of *loss* that seems to permeate the encounter and interview material: loss of voice, loss of professional competence, loss of relationship among colleagues – a series of losses experienced by both Annie and me. The problem is that neither of us had a containing[4] environment to which we could take and process that experience of loss and in such situations facing loss (actual or phantasised) becomes unbearable and rich material for processes of splitting between 'good' and 'bad'. If I am right that loss is a central thread running through the encounter and the organisational experience I think it possible to make a cogent case that 'triumph' or perhaps more accurately 'triumphalism' was at least one factor behind my selection of data from the interview with Annie. For loss, at least from the perspective of object relations theory and the form of group and organisational theory influenced by it, can produce states of mind in which fear, anger and annihilation predominate which in turn lead to forms of psychic defence.

In this regard I am reminded of a point made by Melanie Klein (1940/1986) in a paper on the psychic process of mourning. She writes:

> I wish to stress the importance of *triumph*, closely bound up with contempt and omnipotence, ... One of the ways in which hatred expresses itself in the situation of mourning is in feelings of triumph over the dead person [lost object]. ... In my experience, feelings of triumph are inevitably bound up even with normal mourning, and have the effect of retarding the work of mourning ... In my view, this 'narcissistic satisfaction' [when ego severs attachment to lost object] contains ... the triumph.
> (1986: 157, 161)

So there Annie and I were, face-to-face in the context of a project exploring the experiences of black women social workers and in which the affective atmosphere is thick with a sense of obstruction, abuse and annihilation – no wonder she was easy pickings for a highly defended researcher who phantasised about getting back at her and thus 'commanding' her. And one who was equipped with a theoretical and methodological approach that facilitated the production of an adequate analysis, whilst disguising the element of vengeance and psychic defence that were secretively inscribed in that analysis.

For I was battered in that double sense of encased in and bashed by experience as I felt stripped of my humanity (another bit of 'the icing on the cake'). I was incapable of hearing, feeling or connecting with anything other than this woman's recourse to racist discourse. Totally unable to recognise or even countenance Annie's sense of being de-professionalised and demonised if she asked for help. I was thus unable to engage with the full range of emotional experience generated between us. I was not able to use that multi-faceted experience as an analytical tool and as something from which I might learn and which might have enabled a more textured analysis of the processes and experience of racialisation and gendering. To get to that place I would have had to consider questions that were too difficult to even put into words let alone face and process. Such as whether the circulation of an affective economy that includes this kind of triumph also helps us understand our investments in particular intellectual projects. To ask whether we think expending intellectual energy in the direction of disrespect, trauma, pain will help us to 'master' – triumph over – our own traumas, our own pains as we go about our work as qualitative feminist researchers? These are among the questions that are now among my intellectual and political preoccupations. At the time I did not have the emotional, theoretical or methodological resources that would have been necessary to consider the link between intellectual and creative work, on the one hand, and subjectivity, on the other.

Organisation as multicultural and affective zone

Earlier I outlined the way in which I had been thinking organisations as sites for the production of racialised and gendered difference at the time of the original publication. I also stated that there were three secrets interred within the earlier research: the secret of emotional experience; the secret of the relation between that emotional experience and data selection; and the secret of the censoring and persecutory organisation. Now, having established the ground upon which these 'secrets' took root, I want to offer a different way to think organisational process as I near the end of this new pathway through the original research encounter.

Within the UK (and indeed other parts of northern Europe) public-sector organisations have been placed on the frontline of attempts by government to foster their preferred approaches to the management of ethnic and other forms of social diversity. As such public-sector organisations are zones of *multiculturalism*: that is they are the administrative units charged with implementing the policies that are aimed at governing populations marked by the postcolonial logics of difference.

But they are also zones of *multiculture* (Hesse, 2000): that is spaces of encounter and negotiation across numerous forms of difference – sexual, cultural, religious, gendered and classed. In this conception of multiculture it is the indeterminancy of the meaning and reach of cultural difference that is foregrounded and which marks out a space of what Hesse calls undecidability. In my reading, designating zones of multiculture as sites of *negotiation* and including public-sector organisations among these suggests that they are also sites of inter-subjective encounter and experience in which all the vagaries of intra-psychic and inter-subjective anxiety and possibility are also present.

Yet as a field of practice and interaction, it is precisely the ambiguity, or undecidability of the multicultural that is in play in the everyday of organisational sociality. As I indicated earlier, from a psychodynamics of organisation perspective this ambiguity with its lack of clear boundaries makes such organisations fertile ground for the mobilisation of psychic defence mechanisms at individual and group level. Thus the conjunction of multicultural ambiguity with unstable and changing work contexts impacts upon the extent to which individual and/or organisational defences are mobilised. Such conditions characterised the social services department in which Annie worked and which I entered as researcher.

In such circumstances what Hirschhorn (2000: 26) calls 'normal psychological injuries' are part of the quotidian fabric of working life. Such injuries 'are the normal, expectable hurts that people experience as they try to collaborate with others in implementing an organisation's primary tasks within an *uncertain environment*' (my emphasis). In framing the issues in this way he points to the organisational situatedness of interpersonal relations and the psychodynamic processes evoked as people work in pursuit of the primary task. What then have to be negotiated are the demands, ambitions and anxieties provoked by the assumption of organisational roles, including those of competency and what is deemed sayable, how and to whom.

Through the analytical lens offered by systems psychodynamic approach the demands of group and organisational life are fertile sites for the generation of paranoid phantasies in which ontological security is threatened. Jacques (1955) suggested a profoundly interactive relation between the psychic and affective world of individual members and those organisations of which they are a part. Other writers, as noted earlier, have suggested that individuals symbolically internalize the institutions with which they are connected (Armstrong 2005) and thus there is a dynamic interplay of projection and introjection of affective states, including the anxieties generated by the very character of group and organisational interaction. Thus boundaries, psychic and structural, are central to the anxieties and ambivalences of individuation/group membership. I also want to insist that the *academic researcher* also be placed within this formation and thus subject to the same conditions, vagaries and anxieties.

If I now 'know' this, the discourse analytic perspective that was my intellectual armament at the time offered me much *but* had no way of alerting me to this way of thinking human relatedness. Had I been able at that time to recognise the inter-subjective emotional dynamics of my encounter with Annie, including my own intra-psychic conflicts that it seems evident had been animated I might have been able to use this understanding together with my own pain as an analytic resource rather than a cause for triumph and quest for (defensive) domination. I might have attempted to read the 'possession' extract against or alongside the grain of the second (sequentially earlier) extract. This might have enabled me to recognise that Annie's attempt to seek refuge in whiteness (*for I still have no doubt that she does resort to this*) and her organisational position were defensive responses through which she was seeking to bring some stability and meaning to a here-and-now that was profoundly unstable and ambiguous as the organisation struggled to meet both the challenges to racialised and gendered power and the new systems of service delivery. In that context I might have read the extract about being able to ask black people for help when at a loss as reaching for a connection: as an ambivalent and ambiguous claim of (frightening?) responsibility. At the same time a closer cross-reading of those extracts might have suggested that the claim about 'moving up too fast' be heard as a kind of displacement of Annie's own here-and-now anxieties about her ability to do her job in a context of organisational chaos and censorship in which the ambiguities of multiculture were pronounced.

This would have offered a very different analysis: not one that totally replaced the earlier theoretical and methodological approach and arguments made but which expanded and deepened them. And, in the context of this volume, this analysis would have offered a more complex form of researcher reflexivity, one in which the vengeful and pained secretiveness was replaced by a more creative, even if private, secret space in which a different kind of thinking was possible and in which discursive constitution of sameness and difference sat alongside a commitment to capture something of human experience – and learn from it.

Notes

1 The journal *Organisational and Social Dynamics* is a particularly good source for an illustration of the range, objects of enquiry and methodological and theoretical emphases encompassed within this approach.
2 All names of research participants are pseudonyms.
3 In the 2002 publication I cross-read this section of account from Annie with an account from Shirley, one of the team managers mentioned here.
4 Here I am using the notion of containing in the sense proposed by Bion (1962).

References

Armstrong, D. (2005) *Organisation in the Mind*, London: Karnac.
Bion, W.R. (1961) *Experiences in Groups*, London: Tavistock Publications.
—— (1962) *Learning from Experience*, London: Tavistock Publications.
Britton, R. (1992) 'Keeping things in mind', in R. Anderson (ed.) *Clinical Lectures on Klein and Bion*, London: Routledge.

Canham, H. (2002) 'Group and gang states of mind', *Journal of Child Psychotherapy*, 28 (2): 113–27.

Clough, P. (2002) *Narratives and Fictions in Educational Research*, Buckingham: Open University Press.

Foucault, M. (1978/1990) *The History of Sexuality,* Vol.1: An Introduction, New York, Toronto: Vintage.

Freud, S. (1905) 'On Psychotherapy', *Standard Edition*, 7, London: Hogarth.

—— (1921) 'Group psychology and the analysis of the ego', *Standard Edition*, 18, London: Hogarth.

Hesse, B. (2000) 'Introduction: un/settled multiculturalisms', in B. Hesse (ed.) *Un/settled Multiculturalisms. Diasporas, Entanglements, Transruptions*, London: Zed Books.

Higginbotham, E.B. (1992) 'African-American women's history and the metalanguage of race', *Signs*, 17 (2): 251–74.

Jacques, E. (1955[1985]) 'Social systems as a defence against persecutory and depressive anxiety', in M. Klein, P. Heimann and R.E. Money-Kyrle (eds) *New Directions in Psycho-Analysis*, London: Tavistock [Karnac] Books.

Khan, M.M.R. (1977) 'From secretiveness to shared living', in K.A. Frank (ed.) *The Human Dimension in Psychoanalytic Practice*, New York and London: Grune and Stratton.

Klein, M. (1940/1986) 'Mourning and its relation to manic-depressive states', in J. Mitchell (ed.) *The Selected Melanie Klein*, London: Penguin.

Lawrence, W.G. (1979) 'Introductory essay: exploring boundaries', in W.G. Lawrence (ed.) *Exploring Individual and Organizational Boundaries: a Tavistock Open Systems Approach*, London: Karnac.

Lewis, G. (2000) *'Race', Gender and Social Welfare: Encounters in a Postcolonial Society*, Cambridge: Polity.

——(2002) 'Categories of exclusion: "race", gender and the micro-social in social services departments', in E. Breitenbach, A. Brown, F. Mackay and J. Webb (eds) *The Changing Politics of Gender Equality in Britain*, Basingstoke: Palgrave.

Menzies-Lyth, I. (1959 [1988]) 'The functioning of social systems as a defence against anxiety', in *Containing Anxiety in Institutions: selected essays*, vol. 1, London: Free Association Books.

Mitchell, R.G. (1993) *Secrecy and Fieldwork, Qualitative Research Methods Series*, no. 29, London, Thousand Oaks, New Delhi: Sage.

Scott, J. (1988) *Gender and the Politics of History*, New York: Columbia University Press.

Stein, H.F. (2008) 'From organizational meaning through splitting to organizational meaning through integration: healing the great divide', *Organisational and Social Dynamics*, 8 (2): 298–321.

17 Breaking the silence

The hidden injuries of the neoliberal university

Rosalind Gill

Introduction

How are you?

I am totally stressed at the moment, to be honest. Work is piling up and I'm just drowning. I don't know when I'm going to have time to start on that secrecy and silence book chapter – I'm so, so late with it now, and I feel really bad that I'm letting Róisín down, but I literally never have a second.

I know, I know exactly what you mean.

I mean, I had 115 e-mails yesterday and they all needed answering. I'm doing 16-hour days just trying to keep on top of it. I feel like I'm always late with everything, and my 'to do' list grows faster than I can cross things off it. It's like one of those fungi in a horror movie that doubles in size every few hours! (Laughter) And I never ever have chance to do any of my own work. I'm sleeping really badly and it all just feels completely out of control …

It's the same for me. Reading? What's that? Thinking? No chance! And you feel *awful*, don't you. With me I feel like I'm constantly stealing time from the kids too – I'll go off to check messages in the middle of a game of Monopoly or something. Sometimes I just feel like quitting.

Yeah I know. It just gets worse. Still hoping to win the lottery, then? (Laughter) But how *are* you?

Do you really want to know?! (Laughter) (Yeh) well, awful actually. I'm really fed up. I heard yesterday that my article for x journal was turned down. (Oh *no*!) You know, the one I worked on for ages and ages. I poured so much of myself into that piece (I know). And one of the referee's comments was vile – it said something like 'my first year undergraduates have a better understanding of the field than this author does – why are they wasting all of our time'. When I read it it was like a slap in the face, Ros. It was all I could do not to burst out crying in the postroom, but I had a lecture right afterwards so I somehow managed to pull myself together and go and do that. But last night, I just didn't sleep (Poor you) I just kept on going over and over with all these negative comments ringing round my head. And you know the worst thing is, they are right: I *am* useless (No you're not),

> I'm a complete fraud, and I should have realised that I was going to be found out if I sent my work to a top journal like that.

This is a transcript of a conversation I had with a female friend in the few days before (finally) beginning work on this chapter. Both speakers are white, both work in 'old' (pre-1992) British universities and both are employed on 'continuing' contracts – thus are already marked as 'privileged' in multiple ways in the contemporary academy. Mine is easily recognisable as the voice which worries about how late this article is! Some readers may find this fragment of conversation rather odd, but I suspect for many more it will appear familiar and may strike deep chords of recognition. It speaks of many things: exhaustion, stress, overload, insomnia, anxiety, shame, aggression, hurt, guilt and feelings of out-of-placeness, fraudulence and fear of exposure within the contemporary academy. These feelings, these affective embodied experiences, occupy a strange position in relation to questions of secrecy and silence. They are at once ordinary and everyday, yet at the same time remain largely secret and silenced in the public spaces of the academy. They are spoken in a different, less privileged register; they are the stuff of the chat in the corridor, coffee-break conversations and intimate exchanges between friends, but not, it would seem, the keynote speech or the journal publication or even the departmental meeting. For all the interest in reflexivity in recent decades, the *experiences of academics* have somehow largely escaped critical attention. It is as if the parameters for reflexivity are bounded by the individual study, leaving the institutional context in which academic knowledge is produced simply as a taken for granted backdrop.

What would it mean to turn our lens upon our own labour processes, organisational governance and conditions of production? What would we find if, instead of studying others, we focussed our gaze upon our own community, and took as our data not the polished publication or the beautifully crafted talk, but the unending flow of communications and practices in which we are all embedded and enmeshed, often reluctantly: the proliferating e-mails, the minutes of meetings, the job applications, the peer reviews, the promotion assessments, the drafts of the RAE narrative, the committee papers, the student feedback forms, even the after-seminar chats? How might we make links between macro-organisation and institutional practices on the one hand, and experiences and affective states on the other, and open up an exploration of the ways in which these may be gendered, racialised and classed? How might we engage critically with the multiple moments in which individuals report being at breaking point, say 'my work is crap' or 'I'm going to be found out' – as well as those moments of gratuitous attack and cruelty, so often seen – for example – in anonymised referee processes (yet rarely challenged) – and connect these feelings with neoliberal practices of power in the Western university? In short, how might we begin to understand the secrets and silences within our own workplaces, and the different ways in which they matter?

I cannot hope to address all these questions in this short piece, but it feels important – indeed urgent – to put them on the agenda. This is not an exercise in self-indulgence or narcissism or even an opportunity to have a good moan – for part of what interests me is precisely how the strata of communication, of which the conversation above is an example, remains hearable *as* a 'moan', as an expression of complaint or unhappiness, rather than being formulated as an analysis or a (political) demand for change. Rather this chapter is the beginning of an attempt to redress our own collective silence, our failure to look critically at 'our own back yard', with the broad aim of understanding the relationship between economic and political shifts, transformations in work and psychosocial experiences – and starting a conversation about how we might resist.

Situating the experiences

It seems to me that four different literatures are pertinent to this project. First, there is the extensive literature about the transformation of work, writing about which shades into social theory more generally, with accounts of late capitalism, network society, liquid modernity, knowledge society, or post-Fordism (Bauman, 2000; Beck, 2000; Hardt and Negri, 2000; Boltanski and Chiapello, 2005; Sennett, 2006). Key themes include a stress upon risk, individualisation, insecurity and rapid technological change leading to the need for constant updating and reskilling (the requirement to become what Manuel Castells (1996) calls 'reprogrammable labour'). The recent upsurge of interest in cultural labour represents a particularly relevant subset of this literature which is arguably more empirically informed than general accounts and examines the experiences of work in cultural industries such as web design, television, film or fashion. Studies have highlighted a number of relatively stable features of this kind of work: a preponderance of temporary, intermittent and precarious jobs; long hours and bulimic patterns of working; the collapse or erasure of boundaries between work and play; poor pay; high levels of mobility; passionate attachment to the work and to the identity of creative labourer (e.g. web designer, artist, fashion designer); an attitudinal mindset that is a blend of bohemianism and entrepreneurialism; informal working environments and distinctive forms of sociality; and profound experiences of insecurity and anxiety about finding work, earning enough money and 'keeping up' in rapidly changing fields (Ursell, 2000; Gill, 2002; McRobbie, 2003; Ross, 2003; Banks, 2007; Gill and Pratt, 2008). These findings seem to resonate powerfully with many of the predominantly secret or silenced features of life in the contemporary Western university.

A second, but much smaller, body of work is the literature about structural transformations in higher education, which highlights the increasing corporatisation and privatisation of the university, and the impacts of this (Graham, 2002; Washburn, 2003; Evans, 2005). These include the importing of corporate models of management into university life; the reformulation of the very nature of education in instrumental terms connected to business and the economy; the transformation of students into 'consumers'; and the degradation of pay and working conditions for academics, as well as the increasing casualisation of employment, yet with little organised resistance from trade unions or other bodies. Critical work (and not all of this writing could be considered so; some of it is merely nostalgic for the era of elitist values and the 'gentleman scholar') speaks of the 'corporate university' and of 'academic capitalism', and considers the takeover of higher education by a logic of the market.

Third, scholarship concerned with the micro-politics of power in the academy is also highly pertinent to this project (Gillies and Lucey, 2007). Often feminist in orientation, and also sometimes informed by psychoanalytic thinking, this work challenges the popular image of the 'ivory tower' as 'a rarefied haven of detached reasoning and refined culture' (ibid.: 1) to look instead at the operation of power at different levels and in contradictory ways in the contemporary university. Power is understood relationally and this work also directs attention to unconscious forces in operation at both institutional and interpersonal levels. What is particularly valuable is the emphasis upon the small-scale, micro-negotiations of power in the academy – from the dynamics of a PhD supervision, to discussions about workload or promotion.

Finally it would seem that Foucaultian-inspired writing about neoliberalism represents another important source for thinking about contemporary working life in the academy. Key concepts include the notion of 'compulsory individuality' (Cronin, 2000), the idea that individuals are now increasingly required to tell the story of their lives as if they were the outcome of deliberative planning and choice (Rose, 1990; Walkerdine et al., 2001), and the critical interrogation of 'audit culture' with its attendant obligation to make everything 'auditable', rendered knowable and calculable in terms of quantifiable 'outputs' (Power, 1994; Strathern, 2000). Extending from discussions of economic rationality, critical scholarship about neoliberalism directs our attention to new and emerging forms of discipline, which operate as technologies of selfhood that bring into being the endlessly self-monitoring, planning, prioritising 'responsibilised' subject required by the contemporary university. She requires little management, but can be accorded the 'autonomy' to manage herself, in a manner that is a far more effective exercise of power than any imposed from above by employers.

In combination these distinct literatures have much to teach us about the changing nature of academic labour, but what is needed, I want to suggest, is an approach that can *think them together* in such a way as to explore the relations between transformations in capitalism, new forms of governmentality and psychosocial experiences of working in the university. In attempting this, I begin from *experiences* in the academy – experiences that are often kept secret or silenced, that don't have 'proper channels' of communication. My 'data' are entirely unscientific, but nevertheless, I contend, they tell us something real and significant about our own workplaces. They consist of conversations and e-mails from friends or colleagues, university memos, letters from journal editors and other 'fragments' from daily life (all anonymised except where they are mine) collected over a period of one year. I wanted to start from experiences, rather than from theory or from accounts of changes in capitalism, work or higher education, because – despite all the contestation around that term, particularly within feminism – it seems to me that it is this level that remains silenced in most fora – yet insistently asserts itself in our aching backs, tired eyes, difficulties in sleeping and in our multiple experiences of stress, anxiety and overload.

Precarious lives

> Don't get me wrong, I'm really glad to have this job, but because the contract is so short – again – I'm going to have to start looking for another one more or less right away.
>
> (Career early academic, 30s, on one-year contract for the third time)

> I'm actually doing four part-time jobs at the moment. It was only going to be three – which was just about manageable – but then someone went off sick at x (university) and they asked me to step in. I know it's mad, but there's just no way I could turn it down because they might be one of my only chances of getting a full-time job next year. So I've got to show willing and get my foot in the door. But I'm telling you, it's really killing me – you should see my timetable, and on Thursdays I'm doing like 400 miles going between jobs, and when I'm sitting in the car I am just so stressed, my knuckles are white on the steering wheel, and I keep thinking that if I hit traffic or there's an accident or something the whole thing will completely fall apart and I'll have blown it.
>
> (New post-doc, 30s)

> I've been killing myself trying to finish this paper, because if I don't get it into a good journal they won't enter me into the RAE, and if that happens I can forget about promotion altogether, and my days are probably numbered. Teaching-only contract here I come! I feel like I'm clinging on by my fingernails.
>
> (Lecturer, 40s)

Precariousness is one of the defining experiences of contemporary academic life – particularly, but not exclusively, for younger or 'career early' staff (a designation that can now extend for one's entire 'career', given the few opportunities for development or secure employment.) Statistical data about the employment patterns of academics shows the wholesale transformation of higher education over the last decades, with the systematic casualisation of the workforce. Continuing contracts – understood in the US as tenure-track appointments – now represent only just over half of academic posts, with 38 per cent of all academics in higher education on fixed-term contracts in 2006–7 (Court and Kinman, 2008). While, in the past, short-term contracts were largely limited to research positions and tied to specific, time-limited projects, today they also characterise teaching posts which are frequently offered on a one-year temporary basis at the bottom of the pay scale. However, even these posts constitute the 'aristocracy of labour' when compared to the proliferation of short-term, part-time teaching positions, contracted on an hourly paid basis, in which PhD students or new postdocs are charged with delivering mass undergraduate programmes, with little training, inadequate support and rates of pay that – when preparation and marking are taken into account – frequently fall (de facto) below the minimum wage and make even jobs in cleaning or catering look like attractive pecuniary options. Alongside such jobs is the newly created stratum of 'teaching fellowships' in which, as a cost-cutting measure for university management, work once rewarded with a lectureship is repackaged for lower pay, stripped of benefits (e.g. pension) and any sense of obligation or responsibility to the employee, and offered purely on a term-time basis, frequently leaving teaching fellows without any source of income over the summer.

There is much that can – and should – be said (angrily) about this – about the HE policies of successive governments, about the complicity of relatively secure staff in this erosion of pay and conditions for their colleagues, about the failure of a collective response to the decimation of a profession, indeed of a vision of the university and intellectual work itself. But what also needs discussion are our *experiences* of this kind of precariousness. How is the 'brave new world of work' elaborated by social theorists (Beck, 2000) experienced by those who live it in academia? What are the *costs* of the shift from relatively secure work to poorly paid, informal and discontinuous employment? The extracts presented here speak of some of these. They include chronic anxiety and stress brought about by long hours, high costs of travelling and the inability to plan ahead because of endemic insecurity about one's position. The Health and Safety Executive calculates that 13.8 million working days annually are lost to work-related stress, anxiety and depression, and the University and College Union's 2008 survey found academics reporting 'very high stress levels, considerably higher than average', which had increased from earlier surveys in 1998 and 2004 (Court and Kinman, 2008). Despite their profound impact upon our lives, these things are rarely spoken of within the academy, and, if they are, they tend to be treated as individual, personal experiences rather than structural features of the contemporary university. Moreover, academics are notoriously bad at talking about (poor) pay, perhaps seeing mention of it somehow as calling into question their commitment or integrity. As Andrew Ross (2000) has argued, the academic's refusal to grubby his or her hands with talk about money is related to the idea of scholarship as a 'noble' calling or vocation – a fact that is probably not unrelated to our failure over many decades to secure pay deals that even keep pace with inflation. Financial hardship can be masked – and rendered difficult to speak of – by academics' educational and cultural capital.

It is perhaps the same 'sacrificial' ethos that silences accounts of the personal costs of insecure and precarious work within universities. Having to commute long distances, or to live apart from partner and friends, are among these, as we become an increasingly mobile, fragmented workforce. Another cost for some is not being able to have children. This impacts disproportionately on female academics who, it would appear, are significantly less likely to have children than both their male counterparts in academia, and women in other types of employment (Probert, 2005; Nakhaie, 2007). Part of this difference may be accounted for in terms of the lower numbers of female academics who *want* children, but recognition of this should not blind us to the fact that increasing numbers also feel unable to do so and sustain an academic career, either because the length of time it takes to get a secure job (degree, Master's, PhD, series of temporary contracts) makes it too late, or because the intense day-to-day demands of contemporary academic employment make it extremely difficult to manage. A study at the University of California found that women academics with children were working 100 hours per week, when housework and childcare were added to academic labour (Mason et al., 2006). It might be argued that the rapid influx of women into academic positions within universities in the last 30 years has come at the cost – for some of them – of having families. This resonates × are trends towards gender equality, but in which more complex forms of discrimination and inequality are emerging.

Fast academia: the intensification and extensification of work

> NB In completing the online form, please do not enter a total number of hours greater than 37 per week, as this will cause the form to be void. If you have worked more than 37 hours in the relevant week, please enter your responses as percentages of time worked, not as hours.
>
> (Guidance to staff on completing the TRAC form, x University, 2007)

> I think I'm a bit too either addicted or compulsive about it or obsessive about it … I worry that I'm going to miss something that I ought to be attending to, I worry that if I leave it for a day, then I'm going to come back and then just have 60 or 70 e-mails at the end of the day … so to that extent my e-mails are completely Sisyphean. It is never ending. It's like my To Do list. I'm down from 70 things to do on my To Do list to 30, but that 30 keeps on – it's a perpetual 30.
>
> (Male professor, 61 – quoted in Gregg, 2009)

A punishing intensification of work has become an endemic feature of academic life. Again, serious discussion of this is hard to find either within or outside universities, yet it is impossible to spend any significant amount of time with academics without quickly gaining an impression of a profession overloaded to breaking point, as a consequence of the underfunded expansion of universities over the last two decades, combined with hyperinflation of what is demanded of academics, and an audit culture that, if it was once treated with scepticism, has now been almost perfectly internalised. (Indeed, as I write this, I'm being informed by email of the need to be 'REF-ready', even before the terms of the new research assessment audit – the so-called Research Excellence Framework – have been announced).

The intensification of academics' labour is borne out not only by anecdotal evidence (of which most academics could supply reams) but by all the available research on working hours. A report by the TUC in 2005 (quoted in Court and Kinman, 2008) found that academics and teachers were more likely than any other occupational group to do unpaid overtime. A large proportion were working hours in excess of the European Working Time Directive, and 42 per cent said that they regularly worked evenings and weekends in order to cope with the demands of their job. The reason given was very simple: the volume of work demanded of them. This is like an 'open secret'. Indeed, awareness of it on the part of those managing universities meant a change to auditing procedures that was, quite literally, built into the software of the TRAC system for monitoring how academics append their time (see above). This made it impossible for staff to record the total number of hours worked, if these exceeded those for which they were nominally contracted. In this way, academics' working hours were systematically and quite deliberately rendered invisible, operating as a silencing mechanism.

There are of course a whole range of much more subtle and pernicious techniques for silencing complaints and neutering resistance, which operate at the micro level of 'collegial' relations, as well as within the academic subject himself or herself. One female lecturer told me:

> I was at breaking point. I went to see my mentor to complain about my workload. I mean, I'm really, really conscientious – you know that – and my mentor just said: 'Welcome to modern academia. We're *all* working these crazy hours. I'm sorry to be blunt, but you know what you have to do: if it's too hot, get out the kitchen.'

The 'kitchen' of academia is, it would seem, too hot for almost everyone, but this has not resulted in collective action to turn down the heat, but instead to an overheated competitive atmosphere in which acts of kindness, generosity and solidarity often seem to continue only in spite of, rather than because of, the governance of universities. Increasingly, requests to perform activities that would once have been considered part of the 'civic' collegial responsibility of being a university lecturer (such as examining PhDs, refereeing articles or reviewing grant proposals) take on a tone of pleading desperation, as journal editors or course managers find no one prepared to do the necessary work. This is a collective, structural problem that is a direct result of workloads which leave many people with no 'slack' to take on *anything* beyond that which is directly required of them. Yet once again there is no discussion of this as an institutional or organisational issue. Instead universities 'help' staff to deal with these new intensified conditions with a barrage of 'training courses' (most of which we have no time to attend) which cover topics such as 'time management', 'speed reading' and 'prioritising goals', and require each individual to work on the self to better manage proliferating workloads, as if there were a technical fix (*oh it'll all be alright if I only check emails once a day – why didn't I think of that?! I'll just pick all 115 of them up at 5 o'clock then I can stay up all night answering them!*), while actively refusing any 'reality check' on the sustainability of contemporary academic workloads.

This is particularly ironic given that academics hardly need any *more* training to perfect their polished self-discipline and self governance! We appear, on the contrary, to be model neoliberal subjects whose working practices and 'psychic habitus' (to stretch Bourdieu a little towards my psychosocial concerns) constitute us as self-regulating, calculating, conscientious and responsibilised. The 'freedom', 'flexibility' and 'autonomy' of neoliberal forms of governmentality have proved far more effective for extracting 'surplus value,' or at least vastly more time spent working than any older modalities of power (though, of course, feudal and other forms co-exist quite comfortably with these in the operation of universities).

Meanwhile, critical of yet trapped within the same logic of individual solutions and techniques of the self, I ask my friends how they cope with things such as daily requests to referee articles (I'm looking for ideas to help me deal with this): 'I only referee for journals I'm on the editorial board for'; 'I do 20 each year and when I've done those 20 I resolutely refuse any more'; 'I look at the topic and will only do it if it is very close to my own interests'; and so on. I am struck by the amount of thought and emotional labour has gone into this: so many different responses, so many carefully thought through personal strategies, so much energy invested in navigating a course between being a good ethical 'citizen' of academia, and *surviving* – that is, not going under, getting sick or giving up one's own work entirely. But all of this is almost entirely secret, a panoply of privatised responses for managing the unmanageable.

And it misses too all the emotional costs that come not only from work done, but also from work not done. A colleague asks me to examine his student's PhD. I agonise for two days: I want to help out, it sounds an interesting thesis, it feels important ethically and politically to do this stuff, and I know the student really wanted me as her examiner … but I am already examining two other PhDs that month, I'm behind on everything, my mum's ill, and I can feel I'm getting close to that place where I will collapse. … Deep breath: I say, 'No, sorry, I can't do it'. I am immediately flooded with guilt, I feel a bit shabby, a little bit less than the human being I want to be; I try not to think about the student's disappointment.

Always on: academia without walls

Alongside the intensification of work in academia, we are also experiencing its marked extensification (Jarvis and Pratt, 2006) across time and space. Paradoxically, as university lecturers have increasingly reported that noise, open-plan offices, interruptions and student demands mean that 'you can't work at work' everywhere else has opened up as a potential site for academic labour! How convenient. Autonomous Marxist writers call this the era of the 'socialised worker' and the 'factory without walls', a phase of capitalism in which labour is deterritorialsed so that 'the whole society is placed at the disposal of profit' (Negri, 1989: 79). Work in today's universities is, it would seem, *academia without walls.* This is the outcome of multiple determinants but is facilitated by information and communication technologies that render it possible to be 'always on' (Gregg, 2009)

Ever speeded-up mobile technologies intermesh seamlessly with the psychic habitus and dispositions of the neoliberal academic subject: checking, monitoring, downloading whether from BL (British Library), beach or bed, trying desperately to keep up and 'stay on top'. Two things are striking about Gregg's data (interviews with white-collar workers in Australia) as well as my own more informal conversations with academic colleagues and friends. First, there is the palpable *anxiety* that pulsates through these accounts: anxiety about falling behind, missing something important, going under. And second is the way in which this is framed almost entirely in individualistic discourse. Once again, it would seem that these are privatised anxieties that are understood to reflect on the value and worth of the individual, rather than the values of the institutions that make intolerable demands. Indeed, it is notable how much self-contempt runs through such accounts, and the way they draw on the language of pathology. In the extract that begins this section, the male professor characterises himself as variously 'addicted', 'obsessive' and 'compulsive' when he might more accurately be seen as enacting quite reasonable strategies in order to cope with an entirely unreasonable workload. 'Addiction' metaphors suffuse academics' talk of their relationship to e-mail, even as they report such high levels of anxiety that they feel they have to check e-mails first thing in the morning and last thing at night, and in which time away (on sick leave, on holiday) generates fears of what might be lurking in the inbox when they return. Again, inventive 'strategies' abound for keeping such anxiety at bay, e.g. putting on your 'out of office' reply when you are actually in the office.

However, it is not only the always-on culture of e-mails that has led to the marked intensification of our workloads and the almost constant experience of high levels of stress. In fact, it is paradoxical given how much time we spend on it, that e-mail is mostly experienced as what stops us getting on with our 'real' work – which is itself intensifying all the time, as a consequence of what Gregg (2009) calls 'function creep' – the requirement to do more with less. In teaching, for example, it is no longer enough to give a lecture and run some seminars, we are also expected to produce a set of resources for use on the new online communications platforms such as WebCT, Blackboard and Moodle. 'It is not acceptable simply to upload your lecture notes', comes the guidance from one university. 'We encourage you to use WebCT *creatively*, with quizzes, hyperlinks, visual materials, etc. To learn more about the potential of WebCT for innovative teaching, come along to one of our training courses.' Oh great, I would think facetiously on receiving yet another memo like this, another training course! And yet the pressure that is produced by such constant exhortations to be more creative, teach more innovatively, be at the cutting edge (etc.) is undeniable – particularly because it meets an *already existing set of desires and ethics* around being professional and wanting to do a good job.

Mostly, though, it is in relation to research that people feel most under pressure for it is here that our 'worth' is most harshly surveilled and assessed, and where we are subject to ever greater scrutiny. For it is not just a matter of whether you publish, but what you publish, where you publish it, how often it is cited, what 'impact factor' the journal has and whether you are 'REF-ready'. Reading Nigel Thrift (2000) on 'fast management' (itself a development from the notion of 'fast capitalism'), I was struck by the parallels with academia: our need to be ever faster, more agile, and with what Thrift calls 'hair trigger responsiveness' so that we are able to adapt to new calls for papers, new funding streams and fit in with every changing fashion on engaging 'research users' and stakeholders. In Thrift's terms, we are subjects who are required to cope with a state of permanent 'emergency as rule'. This is a form of governmentality that is even more pernicious than the notion that 'you are only as good as your last job' (Blair, 2001). Instead, you are only as good as your last paper, and that now has a half life that is shorter than ever. Welcome to fast academia.

Toxic shame

> This paper will be of no interest to readers of x (journal name). Discourse analysis is little more than journalism and I fail to see what contribution it can make to understanding the political process. It is self-evident to everyone except this author that politics is about much more than 'discourse'. What's more, in choosing to look at the speeches of Margaret Thatcher, the author shows his or her complete parochialism. If you are going to do this kind of so-called 'analysis' at least look at the discourse of George Bush.
>
> (Referee 2's comments accompanying journal rejection)

> I haven't been able to tell anyone at work about it. I just feel so humiliated. This will confirm everything they already think about me.
>
> (Lecturer, 40s, on hearing that she had not been successful in getting a grant)

> I coped with it once, Ros, but how can I deal with this again? After two knock-backs for promotion I just don't know if I can carry on. I've worked my balls off for that place, but they've just made me feel like I'm nothing.
>
> (Senior lecturer, 50s, on hearing his promotion application had been rejected for a second time)

The quotation that leads this section is a referee's report I received the first time I ever submitted a paper to a journal, back in 1990. I laughed (bitterly) at the accusation of parochialism from this particular North American journal, and even more at the suggestion that this would be put right by focusing on the US(!). But that was small comfort because mostly I felt belittled, hurt and upset at this dismissive rejection of work that I had thought about, developed and crafted over months of careful scholarship. Maybe I wasn't 'good enough' for academia. I had felt optimistic and proud to have written my first 'proper' academic paper. Eight months later when the rejection letter came, disheartened, I could not bear to look at it again. It remained unpublished and some years passed before I submitted another paper to a journal.

I am older, more experienced, and (a bit) tougher now. But I have witnessed the same thing happening many times to friends and PhD students; seen them crying after opening such letters (as my friend reports at the start of this chapter), looking bewildered, devastated. I often wish I could protect them, but all I can do is try to prepare them for what one former student eloquently describes as part of the (sometimes brutal and dehumanising) process of 'becoming Throsby' (her surname) – that is, achieving full academic citizenship.

For me this raises (at least) two kinds of question. First, what is going on when such hostile and dismissive judgements are made by one's peers? The comments my paper attracted nearly 20 years ago were quite mild and innocuous compared to many I have seen more recently, as journals 'open up' their reviewing processes and send all the reviews to each reviewer. When did it become acceptable to write of a colleague's work 'this is self-indulgent crap' or 'put this manuscript in a drawer and don't ever bother to come back to it' – both comments I have read in the last year on colleagues' work. What are the psychosocial processes that produce this kind of practice? I would argue that this has nothing to do with a notion of 'academic freedom', nor is it merely about intellectual differences or the normal cut and thrust of academic debate – all things that must be preserved – but is produced by the peculiarly toxic conditions of neoliberal academia. To understand it we have to think psychosocially in a way that can connect the pressures, competitiveness and frustrations of contemporary academia with the reviewers' own experiences of being treated with contempt and derision. Might it be an example of repressed rage bursting out as an attack against someone who is not the cause of it? Or is it is better understood, by contrast, as one of the few sites where academics may feel that they can exercise some power – thus they 'let rip,' occasionally cruelly, under the cloak of guaranteed anonymity.

The second set of questions it generates, however, focus on the 'receiving end' of negative reviews to ask what it is that happens when rejection (itself an absolutely normal, routine feature of academic life) translates so quickly and so readily into what I would suggest is a kind of toxic shame? It is the outcome partly of the particular biographies most of us bring, which may sometimes include struggle, but *always* feature 'doing well' (passing exams, achieving plaudits, winning prizes). Being hard-working, self-motivating and enterprising subjects is what constitutes academics as so perfectly emblematic of this neoliberal moment, but is also part of a psychic landscape in which *not* being successful (or lucky!) (i.e. not being the one in five who gets their research application funded, or the one in 15 whose paper is accepted for publication in the 'good' journal) is misrecognised – or to put that more neutrally, made knowable – in terms of individual (moral) failure.

This individualising discourse devours us like a flesh-eating bacterium, producing its own toxic waste – shame: I'm a fraud, I'm useless, I'm nothing. It is (of course) deeply gendered, racialised and classed, connected to biographies that produce very different degrees of 'entitlement' (or not). This affective response in turn is profoundly silencing and isolating – and how could it be otherwise; we don't want to 'show' our ugly failure, any more than it might already be evident, so we are careful about who we tell of our rejection – a partner, yes, close friends, perhaps, but not (as the above extract illustrates) necessarily one's colleagues, if they are felt to be hostile or competitive rather than solidaristic. When students tell me of receiving a rejection from a journal, they have often kept it secret for some time while they try to process the feelings it has engendered. When I tell them it has happened to me, and to every academic I know, they are surprised, having immediately and automatically internalised the experience as their own shameful failure. Some will have concluded that they really aren't good enough, they can't 'hack it'. But others will have already devised 'solutions': I must try harder, read more widely, understand theory better, and so on – the solution, then, for 'us' good neoliberal subjects, simply to work *even harder*.

Pleasure

All this happens in a context in which not only has the boundary between work and play (or non-work) become completely corroded, but in which we are deeply invested in and passionately attached to work – indeed, we often draw no distinction between our work and ourselves (and again there are powerful parallels with creative workers here). As Angela McRobbie has pointed out in relation to the fashion industry and other creative work,

> professed pleasure in work and indeed passionate attachment to something called 'my own work' where there is the possibility of the

> maximisation of self-expression, provides a compelling status justification but also a disciplinary mechanism for tolerating not just uncertainty and self exploitation but also for staying unprofitably within the creative sector and not abandoning it altogether.

I believe that we could substitute 'academics' for 'creatives' in this powerful analysis without losing any of the force of this argument. We therefore need urgently to think about how some of the pleasures of academic work (or at least a deep love for the 'myth' of what we thought being an intellectual would be like, but often seems at far remove from it) bind us more tightly into a neoliberal regime with ever-growing costs, not least to ourselves. Lauren Berlant's work on 'cruel optimism' may be helpful here in showing how such passionate investment (e.g. in the myth of the academic good life) allows us to survive, whilst simultaneously making things worse.[1]

Conclusion

In this chapter I have looked at some of the secrets and silences of academic life. I have tried to argue that academia represents an excellent example of the neoliberalisation of the workplace and that academics are, in many ways, model neoliberal subjects, with their endless self-monitoring, flexibility, creativity and internalisation of new forms of auditing and calculating.

Neoliberalism found fertile ground in academics whose predispositions to 'work hard' and 'do well' meshed perfectly with its demands for autonomous, self-motivating, responsibilised subjects. This is gendered, racialised and classed, too, to be sure, in ways that merit urgent attention that I have been unable to give in this short piece. The lack of resistance to the neoliberalisation of universities is partly a result of these divisive, individualising practices, of the silences around them, of the fact also that people are too exhausted to resist and furthermore do not know *what* to resist or *how* to do so. But it is also understandable, I suggest, in terms of the inherent pleasures and fulfilment that many people derive from their work (when they find time to do it) or at least the promise of/idea of it, as well as to the seductions of relatively autonomous working lives – though this autonomy is eroding fast, as universities import business models which require, for example, that all e-mails be answered within 24 hours, or that academics are present in the office five days a week. In reality, the much-vaunted autonomy often simply means that universities end up extracting even more labour from us for free, as we participate in working lives in which there is often no boundary between work and anything else (if indeed there is anything else).

In this chapter, by focusing on experience, I have tried to show some of the costs of this – highlighting insecurity, stress, anxiety and shame as some significant examples.[2] In this 'emergency as rule' (Thrift, 2000) world, these are some of the secrets, silences and hidden injuries of the neoliberal workplaces we inhabit. The challenge is how we might begin to resist.

Postscript

This chapter almost didn't get written. One reason for this is precisely the working conditions outlined above. However, there was another 'internal' block that almost prevented me from committing these ideas to paper: an anxiety about the seeming narcissism and self-indulgence of such a piece. Part of me felt that merely pointing to some of the 'injuries' of (British) academic life had a somewhat obscene quality to it given our enormous privileges relative to most people in most of the world. As Kate Soper (1991) put it in another context – 'no one is starving you, torturing you or even denying you the price of a tube ticket to a conference about postmodernism'; what right, then, to spend a whole chapter talking about myself/ourselves as if *we* had any real problems?! This feeling was intensified by the fact of writing this in January 2009 as Israel relentlessly bombed the population of the Gaza strip. The times when I was not trying to finish this piece were spent either demonstrating outside the Israeli embassy in London or weeping tears of impotent rage as I witnessed daily the appalling suffering of hundreds of thousands of Palestinians on my screen. Against that context the costs of the neoliberalisation of academia hardly seem a 'worthy' subject for a politically engaged, critical intellectual …

Yet, of course, this too can become a silencing dynamic, allowing us only to speak of extremes of injustice and suffering, as if the mere fact that others 'have it worse' disentitles one from any kind of criticism, from saying anything about our own experiences. On balance, then, I decided to write it and I hope that the ideas about the psychosocial aspects of neoliberalism that it tries to develop will, ultimately, be seen as part of a wider project to *make intelligible contemporary modalities of power*, and thus as connected ineluctably to the struggle for a better, more just world.

Acknowledgements

Thanks to Stephen Court at the University and College Union for his invaluable assistance in obtaining statistical data relating to academic employment and workplace stress. I would also like to thank several friends and colleagues for suggestions and feedback that have been helpful and inspiring. I'm grateful to Mark Banks, Sara Bragg, Kathy Davis, Natalie Fenton, Breda Gray, Melissa Gregg, Clare Hemmings, Gail Lewis, Angela McRobbie, Andy Pratt, Róisín Ryan-Flood, Christina Scharff, Stephanie Taylor and Imogen Tyler. My special appreciation to Bruna Seu for sharing her wit and wisdom about academic life over many years of stimulating and supportive conversations.

Notes

1 I am grateful to Clare Hemmings for drawing my attention to this.

2 I might also, however, have talked about illness, as both morbidity and mortality rates look bleaker and bleaker for our profession, and colleagues report 'I get sick all the time'.

Bibilography

Banks, M. (2007) *The Politics of Cultural Work*, Basingstoke/New York, Palgrave Macmillan.

Bauman, Z. (2000) *Liquid Modernity*, Cambridge, Polity Press.

Beck, U. (2000) *The Brave New World of Work*, Cambridge, Polity Press.

Blair, H. (2001) 'You're only as good as your last job': the labour process and labour market in the British film industry. *Work, Employment and Society*, 15, 149–69.

Boltanski, L. and Chiapello, E. (2005) *The New Spirit of Capitalism*, London/New York, Verso.

Castells, M. (1996) *The Rise of the Network Society*, Cambridge, MA, Blackwell.

Court, S. and Kinman, G. (2008) 'Tackling stress in higher education'. London, University and College Union.

Cronin, A. (2000) Consumerism and compulsory individuality: women, will and potential. in Ahmed, S., Kilby, J., Lury, C., McNeil, M. and Skeggs, B. (eds) *Transformations: Thinking through feminism*, London, Routledge.

Evans, M. (2005) *Killing Thinking: The Death of the University*, London, Continuum.

Gill, R. (2002) Cool, creative and egalitarian? Exploring gender in project-based new media work in Europe. *Information, Communication and Society*, 5, 70–89.

Gill, R. and Pratt, A. (2008) In the social factory? Immaterial labour, precariousness and cultural work. *Theory, Culture and Society*, 25, 1–30.

Gillies, v. and Lucey, H. (eds) (2007) *Power, Knowledge and the Academy: The Institutional is Political*, Basingstoke/New York, Palgrave Macmillan.

Graham, G. (2002) *Universities: The Recovery of an Idea*, Exeter, Imprint Academic.

Gregg, M. (2009) Function creep: communication technologies and anticipatory labour in the information workplace. *New Media and Society.*

Hardt, M. and Negri, T. (2000) *Empire*, Cambridge, MA, Harvard University Press.

Jarvis, H. and Pratt, A. (2006) Bringing it all back home: the extensification and 'overflowing' of work: the case of San Francisco's new media households. *Geoforum*, 37, 331–39.

Mason, M.A., Goulden, M. and Wolfinger, N. H. (2006) Babies matter: Pushing the gender equity revolution forward. In Bracken, S., Allen, J. K. and Dean, D. R. (eds) *The Balancing Act: Gendered Perspectives in Faculty Roles and Work Lives.* Sterling, Virginia, Stylus Publishing.

McRobbie, A. (2008) 'Be Creative' Unpublished paper delivered at Barcelona Museum of Contempotart Art. November.

McRobbie, A. (2003) Club to company. *Cultural Studies*, 16, 516–31.

Nakhaie, M. R. (2007) Universalism, ascription and academic rank: Canadian professors 1987–2000. *Canadian Review of Sociology and Anthropology*, 44, 361–86.

Negri, T. (1989) *The Politics of Subversion: A Manifesto for the 21st Century*, Cambridge, Polity Press.

Power, M. (1994) 'The audit explosion'. London, DEMOS.

Probert, B. (2005) 'I just couldn't fit in': Gender and unequal outcomes in academic careers. *Gender, Work and Organization*, 12, 50–72.

Rose, N. (1990) *Governing the soul: the shaping of the private self*, London; New York, Routledge.

Ross, A. (2000) The mental labour problem. *Social Text*, 63, 1–32.

—— (2003) *No Collar: The Humane Workplace and its Hidden Costs*, New York, Basic Books.

Sennett, R. (2006) *The Culture of the New Capitalism*, New Haven, CT, Yale University Press.

Soper, K. (1991) Postmodernism, subjectivity and the question of value. *New Left Review*, 186, 120–28.

Strathern, M. (2000) The tyranny of transparency. *British Educational Research Journal*, 26, 309–21.

Thrift, N. (2000) Performing cultures in the new economy. *Annals of the Asssociation of American Geographers*, 90, 674–92.

Ursell, G. (2000) Television production: issues of exploitation, commodification and subjectivity in UK television markets. *Media, Culture and Society*, 22, 805–25.

Walkerdine, V., Lucey, H. and Melody, J. (2001) *Growing Up Girl: Psychosocial Explorations of Gender and Class*, Basingstoke, Palgrave.

Washburn, J. (2003) *University, Inc.: The Corporate Corruption of Higher Education*, New York, Basic Books.

18 Silence and secrets

Confidence in research

Suki Ali

Confidence in research

Writing about secrets while maintaining an ethical stance can be difficult. This is certainly so for my own work as an ethnographer who wants to write in a grounded way, drawing upon examples from research without breaking confidences. Perhaps it would be possible or even preferable for me to simply use hypothetical examples. But these can seem rather hollow and trite – a little too tidy in the light of the much more messy and sometimes painful realities of extensive fieldwork that often provides such rich material. I have decided to focus upon a range of inter-related *issues* that emerged whilst doing ethnographic fieldwork. Fictional or not they are reflective of some of the complexities I encountered whilst in the field. The research explored gendered processes of racialization and was conducted with both children and adults from a range of backgrounds. Although primarily tied to three key ethnographic sites (primary schools), it did spill over into other spaces, such as interviews in family homes, field trips with children and other events. It is important to note that although some of the issues I discuss here are perhaps more likely to occur in work with children or to have a greater impact or import with them, many of them would be relevant to a range of research encounters.

When first engaging the meaning and impact of 'secrets', it is inevitable that it leads into a consideration of a whole range of related concepts and topics. The secret is a concept that is particularly enmeshed within discourses of privacy, confidentiality, discretion and disclosure. It is almost impossible to think of secrets without thinking about how they are often linked to lies or at least evasions of truth telling, of the silences that are present (absences), and how silences maintain secrets, withholding, the fear of revelation. In short thinking of secrecy brings us centrally to what can be known, what not, what can be said and not said, and in the case of visual research, what can be seen and shown and what cannot. What can we see, what do we think we see, what do we need to know to 'see' better? Should we ever push to find the 'truth' that is lying behind the silence, the silence maintaining the secret? Should secrets never be told? The way in which we approach these questions is of crucial importance to feminists and other reflexive researchers. They are not purely a matter of ethics, nor yet of method, but are bound to both, and framed within particular political understandings of the research process.

In the following sections I will explore some of these issues as they emerged in ethnographic research into 'race', ethnicity and cultural practices through gendered racialization. The bulk of the research was carried out over a year, and involved working directly with children, with some teachers, and to a lesser extent with parents. Although the main issues were framed within work into mixedness and 'identities', it was of equal importance to situate these within a broader understanding of processes of racialization and their relation to ethnicity and to the politics of belonging (see Ali 2003). The research explored both the discursive regimes that formed the understanding of 'race' in school environments but also engaged children's familial narratives of home and belonging. It was evident that working with children from the 'middle years' raised particular concerns about the 'sensitive' nature of the topics, not only in discussing 'race' and racism, but, of course, having them think about their own and others' family lives. The whole process required the development of 'confidence' in its many forms.

If we are to have confidence in our research we need to be constantly aware of how this research impacts upon others. This is an obvious point to make as it might be understood that the reason for doing research named 'feminist' is for it to be socially and politically relevant and for it to effect change of some kind (see, e.g., Harding and Norberg 2005). It is, however, equally important to think about the research process itself. Concerns about impact are perhaps less obvious when researching with objects, although of course this need not be the case. When working with people, we are most likely to be brought up against the ways in which having and building confidence in research places us in a variable and dynamic relationship with power and control over every aspect from drafting funding proposals through to access to respondents, data collection, analysis and the subsequent dispersal of 'outputs'. Some kinds of evasions and omissions might be considered as 'silences' or 'secrets' and thus an inevitable part of the data collection process. But if the unspoken and unrepresented come to be used as data, does this amount to a betrayal of the confidentiality and consent gained from participants? Is this, bluntly put, an abuse of power? Can we consider it a 'tactics of evasion' as choices made by children to construct their own narratives, or are they the outcome of intrusive research methods which break with the ideals of feminist research methodologies? These questions are unanswerable, and serve only to act as a framing for politically engaged, ethical research practice.

Accessing the confidential

Access as informed consent

One of the first areas in which secrets and confidences, disclosure and discretion appear is in gaining access to particular respondents by eliciting 'informed consent'. When working with children, young people and other 'vulnerable' groups it is particularly important that what constitutes the 'informed' part of the consent is held up to the closest scrutiny.[1] It is well known that the basis for gaining consent is tied to the imperative to avoid harm as well as to act in a morally responsible, ethical fashion. Therefore, although some 'consent' might be isolated to a requirement of ethical practice in relation to 'data collection', it is of course essential that we give careful consideration to ethical implications upon leaving the field, and in the data analysis and publication phases. Sisela Bok's (1989) discussion of secrets in social science research is rightly scathing about some of the more dubious work that has been done covertly. She illustrates this citing a case in which the researchers completely misrepresent who they are and what they are doing, 'masquerading' as religious cult members in order to gain information. The first edition of her book came out in the 1980s – not so long ago, yet I would hope that the kind of covert research she cites would be unlikely to happen today.[2] Importantly, in the examples she gives there are clear boundaries between confidences and consent. In such cases the researcher is the one who holds the secrets and who, in her mind, is quite simply lying and deceiving in order to collect data. While it may be desirable to disclose as fully as possible what research is about in order gain full consent, Ramazanoğlu and Holland note that informed consent 'is a particularly difficult issue in any social research, since researchers often do not want to inform the researched or their gatekeepers too fully because of the possible impact on data production' (Ramazanoğlu and Holland 2002: 157). In the case of gaining consent to work with young people on sensitive topics, despite the overt nature of the research, it may often be the case that certain areas of interest are quickly passed over, some 'not mentioned' until a later date and so on. Such hazy explanation might not be intended as deliberately misleading, rather it often arises from a concern that too much explanation of the topic will not only impact upon the type of data collected but on the way in which respondents themselves will come forward. If the respondents do not take part there is no research, or if they are given a lot of information it becomes a different kind of research, one that might not fully get to the accounts given by people who live the topic under consideration. This management of information then is not so much 'secrecy' as a form of withholding which seems justifiable in one respect, but if held to the absolute standard of total disclosure, is ethically dubious.

Confidentiality and consent

In research into 'sensitive' subjects, the promise of confidentiality is often the key to obtaining information through informed consent. My own experience of discussing issues of confidentiality with children really opens up the problem with the 'informed' part of the consent. I realised that often children simply did not understand the word and found myself having to explain to them what this meant. This proved to be an extremely revealing exercise in and of itself. In conversation with Marita (aged 8) one day I found the weakness in my explanation confronted in no uncertain terms. I had already obtained school approval to work with certain classes and had sent letters home to parents and carers explaining what I hoped to do and offering them the opportunity to speak to me and to withdraw their child from the research. In addition to the participant observation, the preliminary stages of the research which was specifically with children, involved whole-class participation in discussion. I then conducted focus group discussions with friendship groups. I followed these with individual and/or pair interviews and some children were also invited to produce photographs with disposable cameras and then discuss these. Marita was one of the children with whom I hoped to conduct a more formal interview. We set up some time to talk in a 'private space' in the school. I had not originally told children that I was interested in mixedness per se as I wanted to see if they would name it as part of their repertoire of identifications. Here then was a kind of withholding on my part. At the focus groups I began to introduce the topics under investigation more broadly. Following these sessions, the children of course began to discuss my presence and the research. I had numerous children interested in joining the research who began to claim 'mixedness' – mainly because it meant they could occasionally get taken out of class. This was all valuable and interesting 'data'. When Marita arrived she knew already that the research was about 'race' and 'mixed race' and had worked out that her own self-identified mixedness in particular was one of the reasons she was there. She was an extraordinarily articulate child who could express things about her own life and identity in extremely sophisticated ways. Her parents had obviously discussed 'race' and racism with her, and she was attending a school which took a very proactive approach in dealing with these kinds of topics in an open and direct way. It was then no surprise when she confronted my somewhat vague account of what it meant for her singular contributions to be 'kept confidential'.

I began by asking if she might be interested in talking to me in more detail about the topics we had begun to discuss in the focus groups. I had already said at the very beginning that I hoped that the research might be useful to people when they were dealing with these issues. I reminded her of this and said to her that in these further sessions what she said would be 'confidential' and asked if she understood this word. When she responded negatively I explained that what she said would be 'private', 'a bit like a secret' between us and that what she told me would not be told to the parents, teachers or other children. With no hesitation she retorted, '[w]ell why are you taping everything then if it's a secret?' I realized immediately that to describe this material as 'secret' in the terms she understood it was not accurate as that would mean I would never tell anyone about it. She thought that not only would I not mention the content, but I would also not use anything she said verbatim at all. I further explained that although I might use some of the words she said in the research, no one would know it was her speaking because I would be careful to anonymise her and others' responses. At this point it became very clear that I had indeed been in error. I was not promising total confidentiality, I was promising anonymity which is a rather different beast. I had also said that children could tell people what they had talked about what had happened in our interviews, and that they were not bound by these same rules of confidentiality; it was up to them if they talked about things, but I couldn't tell people what they had said. Again, giving this latitude meant that actually the material was potentially not confidential at all. But I felt I could not bind the children themselves to a kind of secrecy in relation to the interview. I soon found myself modifying what I said to children to emphasise anonymity but adding that I would indeed be using their words, even if paraphrased, collectivised and not directly quoted. I learnt the hard way how complex these issues are as you are immersed in a research site and having to think 'on your feet'. It is even more complicated by the kinds of relationships that were already developing.

Trusting in confidentiality

The process of gaining consent through the promise of confidentiality is one that engenders trust in the research process and marks a shift in research relationships. In work with children, the consequences of this are steeped in an awareness of 'power relationships', or to be more accurate on the dynamics of power. When I first began the research project I was repeatedly told that it was unworkable because children would not understand what it was that was being asked of them, that the information they gave would be unreliable, or that they were particularly vulnerable and were open to being pushed into discussing things that could be disturbing to them. In these accounts we see the idea of 'informed' consent in its purest form, as it was developed in biomedical settings. There is a model of a universally recognisable, rational citizen at its heart, one that can, if given enough information, make a judgement about harm. 'The child' here is by common understanding not-yet-rational, and was therefore for many simply off limits. In this case, sets of rules and guidelines for this ethically approved informed consent can mean constraints upon what kind of research can be done with whom. As Halse and Honey note: 'The epistemic tensions between the discourses of the universal, rational subject of scientific realism and those of the multidimensional, particular and social subject of interpretive, qualitative research create messy moral dilemmas' (Halse and Honey 2005: 2157). As a researcher, I felt myself less concerned with morality per se. The desire to work with potentially difficult areas with children required a highly reflexive engagement with my own processes and decision making; one that I would characterise as both ethically and politically informed rather than 'morally' guided. In gaining access through promises of confidentiality I felt that I was trying to be as open as I could about the research in order to show that confidences would be held and respected. In offering up confidentiality, I also offered trust, and something like a relationship. This was quite difficult to maintain if children themselves chose to reveal things about our discussions. However, it became even more difficult as the ethnography progressed. Relationships deepened and stretched and the multiple methods of data collection began to expose secrets – not in the sense of revealing material that was intended to be kept hidden, but in the many facets of the same versions of events were revealed by different people and in different contexts. Some of these issues are explored further below.

Confidences given

Not telling tales

Gaining trust means that we often become confidantes to our respondents. However, the practice of giving information to the researcher, the offering of confidences, was by no means certain, and was certainly not expected. The research was not intended to be invasive; quite the reverse. I constantly worried about intrusive practice: I was concerned with the practicalities of asking questions in ways that were respectful, of stopping when I saw discomfort, but of gentle probing where children appeared comfortable but were perhaps not quite engaging the issues directly. I also had to be careful not to be invasive with my presence in the playground. It became a bit of a joke that my tape-recorder was something of a magnet to the children. That at least was an open and generous response to my evident presence. What was not comfortable for me was to be doing semi-participant observation in the playground, i.e. to be 'hovering' in the vicinity, silently witnessing events while children were unaware. I rarely did this kind of thing, in playgrounds or in class. However, of course children got used to my presence and began to take it for granted in the 'public spaces' and to extend their trust in me in 'private spaces'. These developments meant that some way into the research it became evident that confidences were being both offered and withheld. The two obvious ways in which this manifested was that in some instances children might reveal secrets they wanted me to keep, whereas in other cases they withheld information that subsequently came to light – silences were broken.

The issue of trust, ethics and power was most poignantly revealed the first time a child recognised that confidentiality meant that I would not 'tell'. In one case a child talked about behaviour from an adult that bothered her. She made me promise that I would not tell anyone this. I felt this as an acute burden and in this particular case a very difficult ethical dilemma.[3] I had to make a judgement that may have broken her confidence but might have been more important in terms of any possible impact upon her welfare. After taking some advice (of course anonymising the child), I negotiated with her that she would speak to someone else that she trusted who could help her.

In another very emotional moment at the end of my fieldwork, one child asked if she could have my home phone number, because 'Who am I going to talk to when you go?' This might have been expected with some of the children who were particularly involved in the research; however, in this case I had not, I had thought, developed a particularly close relationship with the child. Yet at this moment I worried that she had indeed seen me as someone who she could trust to talk to about things that she could not do with others in her social circle. I had always made clear to the children that there was a finite amount of time that I would be with them, and that although we were 'friendly' I was not their 'friend'.[4] Again I sought advice and decided that it would not be appropriate for me to give out my home number to her, and that the research-friendship relationship would be drawing to a close.

These very clearly problematic revelations were offset by the more everyday ways in which quite personal information was given. In many cases these were the simultaneous revelation of and reinforcement of materials that might at the very least be considered private if not exactly secret. Much of this was about family life. Monika Konrad (2005a, 2005b) is one of many social scientists to note that families are made through secrets as much as revelations. It was therefore no surprise to find that in asking about understandings of 'home' and 'belonging' children would offer up personal information that felt extremely private and intimate. Often I was told of one person's disapproval for another; of absent family members; of anti-social or eccentric behaviours; of illness. These were disclosures that were, to say the least, candid. I made a decision not to use such materials. By removing them I had corroborated to an extent what the doubters had suggested. The withholding suggested that I knew better how to manage the social positioning of the discussion/interviews/chats, and that I judged from an adult position that these were things best not disclosed. I theorised the ways in which children often spoke in different ways in different sites – playground, classroom, interview – as different kinds of 'speech genres' (Bakhtin 1986). I suggested that the children were freer speaking to me in certain kinds of environments than others, that this was sometimes wilful, and at others was a failure to understand the generic form of interaction. I occasionally felt that even if the children did not think things were secrets as such, they were best kept private and should not be disclosed to others. While still in the field, in the schools, I was often put under considerable pressure by teachers to reveal what children were saying, and ever fearful that it might be possible to connect specifics to individuals, I prevaricated for some time before reporting back in very generalised terms.

Family confidential

It was not unexpected that children would be unclear about what might be appropriate to tell me. What was more surprising was where, for example, parents or carers would expect a child to have disclosed information that they had in fact withheld. In such moments the ways in which secrets structure families were revealed in very immediate ways. For example, one mother expected her child to have revealed some significant and foundational aspects of her own childhood. He had not, and she was extremely surprised by this as it was something that they had discussed at length and in her mind was not a 'secret' to them and their family. In this case it might be interpreted as a decision made by a child to 'protect' his mother. This was not the only time a child did not disclose material as a form of 'protecting'. In a separate case I discovered that a child had totally avoided mentioning a death in the family. I found out about it in a discussion with her mother who confirmed that it was something not spoken about. If not a secret as such, it was a part of their lives that was not generally discussed with outsiders. By the time she told me she knew that her daughter trusted me, and so she revealed something her child had remained silent about. This case is one of the few in which a full discussion of the data would have seemed morally repugnant, despite its 'academic' worth. It was a very 'interesting' example of the ways in which family secrets are part of genealogies of belonging. In this case the impossibility of disclosure required some evasions on the part of the child, who managed to narrate a family story that informed her present understanding of herself as gendered and racialised without reference to this incident.

Seeing silence

These silences were echoed in the way in which children used the photographs to show 'home' and 'family'. In one instance, a child took a set of images that had no people in, no pets, no personal items – just a garden, a front door and a car (see Ali 2006 for a more in-depth discussion of this). I interpreted this as the child using a 'tactics of evasion' to maintain some agency in the research process. She showed things that she claimed were important to her; an upwardly mobile lifestyle represented in material things, specifically her home and car. I wondered if she simply did not want to portray her family members, and this was itself an issue of privacy and discretion – a form of withholding. Others might have suggested that the visual silence was a rather bleak portrait of a psychic emptiness for a child who was an outsider, a minority in 'racial' and ethnic terms within her school, and the subject of some rather unsavoury 'teasing'. Now I wonder if the silences were created by a research practice that despite my best intentions was, after all, intrusive. In this case, despite 'listening with my eyes' (Back 2006), I did not hear anything with any certainty about these images. I felt it would be inappropriate to 'push' to discover what 'lay behind' the silence as the child was quite shy and nervous. I was clear that I did not reach 'the truth' of the images. Working with children and their families meant that wherever possible I simply did not use material that had come to my attention in this more probing way. I did not re-present the material – at least, not directly. However, it might be argued that in taking part in discussions about absences/silences that is often seen as the bread and butter work on 'reflexivity' and (sometimes crude) psycho-social approaches to data analysis and representation, the confidences with which I was entrusted have indeed been broken.

Confidence tricks? Show and tell?

How then do we deal with secrets both maintained and revealed within data collection? Michael Taussig suggests that:

> So easily we join truth and secret; with rapture we skid between them, envelop the one in the other: truth = secret. Yet embedded within this ingrained poetry of daily habit there exists something not so obvious, a finely-tuned theatrical process, thanks to which, as Benjamin sees it, the revelation shall do justice to the secret.
>
> (Taussig 1999: 2)

This is an interesting notion and one that resonates with the issue of finally writing research for publics. Taussig goes on that the key issue is to make sure revelation stands up to its task. 'And this carefully contrived process of the just revelation, be it noted, stands in juxtaposition to exposure, which, Benjamin warns, would only destroy the secret (ibid.).' The writing up of research is the point at which the 'just revelation' becomes most difficult to manage.

Using visual materials during the research, I accumulated an extensive archive of photographs. Children took photographs of places, people and things that meant 'home' and 'family', and were so enthused that they often took to bringing in more intimate family snaps from family albums. I did not use any of these in subsequent publications as I felt that I could not possibly maintain confidentiality and produce images of these people and places. It was perhaps a methodological flaw that I should have considered, but at the outset I was, naively, under-estimating the numbers of children and families who would become involved and the levels of intimacy that would be revealed. It was an easy decision to reach to withhold the images and at least recognise privacy, if not secrets as such. The 'outputs' that have gone into the academic arena have been entirely shaped by the visual methodologies, but they have been an absence that shaped what was present. If they had been included would they reveal a greater truth? Would looking at the image of the empty garden help the viewer/reader understand the research as a whole better? I am not sure that it would. If I had engaged with these issues and asked for consent for the images to be used, I would have lost the anonymity of the whole project and if not all, many secrets would have been revealed. This did not seem to be a 'just revelation' but much more like 'exposure'.

Withholding most images might have been an 'easy' decision, but others were in a greyer zone. Some information that we are given might be anonymised and used in ways that do not reveal the secrets with which we have been entrusted. Yet in this moment we make choices that feel akin to a betrayal of the principles of confidentiality, and slide more into the realm of anonymity and the maintenance of privacy. Even with the clear decision not to reveal people or places that could be recognised, I did use a couple of the images of objects such as favourite pencils, rabbits and dolls in a small number of presentations. In these settings, with control over the images as material objects, I felt that anonymity was preserved. But again it cannot be refuted that some of materials that were given 'in confidence' were revealed. So while the content of the images was intensely intimate if not secret, it was often part of the range of material that had come under the remit of the 'confidential' nature of the research. I did not always negotiate these dilemmas well. For example, I did at first refer extremely obliquely to the example of the disclosure of a death in the family in a draft manuscript. I used it precisely to illustrate the way in which children chose to exercise their own discretion and to keep family secrets in making their own family narratives. Despite the fact that I thought this legitimate, and that it protected those involved, one of the readers for the manuscript thought it insensitive to refer to it at all. I removed it immediately. Now, another few years later, I mention a death. The discussion here has, I believe, been vague enough for it not to reveal what was secret about the whole story. Some of the images such as the 'problematic ones' which I had taken out have also been described and analysed in other places (as mentioned above). Now I return to these again. When giving consent based upon confidentiality did respondents think these disclosures would take place? Are they actually disclosures or so distorted as to be fictional vignettes based upon truth? Does their partial revelation provide a bigger, better truth? Has what I have revealed been the 'truth' at all? These questions are interesting at an epistemological level and crucial at the methodological and in practice.

Maintaining trust, building confidence

Working ethnographically with children over time meant that I inevitably built up research relationships. I became what I described above and elsewhere as a 'researcher-friend' to some. This is again a rather ambiguous position to occupy. I was never 'like them' or 'one of them' but neither was I teacher or a school official. It is the function of ethnography that it is in-depth and prolonged engagement with respondents. It is the way that we build up a picture of the area we are interested in understanding. Simply interviewing children would not have provided the rich data which ethnography did. Informal discussion, observation and so on give a different kind of information for analysis. The trust and confidence bestowed upon me was nothing short of remarkable and I am extremely grateful to all the participants. The production of anonymity and maintenance of privacy was crucial to the process, the gift of confidences accepted with respect and often returned from myself. Withholding some information is inevitable; disclosure of some is of course compulsory. How this is done is part of our research practice; we can only hope that certain kinds of revelation do indeed do justice to the 'secret'.

Secrets and silences are an integral part of research. We cannot evade them, and nor should we try to. The best we can do is engage with them with a clear research agenda and with the honesty and sensitivity to acknowledge when this must be superseded by ethical behaviour. This requires flexibility that cannot be found in rigid rules about ethics procedures, consent tick lists and so on. Although focusing upon what might be considered difficulties with these issues, it is important to note that in order to have confidence in research we need to consider how the role of confidence is also often a positive. It indicates some successes. Participants do often feel confident in research, confident that it is useful, interesting or worthwhile. They take part willingly for any number of reasons. In so doing they often develop confidence in researchers (especially in ethnography) and this can be productive and rewarding for both. Dealing with these complexities needs to be an integral part of our research practices, and cannot rest solely on an abstracted notion of ethics. Nor are they restricted to any one part of the research process. We need to train researchers to deal with these issues in grounded ways. There are often no hard and fast rules to apply, yet we need strong political and ethical guidelines to help when making decisions fast while in the field. It is the only way to feel positive about the silences and secrets that we need in order to produce socially responsible research.

Notes

1 A large amount has been written on 'consent' within research and especially in relation to children as a particular kind of 'vulnerable group'. Some of my key early resources were Maybin 1993; Mayall 1994, Alderson 1995, Mauthner 1997; Alldred 1998.

2 I am not suggesting covert methods should simply never be used, but that they need to be considered carefully.

3 There are of course legal matters that are pertinent here. I was bound to uphold the school's policies and legal imperatives on disclosure of, for example, sexual abuse.

4 For further discussion of these distinctions see, e.g., Hey 1997; Skeggs 1997; Hirsch 2005.

References

Alderson, P. (1995) *Listening to Children: Ethics and Social Research*, Ilford: Barnados.

Alldred, P. (1998) 'Ethnography and Discourse Analysis: Dilemmas in Representing the Voices of Children' in J. Ribbens and R. Edwards (eds) *Feminist Dilemmas in Qualitative Research: Public Knowledges and Private Lives*, London: Sage.

Ali, S. (2003) *Mixed-Race, Postrace: Gender, New Ethnicities and Cultural Practices*, London and New York: Berg.

—— (2006) 'Racialising Research: Managing Power and Politics?', *Ethnic and Racial Studies*, 29 (3): 471–86.

Back, L (2006) 'Listening with our Eyes: Portrait as Urban Encounter', in C. Knowles and P. Sweetman (eds) *Picturing the Social Landscape. Visual Methods and the Sociological Imagination*, London and New York: Routledge.

Bakhtin, M.M. (1986) *Speech Genres and Other Essays*, ed. C. Emerson and M. Holquist, trans. V.W. McGee, Austin, TX: University of Texas Press.

Bok, S. (1989) *Secrets: On the Ethics of Concealment and Revelation*, New York: Vantage Books.

Halse, C. and Honey, A. (2005) 'Unravelling Ethics: Illuminating the Moral Dilemmas of Research Ethics', in *Signs*, 30 (4): 2141–62.

Harding, S. and Norberg, K. (2005) 'New Feminist Approaches to Social Sciences Methodologies: An Introduction', *Signs*, 30 (4): 2009–15.

Hey, V. (1997) *The Company She Keeps: An Ethnography of Girls' Friendships*, Buckingham: Open University Press.

Hirsch, G.E. (2005) 'Friendship, Friendliness, and Feminist Fieldwork', *Signs: Journal of Women in Culture and Society*, 30 (4): 2163–72.

Konrad, M. (2005a) *Nameless Relations: Anonymity, Melanesia and Reproductive Gift Exchange between British Ova Donors and Recipients*, Oxford: Berghahn.

—— (2005b) *Narrating the New Predictive Genetics: Ethics, Ethnography and Science*, Cambridge: Cambridge University Press.

Mayall, B. (ed.) (1994) *Children's Childhoods: Observed and Experienced*, London: Falmer Press.

Maybin, J (1993) 'Children's Voices: Talk, Knowledge, Identity', in D. Graddol, J. Maybin, and B. Stierer (eds) *Researching Language and Literacy in Social Context*, Milton Keynes: Open University Press.

Mauthner, M. (1997) 'Methodological Aspects of Collecting Data from Children: Lessons from Three Research Projects', *Children and Society*, 11: 16–28.

Ramazanoğlu, C. and Holland, J. (2002) *Feminist Methodologies: Challenges and Choices*, London, New York and New Delhi: Sage.

Skeggs, B. (1997) *Formations of Class and Gender: Becoming Respectable*, London: Sage Publications.

Taussig, M. (1999) *Defacement: Public Secrecy and the Labor of the Negative,* Stanford, CA: Stanford University Press.

19 Shameful silences

Self-protective secrets and theoretical omissions

Bruna Seu

The topic of silence is key in this chapter in two ways. The first is about content – women's shame experiences – as silence is precisely what makes shameful experiences so powerful and never ending. Because the telling of the experience exposes the subject to yet more shame, silence might be used as a defence, thus inadvertedly confirming and perpetuating the negative self-attribution. Second, silence is inevitably involved in my reading of the women's accounts as the researcher. This is the silence that breeds in the gaps between theoretically and methodologically 'possible' readings.

The two types of silence feed into each other in a potentially never-ending loop. Part of what makes it difficult to explore is shame's intrinsic silent nature: whilst guilt compels to confess, so that she, who feels guilty, may ask for forgiveness, shame makes people withdraw into self-protective silence. The shameful woman, desperately longing for acceptance, fears that the listener will confirm what she expects: that the shameful experience is a reflection of her failing, inadequate self. Silence might therefore be safer.

Breaking the silence in a reparative way, then, is particularly crucial. Good therapists and friends do this all the time: the benign mirroring back of positive recognition comforts and heals. On similar lines, and wanting to contribute to the emancipatory project of bringing women's voice in from the margin, I attempted a psychoanalytic discursive feminist reading of women's experiences of shame.

I had been struck over the years, by how large shame figured in my, my female friends' and patients' experience. Shame appeared to be an invisible force that held women back and silently tortured them. My motivation for the research project came from the desire to grapple with this force and unpack women's experiences and so I set out to ask 20 women about their experiences of shame. Being a psychoanalytic psychotherapist and a feminist, I began from what I knew to try to understand what was so difficult and painful about shame. It was in the complexity of such a project that I began to hear the silences: how, by using exclusively a psychoanalytic reading, women would be cornered into essentialist inadequacies and pathologising attributions; how, however, to do away with the recognition of the role played by unconscious dynamics and history, women's actions and narratives might appear as one-dimensional rhetorical games without a sense of why they would want to maintain such an identity for themselves. To a certain extent feminist readings of shame have also tended to flatten women's experiences by victimising them. Bartky, for example, and other feminist writers have looked for the roots of women's uncertain sense of self-worth in processes of socialisation in patriarchal societies. Unfortunately, such explanations have often heavily relied on individual/society, oppressor/oppressed dichotomies which hinder the recognition of women's collusion in the process of oppression in terms of self-surveillance and taking on a devalued subject position, thus neglecting more subjective, personally historical and unconscious reasons.

This chapter attempts to grapple with the possible and impossible readings that current theoretical approaches provide. My claim is that, despite the epistemological and methodological contradictions, it is imperative, politically and in terms of scholarship, that we bring all these readings together to enable the full richness of women's experiences to be heard. Only through a feminist psycho-social reading might we be able to avoid silencing some crucial aspects of women's accounts.

I will argue for the necessity to theorise women's shame as over-determined in three ways: first, in the way suggested by Bartky's (1990) feminist interpretation of shame as women's existential experience of 'being in the world' in a male-dominated society. This position allows for a reconceptualisation of women's shame not as private feeling or shortcoming, but as a political statement of their oppression. The second way looks at the ambiguity and struggle involved in 'being subjects of power': i.e. being determined by pre-existing conditions but also able to strategically use the shameful subjectivity. This does not ignore the material conditions of power, but returns agency to women by removing them from a position of passive victims.

The third way in which I conceptualise a shameful subjectivity as over-determined is in being arbitrary but not accidental. The discursive approach, although focusing on agency, leaves unanswered the question of why one subjectivity is privileged over another, when a choice is available. Without an insight into the role played by women's internal world in the perpetuation of their own oppression and their collusion with it, we are in danger of attributing a one-dimensional and mechanistic quality to women's subjectivities. History and biography are essential to understanding subjectivity. History is the context within which the subject is constructed and conversely, where the subject constructs a historical version of events. By bringing together Foucauldian ideas of self-surveillance and positioning in discourse, with a psychodynamic theorisation of shame as resulting from a constant negotiation between external forces and internal agencies, this chapter argues for an understanding of women's shame as discursively, politically and psycho-dynamically over-determined. Consequently, it also argues for the necessity of a multiplicity of readings to make adequate sense of such over-determination.

A proper engagement with the epistemological, theoretical and methodological intricacies of this debate is beyond the scope of this essay.[1] Instead, I will ground the thinking in the data by exploring the usefulness of using both methodologies and by highlighting what is missed when only one of them is employed.

I will start by framing the topic in terms of what has been argued about shame from a psychoanalytic and feminist angle. I will then explain my theoretical approaches in some more detail, before looking at two long extracts from two different women: Rita and Mae.[2] I will conclude by discussing some of the pitfalls, challenges and dilemmas for feminist research.

Theoretical resources: psychoanalytic, discursive and feminist readings of shame

Shame is an acutely 'painful experience about the self, in which the subject feels they 'could die' or 'crawl through a hole' (Lewis 1987). One of the functions of shame is to act as a boundary between the private and public aspects of oneself (Pines 1987). Shame, as the guardian of boundaries, protects the separate, private self and prevents intrusion. Shame guarantees the self's integrity. Therefore, shame anxiety is experienced when one's dominion over one's 'innermost self' is threatened or temporarily shattered (Wumser 1981). More specifically, shame is the experience of being exposed in a situation where the self is seen as a lesser, inadequate self.

The construction and the loss of the public self, or 'loss of face', has been linked to the root of the word shame which comes from the Old High German root, *scama*, 'to cover oneself'. *Sceme* is 'cover, mask'. As implied in the root of the word, shame experiences embody a sense of deep exposure (Lynd 1958), of bodily or psychological nakedness (Yorke 1990). Therefore, the 'purpose' of shame has been repeatedly connected to hiding and disappearing in order to isolate the person from the danger of exposure (Wumser 1981; Lewis 1992). Biblically, this is graphically expressed by Adam's fall and the attempt to hide, which represented the exposure before God (Lewis 1992), and observations of the phenomenological expression of shame (head bowed, avoidance of gaze, shrinking of the body) support the idea that shame engenders a wish for concealment and avoidance. In shame one wants to change oneself into another being or to hide – not to be seen any more. The mask (or façade), changes the shameful one who fears to be seen, into one who is seen and is strong. Shame is the wrath over one's imperfection and limitation (Hegel in Wumser 1981: 306). Thus, shame is intrinsically linked with secrecy and silence.

Part of my feminist take in this chapter is to remove shame as an experience from an intrapsychic, personal explanation which sees it as a reflection of women's true identity and flaws. Instead, I reconnect these experiences to broader social issues and women's experiences in a patriarchal society. Methodologically, this is achieved through Foucauldian discourse analysis

(Parker 1992, 1994) and discursive psychology (Potter and Wetherell 1987; Edwards and Potter 1992). The discursive analyses explore whether the extracts offer the possibility of alternative subject positions which women could take. Hence, the accounts are explored in a way that take in some of the broader social issues to which they allude (Burman and Parker 1993), as well as what function the accounts serve; in particular, what version of events that account is designed to counteract (Potter and Wetherell 1987). A Foucauldian analysis seemed the most appropriate tool to read women's accounts of shame as the taking on of an identity that is diminished and under constant (self-) surveillance, as a subject position made available by hegemonic and pervasive 'articulation' of gender discourses (Laclau and Mouffe 1985; Edley and Wetherell 1995; Frosh et al. 2003).

In short, the Foucauldian approach to discourse is used to examine constructions of subjectivity, selfhood and power relations, whilst discursive psychology focuses on how the participants use language and discursive resources during the interview process (Willig 2002). The employment of these two types of discourse analysis allows the capturing of the complex power negotiations and strategic uses of positioning. Judith Butler has provided a sophisticated theorisation of this complexity 'painful, dynamic, and promising, this vacillation between the already-there and the yet-to-come is a crossroads that rejoins every step by which it is traversed, a reiterated ambivalence at the heart of agency' (Butler 1997: 18). Despite its high potential in the unravelling of this 'vacillation', discourse analysis arguably falls short at two levels. One, it does not sufficiently theorise emotions; hence the 'painful' quality of the vacillation cannot quite be captured by an analysis of text. Second, the 'already-there' is never explored in the 'personal' dimension of the biographical history of the subject. Psychoanalysis fills that gap. First, it is an invaluable tool in the understanding of the emotional dimension of women's shame, both as a contributor to the script and because of a rich theorising of the affective side of power. Second, it fleshes out agency with history thus adding complexity to functions of shameful subjectivity. As Frosh et al. (2003: 41) point out, psychoanalysis restores agency or 'authorship' to the subject which 'enables us to ask questions about why and how specific formations of subjecthood come about; that is, what purpose they serve, what anxieties are actively defended against, what aspirations fulfilled'

It is crucial to point out, at this point, that what follows is not intended as an analysis of the participants, but the application of psychodynamics to the narrative (Roseneil 2006). This is done reflexively and tentatively. I will return to the ethical dangers of applying the analytic tool of interpretation outside of the safe boundaries of a consulting room.

For the purpose of this chapter, I will ignore the epistemological contradictions and pitfalls involved in attempting to bring together these different theoretical approaches (see Seu 2006 for a fuller discussion), and concentrate on the strategic function of this 'bringing together' in providing a more nuanced and complex account of shame that draws on both psychoanalytic understandings and discursive work. This is a breaking of silence in itself as, without this move, some crucial aspects of women's experience would be silenced. My intention, therefore, is to illustrate, rather than foster, the silences and to show what the price of prioritising one reading over another is. I will do that by using two extracts from two different women, Rita and Mae. I had asked them to define shame and to tell me of an instance that came to their mind when they had felt shame. Their stories are very different: Rita talks of shame in terms of her reaction to being flashed at on a train, while Mae focuses more on her ongoing sense of inadequacy. Within an overall feminist framework, I examine what discursive and psychoanalytic readings could allow and prevent these women from saying.

Rita's story

I will start with Rita. The challenge here is how to use psychoanalytic concepts and yet resist their ontological and epistemological implications. Theoretical frameworks determine what can be thought. It determines the limits within which a phenomenon can be read and understood. It provides the range of possible meanings. Theories produce and carry world-views and so do concepts created within that theoretical framework. This restricts the use of those concepts to the ideological boundaries allowed by the world-view underpinning the theory. As psychoanalytic concepts only make sense within a specific formulation of how the human mind works, one needs to be aware of the whole meta-psychology embedded and filtered through every concept, even when their relation with patriarchy seems very remote. The challenge, therefore, consists in being able to think within and outside a theory at the same time. The question, then, is how to not throw the psychodynamically insightful baby out with the patriarchal water.

RITA: One day I felt so ashamed, I was in the tube, about 2 years ago. I am short-sighted and I wasn't wearing my contact lenses. In that compartment there were only 2 women, no men, when we got to [the station] a man came into the compartment and he came to where I was sitting, opposite to the other lady and I had the strong feeling that he wasn't wearing any trousers and he flashed, now because I wasn't wearing glasses or contact lenses I wasn't sure that that was real, but the girl, I could tell, I was just thinking, you know, it looks like this man is flashing, he was actually flashing, now because I didn't realise immediately I didn't take my gaze away from him as quickly as I should have done, but when I realised, oh my God!, and he must have realised that I was looking at him, but I just couldn't tell (.) when I realised I just got off and walked off, very very embarrassing, I couldn't tell anybody, I was petrified even to go to the police.

BRUNA: Why do you think you were embarrassed?

RITA: I think because it took so long to realise that he was actually flashing, I should have just ignored the whole thing, but I wasn't aware (.) the embarrassment, I was so ashamed I didn't even report it, because where do you start, you have to describe the person (.) I definitely felt ashamed.

BRUNA: What do you think would have happened?

RITA: Well I would have had to describe the person which means that you spent so long looking at them and the implication of describing a person who was flashing is that you had a confrontation, although it was just eyes, it meant that I stared at the person.

BRUNA: Are you saying that you felt ashamed because you were actually looking at him?

RITA: Yes (laugh), if I had spoken to the other girl, but we both got off and just scurried away not knowing what to do […] and if I had been wearing my glasses it would have been worse, because all the time I was wondering 'is this real?'

BRUNA: Do you know why it would have felt worse wearing glasses?

RITA: You know when someone does something to me I try to assess if they are mad or not (.) at that time of night, being a woman and travelling at that time of night (9 pm) you worry that you'll get attacked (.) you have so many thing going on in your mind, gosh I have escaped it could have been worse, and then the anger, and then you start worrying maybe I'm travelling late and I shouldn't, so many things going on in your mind (.)

BRUNA: So did you feel you had done something you shouldn't have done?

RITA: My boyfriend said: 'you shouldn't travel late, because you put yourself in this position', so he made me feel guilty that I was travelling late, contributing to things like that.

BRUNA: As if it was your fault (.)

RITA: Yea and then you think, God why can't I travel when I want! […] they happened together, one after the other, I felt ashamed because I didn't even report it and then I felt guilty because I was travelling late and everything happens at once after that and you start wondering 'is it me?'

How might a psychoanalytic reading illustrate what Rita is experiencing here?

Freud argued that a special connection existed between femininity and shame. In fact, he claimed that shame was the '*feminine feeling par excellence*' (Freud 1933: 132), having as its main purpose the concealment of genital deficiency. The role of the penis and the infamous penis envy are, according to Freud, crucial in the formation of femininity and are responsible, amongst other things, for women's vanity in a vain attempt to compensate for their sexual inferiority.

It is also important to bear in mind that, because of the attention paid to unconscious dynamics, a psychodynamic approach would distinguish between a reason and a cause. Something happens, often an external event, which triggers the feeling (the reason), but that event is made traumatic because it sets off unconscious, intra-psychic reactions (the cause).[3] In the context of this extract, the inter-psychic *reason* is the exhibitionistic act. To explain the *cause* for the intra-psychic emotional state it produced, two readings are possible: one is a classical Freudian reading whereby shame is the reaction-formation to Rita's voyeuristic impulses. In other words, Rita's voyeuristic impulses pressed for satisfaction (and partly succeeded), but this was followed by shame functioning as a repressing force, transforming the forbidden pleasure into its opposite: an unpleasant feeling of shame. This reading is supported by the concurrent experience of guilt for the fleeting satisfaction of her impulses. Confirming this, Rita does say that going to the police would have involved confessing that she had looked at the man's genitals for too long.

Another available psychoanalytic reading connects shame to the ideal-self formulation. There is widespread agreement in the literature that low self-esteem derives from a discordance between wishful self-images and a self that appears to be failing, defective, inferior (Lewis 1971; Sandler 1986; Pines 1987; Silberstein et al. 1987) These conflicts are apt to evoke feelings of inferiority and shame (Wumser 1981; Sandler 1986).

There are many aspects of the ideal self that Rita felt she failed to meet. In moral terms she failed to immediately turn away. In terms of personality she also failed, by being deeply affected and confused instead of being sufficiently in control to ignore the man. Finally, she also felt she failed in not having gone to the police.

This is what the theory allows us to see. I am not suggesting we should disregard these possible readings. Instead I want to explore what it is that it does *not* allow us to see and what the possible material implications of that are. I want to argue that, far from being just a personal intrapsychic conflict (as the two psychoanalytic readings would construct), the shame Rita is describing is being negotiated at many different levels within socially constructed parameters. In order to do that, I will approach Rita's narrative not as reflective of a hidden internal truth but as text. I will deconstruct the text on the basis that language is not a transparent medium, but a form of social action because it *constructs* rather than merely describes the self, people's experience, social and psychological phenomena (Wetherell and Potter 1992; Potter 1996). The immediate implication of this move is that Rita ceases to be simply an agglomerate of impulses, conflicts and intra-psychic dynamics and becomes a social agent acting within and affected by specific historical circumstances.

When looking at Rita's story it is interesting to notice that the area the shame relates to (sexual exhibitionism) transpires only later, as initially Rita is too preoccupied with justifying herself. Rita thus first focuses on herself, making a point of positioning herself as incapacitated. I read this as a rhetorical move, a disclaimer (Wetherell and Potter 1992). By positioning herself as disabled and relatively helpless Rita is warranting her position of blameless victim, thus counteracting possible accusations or attributions that might come later. The fact that this involves Rita (the victim) tells us that her position of victim has to be strengthened and warranted from the beginning.

The invitation to trust her innocence is clearly made through the statement that she wasn't sure if it was real, where she uses her short-sightedness as her strongest defence point. Why does she need to do this? Why all this priming of the listener?

If we take a step back it might be helpful to remind ourselves that a cornerstone of any psychoanalytic investigation is to make the unconscious conscious. Freud (1933), for example, reconstructed the meaning of human motivation by arguing that people are not guided by rational and conscious thought processes, as the Enlightenment claimed, but mainly driven by unconscious mechanisms. One of the basic implications of this epistemological shift is that the reason people give off why they are doing something is not necessarily the 'true' reason. So, does the 'lady protest too much', then? Rita says that because she couldn't see properly, she looked for longer than she should have done. Around this she constructs one of the shameful/embarrassed positions (the other being that of humiliation), about having looked at the flasher's genitals for too long. This is where the opening of the story makes sense, because it implies that Rita only looked at his genitals because she could not see properly and she could not tell what she was looking at. Rita claims that it was an accident, but for a classical Freudian she 'really' wanted to look. The question is, is it simply that she is somehow aware of her unconscious desires or that she has internalised the lesson that in our society assaulted women are automatically under accusation?

It seems that Rita expected this to happen, as she is very keen to prevent the intimation that she might have done anything to encourage or bring the event on herself. Consistent with this, she is the one who leaves the train, resorting to withdrawal and silence as defence. She explains the silence as a way of protecting herself from having to admit that she had looked at the man, further positioning herself as the shameful and the guilty one, as she explains in more detail later. By taking this position, Rita turns the situation into a personal problem, hiding the reality that she would have found herself being interrogated, not taken seriously and perhaps even humiliated by the police. Although her constant doubt about what was happening further weakens her position, her refusal to go to the police might have been a realistic appreciation of the situation and represent her resistance to being further humiliated by a system which wouldn't give her a genuine chance to have a voice (Marks 1993). Thus she chooses silence.

In my mind it is crucial in this story that from the beginning the speaker's concern is around attribution of blame, particularly because the extract offers other alternatives to being shameful and a victim. For example, there is the position of anger for having being assaulted and for not having the freedom of travelling when she wants to because she is a woman. However, the anger is gravely undermined by the self-blame and Rita settles for positioning herself as shameful from the beginning.

It is this self-blame that I am most interested in. There is nothing wrong per se in interpreting unconscious motives and perhaps, as many argue, this is precisely what psychoanalytic practice offers. So it might have been 'right' and perfectly justifiable and in fact perhaps productive, if Rita were in therapy, to interpret her conflicts and repressed voyeuristic wish. The point is that that interpretation would also reinforce current social practices of expecting women to prove their innocence when attacked. If, as a researcher, I were to do that, I would be saying, in effect, that Rita was secretly pleased to have been confronted by the exhibitionist, perhaps even, as her boyfriend clearly implied, that she was 'asking for it'.

At this point I seem to have argued myself into the feminist vs. psychoanalytic corner, with the psychoanalytic losing out. It is hard, in other words, to see what a feminist project would have to gain from a psychodynamic reading. What it has to offer is an insight into the internalisation of the power dynamics that are played out between Rita and her boyfriend. We have an actual silencing here, thus this story is not just about shame but about *who* does the silencing. Rita gave her boyfriend the power to validate her reality (whether primarily because he is a man or a partner is unclear), but he instead chose to blame and Rita, to a large extent, agrees and is silenced. We can here see the small, cumulative steps of oppression, patriarchal power as expressed in its banality through the small, everyday incidents by which women's position is reiterated and reinforced. It still does not explain, however, why Rita voluntarily submits herself to this or does not resist the attribution of blame. Psychoanalysis offers a compelling and sophisticated explanation of how such self-surveillance comes about as the product of internalization of external oppression. It is hardly surprising that, historically, feminists turned to psychoanalysis when increased consciousness of women's oppression proved to be a poor match for the ostensibly voluntary repetition by women of their own oppression (e.g. Mitchell 1974; Chodorow 1978; Benjamin 1990; Orbach 1993 just to mention a few). Feminist therapists came to realise that the most powerful and elusive enemy was the 'enemy within' and that in order to understand and prevent the 'persistent stumbling blocks to emotional change' they had to give more attention to unconscious processes (Eichenbaum and Orbach 1983: 13). There is a wealth of clinical accounts illustrating the therapeutic approach to these processes, but very little in-depth analysis of data that explores the manifestation of this dynamic that takes into account the interplay of internal and external oppression.

The next section offers another illustration of the necessity of employing both discursive and psychoanalytic readings to capture more fully the complexity of women's experiences of shame. The participant, Mae, is talking about shame in terms of a sense of inadequacy; another of the 'shame umbrella of feelings' (Lewis 1987), and of hiding behind a façade (Wumser 1981)

Mae's stories

What preceded the extract was Mae's detailed description of how she tunes into what people expect from her in different circumstances, in order to 'gain acceptance'.

MAE: Oh, yes, inadequacy is a very very clear strain in my life and I have always felt inadequate and it is amazing how powerful that feeling inadequate is, physically wrecked me, the sense of inadequacy has actually left me with a chronic disease, […] At the end of my degree, honours degree, I was incredibly ill because of feelings of inadequacy, hospitalised and managed to get all the work done, to sit the exams and at graduation which happened four months later, I discovered that I had been awarded the government award as outstanding student, and I was shocked because again academic success is irrelevant because I am not a perfect human being you see (laughs) and now five years later I still don't believe it, don't really believe that they gave me the award because I was a good student, but because I survived a bad illness

BRUNA: Actually it sounds very powerful.

MAE: Yes, amazingly powerful, a real theme in my life.

BRUNA: Do you feel it stops you from doing things?

MAE: Uhm, it really does. I have been told that I have a good singing voice and I have been told that I am a very good pianist, by adolescence or earlier than that, feelings of inadequacy actually led me to stop all that, actually stop playing the piano completely, which appalled people who knew what I was like before I stopped, it is only recently that I have actually found the courage to do chorus singing and even in that situation when I go to rehearsals and I am in the midst of whole people singing I feel inadequate and yet everybody on the outside says, 'No, you are OK, you have a very good voice, what is the matter?'

BRUNA: This is very interesting, the analogy is so graphic, it feels like you are terrified of being singled out, in the chorus you can hide.

MAE: Yes, I can hide, the thing is that as a young child I was singled out by, it is such a long story, my mother is a frustrated concert pianist, that encapsulates the story and she had four children, I am the eldest and she allocated an instrument to each child, I came first so I got the piano and I showed a talent, my mother's extraordinary persistency and support, but I also showed talent in other activities at school, the nature of the school is such that if someone shows a talent it makes other people feel inadequate, if you are showing (.) shining there is an attempt to block the light, not to encourage to shine and yes, from a very young age I felt singled out and it got more and more complex as I grew older and now I don't want to – that's rubbish (with anger) – of course I would like to be singled out, of course I would like to achieve, of course I would like to be wonderful, but I don't allow it.

BRUNA: Why?

MAE: Because it puts me on the outside, it makes me different from the rest, and yet there is conflict between wanting to be different and yet it is scary out there, it's too scary being different, it is easier to be just one of the crowd, boring as hell, but easier.

BRUNA: Because it's scary?

MAE: Yea, it is scary being on the outside saying, 'I am talented, I can do this, I am good at this', it is scary because you have your own expectations to fulfil, you have other people's expectations to fulfil and it puts you outside, you are not run of the mill.

Lewis's (1971) exploration of women's higher field-dependency and proneness to shame might be relevant here, as is the rich feminist literature about women playing a series of roles and adapting themselves to others' needs (Gilligan 1982; Orbach 1993). Walkerdine (1990) has also looked at this phenomenon and has argued that women role-playing is a cover on top of a repressed, true self that has been inhibited by layers of social conditioning. She talks of some of her students who found it hard to identify with their success and experienced the 'outstanding student' as existing 'outside [their] body […] instead [they] feel [they] [are] hopeless, consistently panic about [their] performance and appear to have little confidence in [themselves]' (Walkerdine 1990)

Although I have reached similar conclusions to Walkerdine's, many of the feminist explanations seem dissatisfying as they do not allow space for the possibility of a different story, nor do they explore the agentic and strategic uses of positioning. What is obscured is that success might *actively* be rejected as it might provoke rejection, on the one hand, because it would mean transgression of what is the expected passive position for women, and on the other, because it might invite envious attack. Arguably, then, the employment of a façade is a helpful disguise which attributes the rejection to what is experienced by women as their intrinsic unlovability.

The first clue that there might be an investment in clinging to the shameful position is the existence of more than one position available to Mae. The first subject position in the account is that of the inadequate student. This is consistent with the previous narrative and is strengthened by the anecdote introduced later on. The feelings of inadequacy were such as to 'cause' Mae to be hospitalised. The self here is constructed as inadequate, fragile, ill. The comment at the end about the award being given to the survivor of the illness refer to the self she implies is the one worth recognition; the only one she obviously feels is 'her'. The other self, the outstanding student, she constructs as a lie and as such, she disowns. This is, more or less, as far as most feminist readings would take the situation.

When looking at it discursively, however, the narrative acquires extra complexity. To begin with, the inadequate student is positioned as *other* to the survivor (although she arguably attempts to polarize the situation between the two – something which will be discussed shortly). It is important to recognise the existence of this self which fights and wins because, although Mae disowns the outstanding student as a lie, a façade and not her true self, the '*survivor* as her true self' is available for her to identify with. In fact, the account states her belief that this is the self that, deservedly, got the award.

In this light, then, we can make sense of the contradiction introduced soon after when, although distancing herself from the outstanding student, she also says: 'at the end of *my* degree, honours degree', thus taking the degree as her own and implying pride in the fact that it was an honours degree. This is further substantiated in the next line where she says that *despite* [this is my reading; Mae says 'and'] the illness she managed to get all the work done and sit the exams. I say 'despite' because it is obvious that the 'I' who sat the exam was in conflict with something else. Mae's oppression, expressed through an internalised sense of inadequacy and inferiority, militates against her success. Her familiar shameful position is hard to dislodge and a conflict is created by the possibility of an alternative position of success. Mae's 'dismissive voice', then, would represent her active refusal to identify with her success. This is achieved by emptying it of value.

Therefore, what is repeatedly stressed in this extract is that, despite the existence of alternative, more positive and successful representations of herself, there is almost a determination not to take that position. This is warranted by construing what is seen on the outside, the successful, positive representation, as a façade and a lie. This could also be read as a manoeuvre to avoid conflict and gain acceptance, but brings it back to a space where different actions within the text are possible, rather than resorting to external influences and women's passivity. Nevertheless, even though this is liberatory in contrast with a mechanistic understanding of women's oppression, it still does not tell us much of why, when available, Mae prefers the losing, shameful position.

This is a crucial consideration in the light of something else – another fragment of self? – being slipped in when Mae says: 'academic success is irrelevant because I am not a perfect human being you see (laughs)'. Even though she attempts to undermine the importance of this statement with laughter, through this utterance another possibility appears. Mae seems to be suggesting that the conflict resides elsewhere, not in the belief that she should have less success, but *more*. This is, however, not pursued and dismissed through laughter, whilst the victim line is pursued till the end. How can we make sense of this important contradiction? How can we begin to understand Mae's struggle and ostensibly self-inflicted oppression?

Unfortunately, a discursive reading cannot answer these questions. It has been pointed out that the abandonment of a modernist understanding of the self would also imply that all attempts at understanding history are fraudulent – both the collective history of a people and its culture and the private history of each individual self (Frosh 1991: 29). And yet, if we do disregard history, can we really make sense of choice?

The last section of the extract throws some light on crucial aspects of Mae's personal history, which might account for some of her painful choices.

Mae begins line 30 by, again, positioning herself as inadequate and claims that it is this feeling of being inadequate that stops her from performing. She tells us that recently she has found the courage to perform again, but only when she can hide or disappear in the chorus. What emerges after this representation and in contradiction with it, is that she is a gifted pianist in comparison to her mother who is a 'frustrated' pianist. In her account, she first praises her mother for her support, but then adds that the result of this, her 'shining', made other people feel inadequate and therefore the light was blocked.

A possible interpretation of this extract is that it contains an oblique reference to the ambivalent feelings of Mae's mother to her daughter's success. Perhaps by 'shining', Mae feared she might be making her own mother feel inadequate. At an unconscious level, Mae might have feared provoking an envious attack from her mother, or internally from her maternal introject. That not withstanding, Mae might have felt uncomfortable and guilty for having had opportunities which were closed to her own mother. Where was the boundary between her mother realising her own aspirations through her daughter and resenting her for that? The line 'if someone shows a talent it makes other people feel inadequate' is particularly poignant and charged for Mae. In respect of this chapter, these personal conflicts and dilemmas are considered many times amplified in the wider context of conflicts evoked by success for women. Hence, the rejection due to 'shining' too much, to being too good, would be reinforced and over-determined many times over.

It is not surprising, then, that in total opposition to the initial representation, the possibility of achievement is presented as desirable and that it is Mae herself who does not allow it. The position of being singled out for her success is presented as highly desirable and wonderful but at the same time as 'too scary', because it would make her different. What is scaring her then, as is stated clearly at the end, is the possibility of owning the successful performance, the 'façade' as the true self, talented and capable.

Discussion

In this chapter I have tried to break the theoretical and experiential silence around women's experiences of shame, by illustrating the benefits offered by multiple theoretical readings. I will now briefly summarise what are, within the agenda of a feminist research project, the risks and potential silences involved in using only theoretical resources, and the benefits of opening to multiple ones, to capture the complexity of the experience and to offset the limitations of each theoretical approach used on its own.

What we gain with a discursive reading is the returning of agency to women and the overcoming of the dichotomy victim/oppressor that comes with some feminist literature. On the other hand, a discursive approach might construct women as disembodied, impersonal accumulations of positioning.

What we gain from a psychodynamic reading is a more complex picture of internal and external oppression and the dynamic fluidity between them. But this also brings the dangers of essentialist/patriarchal trappings of some psychoanalytic theorising as well as the potential risk of 'psychologising' (Wetherell 2005) and pathologising the participants.

There are also the ethical dilemmas and risks involved in 'wild analysis' when specific psychoanalytic tools (e.g. interpretation, transference, countertransference) are used outside the safe boundaries of mutually agreed professional contracts and specific, technically sophisticated, therapeutic settings. This is accompanied by the uncomfortable feeling that there is something exploitative, inappropriate and abusive in claiming a privileged access to participants' unconscious, in itself, and without the participants' consent. I therefore feel compelled to reiterate that I am in no way claiming such access, but that my strategic and self-conscious hinting at unconscious processes is used to highlight the need for a method that would capture the dynamics of power beyond positioning in discourse. Beyond the above disclaimers, then, what is crucially gained, through a psycho-social analysis is a glimpse into the disempowering effects of internalisation and how discursively, politically and psychodynamically over-determined shame (albeit resisted and reconstructed by these women) can lead to learnt helplessness.

Notes

1 See Hollway 2005; Spears 2005; Wetherell 2005 for a recent debate on these issues.
2 The names of participants have been changed to preserve anonymity.
3 The shift from trauma caused by an external event to trauma due to internal conflict was one of the crucial factors in Freud's controversial abandonment of the 'seduction theory' and the shift from the 'Affect-Trauma' to the 'Topographical' model of the mind.

References

Bartky, S.L. (1990) 'Shame and gender', in *Femininity and Domination*, London: Routledge.

Burman, E. and Parker, I. (1993) (eds) *Discourse Analytic Research: Repertoires and Readings of Text in Action*, London: Routledge.

Benjamin, J. (1990) *The Bonds of Love. Psychoanalysis, Feminism, and the Problem of Domination*, London: Virago.

Butler (1997) *The Subject Life of Power. Theories of Subjection*, Stanford, CA: Stanford University Press.

Chodorow, N. (1978) *The Reproduction of Mothering*, London: University of California Press.

Edley, N and Wetherell, M. (1995) *Men in Perspective: Practice, Power and Identity*, London: Prentice Hall/Harvester Wheatsheaf.

Edwards, D. and Potter, J. (1992) *Discursive Psychology*, London: Sage.

Eichenbaum, L and Orbach, S. (1983) *Understanding Women*, London: Penguin.

Freud S. (1933) 'Femininity', in *New Introductory Lectures on Psychoanalysis*, London: The Hogarth Press: 139–68.

Frosh, S. (1991) *Identity Crisis: Modernity, Psychoanalysis and the Self*, London: Macmillan.

Frosh, S., Phoenix, A. and Pattman, R. (2003) 'Taking a stand: using psychoanalysis to explore the positioning of subjects in discourse', *British Journal of Social Psychology*, 42: 39–53.

Gilligan, C. (1982) *In a Different Voice*, London: Harvard University Press.

Hollway, W. and Jefferson, T. (2005) 'Panic and perjury: a psycho-social exploration of agency', *British Journal of Social Psychology*, 44 (2): 147–63; and reply to two commentaries on the above in the same issue: Hollway and Jefferson, 'But why did Vince get sick? A Reply to Spears and Wetherell', 175–80.

Hollway, W. Spears, R. and Edwards, D. (2005) 'Psychoanalysis', part of 'Three Views on hate', *The Psychologist*, 18 (9): 844–46.

Laclau, E. and Mouffe, C (1985) *Hegemony and the Socialist Strategy*, London: Verso.

Lewis, H.B. (1971) *Shame and Guilt in Neurosis*, New York: International Universities Press, Inc.

—— (ed.) (1987) *The Role of Shame in Symptom Formation*, Hillsdale, NJ and London: Lawrence Erlbaum Associates Publishers.

Lewis, M. (1992) *Shame, the Exposed Self*, Hillsdale, NJ and London: Lawrence Erlbaum Associates Publishers.

Lynd, H.M. (1958) *On Shame and the Search for Identity*, New York: Harcourt, Brace.

Mitchell, J. (1974) *Psychoanalysis and Feminism*, London: Pelican Books.

Orbach, S. (1993) *Hunger Strike. The Classic Account of the Social and Cultural Phenomena Underlying Anorexia Nervosa, Bulimia and Other Eating Problems*, London: Penguin.

Parker, I. (1992) *Discourse Dynamics; Critical Analysis for Social and Individual Psychology*, London: Routledge.

—— (1994) 'Reflexive social psychology: discourse analysis and psychoanalysis', *Free Associations*, 4 (32): 526–48.

Pines, M. (1987) 'Shame – What psychoanalysis does and does not say', *Group Analysis*, 20: 16–31

Potter, J. (1996) 'Discourse analysis and constructionist approaches: theoretical Background', in J.E. Richardson (ed.) *Handbook of Qualitative Research Methods for Psychology and the Social Sciences*, Leicester: British Psychological Society.

Potter, J. and Wetherell, M. (1987) *Discourse and Social Psychology: Beyond Attitudes and Behaviour*, London: Sage.

Roseneil, S. (2006) 'The ambivalences of Angel's "arrangement": a psychosocial lens on the contemporary condition of personal life', *The Sociological Review*, 54 (4): 846–68.

Sandler, B.R. (1986) 'The campus climate revisited: chilly for women faculty, administrators, and graduate students', Project on the Status and Education of Women, Association of American Colleges, Washington, DC.

Seu, I.B. (2006) 'Shameful selves: women's feelings of inadequacy and constructed façades, *European Journal of Psychotherapy and Counselling*, 8(3): 285–303.

Silberstein, L.R., Striegel-Moore, R. and Rodlin, J. (1987) 'Feeling fat: a woman's shame', in H.B. Lewis (ed.) *The Role of Shame in Symptom Formation*, Hillsdale, NJ and London: Lawrence Erlbaum Associates Publishers.

Spears, R. (2005) 'Where did Vincent's van go? A commentary on Holloway and Jefferson'. *British Journal of Social Psychology*, 44, 165–168.
Walkerdine, V. (1990) *School Girl Fictions.* London:Verso.
Wetherell, M. (2005) 'Interpretative repertoires', in V. Jupp (ed.) *The Sage Dictionary of Social Research*, London: Sage.
Wetherell, M. and Potter, J. (1992) *Mapping the Language of Racism: Discourse and the Legitimation of Exploitation*, Hemel Hempstead: Harvester Wheatsheaf.
Willig, C. (2002) *Introduction to Qualitative Research*, London: Sage & Open University.
Yorke, C. (1990) 'The development and functioning of the sense of shame', *Psychoanalytic Study of the Child*, 45: 377–409.
Wumser, L. (1981) *The Mask of Shame*, London: Johns Hopkins University Press.
Yorke, C. (1990) 'The development and functioning of the sense of shame', *Psychoanalytic Study of the Child*, 45: 377–409.

20 Living in the real world?

What happens when the media covers feminist research

Deborah Finding

Scene: The scene is set in a meeting of F.R.A. (Feminist Researchers Anonymous)
Location: The Real World

DEBORAH: Hi, I'm Deborah, and I'm a stupid humourless nitwit; an asinine political wonk who makes people want to vomit; a PC whinger with too much time on her hands; a worthless dickhead without even half a brain; a monotonous, bitter, narrow-minded academic who would do anything to become a celebrity, a pompous do-gooder with nothing better to worry about – whose research can only be described as a useless turd, tripe, or presumptuous rubbish that wastes both time and money; a dull-witted prude who should just shut up, and a git with a lazy intellect, not to mention being a smug bitch with no life who doesn't know shit about sociology – or any actual form of human interaction – who has spent her whole life masturbating over equations because she can't get laid.
ALL: Hi, Deborah! Welcome to the Real World!

Introduction

Although not all in the same sentence, or amalgamated in the same ways, all of the words and phrases in the speech above were used to describe me – over a period of weeks in October and November 2008 – in response to media coverage of a piece of research that had been published a short time earlier. I was approached to write a chapter for a book collection of academic essays on the BBC TV comedy sketch show *Little Britain*. The basis of my chapter, entitled 'The only feminist critic in the village? Figuring gender and sexuality in *Little Britain*' (Finding 2009), was that when *Little Britain* provides us with characters based on particular stereotypes, it feeds into our recognition of, and disgust at, these figures. Following Tyler's use of figurative analysis (Tyler 2008), I argued that the 'chav mum' presented in the character of Vicky Pollard harks back to the 1980s tabloid demonisation of the working-class single mother; that the character of Ting Tong (an unattractive yet seemingly empowered mail-order bride) is a damaging misrepresentation of the realities faced by women bought for sex, and that the ridiculous pursuit of homophobia brought about by the character of 'only gay in the village' Daffyd only works as a joke if we do, in fact, live in a pro-gay utopia without prejudice or discrimination. The essay concluded that these characters (and others) are not simply 'figures of fun' but represent targets of real hatred, of the type we have seen in comedy, such as that of Bernard Manning, in the past.[1]

Due to the space constraints of the edited collection, I was asked to take out my analysis of one of the characters, Vicky Pollard, as there were other chapters in the book dealing with class issues. Although I agreed to this, I felt that the missing section was important to my argument, and that there was still more to say. As such, I wrote an extended version of the chapter, which was published as a working paper by Media@LSE in July 2008. In mid-October, I was contacted by the Head of Press at LSE, who said he had enjoyed the paper, and would like to publicise it in the media, given its timeliness,[2] if I was amenable to this. We agreed that he would write a short press release, send it out and see what happened.

At the time of writing this chapter (December 2008), what happened – the chain of events following this press release – is only just coming to an end, and as such, I cannot claim any critical distance from it in which to write. However, in a collection exploring the hidden aspects of feminist research – that which we normally keep secret – perhaps it is enough to acknowledge this, and write from this space anyway. I believe that this episode may offer insight into one area of research practice that is often not discussed: the public reception of our work. In particular, I suggest that the vitriolic responses I received to press coverage of my research, as well as to the follow-up piece I wrote shortly afterwards for the *Guardian*, may be understood themselves as a kind of (violent) silencing practice, and may, moreover, tell us something important about what happens when feminist research 'goes public'.

Given that most support from friends, family and colleagues over this time has taken the form of suggestions to not read the comments because the people writing them are 'not worth it', one might ask why I want to engage with these comments by giving them the space and attention of a book chapter. The answer is simple: I am unable to accept the 'don't take it seriously' advice, because I believe that some serious things are going on in these responses. My original research attempted to highlight a return to the 'old' (racist/sexist/homophobic, etc.) comedy, and place this return within a post-feminist context, in which those discriminated against have to either participate in, or at least laugh at their own exploitation in order not to be branded 'humourless'.

In his memoir *Dreams from My Father*, Barack Obama admits his rage at the phrase 'can't you take a joke' (Obama 2004: 80), following as it invariably did, racist humour directed at his family.[3] Scholars from Freud onwards have shown that a joke is never 'just a joke', but a reflection of attitudes and fears, which can then be reflected in a number of ways from media output to government policy. It has been fifteen years since the publication of Catherine MacKinnon's classic feminist text 'Only Words' (MacKinnon 1994), in which she identifies hate speech as anything but 'only words'. Similarly, Gill Valentine, whose work concerned with her own hate-mail experiences[4] I reference throughout this chapter, titled her paper 'Sticks and Stones May Break My Bones'. She omits the second half of the well-known phrase ('but words will never hurt me') as it is clearly shown to be untrue in the context of her work, but leaves the physical threat of the first half in order to demonstrate the fear of physical harm that her experiences engendered.

If it is important to look at the comments as potentially indicative of something more sustained and systematic than 'just a few weirdos letting off steam', how is this to be accomplished? It would not be possible to go through every comment or email, highlighting themes in each one. Instead, I have identified several categories, through which I discuss comments, or parts of comments, in order to analyse the ways they work to either silence the researcher or diminish the research. These are:

1 Protecting the show and enjoyment of it from negative research conclusions
2 Personalising the show and the research
3 Using the characters of *Little Britain* as a way of attacking the researcher
4 Misconceptions about academia and academic research
5 Misrepresentation of the researcher

In order to do this, it is important to note that there are several actors, or groups of actors in play here, namely:

The creators of *Little Britain* (Matt Lucas and David Walliams)
The characters of *Little Britain* (Vicky Pollard, Daffyd, etc.)
The audience of *Little Britain*
The researcher (me)
The media
The audience of the media coverage

Any pair of actors from that list comes with its own interesting relationship, complete with its own power dynamic. My original research paper explored the relationships between the first three actors: the creators, the characters (figures) and the audience. This chapter focuses primarily on the three actors that come into play because of the research paper: the researcher, the media and the audience of that media coverage.[5]

1 Stop spoiling it for the rest of us: protecting the show and enjoyment of it from negative research conclusions

Although most of the quotes I use in this chapter are short comments from message boards, or excerpts from blogs, I thought it would be worthwhile to include one email verbatim, in order to show that there are often a number of things occurring simultaneously in the responses, as well as to give a more complete contextual understanding in this instance:

> Dear Sirs[6]
>
> We are all too aware we have horrible and disgusting things happening in our world. *Little Britain* is pure comical genius, for it to be slated in this way is ridiculous. If you're taking it seriously and don't find it funny, then don't watch it because you obviously don't have the sense of humor for it. It's not for analysing. Everyone knows it's just fun and not serious, the majority of people in this country takes the over the top jokes on the chin and enjoy it. Stop ruining things for people and ridiculing this programme just because you think it's 'politically incorrect'. Lighten up like the rest of us, it's hilarious! I'm sure you have more important things you could be writing about.
>
> (Name and email address supplied)

Although most of the themes in this email will be explored in other sections of this chapter, it is the sense that my research could somehow be 'ruining things for people' who like *Little Britain* that interests me here. The author of this email presents the show as somehow fragile and capable of being 'taken away', if either a majority, or someone in a position of power, agrees with my findings. The idea that the world is a bad enough place without researchers trying to 'spoil' things that make people laugh (whether or not this laughter might be rooted in hatred) was one that arose on several occasions. For example, these two posts from the discussion forum following the report at the Australian website 'Big Pond Movies':[7]

> GREAT! This is all we need; another monotonous, narrow minded academic trying to bring us all down. Thank you very much Deborah Finding.
>
> Chief (29/10/2008 5:04:48 PM)

> Academic git!!! Too much time on her hands!!! There are more fair dinkum!!!! Get a life and forget Political correctness … there's enough horrible stuff going on in the world. … let us laugh once in a while!!! Unbelieveable [sic]!!!
>
> suzimac4 (29/10/2008 3:30:04 PM)

The notion that (ironic) comedy gives relief from the process of 'PC'-ing our thoughts and actions is one that was explored in depth in the original research paper. As Whelehan (2000) points out with reference to 'New Manism' giving way to 'New Laddism', it is far more exhausting to have to change behaviour than it is to return to the old behaviour and call it ironic. The main point of these comments (and others like them) seems to be 'Please let us laugh at this – whether it's right or not', and those writing the comments seem not to notice or mind the head-in-the-sand aspect to this approach.

2 Do you think you're better than me? Personalising the show and the research

I was called by a representative from LBC[8] radio and asked to speak live to one of their DJs, James O'Brien, about my research, 'because he thought it was really interesting and he totally agrees with you that it panders to prejudice'. Having had previous experience of radio work in my last job, I was well aware of the techniques used to get people to agree to do the shows, such as assertions of agreement from the host or of an opportunity to explore the issues in more detail than they have been up to that point. Although my cynicism prevented me from immediately accepting the offer, after some consideration, I agreed to take part, having decided that even a somewhat antagonistic discussion of the issues raised in my research was better than none. However, the hostility I encountered on the show was far greater than the antagonism I had prepared myself for. The following is an except from the beginning of the interview:[9]

JAMES O'BRIEN: It [*Little Britain*] is funny though. I know I'm a quite nice bloke Deborah, we've never met but I'm not in any sense someone who is regularly going around looking for people to attack or bully and the Vicky Pollard sketch makes me laugh. Does that make me a bad person? Does it make me naïve, misled, deluded or evil?

We can see several techniques at work here. First, O'Brien personalises my research, rather than discussing the issues themselves. By aligning himself with the show (he finds it funny), he dares me to criticise it – and by implication, him. By asserting that he is a 'nice bloke', drawing on his radio (self-given) reputation as a 'man of the people', salt-of-the-earth type, he asks me to either agree with him *or* call him a bad person ('naïve, misled, deluded or evil') because he laughs at the show. Both potential answers leave me in a lose/lose position. If I say that I am sure he is a good person, and that it's OK that he laughs at the show, then he is in a perfect position to say 'well, what's the problem then?' and that I have contradicted my own research findings. I cannot say that I think he is a bad person (note how he describes this in extremes such as 'evil' to make it impossible for me to align myself with this position): first, because I do not know him; second, because it is his show, so that would immediately put me in a very vulnerable position; and third, because it would set me up as arrogant – thinking it was my place to judge whether people were good or bad. It was the third accusation he wished to make against me, it became clear as the interview went on, and I was not able to deflect with my response, which was laughing and trying to address the issue instead in my answer.

I attempted to explain in non-academic terms why I thought the Vicky Pollard character was potentially problematic (kids calling a little girl a 'chav' or a 'Vicky Pollard' in the playground because she lives in a council estate or her mum wears a tracksuit; newspapers using 'Vicky Pollard' as shorthand for 'single mother', therefore creating and sustaining the negative associations). However, this was difficult as O'Brien did not allow me to finish many sentences during the course of the interview and would immediately contradict me once I had said anything at all. Even though some of his comments did not really make sense, he asserted them so strongly and so quickly that it was hard to discern this at the time – and it did appear, superficially, that we were having a debate, although retrospectively, this was not really the case. The following extract demonstrates the level on which this 'debate' took place:

JAMES O'BRIEN: I don't think Vicky Pollard is the problem. Newspaper demonisation might be, but Vicky Pollard does not make people hate single mothers.

DF: But can you not see a connection between Vicky Pollard and tabloid demonisation of single mothers?

JAMES O'BRIEN: No, because one is comedy and one is demonisation and there's a flipping wealth of difference between the two, you only need a dictionary to work that out.

Rather than answering my question about whether he could really not see a connection between a portrayal of a single mother on a TV show and a portrayal of single mothers in the tabloids, he instead relies on the argument that there cannot be a connection between 'comedy' and 'demonisation' because they are different words. By taking my premise (that there is a connection between the two things) and repositioning it (as though I was arguing that the two things were numerically identical), he does not have to engage with the issues. Instead, his response positions me as ridiculous: I would only have to look at the difference between the two words in a dictionary to defeat my own argument, but clearly I am too stupid to do this.

O'Brien then proceeded to interrogate me about things he assumed were in the research paper, but were not. At this point, I remarked that it was difficult for us to have a conversation about the content of a paper that he obviously had not read, which he then had to concede that he had not. The interview ended when he kept asking me to say that I thought I was more intelligent, educated and sophisticated than most people who watch *Little Britain*, and I kept refusing. Again, either answer left me in a lose/lose position. Had I agreed that I thought I was somehow 'better than' others, I would have been open to accusations of arrogance, snobbishness and prejudice. However, the problem with answering 'absolutely not' and 'definitely not' (as I did) is that it inevitably leads to the conclusion that my research findings carry no more weight than an opposing sentiment articulated by someone who has given the issues no consideration at all.

This is perhaps a more prevalent issue for those of us who write on popular culture than it is for scientists. Our research topics are, by their nature, accessible and part of everyday life. As such, anyone can have an opinion, and the researcher struggles to make their research understood as more than 'just an opinion'. Given that only a tiny minority of commenters actually read any part of my research in addition to the media coverage of the press release, it was widely assumed that my 'research' only consisted of me watching the show and writing down what I thought of it. No strength or validity was given to my position on the grounds that I had spent time researching the topic, placing it in historical and social context, before constructing a logical argument to support it. In addition, my position at the Gender Institute at LSE did not bestow any 'expertise'[10] upon me either – rather, in many cases, it actually served as a reason that my research could be dismissed, as the subjective rantings of someone with a feminist agenda to push.

3 Beatings: using the characters of *Little Britain* as a way of attacking the researcher

There was a strong negative response to my claims the characters of *Little Britain* are being used as a stick with which to beat those they come to stand in for (e.g. Vicky Pollard for single, working-class mothers). It was suggested that the reason I might not like the show was because it was somehow 'too close to home for me' – that I recognised (and was unable to laugh at) myself in one of the characters I critiqued:

> *Little Britain* is a wonderful show – and such talent! It is obvious to anyone with half a brain that it is all meant in fun. Perhaps one of the charactors [sic] too closely resembles the Researcher? Can't wait til [sic] they visit Australia again.
>
> Nancy (29/10/2008 4:08:08 PM)[11]

There were also comments suggesting that I provided enough fodder to be turned into a character on *Little Britain*, e.g.:

> Lets [sic] all laugh at the stupid researcher!!!! Could be a new character?
>
> rocknroll [sic] (29/10/2008 3:35:24 PM)

However, it was more common for those commenting to actually reference or channel characters from *Little Britain* in order to make their point. Consider these three, all taken from the same website:

> Well I am over 70 and I piss myself @ Little Brit and the no PC crap. So … computer says no to mirthless academix (whats it got to do with economix?) [sic]
>
> sceptborg (29/10/2008 6:57:32 PM)

> shut up i aint done anythin or sumfthin or nothin. i am well gonna give that debra findings beatings, just ask trish. you now trish trish.
>
> vicky p (29/10/2008 6:07:00 PM) [sic]

> Hello Martin, it's Linda. I've got Deborah with me. You know Deborah? Yes the academic with the stick stuck up her ****! Yes the one who doesn't have a life and now doesn't have a grant to do useless studies with!
>
> Sandy Ronchi (29/10/2008 3:47:00 PM)

These comments utilise the *Little Britain* characters Carol Beer (Computer-Says-No Woman), Vicky Pollard and Linda Flint, respectively. They show us some of the ways in which these characters exist outside of the original text and act as conduits for, and defences of, the behaviour of real people towards other real people.[12]

The first comment does not take on the 'Computer-Says-No' character throughout the whole comment. Rather, the line 'computer says no to mirthless academix [sic]' is a way of bolstering the commenter's position (that I am a mirthless academic) by using a character's catchphrase to say it. If people feel positively about a recognisable/funny catchphrase, they are more likely to go along with the comment associated with it. This is a common technique in many fields, such as business negotiation, relying on the notion that laughing is half-way to agreeing.

The threat against me (beatings) in the second comment is undercut by the fact that it is obviously supposed to be said by Vicky Pollard (the commenter even signs her[13] name 'vicky p'). As such, I am expected to take it as 'just a joke', as merely something that a fictional character would say in this context, were she real, rather than as evidence of the commenter's hostile/violent feelings towards me. My original point, that the characters of *Little Britain* provide us with figures to project our negative feelings towards particular groups, is expanded here. The character of Vicky Pollard is not, in this case, being used to project hatred onto a working-class single mother. Rather, she is being utilised for her un-boundaried, 'chavvy' nature and style of speaking. It would be crossing a line for the commenter to threaten me herself, but speaking through Vicky Pollard gives her free rein to say anything while still being able to hide behind the 'just a joke' defence.

Similarly, the third comment utilises Linda Flint, the university employee whose 'PC training' cannot contain her racist/sexist/homophobic etc. outbursts when describing her students. In my original chapter, I suggested that this character might provide a more sophisticated critique of the superficiality of Human Resources departments' attempts to alter discriminatory behaviour (but not prejudiced thinking). However, in this case, there is no evidence of this, more generous, interpretation. The character is simply being used to say mean things. Somewhat ironically, it was my original intention to interpret the character only in this way: as providing a relief-filled outlet for all the things people feel but are no longer 'allowed' to say in an era of 'political correctness gone mad'. Again, the woman commenting uses somewhat violent imagery in her post, describing me as 'the academic with the stick stuck up her ****', before then describing my situation as 'the one who doesn't have a life and now doesn't have a grant to do useless studies with'. The implication here is that my research is so bad that my funding will be taken away. The theme of money, which featured quite heavily in the comments, will be explored in the next section.

4 Why not do something useful? Misconceptions about academia and academic research

It is constantly assumed that government money is being used (wasted) to fund research such as my *Little Britain* paper:

> Get a life. And to think, someone is paying her to come up with this bull.
> BPM (29/10/2008 3:49:04 PM)

Phrases such as 'waste of taxpayers' money'[14] are commonly used to deride research not seen to be worthwhile by the tabloids, and imply that the good, hard-working people of this country are being forced to pay for 'useless' research that has nothing to do with them and their lives. The reality is that research in the social sciences and humanities, is – as anyone working in this field in the UK will know – vastly under-funded.

The original book chapter, and subsequent research paper, were a side project to my actual PhD thesis (which in itself was only part-funded[15]), just as this chapter does not constitute any part of my PhD. Since 2004, when I began my PhD, I have been published in books, newspapers and magazines. I have taken part in TV shows and radio programmes. I also have presented work at academic conferences, public debates, model UN meetings and film societies. The vast majority of these things are unpaid – and yet, anyone who wants to have an academic/public intellectual/writing career is expected to do them alongside their main projects.

That studying popular culture – that which is created by, and consumed by, people who live in the 'real world' – can tell us nothing about the real world, seemed to be a popular response. There was generic criticism that the entire field of cultural studies is a waste of time, e.g.

> *Little Britain* is hilarious! She really needs to get a sense of humour and find an actual issue to research, not a TV programme.
>
> Be-Be (29/10/2008 5:43:59 PM)

> That academic obviously doesn't live out here in the real world – basing her study on a TV show, she should check out some of the comments posted on these pages, that'd open her mind to reality.
>
> ......(29/10/2008 12:52:19 PM)

> Research into little Britain? Thats the best joke I've ever heard. Why not do something useful?
>
> Upnorth (10/11/2002 10:01 AM)

In addition, my institutional affiliation was itself a great source of criticism. Because of its name, there was a common misunderstanding of LSE as a university that only studies economics. Therefore, many of the people commenting could not understand why, at a time of great economic upheaval, a researcher from a school of economics would concern herself with a television programme, e.g.

> It makes me wonder why would the london school of economics study a television show, you would think there are far more prudent economic issues to study. Little brittain [sic] is awesome
>
> Brendan (29/10/2008 3:48:32 PM)

That I was supposedly an economist[16] was further proof that a) I did not have a sense of humour, and b) could not possibly have anything to say about popular culture.

5 Who the hell does she think she is? Misrepresentation of the researcher

It will be no surprise to hear that I do not recognise the version of myself presented in the introduction to this chapter. However, this section is not so much an attempt to defend myself, or 'set the record straight', but rather to explore the possible functions that misrepresenting an individual, in response to a belief about their work, perform. In order to do this, I focus primarily on three aspects of myself that were misrepresented during this process: my name, my location and my personal attributes (or assumed lack thereof).

Name

Discussing the ways in which my name was altered during this process may seem minor, but as many scholars and poets alike have indicated, it can be anything but minor. Name-changing can represent slavery, or the emancipation from it (see Lorde 1982), and, as the children's story *Rumpelstiltskin* reminds us, being able to name something removes some of its power. Wilson (2008) suggests that naming is an activity – a process which continually reoccurs and is reconfirmed on a daily basis. If indeed 'the repetition of a name in speech and writing declares and makes public an individual's personal identity and family connections (Wilson 2008: 2), then it stands to reason that a replacement of that repetition with something not of the individual's choosing could represent an attempted disruption of that personal identity and – but to a lesser extent here – family connections.[17]

Two commenters took it upon themselves to abbreviate my name in their remarks. From BPM:

> It's very funny. Absolutely love it. Seems to me that Deb has all of the phobias. ...
>
> jethro (29/10/2008 4:24:19 PM)

And from the *Guardian* 'Comment Is Free':

> Don't try fix what ain't broke Debs. The Brits have goody-goodied themselves into such blandness – muck with comedy and you will all end up as the battery chickens of the world.
>
> Whambham (08/11/2008 3:56 PM)

Using a pet, or more childlike, version of someone's name can act to diminish the person or their status in the situation. Using a shortened version of a person's given name implies a shared intimacy between the speaker and the named. In appropriating this intimacy, the second commenter implies that we are close enough for him to advise me 'as a friend' not to pursue this line of research.

Others went yet further still, such as this commenter from BPM, who actually changes my name in order to make her point:

> Im [sic] glad I'm not Deboring Finding nothing. Watch all their stuff. I say keep it coming.
>
> karen h (29/10/2008 5:58:00 PM)

In changing my name from 'Deborah' to 'Deboring', the commenter embeds 'boring' into my identifier, in order to assert that I am intrinsically boring. Again, wordplay is used with 'Finding nothing' in order to diminish the research.

Location

Valentine explores the ways in which her academic identity (geographer) and sexual identity (lesbian) have been co-constituted, fixing her position as 'lesbian geographer', even when she is not working on projects that relate to sexuality. For Valentine, this was problematic, as she was not 'out' in every context of her life – and was in fact, 'outed' to her parents through hate mail sent directly to them.

There was no mention of my sexuality in my *Little Britain* paper (edited book chapters do not provide the same sort of reflexive space one might find in the methodology chapter of a PhD thesis, or the introductory chapter to one's own book). In the absence of any such detail, I was presumed to be heterosexual. Utilising the argument that unless one is part of a marginalised group, one cannot have a valid opinion, my research on the character of Daffyd was dismissed by some gay posters. Their opinion that Daffyd was funny was seen to trump any argument that the character might be problematic because they were speaking from a gay standpoint[18] and I was not.[19] Having been 'out' in every context as a bisexual, or queer, woman for all of my adult life, being repositioned as heterosexual was a somewhat odd experience.[20]

Sexual location was not the only one to be brought to the fore. My geographical location was also assumed and criticised:

> And this is a woman researcher from england.she has clearly never been to mansfield.I'm from england and its full of stereotypes..and we.like the aussies love taking the piss out of ourselves. I HOPE TO GOD THEY MAKE ANOTHER SERIES!! [sic]
>
> From England (29/10/2008 12:43:41 PM)

The 'London bubble' criticism is one often levelled at the government and the BBC. It suggests that policy decisions, or analyses of society, made in London are flawed because London is not representative (a variation of the 'not living in the real world' argument). Given that London is a migratory city, very few people based at its institutions are 'born and bred' Londoners. The assertion that I had 'clearly never been to Mansfield' appropriated the 'London bubble' discourse in order to highlight that I could not speak for non-Londoners (who don't mind being stereotyped and are able to laugh at themselves). Given that I was born and raised in the North-East of England, much further from London than Mansfield, this comment made me smile. However, there is a more serious point to be made here. Just like the heterosexual repositioning, the geographical repositioning is an attempt to homogenise academics as straight, white, middle-class, liberal Londoners, living in ivory towers with no idea about 'the real world'.

I attempted to challenge this stereotype, and the reassertions of it in response to my research, in the *Guardian* article. I wrote:

> The humourless feminist or PC academic is as much a stereotyped figure worth challenging as the chav mum or the mail-order bride. Since my research on *Little Britain* was published, I have been positioned as both.

Several commenters addressed this point in their comments; for example:

> Humourless feminist stereotypes, certainly, but PC academics are so ubiquitous and ridiculous that they are self-stereotyping and self-parodying. Some stereotypes really do have a basis in reality.
>
> Waltz (08/11/2008 3:36 PM)

This was a common theme – that the stereotypes were acknowledged, but then were still enforced as true; for example:

> And now we get to see how brilliant 'little britain' really are as she is the classic stereotype we all believe-that academics really have NO IDEA ABOUT THE REAL WORLD !She also would fail to see what a dickhead she sounds like to all of us.
>
> amanda (29/10/2008 3:35:33 PM)

Personal attributes – or lack thereof

The first two lines of my original research paper were:

> I started writing a feminist critique of *Little Britain* with a certain amount of trepidation. *Little Britain* is a comedy show, and – in the mainstream at least – feminism and humour are rarely mentioned in the same sentence, unless 'humour' is followed with 'less'.

Had I known the extent to which I would be positioned as a 'humourless feminist' and personally attacked on this basis as a result of this paper, my 'certain amount' of trepidation would have been significantly higher. In many ways, I found the constant assertions that I must have no sense of humour[21] the most difficult of all. It is an impossible situation: most people think they have a good sense of humour, but there is no way to prove this. One cannot make an argument that one has a sense of humour or is funny, although I was often tempted to bring 'evidence' into these discussions by listing all the comedy shows I have been to since being a young teenager. But ultimately, would my professions of love for Eddie Izzard or Rob Newman have got me anywhere? The stereotype of the 'humourless feminist' was strong, and some commenters went out of their way to show that it certainly applied to me. After the previously quoted section from the *Guardian* article about my experience of being labelled in this way, one commenter wrote:

> I wonder why … Deborah Finding is a researcher at LSE's Gender Institute. Her work is concerned with narratives of sexual violence in popular music, and draws upon both trauma theory and feminist cultural studies.

> Sorry, I don't mean this as a personal attack, just that there is often a certain amount of truth in stereotypes, otherwise they wouldn't have any comedic power.
>
> haliborange (08/11/08 4:56 PM)

In taking the very brief biography from the *Guardian* contributor profile, this commenter uses my research interests as proof of my humourlessness. The problem with this is that my academic identity, or part of it, is being used to stand in for my entire identity (which is, of course, how stereotypes work). In writing book or journal chapters, or presenting papers at conferences, Valentine describes the necessity of performing the unified identity 'competent academic'. Due to her self-confidence being severely damaged as a result of her hate mail, Valentine describes this as a 'rather unstable identity'. I would argue that this identity is always unstable, given its inevitably doomed attempt to describe a whole person.

Of course, someone reading the *Little Britain* paper does not need to know that I play tennis, have a mischievous kitten, or prefer red wine to white, in order to critique my research. However, if the critique bleeds from the research to the researcher (or in fact as most comments did, entirely ignores the research in favour of criticising the researcher), this lack of a 'whole person' identity is problematic. Butler suggests that we are constituted in and through our social relations, and therefore have no secure identity that does not exist outside our performances of particular identities at given times. As such, it is important to question how we are being constituted when we perform 'feminist researcher' or 'academic', and what we might be giving up through that process.

Conclusion

Writing an academic response to hateful criticism is, in itself, a strange task. It places a distance between the writer's unstructured personal response to the comments and the necessarily structured form of the written response. This distance is expected, not just in an academic context, but also by friends, family and colleagues, who assume I will 'rise above' such patently ridiculous comments as the ones made about me, and not take them seriously. But being advised to 'just ignore it' because 'it's beneath you' or 'people are just jealous/threatened/weird', while meant as supportive, ultimately silences the felt response to the comments. It is another variation of 'it's just a joke' – albeit a well-meant one – because it suggests that these (only) words should not be taken seriously (because they are not worth it). Valentine (1998) agrees, having found herself, despite on one level 'knowing better', still 'engaged in a constant introspective search either for evidence that the accusations might be right or for proof to convince myself that they are wrong'.

My personal, or felt, response to these comments, is somewhat lost in this chapter, for which I cannot blame the structured form of academic writing, as others have used it to great effect. Brackenridge (1999) writes of the ways in which the responses to her research (threats of legal action, attempted blackmail, media harassment and misrepresentation, hate mail, crank calls, ridicule and personal insults, among others) left her feeling anxious, isolated, politically frustrated and ineffective. Valentine articulates her vulnerability in terms of the public and private spaces she inhabits. She describes the arrival of the morning and afternoon post (previously an excuse to take a work break) as having become two regularly scheduled occasions of dread (Valentine 1998: 322). Everyday objects (envelopes) and sounds (ringing telephones) are no longer innocuous, but now carry meanings 'laden with threat' and 'potent with menace' (ibid.: 321). Rather, my reluctance to include my own felt responses is indicative of my reluctance to admit that these comments did indeed 'get to' me, and that I did not always feel able to dismiss them, as others might have wished me to. For the most part, I protected colleagues, friends and family from the more unpleasant comments, and my feelings about them, focusing instead on the ones that I could present as amusing stories that gave hate mail a somewhat positive spin. It was easier to express glee at the massive academic promotion one commenter had given me by calling me 'Professor Finding' than it was to add that the title had been preceded by ' ... a prude like'. I was delighted to just be mentioned in the same sentence as Judith Butler, I told my PhD consort, even if it was by a commenter asserting that we both 'give academia a bad name'.[22] As such, it is easy to see the ways in which the violent silencing practices of others lead to both self-silencing, and to the 'endless self-monitoring' and the 'toxic shame' that Rosalind Gill explores in her chapter.

Although my aim in this essay was to explore the ways in which hateful comments work against feminists engaged in academic research, rather than to defend myself against the accusations levelled at me, or in some sense 'get my own back', I am aware that I have been able to do both. In discussing the repositioning of myself as heterosexual and Southern by others, I have re-established (in print) my self-identification as queer and heritage as North-Eastern. While engaging with what happens when feminists are described as 'humourless', I have mentioned my own appreciation of comedy and certain comedians in particular, and thus 'proved' that I really do have a sense of humour to anyone reading this chapter. In exploring James O'Brien's comments to me on the radio, I have achieved some wish-fulfilment in positioning them as bullying and somewhat nonsensical – something I was only able to do in retrospect, but wished I had been able to do live on air. Where people assumed that I would never read their message-board or blog comment, I have reposted them and made my own analysis of, or response to, them. That they, in turn, will probably never read this chapter does not matter so much as the fact that I have had a space in which to take some of that power back. The joke may not be on the commenters, but at least I am no longer the punch-line.

Notes

1 This is a very brief outline of the paper, which is obviously more complex than such a short description allows. The full paper can be found online at http://www.lse.ac.uk/collections/media@lse/pdf/EWP13_final.pdf.

2 At the time of publishing, the US version of *Little Britain* was being aired for the first time in the States, to fairly mixed reviews. Just as the press began to cover my research, the radio scandal involving Russell Brand and Jonathan Ross's phone calls to actor Andrew Sachs (joking about Brand's sexual encounter with Sachs' granddaughter, Georgina Baillie) exploded into a media frenzy. Given that both were comedy related, various media grouped them together in order to talk about 'comedy under attack' or question whether or not comedy had 'gone too far'.

3 Also, see Billig (2001) on the ways in which racist jokes are presented as 'harmless'.

4 The hate-mail campaign waged against Valentine was prolonged, vicious and deeply personal, targeting, as it did, not just Valentine (in her own home), but also her friends, family and colleagues. In utilising her work, I do not intend to imply that our experiences are in any way comparable. However, I have found her thoughtful analysis of the ways in which hate mail *works* extremely useful in thinking about this chapter.

5 During the period of media coverage/audience response, I was also made aware of some of these relationships, which would normally remain hidden. For example, both *Now* magazine and the *Daily Star* – who I contacted to request that my name be corrected on their websites – described their relationships with the *Little Britain* creators as 'litigious', and were critical of the individuals involved. *Now* magazine called me to say that they had received a 'cease and desist' letter from the lawyers of Matt Lucas and David Walliams, and asked if I would be interested in them running a story along the lines of '*Little Britain* creators bully PhD student'. Given that the legal action was being taken against the magazine (for a potentially libellous link they had included), rather than against me or my research, I suggested that this would not be entirely accurate.

6 I found this masculinisation (and multiplication!) of myself particularly odd, given that my full name (which is not gender-ambiguous) was attached to the press release, every piece of coverage *and* the email address this commenter is writing to.

7 http://www.bigpondmovies.com/libraries/article_library/aap_newsml/b4c0b725–27aa5–498f-9809-36f89440ff57/

8 London's Biggest Conversation.

9 I am very grateful to Alice Shimmin for providing a transcript of this interview.

10 Others have noted the 'expertise' and 'agenda' factors in dismissing research. See, for example, Brackenridge (1999) on her assumed lack of competence in researching sexual abuse in sport because she is not a clinical psychologist and because she is a lesbian (and therefore inevitably predisposed to negative conclusions about men).

11 All comments in this section are taken from 'Big Pond Movies'.

12 Given that this was the primary argument of my original paper, I am grateful in some ways to these commenters for providing evidence to support and strengthen it!

13 As 'vicky p' is obviously a pseudonym, I have no way of knowing if the commenter is male or female. I use 'her' here for continuity with the gender the commenter has performed.

14 Valentine also speaks of having her previous work (on lesbian geographies) 'lambasted in the *News of the World* as a waste of taxpayers' money' (Valentine: 316)

15 I received several small scholarships for my PhD, but these amounted to less than a quarter of the funding that either of the two major funding bodies would have supplied. As such, during my first two years as a full-time PhD student, I worked three jobs concurrently, in order to make up the difference. I note this, not to elicit

sympathy, but to attempt to challenge the notion that those in academia are somehow taking the 'easy option' by receiving piles of money and doing a small amount of (pointless) work.

16 Hence the 'masturbating over equations' quote at the beginning of the paper, which sounds even more odd out of context.

17 I should note here that not all of the alterations of my name or title were diminishing or insulting. Some relied merely on wordplay (e.g. Angus Robertson's comment, 'I'll tell ya what's funny … a researcher named Finding' on http://www.publicaddress.net/system/topic,1469,field_theory_send_in_the_clowns.sm?i=20), and others made mistakes with regard to my academic title (e.g. calling me 'Professor') that were in my favour.

18 Such as this example, from a blog post entitled 'Economics Promotes Hatred' (Wed., 29 Oct. 2008, 6:36 p.m.) at http://sullensinuous.deviantart.com/: 'well one of the diverse sexual activities i enjoy is fucking other men, and i think Daffyd is brilliant'. See also the blog post entitled 'For What Is A Man Profited, If He Shall Gain A Ph.D, And Lose His Sense Of Humor?' at http://www.feralchild.net/?p=434.

19 This also happened during the course of a TV show discussion on comedy I was invited to. Talking about the representation of disability on the Peter Kay show *Britain's Got the Pop Factor* (an *X Factor* spoof), a speaker in a wheelchair effectively closed down the discussion by saying that if he found it funny as a disabled man, then it was not reasonable for others (who were not disabled) to object to it.

20 Had my sexuality been made explicit, however, it is very likely that is would have been used against me in the criticisms, as Valentine and Brackenridge both discovered.

21 For example this comment, which suggests that I should leave the show to those who appreciate it (i.e. people with a sense of humour): 'Go and do something constructive with your time! No-one cares what you think!!! If you don't like it then don't watch it, Little Brittan is so funny! I bet you don't like Catherine Tate and such like either?' (Samantha (29/10/2008 6:35:55 p.m.). Had the commenter read the original research paper, she would have seen the favourable comparison of Catherine Tate's Lauren character to *Little Britain*'s Vicky Pollard.

22 Or this comment from Aaron posting below the *Herald Sun* article: 'She is WELL on her way becoming the NEXT Germaine Greer: intolerant, sensationalist and brimming with faux intellectual rhetoric.'

References:

Billig, M. (2001) 'Humour and hatred: the racist jokes of the Ku Klux Klan', *Discourse and Society*, 12 (3): 267–89.

Brackenridge, C.H. (1999) 'Managing myself: investigator survival in sensitive research', *International Review for the Sociology of Sport*, 34 (4): 399–410.

Butler, J. (1990) *Gender Trouble: Feminism and the Subversion of Identity*, London and New York: Routledge.

Finding, D. (2008a) '"I can't believe you just said that": figuring gender and sexuality in "Little Britain"', *Media@LSE Electronic Working Papers* 13, London: LSE.

——(2008b) 'Laughter as a weapon', *Guardian*.

——(2009) 'The only feminist critic in the village? Figuring gender and sexuality in "Little Britain"', in S. Lockyer (ed.) *Reading 'Little Britain'*, London: I.B. Tauris.

Lorde, A. (1982) *Zami: A New Spelling of My Name*, London: Rivers Oram Press.

Obama, B. (2004) *Dreams From My Father*, New York: Crown Publishing.

Mackinnon, C. (1994) *Only Words.* London: Harper Collins.

Tyler, I. (2008) 'Chav mum, chav scum: class disgust in contemporary Britain', *Feminist Media Studies*, 8 (1): 17–34.

Valentine, G. (1998) '"Sticks and stones may break my bones": a personal geography of harassment', *Antipode*, 30 (4): 305–32.

Whelehan, I. (2000) *Overloaded: Popular Culture and the Future of Feminism*, London: The Women's Press.

Wilson, R. (2008) 'Surnames after marriage: illegitimacy, patriliny and the nuclear family', presented at ISA Research Committee on Family Research, 9–13 September, Lisbon, Portugal.

21 The place of secrets, silences and sexualities in the research process

Lynda Johnston

Introduction

This chapter examines the research relationship between sexualised bodies, secrecy, silence and place. I attempt to unravel the complexities of acknowledging, or not acknowledging, the researcher as sexually embodied. Drawing on a variety of research situations, I consider my secrets, silences and/or omissions during geographies of sexualities research. When conducting this research it is often assumed that the researcher is the embodiment of the researched; the assumption being, for example, that the researcher will be queer if researching queer bodies and spaces, or straight if researching heterosexual bodies and spaces. I draw on a range of sexuality research places – in both queer and heteronormative spaces – which are illustrative of place and bodies as fluid and negotiated rather than being fixed or stable. Furthermore, the researcher is 'unstable' in that I and others may refashion my sexualised subjectivity in different locations and at different times.

For many years now feminists (Lather 1991, Reinharz 1992) have reflected on research processes and relations of power, not simply because this is 'better' scholarship but because, in emphasising *how* we put together our accounts, we are less likely to universalise on behalf of all places or all people. Instead, the idea is to stress that the knowledge of each person, including and especially the narrator, is only partial and is a product of their particular location (Rich 1986; Haraway 1988). No text is the last word on the matter but each creates and leaves space for other voices and other silences. Feminist poststructuralists try to decentre themselves as narrators and be explicit about their own positioning and assumptions in constructing the text. Being explicit about positioning has often been conflated with discussion, talk and text, yet scholars have been less interested in positionality as it relates to silence, secrecy and omissions.

Adding 'place' as a component of positionality, Wendy Larner argues:

> Working with an understanding of positionality as not only theoretical and ideological positioning, but also positioning in the *politics of place*,

> means recognising that inevitably there will be multiple situated knowledges in any particular context.
>
> (Larner 1995: 187, emphasis added)

Larner's focus on the politics of place is something that feminist geographers have, for a number of years, usefully applied to understand further the complexities of research processes (see, McDowell 1992; Dyck 1993; England 1994; Gibson-Graham 1994; Kobayashi 1994).

Feminist researchers continue to question the politics and complexities of research processes, and I am no exception. Some of my questions that shape this chapter are: How should I present myself to research participants? What are the appropriate methods for including my own embodied account of the research process? What information should I leave out? How and in what ways does place and embodiment matter when considering silences, secrets and omissions in the research process? I also suggest, following Gillian Rose, that:

> A research project is understood not entirely [as] a consequence of the relationship between researcher and researched. To assume otherwise is, once again, to resist the proliferation of power/knowledges that by asserting the unassailable authority of academic analysis.
>
> (Rose 1997: 319)

As other chapters in this collection testify, questions about secrets, silences and omissions add to this proliferation of power/knowledges in the research process.

It is generally agreed that there is no one set of methods or techniques – nor even a broad category of types of method – that should be seen as distinctly feminist. Liz Stanley (1990: 12) advocates feminists 'should use any and every means available'. In general, qualitative methods are advocated by feminists who search for collaborative and non-exploitative relationships with research participants. In particular, many feminist researchers rely on semi-structured and/or in-depth interviews, participant observation and ethnographic methods. 'Qualitative, detailed, small-scale and in-depth case study work is particularly well suited to women studying women. Such methods use to best advantage skills of listening, empathy and the validation of (shared) personal experiences' (McDowell 1999: 236). Rose, however, reminds us that even with 'feminist' methods:

> [W]e cannot know everything, nor can we survey power as if we can fully understand, control or redistribute it. What we may be able to do is something rather more modest but, perhaps more radical: to inscribe into our research practices the absences and fallibilities while recognising that the significance of these does not rest entirely in our own hands.
>
> (Rose 1997: 31)

Attention to absences, fallibilities, silences and omissions is what follows in this chapter as I describe the constitutive relationship between place and sexualised embodiment in the research process. I use a range of queer and heteronormative research settings – lesbian homes, gay urban spaces and heterosexual wedding spaces – to highlight the way in which secrecy and silence discourses about sexuality shift and change depending on the place of research.

Home spaces

My choice of geographies of sexualities as a research topic is motivated by my own personal circumstances. In 1993 I started graduate study in a geography department with a strong reputation for feminism (see Peace et al. 1997; Longhurst and Johnston 2005). Within this relatively supportive academic environment I began a research topic on lesbian homes. I was interested in the relationship between lesbian identity and domestic space and went about conducting focus group interviews with lesbians in their shared houses (some of this research is published in Johnston and Valentine 1995). From the outset my sexual identity constituted the research (a lesbian conducting research about lesbians), yet I was overly cautious about the interactions between myself and the participants and aware that all research situations might be considered landscapes of power (Valentine 2002). It has been suggested that researchers who share the same identities as their research participants are positioned as 'insiders' and as such have access to knowledge that 'outsiders' may not. The way in which the insider/outsider dualism is produced is problematic. The assumption that lesbians interviewing lesbians (and women interviewing women) automatically have insider status has been criticised as a dangerous form of essentialism because the establishment of connections or rapport are uncritically attributed to physical attributes such as sex or race (Kobayashi 1994).

Gill Valentine (2002) discusses and problematises this issue by drawing on the concepts of maximising/minimising shared lesbian identities to produce non-heteropatriarchal space. Being a lesbian conducting research on lesbians 'maximises' a shared identity around dominant discourses of common goals and needs of lesbians. Significantly, in my research, a number of differences became 'minimised' and omitted during data gathering. I suspect that the participants in my lesbian home research assumed that my understanding of 'being lesbian' was similar to theirs, yet I did not elaborate on what 'being a lesbian' meant for me. Nor did I 'reveal' my poststructuralist and queer understanding of sexualised subjectivities as fluid, changing and contingent on place. To my participants I was a 'new lesbian' in Hamilton as I had lived there for only five months at the time of the focus group interviews. The lesbians in this study were all younger than me (in their early 20s and I was 30), most had not travelled beyond New Zealand and Australia (I had travelled extensively), and they had different un/employment experiences to me (I had

had periods of unemployment and a series of low-paid low-skilled jobs so that I could engage in extended periods (months at a time) of mountaineering and rock climbing).

Reflecting back on this research I suspect that the fact that I too shared a house with other lesbians was the most defining feature that structured our research interaction. I made a conscious decision to remain silent about my family background, my age and how my sexuality had shifted and changed over the years and in different places. This silence may have meant that others assumed that I was like them. Indeed, I took several steps to be more 'like' my participants. I dressed casually, 'younger', and wore clothing that might have been considered to be more 'butch' than 'femme' and in doing so I may have essentialised the binary notion that often equates masculinity with lesbian identity and femininity with heterosexuality. In other words, I adorned myself in a way that I saw as consistent with my subjectivity as 'researcher in the specificity of place and context of a particular study' (Dyck 2002: 242). During the research process I used my embodiment to normalise aspects of gender and sexuality (I did not want to feel 'out of place', nor did I want my participants to feel 'out of place' in their own homes), yet my research aims were designed to question and challenge embodied hegemonic norms about places and people. My body was a key research 'instrument' or 'tool' for this research yet during focus group discussions I remained silent about my own experiences of home, as well as my knowledge of some of the participants.

Another issue related to research processes, secrets, silences and sexualities is that I was aware that some of the lesbian participants had experiences of home that they did not speak about during the research process. I respected their silence by also remaining silent and decided not to guide the questioning in a direction that may have made them feel uncomfortable. The focus groups ranged in topics with participants agreeing and disagreeing about their relationship to, and understandings of home. Yet some participants decided *not* to tell all their stories. It was not until after I had completed the focus groups and analysed the data that I realised how important these particular silences were. Melissa Hyams (2004) explores the importance of silences and how easily the researcher can dismiss them from the research. She states that 'silence is most often equated with absence and voice with presence – literally and symbolically' (ibid.: 109). Furthermore, when silence is equated with absence, it marks what should be present but is not. The absence of information in this instance demonstrates the need for the participants to uphold a sense of subjectivity in front of each other and myself.

One of the consequences of 'keeping quiet' about differences between me and my lesbian research participants was that I was accepted into their homes. Other researchers have demonstrated how entering women's homes can redefine the relationship between researcher and researched, usually creating positive rapport (Falconer Al-Hindi 1997; Oberhauser 1997; Avis 2002). On one level a certain amount of trust was necessary to be able to enter the participants' homes and to have them talk about their relationship between identity and domestic space. Conducting focus groups in their home spaces may have subverted hierarchical power relations between the researcher and researched. Apart from my nervousness at the beginning of the focus groups, the interactions unfolded fairly smoothly with plenty of discussion, laughter and eating of the food that I had prepared. My goal was to make each research encounter interesting and enjoyable for participants, not a chore that they were doing to 'help out' another lesbian in their community.

On the surface, women interviewing women or lesbians interviewing lesbians in homes seems an easy task. In my research I had gained the participants' confidence, established easy rapport and I discovered a great deal about their lives, identities and domestic spaces. Even the differences in age, class and life experience seemed not to be an issue but then perhaps this 'easy rapport' happened because of my silences and omissions. It was not my intention to betray participants, but to 'sit back' and have the focus group interviews be more about participants than myself. It is difficult to know whether, given a similar research experience, I would keep quiet about the differences between participants and myself. The specificity of place and time are important factors to consider when deciding, often on the trot, what to say and what not to say. The research space of lesbian domestic homes turned out to be very different to urban spaces of gay pride parades – one of my other research projects.

Queer street spaces

Researching gay pride parades proved to be an extraordinary complex and messy space of both performances and subjectivities occurring between myself and participants. Understanding some of these complexities I remained mindful of feminist poststructuralist knowledge of myself and participants as an incoherent 'decentred site of differences' (Rose 1997: 314) and I employed, once again, feminist methodological tools in order to acknowledge my positionality and hopefully redistributing power between researcher and researched. Yet despite all of my attentiveness, the research process went in a direction that I was not prepared for. Rose (1997) notes that we cannot really know what is going on in any given research encounter and therefore cannot really know how the knowledge is produced. Performances of all those involved in the research process are always in flux.

When I conducted research with organisers and participants of gay pride parades (particularly the HERO parade and festival in Auckland, Aotearoa in New Zealand, but also the Sydney Gay and Lesbian Mardi Gras in Australia, and Pride Scotland, Edinburgh; see Johnston 2005) I became involved in the 'inside', the workings of the pride organisation. Working for and with pride organisations I believed I would have access to participants and be able to gain in-depth participant observation data. I spent a long time in Auckland, working as a volunteer for the HERO Parade. I was also conducting doctoral research, and all other people involved in the pride organisation knew about my dual roles. During this fieldwork, however, several problems emerged. These problems involved shifting power relations between myself and another key gay pride parade worker – the director of the parade.

While undertaking participant observation and voluntary work for an extended period – six weeks – I got to know all of the parade organisers and volunteers very well. We worked together, had lunch together and sometimes socialised together. On the whole I thoroughly enjoyed my experience as a researcher and volunteer for the pride organisation. At several times during data collection, however, I made decisions to remain silent about 'injustices' in the organisation. A situation arose that shifted power dynamics between myself and another parade worker and I decided to 'bite my tongue' as I feared my speaking out might jeopardise the research interaction. The parade director had lost a set of VIP festival tickets and all volunteers were accused of stealing the tickets (after several days the parade director found the tickets and admitted to forgetting where she had put them). There was a great deal of tension at the parade workshop and all volunteers – myself included – found it very difficult to work with the director in the run-up to the parade. In this situation I was very much the parade volunteer, not a researcher, and it brought into sharp focus the difficulty of juggling both roles when addressing injustices.

I was unable to separate my anger over this situation, as a volunteer worker, from my research role, and made the decision not to interview the parade director. This meant that I missed out on what may have been an important interview, and in the process perhaps I had attempted to 'silence' her. I was also faced with the problem of representing this difficult relationship, the anger I felt, and how this shaped my data gathering. Academic protocols, which determine acceptable styles of academic texts, mean that the difficulty remains unresolved. Michael Keith offers an explanation:

> Under conventional rules it would appear that anger as an emotional feature of the everyday world can surface in academic texts only as desiccated anecdote, an object of scrutiny that is a proclivity of the 'Other' that is studied but not of the disciplined self that represents the truth. Anger can only ever be the object of academic gaze, never the legitimate subject of academic style.
>
> (Keith 1992: 561)

Opportunities to document power relations and the anger of others towards the parade director were frequent. Several parade workers were asked by a newspaper reporter to discuss the ways we were 'treated as volunteers'. I remained silent because of my academic position as a researcher.

While I have found qualitative research in the context of feminist, post-structuralist and queer analysis enables a move away from the universalising ideal of research which seeks a single truth, I have also attempted to situate myself in the research process. My sexuality was known at the parade workshop and hence I was studying a world of which I am part, with all the emotional involvement that this creates. The environment of the parade workshop, however, was completely new to me. I had previously been involved in organising all women and all lesbian events but had never been part of a production with, and for, gay men, bisexuals, transgendered, Fa'afafine (Samoan transgender), or Takataapui (Māori gay, lesbian, bisexual and transgender) people. This queer environment is often idealised as the ultimate place where 'any sexuality goes'. My experience shows there are still hierarchical power relations present in 'queer space'. For example, I had conducted a focus group with transgendered paraders at the HERO workshop, a place where those involved in the parade could build their floats. The male to female transgendered respondents indicated that they were more at ease with being understood as heterosexual, rather than being aligned with homosexuality. Many male to female transgendered respondents wanted to be identified as women, and as seeking male partners. One respondent noted that she had more in common with heterosexuals than with homosexuals. The complexities of sexualised subjectivities meant that there were sometimes 'fractions' between different groups in the small space of the parade workshop. Like others in the workshop, I was both an insider and outsider, because of gender, sexuality and race. I suspect that my identity as a pākehā (white New Zealander) was one of the reasons that the Takataapui group declined to be part of a focus group interview. As an observer and volunteer at pride I became caught up in, and constituted by, a set of power relations which produced discursive constructs of gendered/sexed and sexualised embodiment. I trod carefully around these issues of contestation and remained quiet about 'in-fighting' between gay men, lesbians, bisexuals and transgenders at the parade organisation. I also did not want our funders, or the city council, to withdraw their support. In these research situations

> it is impossible for us to unpick how the mutual constitution of gender, class, race, sexuality works in order to identify this as the gender effect. … Dualisms of insider/outsider can never therefore capture the complex and multi-faceted identities and experiences of researchers.
>
> (Valentine 2002: 199).

I have discussed some of the powers at work in queer research spaces and the contexts in which silences, secrets and sexualities are produced. In another geographies of sexuality research encounter – heteronormative wedding spaces – my secrets, silences and omissions became more obvious as participants read my embodied sexuality as not queer.

Heteronormative wedding spaces

Secrets, silences and omissions are more easily tracked within my research spaces of heteronormative weddings. For several years, and as already noted,

I have paid specific attention to non-heterosexual bodies and spaces through my studies of lesbian homes and gay pride parades. More recently, however, I have begun to focus on heterosexual bodies by examining wedding tourism in New Zealand (see Johnston 2006). The valuable work on queer sexualities and spaces continues to grow, but geographers and tourism academics have been slow to examine heterosexuality. My wedding tourism research responds to Phil Hubbard's (2000: 206) claim that 'there appears to be little overt consideration of how moral heterosexual performances are naturalized in a variety of "everyday" social settings, either public or private'. Wedding rituals tend to present a type of 'natural' heterosexuality that conceals historical and material changes. While no wedding works as a transparent window into social structures, they may be, however, powerful markers of a couple's 'normality', morality, productivity and 'appropriate' gendered and sexualised subjectivities.

This chapter began by noting that the researcher's sexual subjectivity is constituted by place, and this continues to be the case. Within overt heterosexual research spaces my secrets, silences and omissions about my sexuality were consciously made. I remained 'secretive' about my queer subjectivity for several reasons. First, and most prominently, wedding spaces are (usually) powerful heteronormative spaces linked to an array of other powerful and hegemonic institutions such as religion, nation state, welfare systems and law. I feared I would be 'othered' and marginalised in these spaces if I announced my sexuality. Second, I made an assumption that the people involved in wedding industries would question my ability to understand, and support, weddings. In the course of keeping secret about the researcher's sexuality, several paradoxes emerged. On the one hand, my embodied subjectivity did not easily 'fit' straight wedding spaces. Weddings are, however, very common events and impossible to escape even when one is 'othered' in relation to heterosexuality. Yet, on the other hand, I performed a type of heterosexual identity when researching wedding spaces.

Accelerated by these feelings of being 'out of place' I felt like the 'annoying university researcher', wanting access to busy people whose job it is to help couples become 'proper' legal citizens, with little to offer in return. Before going into interview situations I consciously asked myself – what sort of information about me would be appropriate in this research context and how should I respond if asked about my experiences of weddings? In a similar way to my research about queer bodies and spaces, I used my own body as a research tool when conducting interviews with people involved in wedding industries. I dressed conservatively and wore make-up in a way that may have been understood as an expression of normative heterosexual femininity. The wearing of an engagement ring became significant during these research encounters. This was my mother's ring (and before her, my grandmother's) and since my mother's death I wear it on a daily basis as constant reminder of her. I was acutely aware that in this research situation, an engagement ring worn on the 'wedding ring' finger would be read in the most dominant way. I did not take it off when conducting interviews.

Another incident of 'passing as straight' occurred when during a visit to a Christchurch wedding company – which is housed in a historic church – a wedding client asked me if I was having my wedding tomorrow? I smiled and said 'no, no, I'm here to talk to Natalie' (the wedding coordinator). The client looked puzzled and muttered 'oh', to which I quickly followed up with – 'I'm doing a bit of research on wedding tourism'. In this situation I remained firmly within my 'researcher' subjectivity, rather than coming out and risk transgressing and disrupting the institutionalised heterosexual space of the church/wedding company.

During wedding tourism interviews with tourism company directors I did not remain completely silent about non-heterosexual relationships and towards the end of each interview I asked if companies catered for same-sex ceremonies. The New Zealand Civil Union Act 2004 provides the criteria for two people to have their relationship solemnised as a civil union (and usually by way of a formal ceremony) and officially registered in New Zealand. A civil union may be entered into by couples of the same sex or by couples of different sexes (see http://www.civildefence.govt.nz/diawebsite.nsf). The usual response from wedding company directors was to discuss same-sex unions in terms of dollar value 'they [gay men] have a lot of money', or, 'they like lavish parties'. One participant, however, seemed uncertain about whether providing same-sex ceremonies was the 'right' thing to do.

DIANE: Yes, I have got one at the end of the year, (Lynda: have you?) yes. (Lynda: Where are they coming from?) From England, yes 'cause I put it on our website when it became legal here. Yeah I put it on there, so yes we've got someone coming out. I'm just waiting for the details to come through.

LYNDA: and is everyone okay with that – your minister and your sub-contractors?

DIANE: Yeah, yeah, [pauses] that's [pauses] it's a hard one, it is really hard. I have the same views as Rob and the other ministers. But it's their day and you know times are changing. Um, I don't know if it's right or wrong but because time is changing, you know you just make it about their day (Lynda: yes, that's right). Yes that's what it comes down to, it's their wedding day and so … [Diane trails off].

This exchange happened towards the end of the interview and it signalled her unease with same-sex civil union ceremonies. While the Act may have legalised same-sex relationships, there still exists much opposition to homosexuality and the public recognition of relationships. At this point in the interview I was relieved that I was 'passing' as heterosexual because of the participant's views. I was uncomfortable with her views, and her church's views, on sexuality. Valentine discusses a similar interview experience. When interviewing couples she notes:

> While I did not deliberately 'pass' as heterosexual during the interview, the assumption of heterosexuality in most everyday contexts (Valentine

> 1993) is so strong that all the interviewees took it for granted that I too was heterosexual and through my performance I did nothing to disrupt this reading of my identity.
>
> (Valentine 2002: 122)

While I document this to assess the extent to which I performed a 'straight' identity (and hence hid a queer identity) I am reminded, on a daily basis, that most bodies are read as heteronormative unless there is an act or performance that actively disrupts heterosexual space.

How ethical then is it to pass as straight by performing a type of heterosexual femininity (and remaining quiet about being a lesbian) to extract information about weddings? There are no easy answers. Indeed, whatever the sexuality is of those being interviewed or doing the interview it is worth considering Helen Callaway's (1992: 30) comment that '[a] deep understanding of our own gendered identities and coded complexities of our being offer the best resources for gaining insights into the lives of others'. Within research encounters we are all gendered and sexualised subjects and research interactions between us are affected by the assumptions about sexualised embodiment, status and authority and about being in or out of place. Feelings of 'in place' of 'out of place' may mean we conceal, hide and/or perform our embodied subjectivities in often ambiguous and paradoxical ways. Linda McDowell (1999: 242) asks is it ethical to 'reveal our research aims, and perhaps our politics, to those we know to be sympathetic to our views, but to disguise our purpose from informants we know would refuse to speak to us if they could read our minds'?

A number of feminist researchers have discussed hiding their researcher identities, but not their sexualised identities. Pamela Moss reflects on her doctoral work and the reasons why she disguised her identity as a researcher:

> I undertook a four-phase research project for my doctoral programme at McMaster University. [In the first phase] I was employed for three and a half months as a maid in a housekeeping franchises service. … Though it was a difficult decision, I went to the employment situation covertly. I figured that this type of complete immersion would allow me particular insights into the labour process that could be gained no other way. I also thought by being inside the process, I would be able to set effective goals for myself as well as participate in setting emancipatory goals for effective social and political change collectively from within.
>
> (Moss 1995: 83)

Moss had concerns about announcing the feminist Marxist theoretical framework of her doctoral study to her employers and other employees, claiming that she would not have gained the same power experiences as other maids if they had known that she was a researcher. During the course of the research Moss walked a fine line between dishonesty and openness particularly when she found that she did not always 'fit in' and felt 'out of place' with her co-workers: she watched different television programmes and ate different food at lunch time.

For much of my time researching wedding tourism I also felt 'out of place', particularly when attending wedding expo fairs. Retailers automatically assumed I was there to purchase wedding items and I did not tell them otherwise. For similar reasons to Moss (1995) who wanted to be immersed in a powerful organisation, I wanted to experience the dominant wedding discourses that construct heteronormative spaces and bodies. Having an 'engagement ring' proved to be a significant marker of heterosexuality when conducting participant observation at a wedding expo in which normative expressions of heterosexuality were in abundance, as shown in Figure 21.1.

I visited all of the promotional displays at this wedding expo and was often asked 'when is your wedding date?' This is not surprising, but perhaps my response was. I could have said 'I'm not planning to have a wedding, I'm here conducting research', or even, 'I'm interested in same-sex civil unions'. I responded, however, with 'Oh, I haven't decided', or 'No date yet'. I also signed up for more information about gift registers, wedding catering and venues and so on. Upon reflection I wanted to 'fit in' at the wedding expo and be read as heterosexual and single in order to gain in-depth information from wedding expo vendors. I also wanted to hide my sexuality in such a

Figure 21.1 Expressions of normative gender and sexuality. Hamilton Wedding Expo, 2005. Image by author.

heteronormative space. It did not feel safe to come out or even to speak 'as a researcher' about same-sex civil unions. Furthermore, how does a researcher tell a wedding retailer that she understands sexuality to be fluid, problematic and contingent upon place? These kinds of interactions tend not to happen when attending a wedding expo. Within the research spaces of weddings I remained silent about my own sexualised subjectivity and attentive to the variations of gendered and sexualised power relations. In this research process my body was read as straight and I was able to understand the ways in which power relations were maintained.

Concluding thoughts

This chapter argues that place is important when considering secrets, silences and sexualities in the research process. I have attempted to understand the ways in which the place of research may reify and disrupt notions of secrecy and silences. Knowledges in the research process are produced through secrets, silences and omissions, just as they are through talk, emotions, observations and other obvious forms of qualitative research methodologies. The relationship between the researchers and researched is crucial in the construction of knowledge. Feminists have paid a great deal of attention to these matters, particularly focusing on power and have written about the 'mutual production of (inter)subjectivities in research encounters … opening up explorations of non-rational and non-cognitive dimensions of research relationships' (Bondi 2002: 10). The spaces of research encounters are complicated, so too are bodies – researchers and researched – in these spaces. It is recognised that research processes are unstable entities and that multiple versions may be presented to colleagues, peers, media, funders, friends, family and research participants. People, places and events have multiple meanings and multiple interpretations all of which need to be considered at different scales.

The notion of situated knowledge has been discussed by feminist researchers for some time now, yet the question of the *place* of the research process has not been given much attention (Rose 1997). Researchers make decisions about what to say, and what not to say – where to speak and where not to speak – on a regular basis and often these decisions are based on how we imagine our selves as researchers; this is not straightforward. Our sexualised embodiment is constructed through topographies of awkwardness and uncertainties, as well as academic authority and experience.

My experience of conducting feminist poststructuralist queer research has not rested easily with the complexities of what to say and what not to say, about myself as a sexually embodied researcher. Even within spaces of supposed sameness (lesbians interviewing lesbian) omissions are made and silences kept during the research process. Upon reflection, my decisions to remain silent at particular times oscillated between concerns for the research process as well as concerns for the research participants – their subjectivities and their places – as well as my own. As a researcher I felt honoured to be able to hear about the constitutive relationship between lesbians and home spaces. During the focus group interviews it would not have been appropriate for me to deconstruct participants' ideas about their sexual subjectivities and spaces, or to push some participants to reveal more, sometimes painful, experiences of home in front of the other focus group participants.

Within the more publicly diverse space of gay pride parade organisations, I again negotiated the complexities of being a researcher and a member of the community I was studying. Several times I had to 'bite my tongue' so that my research would not be jeopardised. I chose not to write about several incidences of 'in-fighting' as I was concerned about the 'public' acceptance of gay, lesbian, bisexual and transgendered groups and activities. In this public queer research space I juggled my secrets and silences according to the public reception of marginalised groups. On the day of the gay pride parade gays, lesbians, bisexuals, transgenders, Takataapui and others minimised their differences and bravely took to the city streets to celebrate their identity. I chose not to write about fractions between different groups in the lead up to the parade.

Researching the spaces of weddings, by interviewing people involved in New Zealand's wedding tourism and by conducting participant observation at wedding expo fairs, reinforced the dominance of heterosexuality. It is within these heteronormative spaces that I was more inclined to consciously keep secret about my own sexuality, as well as treading cautiously when participants discussed same-sex civil unions. After these interactions I was left questioning whether it was ethical for the researcher to 'pass' as straight, or at least, not to mention same-sex civil union ceremonies.

Heterosexuality and its spaces are jointly produced everyday and prominently celebrated during weddings. Straight subjects make and celebrate heterosexual spaces, and it is important to consider how the researcher tentatively negotiates these spaces. Heterosexual spaces and bodies exist through the social and spatial practices that give them meaning and form. It is this focus on place that enables researchers to consider how secrets and silences inform the research process.

Acknowledging these research spaces, and the different sexualised subjectivities that are produced, can contribute to the project of underdetermining heterosexuality and straight space and to the study of sexuality more broadly, which often neglects spatial process.

The absences, omissions, secrets and silences that I have made space for during my research into geographies of sexualities need to be considered within complex discourses of power, subjectivities and research processes. I hope my modest account of research secrets, absences and fallibilities has prompted other researchers to think about sexualised bodies and the importance of place in research processes.

References

Avis, H. (2002) 'Whose voice is that? Making space for subjectivities in interviews', in L. Bondi, H. Avis, A. Bingley, J. Davidson, R. Duffy, V. Einagel, A.-M. Green, L.

Johnston, S. Lilley, C. Listerborn, M. Marshy, S. McEwan, N. O'Connor, G. Rose, B. Vivat and N. Wood (eds) *Subjectivities, Knowledges and Feminist Geographies: The Subjects and Ethics of Social Research*, London: Rowman & Littlefield: 191–207.

Bondi, L. (2002) 'Introduction', in L. Bondi, H. Avis, A. Bingley, J. Davidson, R. Duffy, V. Einagel, A-M. Green, L. Johnston, S. Lilley, C. Listerborn, M. Marshy, S. McEwan, N. O'Connor, G. Rose, B. Vivat and N. Wood (eds) *Subjectivities, Knowledges and Feminist Geographies: The Subjects and Ethics of Social Research*, London: Rowman & Littlefield: 1–11.

Callaway, H. (1992) 'Ethnography and experience: Gender implications in fieldwork and texts', in J. Oxley and H. Callaway (eds) *Anthropology and Autobiography*, London: Routledge.

Dyck, I. (1993) 'Ethnography: a feminist method?', *Canadian Geography*, 37: 50–52.

— (2002) 'Further notes on feminist research: embodied knowledge in place', in P.J. Moss (ed.) *Feminist Geography in Practice: Research and Methods*, Oxford: Blackwell: 234–44.

England, K. (1994) 'Getting personal: Reflexivity, positionality and feminist research', *Professional Geographer*, 46: 80–89.

Falconer Al-Hindi, K. (1997) 'Feminist critical realism: A method for gender and work studies in geography', in J.P. Jones, H. Nast and S. Roberts (eds) *Thresholds in Feminist Geography: Difference, Methodology, Representation*, Lanham, MD: Rowman and Littlefield: 145–64.

Gibson-Graham, J.K. (1994) '"Stuffed if I know!": Reflections on postmodern feminist social research', *Gender, Place and Culture*, 1: 205–24.

Haraway, D. (1988) 'Situated knowledges: The science question in feminism and the privilege of partial perspectives', *Feminist Studies*, 14: 575–99.

Hubbard, P. (2000) 'Desire/disgust: moral geographies of heterosexuality', *Progress in Human Geography*, 24 (2): 191–217.

Hyams, M. (2004) 'Hearing girls' silences: thoughts on the politics and practices of a feminist method of group discussion', *Gender, Place and Culture*, 11 (1): 105–19.

Johnston, L. (2005) *Queering Tourism: Paradoxical Spaces of Gay Pride Parades*, London: Routledge.

—— (2006) '"I do down-under": wedding tourism in Aotearoa New Zealand', *Acme: An International E-Journal for Critical Geographies*, 5 (2): 191–208.

Johnston, L. and Valentine, G. (1995) 'Wherever I lay my girlfriend that's my home: performance and surveillance of lesbian identity in home environments, in D. Bell and G. Valentine (eds) *Mapping Desires: Geographies of Sexualities*, London, Routledge: 99–113.

Keith, M. (1992) 'Angry writing: (re)presenting the unethical world of the ethnographer', *Environment and Planning D: Society and Space*, 10: 551–68.

Kobayashi, A. (1994) 'Coloring the field: gender, "race" and the politics of fieldwork', *Professional Geographer*, 46: 73–80.

Larner, W. (1995) 'Theorising "difference" in Aotearoa/New Zealand', *Gender, Place and Culture: A Journal of Feminist Geography*, 2 (2): 177–90.

Lather, P. (1991) *Getting Smart: Feminist Research and Pedagogy With/in the Postmodern*, New York: Routledge.

Longhurst, R., and Johnston, L. (2005) 'Changing bodies, spaces, places and politics: feminist geography at the University of Waikato', *New Zealand Geographer*, 61: 94–101.

McDowell, L. (1992) 'Doing gender: feminism, feminists and research methods in human geography', *Transactions of the Institute of British Geographers*, 17: 399–416.

—— (1999) *Gender, Identity and Place: Understanding Feminist Geographies*, Minneapolis, MN: Minnesota Press.

Moss, P. (1995) 'Reflections on the "gap" as part of the politics of research design', *Antipode*, 27: 82–90.

New Zealand Department of Internal Affairs (2008), http://www.civildefence.govt.nz/diawebsite.nsf, accessed 5 January 2008.

Oberhauser, A. (1997) 'The home as "field": Households and homework in rural Appalachia', in J.P. Jones, H. Nast and S. Roberts (eds) *Thresholds in Feminist Geography: Difference, Methodology, Representation*, Lanham, MD: Rowman and Littlefield: 165–82.

Peace, R. with Longhurst, R. and Johnston, L. (1997) 'Producing feminist geography "down under"', *Gender, Place and Culture: A Journal of Feminist Geography*, 4 (1): 115–19.

Reinharz, S. (1992) *Feminist Methods in Social Research*, New York: Oxford University Press.

Rich, A. (1986) 'Notes towards a politics of location', in A. Rich, *Blood, Bread and Poetry: Selected Prose 1979–1984*, New York: W. W. Norton and Company.

Rose, G. (1997) 'Situating knowledges: Positionality, reflexivities and other tactics', *Progress in Human Geography*, 21 (3): 305–20.

Stanley, L. (ed.) (1990) *Feminist Praxis*, London: Routledge.

Valentine, G. (1993) '(Hetero)sexing space: Lesbian experiences of everyday space', *Environment and Planning D: Society and Space*, 11: 395–413.

—— (2002) 'People like us: Negotiating sameness and difference in the research process', in P.J. Moss (ed.) *Feminist Geography in Practice: Research and Methods*, Oxford: Blackwell: 116–26.

Index

36406679R00186

Printed in Great Britain
by Amazon